INNOVATIVE DESIGN SOLUTIONS IN LANDSCAPE ARCHITECTURE

INNOVATIVE DESIGN SOLUTIONS IN LANDSCAPE ARCHITECTURE

STEVEN L. CANTOR

97-1583

VNR VAN NOSTRAND REINHOLD
I(T)P® A Division of International Thomson Publishing Inc.

New York • Albany • Bonn • Boston • Detroit • London • Madrid • Melbourne
Mexico City • Paris • San Francisco • Singapore • Tokyo • Toronto

Cover design: Paul Costello

Van Nostrand Reinhold staff:
  Editor: Jane Degenhardt
  Production Editor: Carla M. Nessler
  Production Manager: Mary McCartney
  Designer: Paul Costello

 A division of International Thomson Publishing, Inc.
The ITP logo is a registered trademark under license

Printed in the United States of America

For more information, contact:

Van Nostrand Reinhold
115 Fifth Avenue
New York, NY 10003

Chapman & Hall GmbH
Pappelallee 3
69469 Weinheim
Germany

Chapman & Hall
2-6 Boundary Row
London
SE1 8HN
United Kingdom

International Thomson Publishing Asia
221 Henderson Road #05-10
Henderson Building
Singapore 0315

Thomas Nelson Australia
102 Dodds Street
South Melbourne, 3205
Victoria, Australia

International Thomson Publishing Japan
Hirakawacho Kyowa Building, 3F
2-2-1 Hirakawacho
Chiyoda-ku, 102 Tokyo
Japan

Nelson Canada
1120 Birchmount Road
Scarborough, Ontario
Canada M1K 5G4

International Thomson Editores
Seneca 53
Col. Polanco
11560 Mexico D.F. Mexico

1 2 3 4 5 6 7 8 9 10 BBR 02 01 00 99 98 97

Library of Congress Cataloging-in-Publication Data

Cantor, Steven L.
    Innovative design solutions in landscape architecture / Steven L. Cantor.
      p.   cm.
    Includes index.
    ISBN 0-442-01235-7
    1. Landscape architecture—United States. I. Title.
    SB470.53.C365   1997
    712'.0973—dc20
                                                                    96-11734
                                                                    CIP

DEDICATION

To the creative energies of designers in all fields, with special acknowledgement to the entire cast and production staff of the Mesopotamian Opera Company's April, 1996 production of Sunset Salome, *by Peter Wing Healey and Max Kinberg.*

(DISCLAIMER)

Every work of landscape architecture is unique, and derives from the talents and skills of the designers, the requirements of the program and the nature of the site. Although the reader is encouraged to take inspiration from these projects, only a limited amount of information about each one can possibly be presented in a book of this nature. Therefore, do not attempt the implementation of any similar projects or details without a thorough understanding of the issues involved and a professional expertise in specific, technical areas.

ACKNOWLEDGMENTS

This book could hot have been accomplished without the dedicated efforts of many people. I particularly wish to thank the following:

- The contributing firms and individuals, who have taken time from busy schedules to work with me, provide materials, correct and update the manuscript, and who have trusted me to write about their projects fairly and accurately.
- Frank Plum and Azad Khan, of the Louis Frey Company, Inc., for their help in providing in a timely manner high quality photographs of most of the drawings by Clarke + Rapuano, Inc., and also of some of the drawings by other contributors.
- Gary Evans, for his help in transcribing the interviews.
- Barbara Lupucy, for her legal expertise.
- Vincent Patti, for his spiritual and emotional support.
- Wendy Lochner, for her support and encouragement from the beginning of this project.
- Cornelia Guest, for her assistance in proposal development.
- The staff of Van Nostrand Reinhold, with particular thanks to Jane Degenhardt, Beth Harrison, and Carla Nessler.
- La Wanda Wigfall, for her enduring good spirits whatever the circumstances and her inspiring, creative imagination.
- To my mother Betty, sisters Diane and Sally, and their families, including Tom, Roger, David, Sarah, Becky, Elizabeth, Coal, Jolly and Angus.
- To a core group of friends, family and colleagues who have been unwavering in their enthusiasm and support, including William Gabello; Jeffrey Diehl; Tracy Bidleman; Sarah Dawson and Antigone; Steven Kuehler; Maryanne Connelly; Rob Haimes; Ron Dutton; Sol Morse; Michael Virgona; Keith Garrod and Howard Meltzer; Elena De Lucia; Georgina Martinez; John Phipps; David Hopkins and Brent Cook; Jeffrey and Amy Miller; Doris and Richard Naiman; David Kamp and David Dotterer; Katherine Pfister and Neil Stillings; David Cunningham; Todd Misk; Felix Santiago and Norbert Gasser; Elena Saporta and John Tagiuri and Lili; Andrew Spurlock and John Richardson; Kevin King; Seth Weine; Steven Gilroy; Lewis Cole; Trey Kay and Eleanor Davis; Melissa, Anne and Arthur Beattie-Moss and Phoebe; Linda Hayes and Peter Clark, Sam M. Clark and Cinnabar; Carolyn and David Soloway; Deborah, Hillary, Becka and Tom Bauer, Tarrie and Webster; Michael Garris; Greg Atchley; Nathaniel Altman; Tom Smith; Larry Picard and Sam Gindin; Karen Phillips; Richard Wells; Theresa Brennan; Thomas Riis; Shirley and Sol Kolack; Scott Weinberg; Catherine Howett; Richard Westmacott; Raymond J. Heimbuch; Theresa and James O'Dea; Hyo-Shin Na and Thomas Schultze; Dmitri and Boris Nockaballsikov; Domenico Annese; William Wild; Bernd Lenzen; Alicia Fernandez; Michael Machado; Alex Kraizman; Kevin Maher; Richard Penberthy; Fredrick Redd; George Waffle and Tom Dolle; Tom Fox; Jaime Vasquez; Scott Pfitzner; Daniel Ferris; Shirley Way; Joseph Dunn; Esther Hutton and Paul Herrmann; George Zarr and Denise Robert; Gary Muhlbach; Douglas Anderson; Naida A. Alcock; Jim Boutin, Loren Couch and Sean Massey, Dan Dixon, Frank King, and Gay Circles and Group.

All photos, unless otherwise credited, are courtesy of the contributing firm or individuals.

CONTENTS

INNOVATIVE DESIGN SOLUTIONS IN LANDSCAPE ARCHITECTURE

INTRODUCTION

What is innovation in landscape architecture? When I began research for this book, my approach was to glean from those interested practitioners examples of construction details that they considered *innovative in solving specific design or construction problems*. However, as my work progressed it became clear that for some projects the process that led to a design solution is the most compelling aspect, and not the intricate detailing of some masterfully conceived and unique use of material. On the other hand, some projects draw their strength from the individuality, grace, and strength of unusual detailing in an otherwise straightforward design. Still others are in the middle ground, where idealized design intersects practical construction techniques. Therefore, for some projects I focus on the history and context of the project and the design process, and for others I describe and analyze construction detailing. Where appropriate, I combine discussion of both major areas and also consider construction management issues.

It has surprised me how modestly some very accomplished landscape architects talk about their own achievements, particularly in terms of downplaying their work as being original or innovative. In a world of egotists, it is necessary to educate others and celebrate what we are doing. In landscape architecture, compared to architecture or engineering or other design professions, it has been my experience that we do not share information with one another or have a clear sense of what types of projects people are handling in different parts of the country. Often we are so busy surviving, whether struggling to finish a set of construction documents or finalizing a proposal for the next project, that there is little time to document what we have accomplished or share ideas and experiences with others. This is another goal of the book, to provide basic information about a range of different types of practices and projects, and profiles of people, with the hope that additional discussion and communication will occur.

Some have argued that one reason not to share specific information about detailed design and construction data is to prevent the theft of techniques refined over many years at great cost. I find this a vain argument, as if some people have such an inflated opinion about their own accomplishments that they can declare their work so admirable that idolaters with no ideas of their own have nothing better to do than ape it. If they do, so what? As Ned Rorem has written about composers,

"Minor artists borrow, great ones steal. All art is clever theft. Conscious that he is stealing, the artist seeks to cover his traces. In so doing he expresses himself despite himself. The act of covering one's traces is the act of creation. Art is a misquotation of something already heard. Thus, it becomes a quotation of something never heard."

Landscape architecture combines the disciplined aesthetics of art with the rigorous applications of science and technology, but in wedding these disparate fields, practitioners must share with one another both the intricacies of their creative processes as well as specific techniques.

We often feel that since each site is different, the design applied to that site is unique. Even the simplest detail of construction that is applied to another site must in some ways be transformed to meet the aesthetic and construction requirements of a different situation. If someone is so impressed by a design technique or construction detail that is included in this book that he or she wishes to adapt it for another project, then this is a great complement to the originator, not an act of theft. At the same time, it is an act of generosity to acknowledge one's sources. Music, for example, is filled with examples of one composer's tribute to another, such as Brahms' "Variations on a Theme by Handel."

In the course of my research, I have been fortunate to meet and interview some wonderful people. In a few cases, the perspective I have gained from the interaction has been so significant, or at least so clear, that the interview, with only minor editing, has been incorporated directly into the book. In other cases, I have used the interview as a source of information about the projects and to learn about that person's or office's approach to design. Where appropriate, I have tried to quote directly from the interview or written materials submitted to me in order to give the reader the insight of some particularly spicy, descriptive, or precise use of language that will underscore a major point.

Many people have been generous in sharing their ideas, design approach, construction drawings and details, and photographs with me. It is my hope that I have presented their work clearly and confidently, and that they will be rewarded by a wider audience of appreciation for their work. Opportunities to interact with one another and increase the discussion nationwide about landscape architecture are frequent occurrences in the academic community, but not in practice. Perhaps, this book can contribute to the process.

Originally, my intent had been to group the projects by type; for example: residential applications; restoration, preservation and rehabilitation; parks and recreation; master plans; computer applications; education and research; and institutional and corporate work. This approach has the obvious advantage of comparing and contrasting projects of similar types. However, the disadvantage is that each project, even of the same type, is quite unique, and does not lend itself to easy comparisons. I also considered grouping the projects by region of the country, but again the diversity of work defies easy regional organizations, and often, firms in one location do work in another part of the country. More is to be gained by grouping works by the firm or individual designer, rather than by type. In many cases, I am able to describe several works, often of very different natures, executed by one firm or individual.

It is also important that the reader have a sense of the personality and individuality of the landscape architects and designers about whom I am writing. Therefore, I include in the text a description of the people about whose work I am writing. In the appendix is an index of works by project type and firm.

In order to address and encapsulate this broad content, the book is organized into three chapters. The first includes projects by prominent, large landscape architecture firms with more than 25 employees. The second includes projects by intermediate or small firms with fewer than 25 employees. The third chapter delves into a range of projects by practitioners in the academic and institutional sector, professors at universities and professionals in conservancies and other organizations.

Planting design and horticultural concerns are basic to some, but not all, of the projects in this book. In some cases I do not focus on planting design. In others, the project is at such a large scale, for example, the feasibility studies for the Rockville Facility Right-of-Way, or the master plan for the Sydney Olympics, that planting design is included only conceptually. For those projects in which plant materials are discussed, I have chosen to use the both the Latin names and common names. Since these projects represent a wide variety of locations, and therefore, a range of plant vocabularies, it seems appropriate to include both designations.

For each project I provide the following information to the extent possible:

1. The official name of the project (in a few cases, the landscape architect has requested only a generic description to protect the privacy of the client)
2. Project location
3. Firm/designers (most, but not all, are registered landscape architects, many are ASLA members, a few are architects or in other professions)
4. The client (occasionally, this is generic to protect privacy)
5. Year completed
6. Construction budget (this is not always available—in some cases the landscape architect has determined that the client does not want the cost known)
7. Design process, particularly if unusual
8. Design itself
9. Detail design
10. Construction details of unusual interest
11. Photographs of drawings
12. Photographs of as-built conditions
13. Context: where or how does the project fit into general practice?

One basic question raised by all of the projects presented in this book is how can a landscape architect create the best possible atmosphere in which creative and innovative design can flourish? Clearly, many of the firms and individuals represented within this book have been able to generate creative sparks, nourish them, and sustain them in order to achieve concrete results. The final section of this book is a summary of some aspects of project management that contribute towards this goal.

CHAPTER ONE

THE PRIVATE SECTOR— LARGE FIRMS

Landscape architecture private practice is represented by numerous firms of varying sizes. Compared to engineering and even architecture, there appear to be a relatively small number of large firms. Whereas firms with over a hundred engineers or fifty architects are common, firms of this size in landscape architecture are rare. I choose to designate as "large" the following firms with 25 or more employees.

The range of work they perform is remarkably diverse. Six firms, each in a different location, are profiled: Anshen + Allen, Inc. in Baltimore, MD; Clarke + Rapuano, Inc. in New York City; DHM in Denver, CO; Carol Johnson & Associates in Cambridge, MA; Jones & Jones in Seattle, WA; and Royston, Hanamoto, Alley & Abey in Mill Valley, CA. A profile is presented of the history of each firm and a few of its key personnel. At least two projects by each firm are discussed in order to present its style and design approach, to describe some areas of specialization, and to contrast different types of work.

ANSHEN + ALLEN INC.

Baltimore, MD

Carol Macht grew up on a dairy farm in the beautiful, rolling countryside of Baltimore County, about twenty miles north of Baltimore. In 1956, when Carol was five, her family moved into a modern glass and wood frame house built by her father, a civil engineer who was the owner of a construction company. The house was designed by the architect Henry Hebbeln and landscape architect James Rose—a prominent practitioner who studied at Harvard in the 1930s and who, with Garrett Eckbo and Dan Kiley, was responsible for a not-so-quiet revolution in the approach to landscape design. The house was featured in the 1956 book *Creative Gardens*, by James Rose. He determined the concept for the house, which was on a difficult, steeply sloping site. The house functions as a pavilion in the landscape whose relationship of inside to outside is a critical dimension of the concept. The process of designing and building the house while working with superb design professionals became a fascinating, stimulating, and expanding experience for the young couple that were Carol's parents. The experience of the design process and of living in the house influenced them profoundly. Undeniably, the house and its relationship to the site and its role in the ethos of the family were major influences on the children growing up in it.

Ms. Macht earned a B.A. in architecture at Washington University in St. Louis. Her training in the School of Architecture became a strong foundation for an approach to design and problem solving and an understanding of space and form. After some reflection and appreciation of the role of the early influences of her design life, and stimulated by an influential site and landscape design course "for architects" taught by George Dickie, she decided to continue graduate studies in landscape architecture. She earned her MLA from the University of Michigan in 1975. The relationship of architecture and landscape architecture, respect for the principles that guide excellence in all aspects of design, continue to inspire her work as a practicing professional.

In 1977, Ms. Macht and architects Edward Hord and Lee Coplan joined forces to form the interdisciplinary architecture and landscape architecture firm of Hord Coplan Macht, Inc. Over the next sixteen years, the firm worked on a variety of project types including single and multi-family residential, institutional, and parks and recreational facilities, as well as urban design for private and governmental clients.

In 1993, having grown from three partners and an answering machine to twenty professionals doing a wide variety of architecture and landscape architecture, HCM became one of a network of autonomous, locally led offices of Anshen + Allen, a San Francisco-based architectural firm which specializes in healthcare facilities and institutional design. Ms. Macht and her team of landscape architects continue to support and enhance the work of her partners through site planning and landscape architecture on the variety of the firm's architectural projects. In addition, she continues to develop work that is more strictly landscape architecture or urban design in nature.

Anshen + Allen of Baltimore believes strongly in the increased value and quality it can bring to its clients by offering an interdisciplinary approach to design solution. The ability and need, from time to time, for professionals to "rove" between the two disciplines depending on project requirements and schedules, makes for a lively professional atmosphere of exchange of ideas, sharing and mutual appreciation. The following projects represent a full range of their landscape architecture and site planning work.

PROJECT: *Private residence with music studio*
CLIENT: *Owner*
LOCATION: *Baltimore, MD*

To an existing residence in Baltimore, MD, architect Lee Coplan designed an elegant and airy music studio which includes a soundproof recording/mixing space. His partner, landscape architect Carol Macht, renovated the existing garden into a tightly organized sequence of intimate and private spaces in a modern style that borrows much from Japanese models.

The development of this garden in a wooded area in Baltimore has occurred in three major phases over 12 years. Phase I was developed in concert with the renovation of the existing house for new owners. It consisted of the creation of the bluestone and gravel entry path, curved low stone wall, platform deck entry, and large wrap-around deck on the west and south sides of the house. The deck includes a cut-out area for a gold fish, water lily, and iris pool which abuts the west facade of the house. Phase II was developed to satisfy the

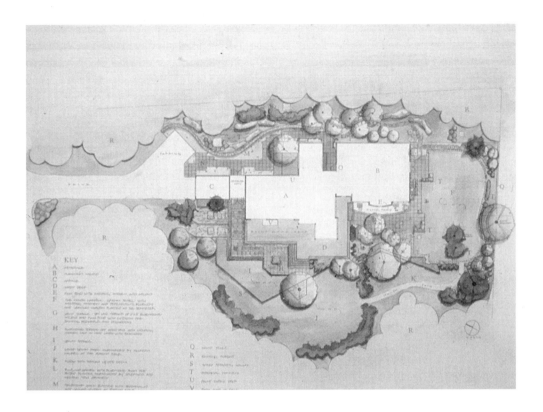

Figure 1-1: *Illustrative site plan, residence (Photo by Blakeslee Group)*

owner's wish for a greater sense of openness immediately around the house and to allow for more sunlight and contrast with the woods beyond. This was accomplished through the removal of some small understory plants and the creation of a large level grass terrace on the west side of the house below the deck. A section of the grass terrace accommodates a small bluestone patio. The grass terrace, defined by a timber retaining wall, sits above a newly created, generous, grassy open space which was carved out of the existing woods. Mountain laurel, rhododendron, and liriope blend with the existing understory plants and forest perimeter.

The most recent phase of garden development occurred in 1991. The garden was inspired by the addition of a music studio made to the south end of the house. This garden consists of three elements: the main west terrace, south garden, and linear east garden. The existing south facade of the house and the new west facade of the studio help to define a space that suggests an outdoor room. The main terrace includes a long, curved fish pool which is contiguous with the west facade of the studio addition. The reflecting pool acts to expand the inside

space and gives the illusion that the studio is floating. One traverses the pool from the door of the studio across "floating" bluestone stepping-stones to the bluestone terrace, dry laid in blue chip gravel. The terrace is constructed within a canopy of existing trees, including red maple and several dogwoods. The grade was raised slightly at the west end of the terrace to create a level surface. An angled timber wall was built to define the edge of the upper level, and to maintain grade at the lower elevation to protect a very large tulip poplar. The deck, constructed as part of Phase I, was revised on the south side to include steps down to the new west terrace and the garden pool. Lumber from the first phase of construction was salvaged for reuse in building the steps.

To the south, in contrast to the wooded terrace, an open grass panel was defined by 1' × 1' bluestone stepping-stones arranged as a curvilinear edge in front of a densely planted border of deciduous flowering trees (redbuds and dogwoods), transplanted flowering shrubs (rhododendrons and azaleas from other areas of the site), new evergreen shrubs (yews and blue hollies) and perennials. Pine trees, planted during Phase I to provide privacy, were selectively removed to

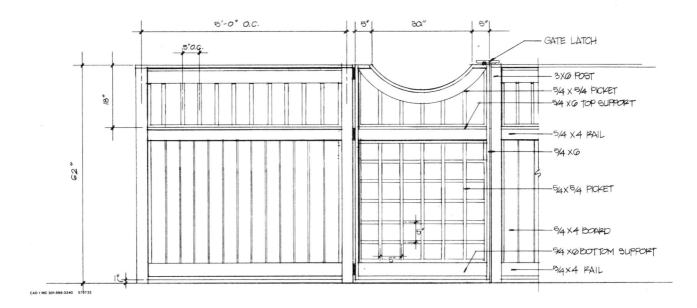

CAD 1 INC 301-565-3340   570732

5'-0" O.C.   5"   30"   5"

GATE LATCH

5" O.C.

18"

62"

3X6 POST
5/4 X 5/4 PICKET
5/4 X6 TOP SUPPORT

5/4 X4 RAIL
5/4 X6

5/4 X 5/4 PICKET

5/4 X4 BOARD
5/4 X6 BOTTOM SUPPORT
5/4 X4 RAIL

5"
5"
1"

Figures 1-2 and 1-3: *Elevation of wood fence and gate, and as-built photograph. The fence consists of solid 5-1/2′ panels constructed of 1 × 4's in a frame of 2 × 4's. The gate is comprised of an open 6″ × 6″ grid of 5/4 square members. (Photo by Anne Gummerson)*

inch-square grid of 5/4 square members. The top of the gate is embellished by a concave curving form, which, together with the open design of the gate, provides a peek into the garden and hints at the openness of space to follow. On either side of the gate, the fence panels are more open at the top to transition from solidness to openness. The fence and gate are suggestive of Japanese design principles in evoking the artifice that these garden spaces represent the universe in microcosm. The half-moon shape of the gate frames and borrows a view of the freer land outside.

The third part of the garden is the east side linear garden which acts as a transition and extension of the front path to the south garden. The existing front walk and curved, low stone wall were extended around the east side of the residence to provide a separate access to the studio for musicians. The extended walk then becomes a more informal, stepping stone path winding through existing large trees and around newly planted redbuds, groundcover of geraniums and ivy, and perennials such as hosta, astilbe, and cimicifuga, to the gate which leads to the garden.

create a more open, sunny, grassy area. Three pines were retained as a middle ground focus to create a sense of depth. Their relatively large size also gave a feeling of age to the newer garden.

The entire south garden is defined by a decorative wood fence which connects to an existing system of black wire fence through the woods. The redwood fencing and gate create a frame for the garden, as they meet the client's requirements to secure the family dog and provide privacy from neighbors. The fence consists of a series of solid 5-1/2′ long panels constructed of 1 × 4's supported by a frame of 2 × 4's. The gate, inspired from images of English cottage gardens, is composed of an open 6-

Directly in front of the entrance to the studio addition is a reflecting pool whose scalloped shape mimics the curve of the building. One enters by walking over bluestone stepping-stones that appear to float on the tranquil surface of the pool. This borrows from the Japanese design principle of using water to symbolize a purification ritual. The pool of water at the base of the building serves also to appear to lighten the mass of the structure.

The reflecting pool is constructed of poured-in-place concrete. Wooden formwork was developed to create the curve. Concrete was poured to form the pool walls and the bottom of the pool, which was then coated with black fiberglass. The supports for the staggered "floating" stepping-stone across the pool are constructed of concrete piers in a dimension smaller than the stepping-stones in order to create the illusion that the stones are floating without an obvious support structure. The pool is only six inches deep, and is filtered and heated. Recessed light fixtures are mounted flush with the side of the piers supporting the stepping stones and emit a soft glow at night to enhance the illusion. (See Figure C–1.) A bluestone coping of stones custom cut to the curve of the pool blends seamlessly with the bluestone patio paving.

In the garden there are three primary pedestrian pavements: 2′ × 2′ bluestone stepping-stones set in blue chip gravel, terraces of rectilinear patterns of 2′ × 2′ bluestone set amidst sweeping gravel forms, and a simpler edging of square 1′ × 1′ bluestone stepping-stones used to separate the edge of planting beds from the lawn. These pavements recall the three different types of traditional Japanese stone paving.

The planting concept throughout is to soften the edges with naturalistic materials, reinforce the sequence of spaces, and provide both textural and color accents. Some examples are plantings of the following combinations:

- redbuds (*Cercis canadensis*), hosta (*Hosta v. Love-Pat*), blue holly (*Ilex meserveae*), and periwinkle (*Vinca minor*)
- dog hobble (*Leucothoe catesbaei*) and yews (*Taxus baccata repandens*)
- Korean dogwood (*Cornus kousa*), blue holly, leucothoe, lily-of-the-valley, and spirea (*Spirea japonica*)
- coreopsis (*Coreopsis verticillata 'Moonbeam'*), mugho pine (*Pinus mugho*), and veronica (*Veronica 'Blue Charm'*)

Figure 1-4: *West terrace with fish pool (Photo by Anne Gummerson)*

PROJECT: *Mt. Washington Pediatric Hospital*
CLIENTS: *Owner*
LOCATION: *Mt. Washington, MD*

In 1984, Hord Coplan Macht, Inc., in a joint venture with Bobrow/Thomas Associates, Inc., of Los Angeles, California, designed the Mount Washington Pediatric Hospital. This 83-bed specialty hospital for the convalescence and rehabilitation of children replaced an outdated 65-bed facility located on a wooded, steeply sloping

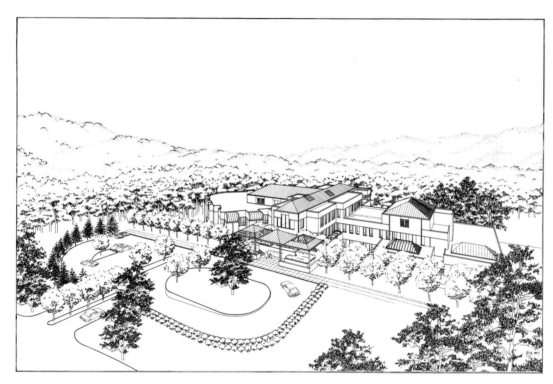

Figure 1-5: *Perspective, Mt. Washington Pediatric Hospital*

site in an established residential community. Careful siting of the building and landscape design efficiently brings cars and services to the facility and provides attractive entries for visitors and staff. Outdoor play areas and garden terraces serve patients and visitors. The facility utilizes state-of-the-art medical technology in a comfortable, homelike environment. In addition to patient wings utilizing unique nursing station designs, the building contains a gymnasium, rehabilitation and physical therapy areas, classrooms, and skylit lobby. Construction phasing permitted the existing facility to remain in service until patients could be moved into the new facility.

Carol Macht directed the site planning and landscape architectural design effort.

The planning of the main entrance offered three specific opportunities and challenges: to announce the entry, to create a covered way into the building from the vehicular drop-off, and to integrate barrier-free access as an integral design element.

The main entrance subdivides into three equal spaces, each of which is framed by a pavilion roof, whose slope matches that of the roofs of the main hospital building. The central pavilion covers the common landing onto which feed the stairs on one side and a U-shaped ramp on the other. The spatial area of both the stairs and the ramp are the same, and each is framed by an overhead pavilion structure. The central landing, to which the stairs and ramp lead from opposite directions, is supported

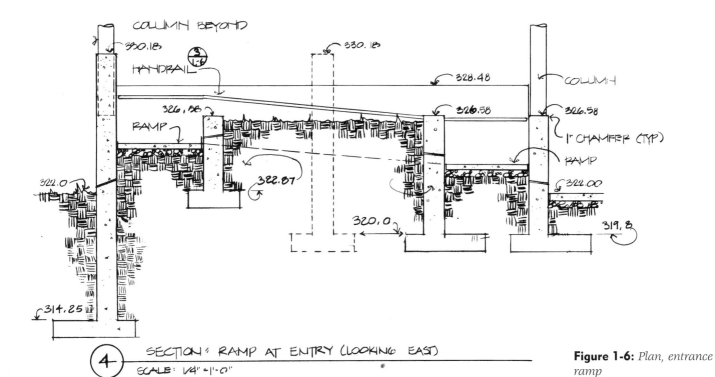

COLUMN BEYOND

330.18

HANDRAIL

330.18

328.48

COLUMN

326.58

RAMP

326.58

326.58

1" CHAMFER (TYP)

RAMP

322.0

322.87

322.00

320.0

319.8

314.25

④ SECTION: RAMP AT ENTRY (LOOKING EAST)

SCALE: 1/4" = 1'-0"

Figure 1-6: *Plan, entrance ramp*

Figure 1-7: *Mt. Washington Pediatric Hospital (Photo by J. Brough Schamp)*

by a concrete wall which forms a parapet wall and also serves as a clear formal element on which the hospital name is mounted. The ramp wraps around a central planting bed that is open to the sky. On the opposite side the reverse is true, as a planting bed wraps around the steps. Through clear geometry and equal allocation of primary space to ramps and steps, the landscape architects have provided a formal entrance which accommodates all visitors.

Figure 1-8: *As-built entrance (Photo by J. Brough Schamp)*

PROJECT: *Church Home & Hospital*
CLIENT: *Owner*
LOCATION: *Baltimore, MD*

In 1857, two Episcopal enterprises in Baltimore, the Church Home Society and St. Andrew's Infirmary, merged into Church Home and Infirmary. They provided medical care for the poor and a home for the aged. The name was changed to Church Home & Hospital in 1943. In 1974 the organization was divided into two separate corporations that still share much of the same space. Church Home & Hospital is located on a steep site covering four blocks adjacent to residential neighborhoods. The facilities include an acute care, not-for-profit, 216-bed hospital, and an 89-bed retirement community with a 22-bed Alzheimer's unit and a 61-bed nursing home. The campus is a grouping of several historic buildings dating from 1836 that have a variety of styles and details. The campus is also changing significantly: A medical office building is under construction, and the demolition of the annex, one of the older portions of the Hospital, is necessary. Anshen + Allen was selected by the administrators to study site conditions, clarify vehicular and pedestrian circulation issues (including service and visitor access), enhance the location of entrances to the major structures on the campus, and create a master plan

that accommodates existing conditions and future growth. The design team, led by Carol Macht, met regularly with a committee of administrators to discuss issues and solutions. Important additional objectives were established: the installation of lighting and other measures to clearly identify the site boundaries and the facilities and increase security, the planning for the space to result from the future demolition of the annex, the design of a unified sign system for the campus, and the clarification and development of a clear campus identity communicated to the community. Finally, the administration needed assistance in developing plans for a vacant site on the west side of campus, the location of a former campus parking lot, the use of which would be cost-effective and flexible enough to allow for potential future use as a building site.

Although Church Home and Hospital is an urban campus only two miles from the central business district, it is adjacent to several residential neighborhoods. The site comprises approximately four city blocks including four main roads: East Fayette Street, North Broadway, North Bond Street, and Fairmount Avenue. The main service entrance to the site is located on North Bond Street and the main visitor entrance is on East Fairmount Street.

Based on an inventory of existing conditions, the design team developed a site analysis that made several problems quite apparent and also highlighted potential improvements. For example, it was important to separate the receiving and loading dock area from the pedestrian and vehicular visitors. Also, several locations, such as the intersection of East Fayette Street and North Broadway, and the main entrance into Church Hospital itself on Fairmount Avenue, were found to have no visual impact

as entries. The proposed demolition of the annex presented several opportunities to open views to the upper terrace of the East building, to provide a connection from the main entrance of the hospital to the upper terrace, and to create an outdoor seating area near the main entry.

The site analysis also defined campus wide objectives to create a unified, attractive, and safe campus environment. Since the campus has developed incrementally over 150 years, it was important to introduce unified design treatment to overcome the seemingly random physical nature of the campus. Therefore, the analysis identi-

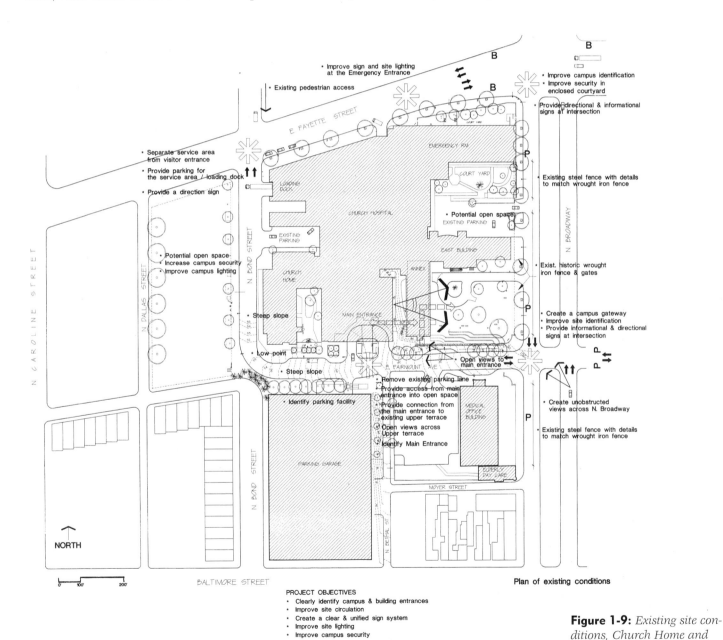

Plan of existing conditions

PROJECT OBJECTIVES
- Clearly identify campus & building entrances
- Improve site circulation
- Create a clear & unified sign system
- Improve site lighting
- Improve campus security
- Develop a campus landscape plan
- Identify campus boundries

Figure 1-9: *Existing site conditions, Church Home and Hospital*

fied and recommended improvements to open spaces, potentials and treatments for street tree planting, paving, lighting, signs, and fencing systems. Based on the conclusions from the inventory and analysis, a master plan for the campus was prepared that established general site design guidelines. Additionally, five areas were selected for special attention, such as the proposed park at West Bond Street and North Dallas Street. The recommendations for the entrance and the vocabulary of fencing types are two good examples of specific plans and general site guidelines.

The master plan proposes "to create a sense of entry, a sense of leaving one realm and entering another," at the main entrance at Fairmount Avenue and Broadway. The cupola logo of the facility would be incorporated into the metalwork of the arch and the design would also include a lighted sign with the name "Church Home and Hospital." Two additional brick piers with precast concrete caps would be built to support the arch and the existing brick walls would be revised to match. As explained in the master plan, "While truck traffic will be discouraged from entering at this location, the arch has been designed with a minimum clearance of 14'-0" which exceeds the Maryland State Highway requirements for overhead encroachments. In addition, a rolled curb median has been proposed; this will act to slow traffic down and increase (along with the additional brick paving proposed) the pedestrian zone." Inside the gateway, pro-

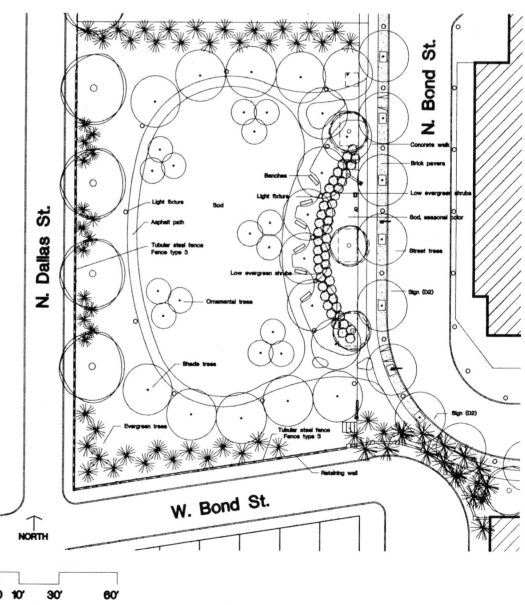

Figure 1-10: *Plan of proposed park space selected for special attention*

posed changes include the "extension of the brick paving past the new Medical Office Building and the creation of a brick paved strip at the edge of the sidewalk that would include street tree planting, new light fixtures, and other site amenities."

Three fence types are proposed to enclose the campus. The designs are an outgrowth of the existing design fabric of the campus. The original wrought iron fencing is complemented by new tubular steel fencing designed to resemble the older original fencing. In some locations, existing fences, whether old or new, are installed on a new brick base between brick piers in order to achieve a consistent, higher fence system while retaining the historical style. Fence Type 1 reuses the existing historic four foot high wrought iron fence currently located on the site along North Broadway. It is proposed to reset this fence on three- to four-

foot-high brick walls between new eight-foot-high brick piers detailed to match the existing brick piers and concrete caps located on campus. Fence Type 2 is a six-foot-high black tubular steel fence fabricated to match the detailing of the historic wrought iron fence. The tubular steel would be set on two- to three-foot-high brick walls between eight-foot-high brick piers with concrete caps to match the existing ones. Fence Type 3 is an eight-foot-high black tubular steel fence, similar to Fence Type 2, but is less costly, and is used to surround the proposed park space which may become a building site. Fence Type 3 also has the advantage of accommodating elevation changes. Finally Fence Type 4 is an alternate that incorporates the detailing of the other three fence types but could be used in areas where security or the wish to limit visibility are issues.

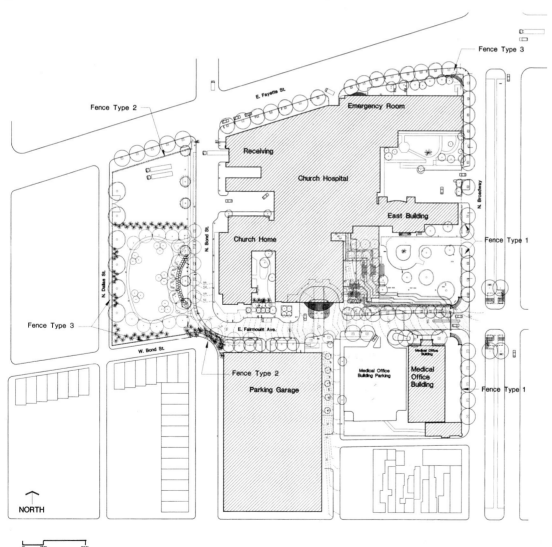

Figure 1-11: *Plan, fence locations*

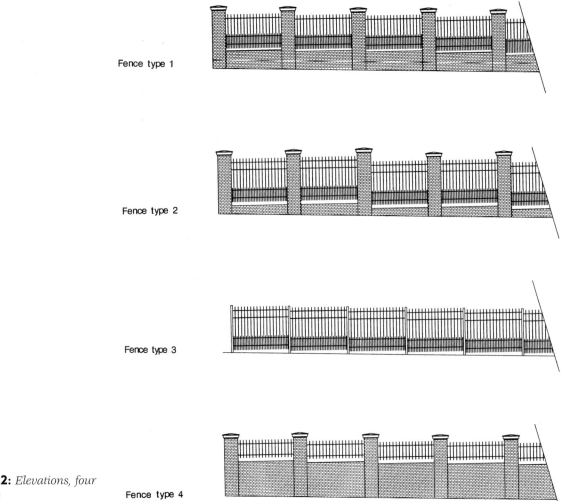

Fence type 1

Fence type 2

Fence type 3

Figure 1-12: *Elevations, four fence types*

Fence type 4

PROJECT: *North Plaza*
CLIENT: *University of Maryland System*
LOCATION: *Baltimore, MD*

Anshen + Allen is developing conceptual site plans for a study of the redevelopment of an existing building entry and service drive for an urban university campus in downtown Baltimore. The existing space extends for one city block for a depth of 50 feet.

The goal of the concept is to create an important, attractive entry to the university facility, while continuing to allow service drop-off functions and minimal, special permit parking. The existing space is dominated by the service drive, which slices through the space, leaving an unsafe condition for pedestrians at the street. The new scheme creates a brick and concrete paver sidewalk which is compatible with the uni-

versity-wide site design improvements which are being implemented throughout the campus.

The renovated building entry includes a new more generous landing which serves as the front porch to the building, an important professional school of the university. Two sets of curvilinear steps, symmetrical about the front door, meet the landing at opposite sides and create a gracious approach to the building while minimizing the visual effect of the cross slope of the sidewalk, as they are separated by a new planter. At the base of the new steps, the brick sidewalk enlarges to create a generous herringbone patterned lower landing. A series of grass terraces, supported by

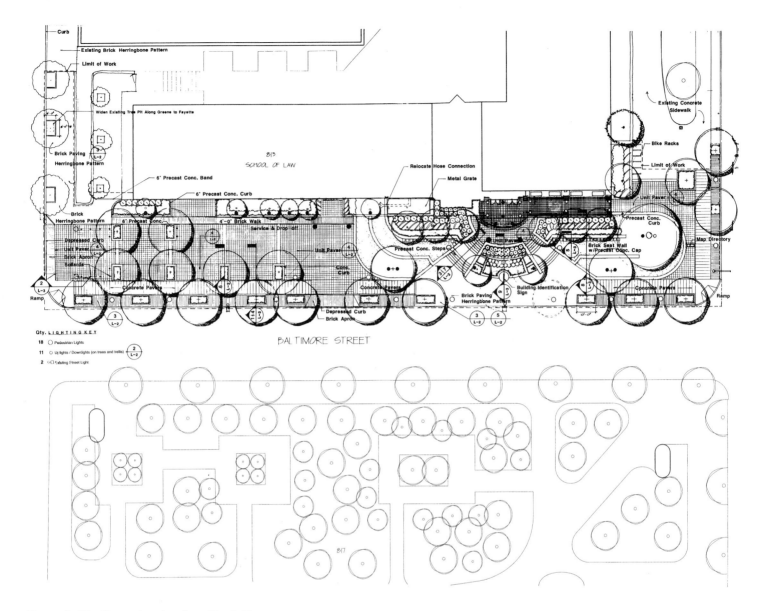

Figure 1-13: *Illustrative site plan, North Plaza*

18-inch seat walls, takes advantage of the elevation change from upper landing to sidewalk, while providing a softer landscape relief and contrast to the surrounding paving.

A steel trellis at the upper landing improves the scale of the building at the entrance, provides a linkage to the on-grade access to the door from the east, and reinforces the new enlarged landing by echoing its form in the overhead projection from the building.

The realigned service drive which allows for continued convenient service deliveries, shuttle bus access, and limited special permit parking, is made of 12-inch-square concrete pavers and contrasting bands of poured-in-place concrete. The concrete bands and/or curbs divide the field of pavers and become borders for planters which accommodate shade trees. Concrete pavers of a contrasting color delineate the four special permit parking spaces.

A vehicular and service court is created, which, when empty of vehicles, can work visually and functionally as a community plaza. The university envisions the possibility of the utilization of this service plaza for school events. New pedestrian-scale 12-foot-high light fixtures, by Paulson, which are consistent with the University standards, are installed along the street within the

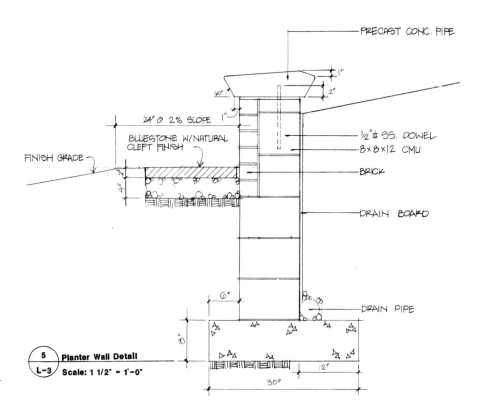

Figure 1-14: *Planter wall detail*

PRECAST CONC. PIPE

24" @ 2% SLOPE

BLUESTONE W/NATURAL CLEFT FINISH

FINISH GRADE

½"# SS. DOWEL
8×8×12 CMU

BRICK

DRAIN BOARD

DRAIN PIPE

⑤ Planter Wall Detail
L-3 Scale: 1 1/2" = 1'-0"

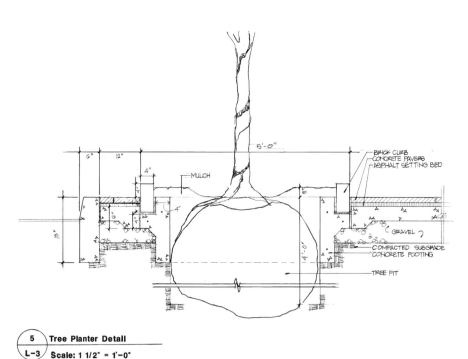

Figure 1-15: *Tree planter detail*

MULCH

BRICK CURB
CONCRETE PAVERS
ASPHALT SETTING BED

GRAVEL

COMPACTED SUBGRADE
CONCRETE FOOTING

TREE PIT

⑤ Tree Planter Detail
L-3 Scale: 1 1/2" = 1'-0"

brick band of the new sidewalk and on the upper landing. Up-and-down lights will be mounted in the trellis and recessed wall lights are recommended at the steps.

New street tree planting, planting within the service plaza, flowering trees, and hedges and perennials which flank the new main entrance and grass terraces, will contribute to transform this non-descript front entry into a green oasis within an orderly, hardscape structure—a fitting frame for an important university building.

The work includes implementation of a vocabulary of site furniture and street pavements for the campus, the creation of an accessible route through the campus facilities, and extensive modulation of open space. These are all types of design development in which Anshen + Allen has demonstrated considerable expertise.

CLARKE + RAPUANO, INC.
Consulting Engineers and Landscape Architects
New York City

The Clarke + Rapuano projects that are discussed here are diverse, recent interdisciplinary efforts that focus on imaginative and creative solutions to landscape architecture problems. The design traditions of the firm can be traced back several generations. A graduate of the landscape architecture program at Cornell in 1913, Gilmore D. Clarke became a professor of city and regional planning there in 1935, and the dean of the College of Architecture in 1939. He was also a civil engineer. Clarke later explained that he decided on landscape architecture as his major while he was waiting in line to register at Cornell. A pleasant fellow in front of him had chosen landscape architecture as his major, and it sounded interesting. After graduation, he was hired by the Bronx River Commission, an agency formed by the New York State Legislature with the mission of cleaning the severely polluted Bronx River in Westchester County. Clarke proposed a pleasure drive along the river with a simultaneous program of clearing and maintaining the river. After World War I he trained with the landscape architect Charles Downing Lay. Clarke was appointed superintendent of construction for the Bronx River Parkway, and became a consulting landscape architect for the Westchester County Park Commission starting in 1923 and continuing until 1935.

By contrast, Michael Rapuano decided to become a landscape architect early in life, although his father, the superintendent of parks in Syracuse, NY had hoped that his son would study law. He graduated from Cornell in 1928, and immediately won a fellowship to study landscape architecture at the American Academy in Rome, where he studied for three years. When he returned to the United States, he was hired by the Westchester County Park Commission and began his association with Gilmore Clarke.

The Westchester County network of parks and its parkway system became a model for many other counties and metropolitan areas in the country. Four design principals of the Bronx River Parkway—controlled access, separation of roadways carrying opposing traffic, curvilinear alignment fitted to the topography, and comprehensive planning of the highway corridor—have become criteria for all modern highways. During the 1930s these criteria became standards for all parkways in New York State, and later for federal parkways in and around Washington, D.C. Their acceptance throughout the country remained limited to such non-commercial highways as parkways until after World War II. With the advent of planning for expressways, freeways, and turnpikes after the war, and finally the planning for the interstate highway system, these design principles were firmly established.

In 1932 President Roosevelt appointed Clarke to the National Commission of Fine Arts, which was created by Congress to advise on art and architecture in Washington. Serving as chairman from 1937 to 1950, he helped determine the design of major aspects of the nation's capital. For example, Clarke persuaded Roosevelt and the War Department to locate the Pentagon on the site of the Old Department of Agriculture experimental farm in Arlington, VA rather than adjacent to the main entrance to Arlington Cemetery, within sight of the Lincoln Memorial.

In 1937 the two men established a partnership for the practice of consulting engineering and landscape architecture, called Clarke + Rapuano. The two principals developed a multi-disciplinary staff in engineering, landscape architecture, architecture and planning. For many years Clarke lived in Ithaca, NY three days a week and devoted his time to the firm in New York City at other times. By 1950, the workload had grown so substantially, that Clarke was obligated to leave his post as dean at Cornell. Shrewd businessmen, they incorporated in 1962 as an engineering and landscape architecture firm, a practice no longer permitted under New York laws. The firm designed many parks over a 25-year period in association with Robert Moses during his tenure as one of New York City's power brokers: He was the New York City Commissioner of Parks and the Chairman of the Long Island State Park Commission and the New York State Council of Parks. The firm's work has included pivotal works in park design, urban development, campus design, world's fairs, corporate and institutional sites, and residential environments. After the two principals' retirement from practice, the firm they founded continued under the ownership of associates whom they had originally trained.

Michael Rapuano died in September, 1975, while working on Jasna Polana, an estate in Princeton, New Jersey, for J. Seward Johnson, one of his clients of many years' duration. Rapuano was planning to travel to Rome to design a garden for Johnson's villa there. That July, Clarke, who wrote sonnets and published several books of his poetry, had written his colleague the following lines:

For five years short of half a century
We worked together in full harmony.
Now, as we part, I know that we shall be
United in a long, rich memory.
We've made important contributions to our art
Where our creativeness will ever be a part
Of history and thus we justified our start
In partnership. In leadership we set a mark!
Our friendship has remained unbroken through the years,
Integrity has been our banner and our guide,
Devotion to high standards brought respect of peers;
May happiness be yours for pride is justified!
Now in the autumn of a most rewarding life,
You still have many years to witness this world's strife!

Sadly, Rapuano only lived a few months longer. Clarke retired from the firm in 1972 and died in August, 1982.

I joined the firm in 1988, well after the retirement of both of the founders of the firm. However, I was fortunate to work with many of the design and engineering professionals who had been with the firm for decades. The current president, Raymond J. Heimbuch, a brilliant engineer in his own right, has continued the firm's tradition of interdisciplinary and practical solutions to challenging site planning and design problems. These traditions are presented in the following contemporary projects.

PROJECT: *Merck World Headquarters*
LOCATION: *Readington Township, New Jersey*
CLIENT: *Merck & Co., Inc.*
DESIGN TEAM: *Kevin Roche, Dinkeloo and Associates, Architects*
  Clarke + Rapuano, Inc., Consulting Engineers and Landscape Architects
  Edmund Hollander Design P.C., Landscape Architects
DATE: *1993*

The Merck headquarters building rises from the rolling terrain of the New Jersey countryside on a 460-acre site. The architects designed a 900,000 square foot hexagonally shaped building to house all administrative services for the company. Its six sides surround an interior, four-acre courtyard of native forest. Despite its size, the building has the grace of a Japanese temple pavilion, and architect Kevin Roche incorporated elements in the fenestration and eaves that are evocative of traditional Japanese temples. One rarely is aware of the size of the building because all of it is not visible at once. The siting and grading absorb the structure into the landscape. The long horizontal forms of each side of the hexagon are unified with simple sweeping roof lines. The three major elements to

be discussed, the nursery of native trees, the miniloffel planters on the terraces of the building, and the treatment of the courtyard, are examples of a project in which, at the request of Merck, every effort was made by the design team and the contractors to wed the building to the site through both large scale site planning and small scale design details. (See Figure C–2)

A loop road system surrounds the building and affords access from major state highways. The roads are designed as parkways with curving alignments that accentuate views towards the building and fit gently into the topography, which features both open fields and mature forests. Most of the building is not visible from any single vantage point. Instead, as one approaches the building by car, walks the site,

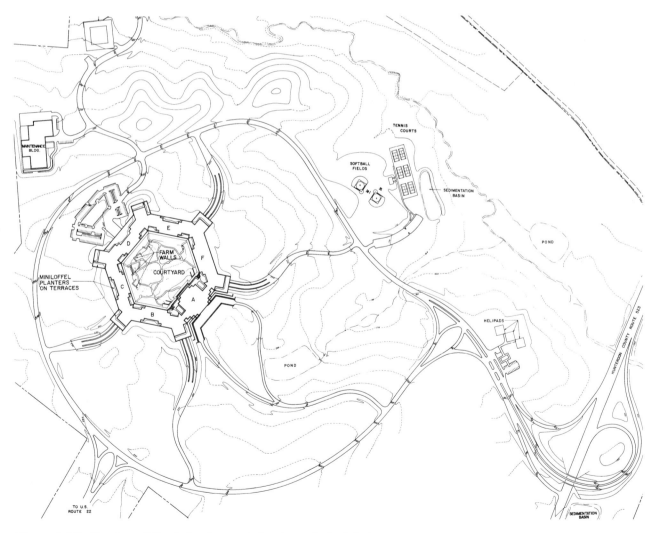

Figure 1-16: *Site plan of Merck development showing principal features*

Figure 1-17: *Aerial view of site under construction (Photo by Sal Boccuti, Ambler, PA)*

Figure 1-18: *Roof lines evoke the grace of a Japanese pavilion (Photo by Steven L. Cantor)*

Figure 1-19: *Grading plan of building shows fluid contouring at its sides in order to transition in the adjacent existing topography*

or explores the courtyard on foot, different aspects of the building become visible, a glimpse at a time. There is one ample, surface service parking lot, but most parking is underground. As a result, the landscape is brought that much closer to the building and seems to flow into it.

On-Site Nursery

The site encompasses mature forests, grasslands and wetlands. As the roads were first being designed, teams of landscape architects would traverse the proposed alignment in the field and adjust it to minimize the impact on major trees and to afford an exciting sequence of views. With an extensive system of roads over four miles long, it was inevitable that some trees would be jeopardized. However, since the layout of the roads was being planned well before their construction, it was determined that many trees could be saved by transplanting them into a nursery for replanting at a later time along the roads. A nursery location was determined and a separate contract was bid to cover the costs of building the nursery, digging and moving to this nursery trees to be tagged by the landscape architects within the road right-of-ways, and finally, replanting the trees from the nursery on the site. The nursery was constructed during the fall of 1988 so that the trees could be dug while in a dormant condition. Replanting occurred during the spring and fall of 1991.

The layout of the nursery, as described in the project specifications, was required to include "a tracking pad to prevent trucks from tracking soil onto local roads, a stone paved area of sufficient size to permit trucks to maneuver as necessary and to park while being loaded and unloaded, and supply wells, pressure system and an irrigation system." Plant materials were tagged in the field, and these tags remained on the trees until replanting. The contractor was required to "keep a log book of all plant material dug and transplanted to the on-site nursery." The log book recorded "the tag number of each plant, its location in the nursery, the scientific name, the common name, the caliper and height for each tree... plus ample space for recording the condition of each plant every month." In this way, quality control was assured; and accurate records made it practical to plan carefully for the replanting of the trees along the new roads.

Standard horticultural and arboricultural practices were applied in all nursery and replanting operations. There were, however, a few unusual details. The plant pits in the nursery were dug to a depth of one half the height of the root ball; the upper portion of the root ball was covered with shredded hardwood mulch. Over the

life of the nursery, this method allowed the trees to grow in a well-drained medium and reestablish fibrous root balls. The trees were irrigated at a rate of one inch per week from well water. During the replanting operations, it was found that a significant number of the areas of fill or undisturbed ground where trees were to be transplanted consisted of silty, poorly drained soils. Where slopes were less than twenty percent, percolation tests confirmed that water would accumulate in the bottom of tree pits. An underdrain drainage system of trenches six inches deep and six inches wide, backfilled with well-graded crushed stone, with an outfall at the base of these slopes, was devised to drain the planting areas. The trees thrived. The mortality rate for both the nursery operations and the replanting operations was extremely low, only about 2 percent of 1,350 trees.

Miniloffel Planters

The alignment of the roads flows into the building at its major entrance. On all sides the topography sweeps forward in its natural form and embraces the building. The transitions to both cuts and fills against the building are curving rather than rigidly engineered, and lead into swales with gentle side slopes. Each floor of the building features terraces facing outward to the site or inward towards the courtyard. Some of these terraces are accessible to the people

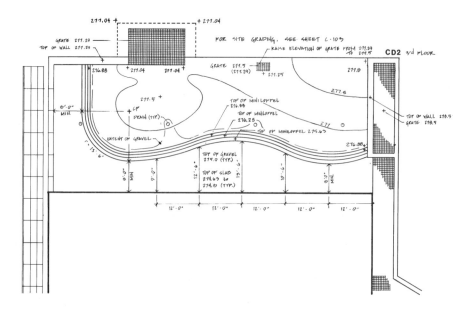

Figure 1-20: *Plan of miniloffel terrace at Building CD*

in the building. Others are intended only as restful, visual compositions that can be viewed from many different angles. These latter terraces are designed so that the plantings within them extend directly into the transitional slopes surrounding the building and harmonize with the existing topography and landscape.

These terraces support planters constructed of graceful convex and concave alignments of pre-cast concrete units, miniloffels, stacked in layers two or three units high. The concrete deck slabs on which the miniloffel planters are built, are sloped to drain to a system of deck drains. A drainage mat was installed on the hori-

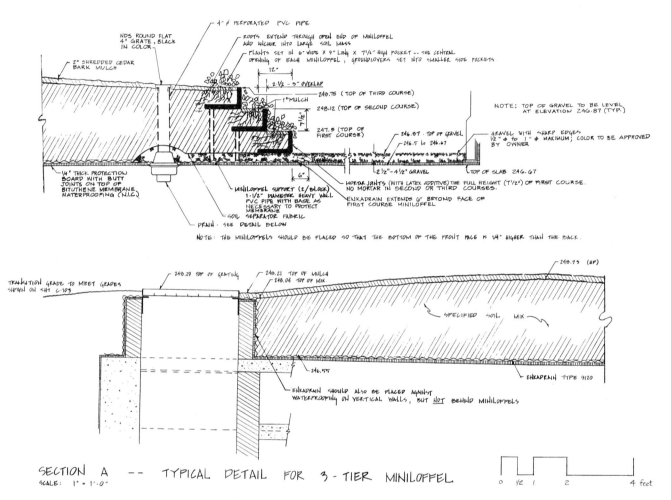

SECTION A -- TYPICAL DETAIL FOR 3-TIER MINILOFFEL
SCALE: 1" = 1'-0"

Figure 1-21: *Detail cross-section of miniloffel construction*

zontal deck slabs and the vertical surfaces of the planters to direct water to the deck drains. A layer of gravel 2-1/2″ to 4-1/2″ was placed over the drainage mat, to achieve a level surface and provide ready access for maintenance. A soil separator fabric was then placed over the gravel and drains. The outline of each miniloffel planter was marked on the gravel layer, and adjusted to create a sinuous form. The miniloffels were then placed one layer at a time. They are sloped 1/4″ front to back for drainage and mortared in place with a mortar mix which were added to an acrylic latex for waterproofing and a coloring agent for matching the brown earth tone of the miniloffels. The alignment of successive courses was staggered like brick so that there are no continuous vertical joints. Partial sections of miniloffels were cut to fit snugly against existing walls or to avoid an unstaggered alignment.

surface of the backfill tie into vertical sections of four-inch-diameter perforated polyvinyl chloride pipe that connect into the underdrain system below the gravel surface of the terrace. The surface of the backfill meets the transitional topography at the rear end of the terrace. Plantings of the same materials continue from the miniloffel planters into the exterior slopes.

Courtyard Walls and Steps

The site planning concept was to set the building into the native landscape. The exact site for the building was selected so that the interior courtyard of four acres would encompass several varied types of landscape: a mature beech maple forest, a meadow on what was formerly pasture, and a transitional landscape of eastern red cedars. In order to anchor the building into the landscape, the building was cut into the existing topography. Since the space in the courtyard is mostly forested and because each hexagonal side of the building is so linear in character and more than three hundred feet long on the courtyard side, the view from any one side of the building into the courtyard creates the illusion that there is uninterrupted space.

There is a large excavation for the building since what is ground level on the exterior side of the building becomes a deep basement level on the courtyard side. The existing topography of the courtyard is a gently rolling plane that rises from elevation 226 to 252. There is a pedestrian entrance into the courtyard from each interior vertex of the hexagon. Since the architectural design of these building entrances is uniform, each is at the same elevation. Two entrances easily meet the existing final grades at the edge of the courtyard, but the remaining four entrances meet substantial cuts, some as great as twenty feet. Therefore, the design of the transition from the building into the courtyard landscape in a graceful manner, while accommodating large numbers of employees, was a major concern.

During construction a work road was built along the perimeter of the courtyard, so that direct access was permitted for the

The height of the planters and the volume of topsoil were constrained by the structural capacity of the terraces. The stacked miniloffels which form the receding vertical face for the planter, were backfilled with a lightweight soil mix and tamped in place one layer at a time. The soil mix consists of, by volume, seven parts of screened topsoil, one part composted manure, two parts approved organic matter (a neutral Ph, weed-free and highly water-retentive, softwood mulch manufactured from paper, bark, and papermill sludge) and two parts perlite. Its total weight could not exceed 85 pounds/cubic foot since the structural capacity of the terrace slabs was 300 pounds/cubic foot, and the maximum desirable height for the miniloffel planters was three feet. Since its weight was a critical factor, a testing laboratory was hired to certify the weight of a sample of the wetted topsoil mixture.

Each miniloffel is planted individually with shrubs or groundcovers that eventually will form a continuous mat obscuring the concrete altogether. Additional backfill is placed behind the miniloffels and extends to the rear ends of the terraces. The backfill is mounded so that in some locations there is enough depth to accommodate small native flowering trees, as well as continuous plantings of native shrubs and groundcovers. Area drains flush with the

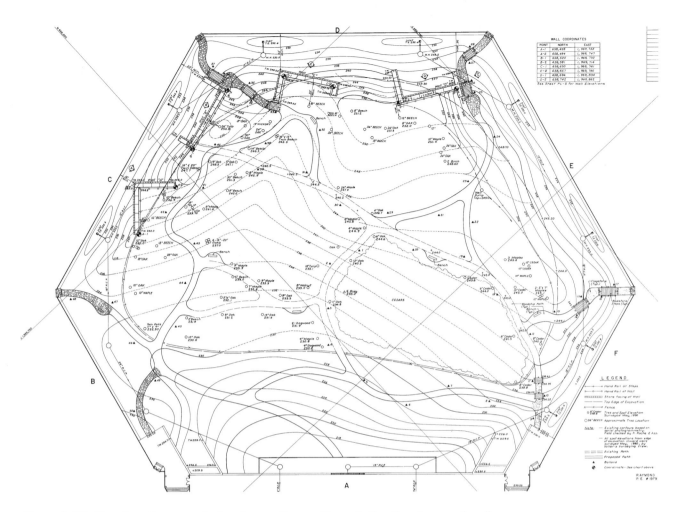

Figure 1-23: *Site plan of courtyard, showing grading and layout of walks, steps, and walls*

building of the infrastructure and shell of the building. Vertical cuts were made against the courtyard landscape creating an island of forest bordered by steep cliffs of cut, as high as 25 feet. The top edge of the perimeter cliff was fenced to protect the pristine interior and avoid accidents. The challenge became a matter of determining how materials—fill, stone and vegetation—could be placed against these cliffs in a manner so skillful that there would be direct links from the building entrances to the courtyard.

It was clear that some system of walls with steps was required. Several schemes were tried using a series of walls parallel to the faces of the building. However, these forms forced a formality for the walls and a rigid geometry for the steps that seemed inappropriate to the natural character of the courtyard. Then several schemes were tried with concentric curving walls with

curving stairs, but again, these were rejected because the concentric pattern seemed such a pale imitation of the spectacular geometry of the building.

Finally, the design team took inspiration from the site's old agricultural landmarks. The region was dotted with old farms, many of which featured beautiful dry laid stone walls built to create level areas for fields or buildings. What if it appeared that the courtyard contained such walls that had been uncovered during the excavation for the building? This artifice became the inspiration for the solution: It was decided to create a series of dry laid retaining walls that bore only a random relationship to the six faces of the building. These walls, rectilinear in character, would appear to rise out of the edges of the courtyard in a random pattern. From each entrance into the courtyard, a walk would lead towards one of these walls, and a series of steps set by them at irregular intervals would climb up to the level of undisturbed grade.

The construction of dry laid stone walls was researched. Based on the soil characteristics and the grading requirements at each location, it was determined that some of these walls would have to be as much as 12 feet high, requiring a wall that would be as much as 8 feet or more at the base; a truly gargantuan undertaking. Some means

Figure 1-24: *Detail plan and elevation of courtyard wall*

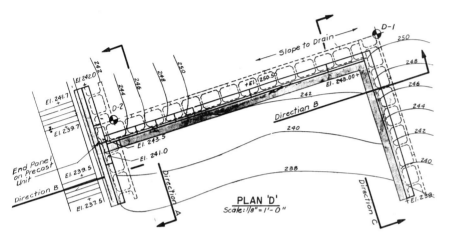

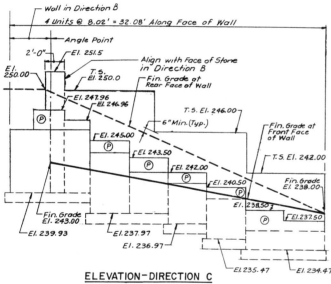

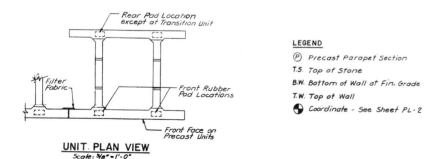

using modern technology was sought to achieve the dry laid effect without such a massive amount of stone. A further limitation was that there could be no poured-in-place concrete. By the time the courtyard was being studied in earnest, most of the structure of the building was already in place. Materials could be brought in through one side of the basement level, but overhead girders prevented the use of tall vehicles, such as concrete mixers.

A solution was developed using pre-cast concrete modular units which could be laid in a rectilinear form and stacked upon one another to form what would become an invisible infrastructure. Its face was then veneered and topped with layers of dry laid stone, stacked like pancakes. Each wall was designed in elevation and section, being planned so that the stone would extend to a depth of 6 inches below and 12 inches above the precast structure. It would never be visible once all of the stone was in place. A Champlain granite was chosen, 70-percent Hudson River blue with a mixture of green, black, pink, brown, and white and with occasional black speckles to include garnet and quartz crystals, harmonizing with the stone facing on parts of the building.

To build the walls, a foundation bed, compacted to 95 percent of modified Proctor maximum dry density, was achieved. If soils were unsuitable, they were replaced. Once the foundation bed was approved, a precast footing and a two inch thick dry pack mortar levelling bed were constructed, with a surface grade not varying more than 1/8" in ten feet. On this firm setting bed, the modular units were placed, one course at a time, with vertical joints staggered with each successive course. The precast units were filled, one course at a time, with a granular fill that was also placed behind the wall. The granite facing and cap over these retaining walls consisted of stone varying in thickness from 1" to 12", but with 70 percent between 4" to 8", with the facing area varying between 1/2 to 3 square feet. In order to provide a level surface for laying stone, courses of standard concrete block were placed on the precast footing and built to a height within one foot of finish grade. The block was mortared to the precast concrete construction and filled with grout. Slotted vertical channels were secured to the face of the block so that the stone facing could be securely anchored to the precast concrete wall. The stone was then stacked against the block, with one anchor for every three square feet of stone surface. All joints in the granite were mortared, but there is no mortar within four inches of the face of the wall to create the effect of dry-laid stonework.

The bluestone for paths and steps adjacent to the walls is a blue-grey to green-grey material. The paths were laid with a random rectilinear pattern, from 12″ × 12″ for the smallest stone varying in six-inch multiples to 36″ × 36″ for the largest. A foundation course of dense graded aggregate was placed, then a sand-cement setting bed, and finally the bluestone with joints no greater than 1/2 inch. Sand-cement material was swept into the joints, fogged with water, and allowed to dry.

The steps were also bluestone. Layers three inches thick were stacked on one another over the same type of base—dense graded aggregate. Since many of these steps were set in fill, the base was anchored firmly with a concrete toe footing, the steel of which was doweled and mortared into the bottom layer of bluestone. Steel dowels are mortared into drilled holes between successive layers of bluestone. At the top of the highest set of steps along each path, a shredded hardwood surface is used to transition into a series of paths throughout the courtyard.

Adjacent to each set of steps are set stainless steel handrails with a two part polyurethane enamel finish and an organic coating with a color and gloss that matches those used throughout the building. Cylindrical footings 12 inches in diameter and 30 inches deep were built adjacent to the steps. Stainless steel pipe was set into the footing, and the stainless steel railing pipe was grouted into it.

The courtyard is large enough to have its own ecosystem, including small populations of animals. A well is drilled within the courtyard, and water can be pumped from

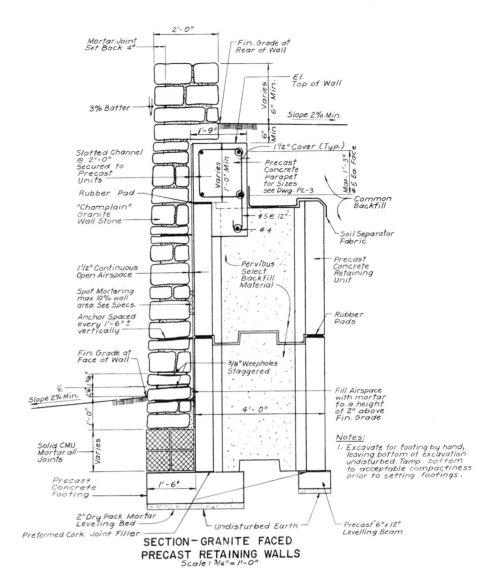

SECTION—GRANITE FACED
PRECAST RETAINING WALLS
Scale: 3/4″ = 1′-0″

Figure 1-25: *Detail cross-section of granite faced precast concrete retaining walls*

it into a gravel recharge trench, two feet wide by three feet deep, which is located at the higher elevation along one entire side of the courtyard. Water can percolate from the trench to replenish the environment during dry periods.

Large quantities of material were required for planting along the extensive system of roads on the site, within the courtyard, and in the miniloffel planters. Since the construction of the building occurred on a tight schedule over several years, the planting could be carefully planned. It was important to be certain of the availability of plant materials when planting operations would begin. Merck arranged with seven different nurseries to pre-purchase plant materials. The nurseries maintained them and grew them to specified sizes. Lists of

Figure 1-26a: *Courtyard walls under construction (Photo by Sal Boccuti, Ambler, PA)*

Figure 1-26b: *Another set of courtyard walls under construction. The massive infrastructure of these "farm" walls will be hidden upon their completion. See Figure C-2. (Photo by Steven L. Cantor)*

these materials were made available to the contractors who were bidding to do the planting work. Most of the plant materials are native and hardy throughout northern New Jersey.

To accentuate the naturalized planting, as many as five or six different sizes of the same species were specified for use in dif-ferent arrangements on the site. For example, ten sizes of red maple (Acer rubrum) were specified, varying in caliper sizes of 3"–4", 4"–5", 5"–6", 6"–8", and 8"–10", each of which was divided between multi-ple trunked trees and single trunked speci-mens. Other trees planted include the fol-lowing:

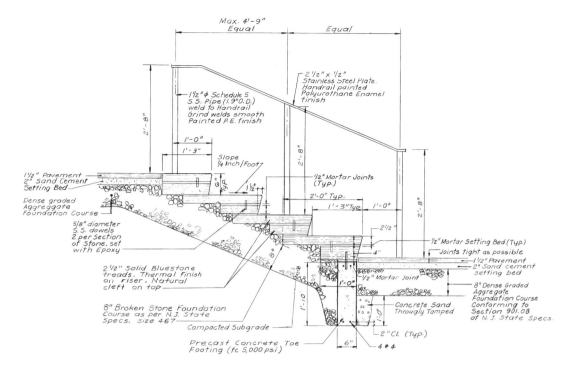

Max. 4'-9"
Equal | Equal

2½" x ½" Stainless Steel Plate. Handrail painted Polyurothane Enamel finish

1½"∅ Schedule 5 S.S. Pipe (1.9"O.D.) weld to Handrail Grind welds smooth Painted P.E. finish

2'- 8"

1'-0"
1'-3"

Slope ¼ Inch/Foot

2'- 8"

1½" Pavement
2" Sand Cement Setting Bed

6" Typ.

1½"

½" Mortar Joints (Typ.)

2'-8"

Dense graded Aggreggate Foundation Course

5/8" diameter S.S. dowels 2 per Section of Stone. set with Epoxy

2'-0" Typ.

1'-3"Typ. 1'-0"

½" Mortar Setting Bed (Typ.)
Joints tight as possible

2½"

8"

4"

1½" Pavement
2" Sand cement setting bed

2½" Solid Bluestone treads. Thermal Finish on riser. Natural cleft on top

½" Mortar Joint

8" Dense Graded Aggregate Foundation Course Conforming to Section 901.08 of N.J. State Specs.

Concrete Sand Throughly Tamped

8" Broken Stone Foundation Course as per N.J. State Specs. size 467

1'-0"

1'-10"

Compacted Subgrade

Precast Concrete Toe Footing (f'c 5,000 psi)

6"

4 # 4

2"CL (Typ.)

TYPICAL BLUESTONE STEPS
Scale 1" = 1'- 0"

Figure 1-27: *Detail section of bluestone walk and steps with handrail*

Figure 1-28: *Flagstone walks and steps under construction (Photo by Sal Boccuti, Ambler, PA)*

Acer saccharinum, silver maple
Betula lenta, sweet birch
Fagus grandfolia, American beech
Fraxinus americana, white ash
Juglans nigra, eastern black walnut
Liquidambar styraciflua, sweetgum
Liriodendron tulipifera, tulip tree
Nyssa sylvatica, black tupelo
Pyrus calleryanna, callery pear
Quercus alba, white oak
Quercus borealis, red oak
Quercus palustris, pin oak
Ulmus americana, American elm

Evergreen trees include the following:

Eleagnus umbellata, autumn olive
Ilex opaca, American holly
Juniperus virginiana, eastern red cedar
Pinus strobus, eastern white pine
Tsuga canadensis, Canadian hemlock

A full range of deciduous and evergreen, understory flowering trees, and shrubs was provided. Understory trees include the following:

Amelanchier canadensis, shadblow
Cornus florida and *c. kousa,* American flowering dogwood and Korean dogwood
Cercis canadensis, redbud
Crataegus oxycantha superba, hybrid hawthorne
Crataegus phaenopyrum, Washington hawthorne

Notable shrubs include:

Hamamelis virginiana, witch hazel
Kalmia latifolia, mountain laurel
Myrica pennsylvanica, bayberry
Rhododendron maximum, rosebay rhododendron
Rhododendron nudiflorum, pinxterbloom azalea
Rhododendron poukanensis, Korean azalea
Rhus copallina, shining sumac
Viburnum dentatum, arrowwood
V. lentago, nannyberry
V. prunifolium, blackhaw

The planting along road cuts and fills included two wildflower mixes, one for wetland areas and the other for upland locations. The wetland mix, composed of 14 species, included:

Eupatorium purpureum, Joe pye weed
Lavatera trimestris, tree mallow
Liatris spicata, gayfeather
Lobelia cardinalis, cardinal flowers
Panicum clandestinum, deertongue grass
Phalaris arundinacea, birds foot trefoil
Viola cornuta, Johnny jump-up

The upland mix included 21 species, such as:

Achillea millefolium, yarrow
Aster novaengliae, New England aster
Andropogon scoparius, little bluestem
Chrysanthemum leaucanthemum, oxeye daisy
Coreopsis lanceolata, coreopsis
Digitalis purpurea, foxglove
Oenothera hookeri, evening primrose
Rudbeckia hirta, black-eyed susans
Solidago graminifolia, lance-leafed goldenrod

The only three species common to both mixtures are New England aster, oxeye daisy and evening primrose. In some areas of the site associated with old fields, wildflowers plants in 1-1/2-gallon containers were planted rather than seeded. There were also considerable areas of bare-root plantings of woodland wildflowers. The grass seed mix used throughout the site was a mixture of spread, chewings, and hard fescue, Kentucky bluegrass, and perennial rye. The Lofts Seed Company of New Jersey provided the specified seed mixes. As

Figure 1-29: *A view of the 300 foot right-of-way near Connecticut Avenue, below which dirt bikers and other vehicles have worn trails into the terrain. The bridge was constructed to accommodate an underpass for the major highway first planned in the 1950s.*

all of these plant materials, trees, shrubs, groundcovers, wildflowers, and grass have become established, the New Jersey rural countryside has merged with the new landscape throughout the site. The building, despite its size, recedes into the landforms, and has been absorbed in a modulated composition that continues to evolve.

PROJECT: *Design Studies for the Rockville Facility Right-of-Way*
LOCATION: *Rockville, MD*
CLIENT: *Maryland National Capital Park and Planning Commission*

The firm Clarke + Rapuano, Inc. (C+R) was hired by Maryland National Capital Park and Planning Commission (MNCPPC) to develop design feasibility studies for the Rockville Facility, an eight-mile-long corridor acquired by the state of Maryland during the 1950s for an outer belt highway which was never built. As areas abutting the right-of-way were developed as residential communities, there was widespread neighborhood opposition to any transportation use of the corridor even as traffic congestion problems worsened. Studies were completed with cost estimates for a linear park, a four-lane parkway and a two-lane parkway in order to help MNCPPC, Montgomery County and other local governments resolve the final land use for this right-of-way.

The corridor is approximately eight miles long by three hundred feet wide, stretching across Montgomery County from west to east. The right-of-way begins just east of I-270 and ends at Northwest Branch Park in the east, intersecting with the future Intercounty Connector. The right-of-way was conceived by C + R as a linear park and/or parkway with a parallel bicycle/pedestrian path, linking the existing parklands crossed by the right-of-way. The topography and natural features, together with safe and proper traffic control and appropriate vertical and horizontal alignment, determined the design criteria for the parkway roads. The existing natural features of the right-of-way also suggested uses for recreation.

Reconnaissance and Data Collection

Maps, aerial photos, planning documents, regulations, and surveys were obtained from MNCPPC, the Maryland State Highways Commission, and other sources. A field reconnaissance of the right-of-way identified physical conditions, including vegetation, and verified visually the existing wetlands mapping. Ten categories of vegetation types were established: meadow, mesic mixed-deciduous forest, wet meadow, lowland forest, pine-tulip woodland, tulip forest, old field, disturbed urban woodland, floodplain forest, and woody old field.

For most of its length, the Rockville Facility right-of-way passes through solidly established residential neighborhoods. There is a predominance of single-family detached homes on lots ranging in size from approximately 1/7 to 1/2 acre, with the smaller lots occurring most frequently. There are also some apartment developments and commercial/office development. The right-of-way is usually 300 feet wide, but it is narrower in a few locations.

The Facility crosses a range of streams and tributaries which drain to the Potomac River. The Northwest Branch of the Anacostia River is designated Class IV, a water quality classification for recreational trout waters. All the other tributaries are designated Class I, water quality suitable for water contact recreation. Only one of these streams, Turkey Branch, parallels the corridor.

A Conceptual Study for Park Use

The Rockville-Facility right-of-way presented an opportunity for interpretation without much parallel in park development. The right-of-way could be viewed as a longitudinal section through an urbanized area, revealing along its way the impact of suburban development on the various natural features of the area's landscape. Viewed in this manner, the Rockville Facility right-of-way suggested a different concept in its use for a park. It was conceived as a "living ecological museum," depicting the interaction of human social activities with the natural environment, rather than as just a series of recreation sites. This approach established the framework for recreation facilities that are appropriate to the natural features of the right-of-way.

The design approach was to allow the existing natural features of the right-of-way—that is, vegetation, topography, streams, wetlands, and floodplains—to suggest the possibilities for recreation, bearing in mind abutting land uses and major points of access and transportation. At this early stage of planning, the study did not address county-wide or neighborhood needs for creation except in the sense that some needs could be met in a park plan for the Rockville Facility.

Each type of vegetation had its own attractive qualities, but some were more generally recognized for their attractiveness,

particularly meadow, wet meadow, lowland forest, pine-tulip woodland, and tulip forest. The preservation and enhancement of such particular types of vegetation were primary objectives in the park development, permitting only the introduction of recreational uses and facilities which would not deleteriously affect the vegetation. In time, it was proposed that this protective management policy take on greater significance, because areas of good natural vegetation in Montgomery County would otherwise be forever lost to development.

The recreational uses most appropriate within a productive management policy were paths for walking, jogging, bicycling and horseback riding; physical fitness courses; and natural trails. Being linear, they were adaptable to the length of the right-of-way, with ready access at every street intersection. Paths and trails could be easily fitted into the topography and could be connected to all picnic areas at suitable locations. These linear uses would be especially appropriate for areas for mesic mixed-deciduous forest, lowland forest, pine-tulip woodland, and tulip forest.

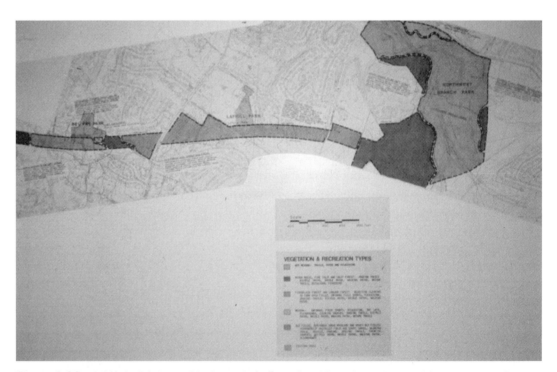

Figure 1-30: *A detail of the portable, hinged 8′-0″ rendered boards used for public meetings. The boards were mounted at eye level so that citizens could easily see their homes in relation to what was proposed. This detail shows the conceptual park plan at Northwest Branch Park, the eastern end of the right-of-way.*

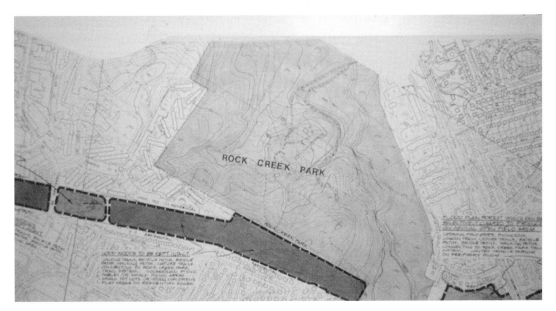

Where the forest types abut residential neighborhoods, particularly multi-family apartment complexes, small tot lots or play areas for young children could be located in the periphery of the woods. Such play areas should be small and located on sites requiring minimal regrading of the land form and little clearing.

The floodplain forest areas, with the exception of Northwest Branch, are generally less attractive than the areas of lowland forest. These floodplain areas, which occupy most of the right-of-way along Turkey Branch between Rock Creek Park and Georgia Avenue, are so dense that selective clearing could be permitted to create open meadows for informal play. Linear paths and trails could, of course, thread their way along the streams.

It was determined that the meadow areas should be maintained as they were, being most suitable for informal play and picnicking. Portions could be given over to tot lots, small play areas, or fitness/exercise equipment. The linear paths and trails could skirt or traverse the meadows. It was recommended that uses in the wet-meadow areas be restricted to interpretive nature trails and passive observation of birds and wildlife.

Ball fields for organized team play were considered only for old fields, woody old fields, and disturbed urban woodland, which are the least attractive of the ten vegetation types. Ball fields required extensive clearing and grading, not only for play but also to accommodate parking for cars. Therefore, such uses were considered judiciously and located in relation to existing transportation arteries to make the fields accessible county-wide.

The Rockville Facility connects a number of county parks and, if observed from the air, would be perceived as a green, open-space extension of those parks. The benefits of incorporating the Rockville Facility into the county park system as a linear connection to those parks are self-evident, particularly in integrating its green open spaces into a regional system.

Four-Lane Parkway

DESIGN CRITERIA

The following design criteria for the preliminary studies were applied:

Design speed . . . . 50 mph
Lane width. . . . . 12'-6" each (two lanes)
Bicycle/pedestrian path . . . . 10 feet
Shoulders . . . . 10 feet
Median. . . . . 30 feet, constant
Curbs. mountable
Maximum grade 6.5%

Two typical sections were suggested: Typical Section A, with curbed roadways and grass shoulders, and Typical Section B, with paved shoulders and curbs at the outside edge of the shoulders. Curbs were proposed in order to direct pavement runoff to a storm

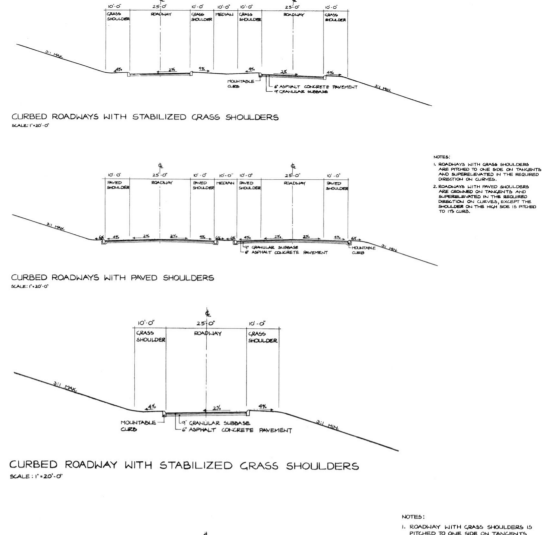

CURBED ROADWAYS WITH STABILIZED GRASS SHOULDERS
SCALE: 1"=20'-0"

NOTES:
1. ROADWAYS WITH GRASS SHOULDERS ARE PITCHED TO ONE SIDE ON TANGENTS AND SUPERELEVATED IN THE REQUIRED DIRECTION ON CURVES.
2. ROADWAYS WITH PAVED SHOULDERS ARE CROWNED ON TANGENTS AND SUPERELEVATED IN THE REQUIRED DIRECTION ON CURVES, EXCEPT THE SHOULDER ON THE HIGH SIDE IS PITCHED TO ITS CURB.

CURBED ROADWAYS WITH PAVED SHOULDERS
SCALE: 1"=20'-0"

CURBED ROADWAY WITH STABILIZED GRASS SHOULDERS
SCALE: 1"=20'-0"

NOTES:
1. ROADWAY WITH GRASS SHOULDERS IS PITCHED TO ONE SIDE ON TANGENTS AND SUPERELEVATED IN THE REQUIRED DIRECTION ON CURVES.
2. ROADWAY WITH PAVED SHOULDERS IS CROWNED ON TANGENTS AND SUPERELEVATED IN THE REQUIRED DIRECTION ON CURVES, EXCEPT THE SHOULDER ON THE HIGH SIDE IS PITCHED TO ITS CURB.

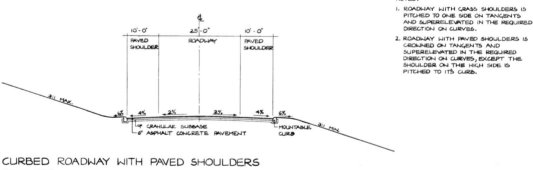

CURBED ROADWAY WITH PAVED SHOULDERS
SCALE: 1"=20'-0"

Figures 1-32 and 1-33: *Proposed typical cross-sections for four-lane and two-lane parkways*

drainage infiltration system, to keep vehicles from encroaching on the grass roadsides, and for a neater appearance. A combined bicycle/pedestrian path running parallel to the roadway was also provided.

ROLE AS TRAFFIC ARTERY

The four-lane parkway design would serve as a major east/west traffic artery, in-

tersecting all important north–south routes that cross the right-of-way. Five major interchanges were proposed. As a four-lane road, the parkway could accommodate a lane for traffic in each direction for high occupancy vehicles at rush hours. With multidirectional grade-separated interchanges, and a minimum of at-grade intersections, the four-lane parkway would facilitate travel through the corridor. It would become an attractive bypass route for congested existing east-west traffic routes.

The bicycle/pedestrian path could accommodate commuter bicyclists and connect to existing bicycle trails. Due to the narrowness of the right-of-way, this path could not be continuous. In some locations the path would end and begin again where there was adequate space. As an alternative, the paved shoulder in Typical Section B could be designated bicycle lanes for commuter bicyclists.

Two-Lane Parkway

DESIGN CRITERIA

The following design criteria for the preliminary studies were applied:

Design speed . . . . 40 mph
Lane width. . . . . 12'-6"
Bicycle/pedestrian path . . . . 10 feet
Shoulders . . . . 10 feet
Median . . . . 30 feet, constant
Curbs . . . . mountable
Maximum grade 7.5%

Two typical sections were suggested: Typical Section A, with curbed roadway and grass shoulders; and Typical Section B, with paved shoulders and curbs at the outside edge of the shoulders. A combined bicycle/pedestrian path on an independent alignment from the roadway was also provided.

PARKWAY CONCEPT AND TRAFFIC ROLE

The parkway was envisioned as a park road linking three major parks, North Farm, Rock Creek, and Northwest Branch, with a curvilinear alignment fitted to the topography. The two-lane parkway crosses the same major north-south routes as the four-lane parkway. Although alternates that included interchanges with the Intercounty Connector were developed, these were not recommended in order to maintain the concept of a parkway linking parks and not highways. Even without this interchange, the parkway would serve as a major east-west route through the county.

Designed to lower standards than the four-lane facility, (that is, lower design speed, fewer lanes), the two-lane parkway

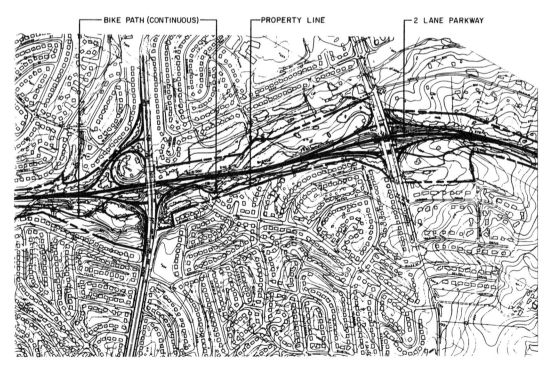

Figure 1-34: *Two-lane parkway alignment plan including the potential underpass which would occur at Connecticut Avenue, seen in Figure 1-29. The alignment of the bike path is generally independent from the parkway's.*

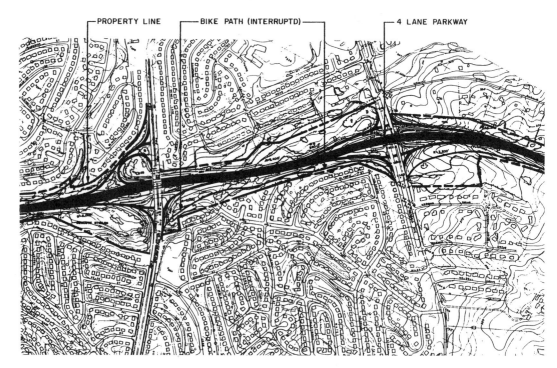

Figure 1-35: *Four-lane parkway alignment plan including the same section of the corridor as shown in Figure 1-34. Note that with the four-lane design, the width of the parkway within the narrow corridor does not permit an independent bike path alignment.*

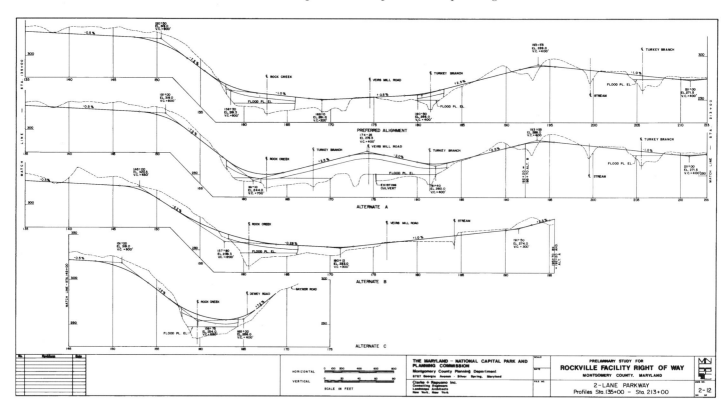

Figures 1-36: *Profiles of preferred alignment and three alternate alignments for a section of two-lane parkway. With the four-lane parkway, options were much more limited.*

was not intended to be a high volume traffic artery. Instead, its role was to provide local access to the several stream valley parks traversed by the right-of-way. However, to increase its trip-carrying capacity during peak periods, the parkway could be designated as a reversible one-way facility during designated hours. One of the

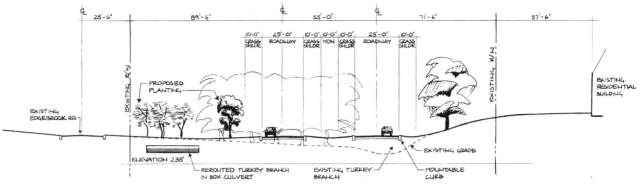

CURBED ROADWAYS WITH STABILIZED GRASS SHOULDERS

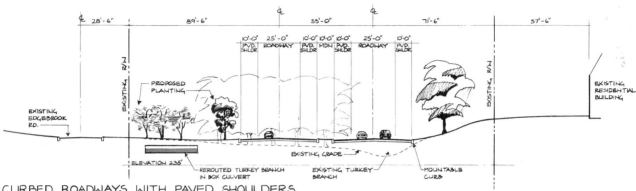

CURBED ROADWAYS WITH PAVED SHOULDERS

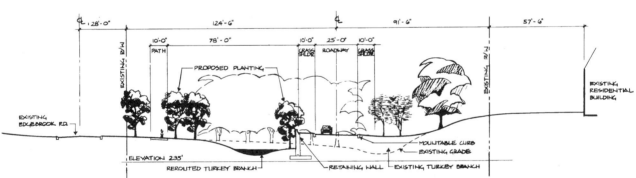

CURBED ROADWAY WITH STABILIZED GRASS SHOULDERS

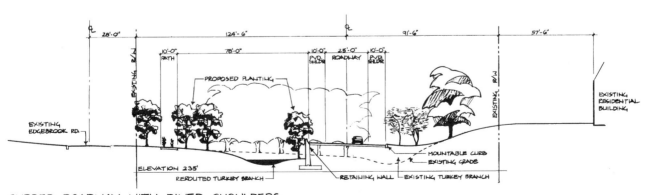

CURBED ROADWAY WITH PAVED SHOULDERS

Figures 1-37 and 1-38: *Cross sections of four-lane parkway and two-lane parkway at stations with profiles shown in Figure 1-36*

lanes, under this plan, could be reserved for use by high-occupancy vehicles (HOV lane).

The bicycle/pedestrian path could accommodate commuter bicyclists and connect to existing bicycle trails. In contrast to the four-lane design, the layout of this path in the two-lane design often moved through varied topography and vegetation as a considerable distance from the roadway. As an alternative, the paved shoulders on Typical Section B could be designated bicycle lanes for commuter bicyclists.

Environmental Issues

IMPACTS ON FLOODPLAIN AND STREAM LOCATION

Throughout the four-lane alignment, all bridges over major streams were designed to span the entire floodplain in order to minimize filling in the floodplain and to avoid impeding flow. Further studies would determine whether these spans may be longer than necessary. The total cost of these bridges was estimated to be $45.4 million, or about 24% of the total estimated cost of the four lane parkway.

Except at Turkey Branch, the parkway route generally crosses streams at right angles, minimizing both the length of bridges and filling in of the floodplain. (See Figure C–3.) However, an 800-foot bridge, a 650-foot culvert, and rechanneling of 500 feet of Turkey Branch were required as the parkway crossed Rock Creek, Turkey Branch, and Veirs Mill Road. A considerable amount of filling in of the floodplain of Turkey Branch was unavoidable as the parkway extended farther eastward. One thousand feet of adjustments to stream meanders in Turkey Branch would be required as the parkway moved through the floodplain of Turkey Branch.

Throughout the two-lane alignment alternative, all bridges over major streams were designed to span the entire floodplain in order to minimize filling in of the floodplain and to avoid impeding flow. The total cost of these bridges in the preferred alignment was estimated to be $15.8 million or about 16 percent of the total estimated cost of the two-lane parkway.

The impacts on floodplains were similar to those of the four-lane parkway, except that the narrower width of the two-lane roadway permitted more flexibility in siting the parkway and substantially reduced the amount of filling and rechanneling required. Therefore, four alternatives at Rock Creek, Turkey Branch and Veirs Mills were considered. The preferred alignment required rechanneling 400 feet of Turkey Branch west of Veirs Mill Road and an additional 950 feet in two locations east of Veirs Mills Road. There was some filling on the north side of the parkway in the floodplain. However, due to an alignment which follows the existing topography while allowing for clearance above the floodplain, this alternate was visually the least obtrusive design. The 1,100 foot retaining wall indicated in the preferred alternative minimized filling in of the floodplain. This retaining wall could be eliminated, but the regrading necessary would increase the fill in the floodplain.

An evaluation of the impact of the two-lane parkway on the floodplain of Turkey Branch was carried out at five selected stations of the parkway. An existing cross-section at each station was compared to a proposed cross-section indicating grades on the parkway. The 100-year storm elevation, taken from the Montgomery County "Flood Plain Information Map," was used in estimating the volume of floodplain capacity lost due to filling and the rise in floodplain elevation. The *average* rise in water elevation along this corridor, which is approximately 1/3 mile long, was calculated to be 6.75 inches. Although precise topographic data would be required to specify the exact impact at any given location in the corridor, the projected increase in water level did not appear to cause a significant impact.

The impact on the floodplain at Northwest Branch and the Inter County Connector was minimized by a parkway alignment that avoids the floodplain as much as possible. The bridges over Northwest Branch, and all bridges over streams, would be carefully engineered not to impede flow during storms.

Since the two-lane parkway could be fitted to the existing topography better than the four-lane parkway, the amount of cut and fill could be minimized. There is ample room in the right-of-way to provide for infiltration by use of open vegetated swales, natural depressions, and stormwater retention and detention structures.

Of the two typical sections, Typical Section A (with grass shoulders) would be more suitable as a park road. Within the 300-foot wide right-of-way, a 25-foot pavement has less visual impact than the 45-foot pavement of Typical Section B (with paved shoulders). The shoulders are aesthetically more pleasing in blending the road pavement into the landscape. On the other hand, Typical Section B is advantageous in that the paved shoulders can be designated bicycle lanes for commuter bicyclists and are also more stable than grass shoulders for disabled vehicles.

IMPACTS ON WETLANDS

Throughout the corridor, there was considerable filling of the wetlands in the four-lane design. Since the width of the right-of-way is 300 feet, and grading width is typically as much as 200 feet, it is questionable whether wetlands could be created within the right-of-way to compensate for those filled during grading operations.

A study was conducted to compare the total area of wetlands in the right-of-way left undisturbed by the two-lane-parkway with the area of wetlands which would be filled by grading operations. Of a total wetlands acreage of 206.76, only 39.76 acres or 19.27 percent, would be filled. Some acres of wetland could be created within the corridor as suitable locations as compensation for those wetlands that would be filled. Further study would be needed to determine if all 40 acres of filled wetlands could be replaced.

NOISE IMPACTS
ON ADJOINING PROPERTIES

In 1983, the Montgomery County Planning Board set forth construction noise guidelines for land use planning and development. These guidelines establish zones of allowable noise exposure levels which depend on the county's traffic volume pattern and population density zoning. The County Department of transportation is currently using a noise standard of 60 DBA Ldn as an interim noise standard for county highway projects. Therefore, any evaluation of the cost of noise mitigation for a new roadway should use this standard for evaluating potential impacts. While these guidelines are being used to achieve overall goals in planning and housing development, the siting of a new parkway in a residential setting might require additional restrictive standards. The Federal Highway Administration (FHWA) uses noise abatement criteria that relate to the highway's peak hour noise levels.

For the purpose of this assessment, there were three conditions under which a direct impact could be declared:

1. If the guidelines set forth by the Montgomery County Planning Board and the County Department of Transportation are violated.
2. If the FHWA peak-hour noise level of 65 DBA is reached.
3. If the projected noise level exceeds the existing average level by 10 DBA regardless of the existing noise level. (A 10dBA change is judged by most people as a doubling or halving of the loudness of sound regardless of the levels at which the comparative sounds are presented.)

In a narrow corridor carrying high-speed, high-volume traffic on the four-lane parkway, it was determined that there would be significant noise impacts, particularly as the parkway winds close to one side of the right-of-way or when topography directs or reflects noise towards properties bordering the right-of-way. With speeds of 50 mph, peak-hour noise levels of 68 DBA and 65 DBA were anticipated at distances of 100 feet and 170 feet, respectively, from the center line of the parkway facility. Noise levels of this magnitude would be considered significant noise impacts requiring abatement by means of sound barriers along a large portion of the right-of-way lines throughout the project.

In contrast, noise levels generated by traffic on the proposed two-lane parkway meandering through the 300-foot-wide corridor were determined not to be of the magnitude to create many noise impacts. Based on a design speed of 40 mph, peak-hour noise levels of 64 DBA and 61 DBA were anticipated at distances of 65 feet and 100 feet, respectively, from the centerline of the park road. It was anticipated that noise abatement would be necessary at a few locations.

STORMWATER MANAGEMENT

The management of stormwater for the parkway was designed in conformance with the regulations of Montgomery County. A two-part stormwater system would be required in which runoff from the impervious pavements of the parkway roads would be routed to an infiltration system while runoff from the roadsides would be directed to the existing natural watercourses.

The roadways for both the two-lane and four-lane parkway designs would have mountable curbs. Runoff would be collected in catchbasins along the curbs and piped to a retention basin. From the retention basin, the stormwater would be piped at a controlled rate to an infiltration basin. Retention and infiltration basins would be located near the low points of the parkway and outside any neighboring floodplain.

The runoff from the landscaped, non-impervious side slopes and undisturbed portion of the surrounding park land would be diverted from the roadway by means of grassed swales and culverts, thus allowing this unpolluted runoff to flow directly into the existing natural watercourses.

Two alternatives for stormwater management were proposed for the parkway: 1) curbed roadways with grass shoulders, and 2) roadways with paved shoulders and curbs at the outside edge of the shoulders. The runoff from both the two-lane and four-lane parkway would be substantially greater with paved shoulders than with grass shoulders, therefore requiring larger retention and infiltration basins.

Building the two-lane parkway without curbs was considered, allowing the runoff from the pavement to be infiltrated in the grass shoulders. The cost of the stormwater management system would be greatly reduced. Such a system would not require as many, if any, retention and infiltration basins, and it would cause less disturbance to the natural features. However, runoff from the roadway pavement would not be separated from runoff from the roadside; such mixing would violate the stormwater management guidelines, since there would be no interception of pollutants from the road surface.

PROPERTY ACQUISITION AND COSTS

Most of the land, 295 acres of the total 350 acres, required for the parkway was already owned by Montgomery County of the State of Maryland as part of the right-of-way. The 55 acres of privately owned land were undeveloped, and included 13.5 acres proposed as additional parkland. The construction costs for the four-lane parkway were expected to be approximately $187.7 million with grass shoulders and $192.4 million with paved shoulders. These figures included the ramp connections to the Intercounty Connector. The costs for the two-lane parkway were expected to be approximately $96.8 million with grass shoulders and $99.9 million with paved shoulders. These costs did not include the extension to the Intercounty Connector, since they were not recommended. With the ramps included, the costs were expected to be approximately $113.7 million with grass shoulders and $117.0 million with paved shoulders. Right-of-way acquisition costs were not included in any of these figures.

Aesthetics

FOUR-LANE PARKWAY

The minimum width of the four-lane parkway from outer shoulder edge to outer shoulder edge is 100 feet, a third of the width of the corridor. In order to achieve a safe and correct horizontal and vertical alignment over rolling topography while providing a sinuous route that fits the landforms and affords good views, it is often necessary that the parkway be aligned off center within the right-of-way. The bicycle/pedestrian route must, at times, directly abut the parkway to permit adequate space for screening the route from the residential areas bordering the right-of-way.

Figure 1-39: *Perspective of two-lane parkway (drawn by Charles Gardner)*

Particularly where the corridor is narrower than 300 feet, yet even throughout its entire length, the grading in each section of right-of-way must be carried out to minimize the impact of the parkway on bordering land uses. At Rockville Pike, Randolph Road must be raised in elevation and the entrance to a shopping center relocated. To achieve an effective site plan, further study is needed. At Veirs Mill Road, where the right-of-way narrows, additional study is needed to show that the right-of-way can absorb the visual impact of the required structures and grading. There remain many difficult site planning, grading and environmental issues to be resolved.

An alternate section with a variable median was studied to provide a different alignment for the eastbound and westbound roads with a greater separation between them. Such a design would permit extensive plantings in the median. Due to the narrow width of the right-of-way, this alternative was rejected as impractical; greater disturbance of existing natural features would occur. Even with the 10-foot-wide median used in the final preliminary design, it would not be uncommon in areas of cut or fill to grade substantially as much as 175–200 feet of the 300-foot right-of-way width.

Two-Lane Parkway

A two-lane parkway in the Rockville Facility right-of-way fit more comfortably into the rolling topography. The curvilinear alignment flows smoothly, flanked by an independent Class I bicycle/pedestrian path linking existing trail systems. The parkway edges would be graded so that cuts and fills blend into the existing topography, matching its character. There is ample width to screen adjacent residential neighborhoods with new plantings and to save large masses of significant vegetation. It was also recommended that comparable recreational uses be provided in areas of the right-of-way adjacent to the parkway.

The following design criteria for parkway character were recommended:

1. Accomplish regrading with cuts and fills fitting the existing topography with the least disturbance to vegetation cover, in a manner consistent with the existing landscape composition, or the creation of a new landscape composition.
2. In wooded areas create an undulating edge starting along the shoulders of the roadway with a variably wide grass strip that extends into gently graded

coves planted with understory and small flowering trees.

3. Preserve the pastoral quality of the open areas (originally fields) along the parkway at a number of locations.

4. Retain specimen trees that serve as focal points in the landscape and plant additional specimen trees to enhance landscape scenes or to create rich visual compositions.

5. Maintain or create vistas where appropriate.

6. Install plantings to screen development that is intrusive or detracts from the natural park quality and, conversely, to screen the traffic on the parkway from the view of development, particularly residences.

7. Where noise barriers are necessary, use landforms and planting to the greatest extent possible as means for mitigating traffic noise.

8. Maintain architectural unity and harmony in the parkway structures (that is, bridges, culverts, walls, noise barriers, guide rails, fences, signs, lighting, etc.) through the use of materials, structural forms, and colors.

9. In constructing interchanges, adhere to the design principles for curvilinear alignment and natural park quality to the greatest extent possible.

10. To reduce mowing needs, maintain open areas as fields of wildflowers, which would require mowing only two or three times a year. (The danger in this treatment is that the fields would quickly revert to shrubs and trees if maintenance became lax.)

Conclusions

Two-Lane Parkway More Suitable

In our study, we developed designs for a two-lane parkway and four-lane parkway (in both cases with opposite roadways separated by a median) in sufficient detail to determine their engineering feasibility. Both parkways would be possible in the Rockville Facility; however, they would differ in their purposes and in their impacts. Clearly, the four-lane parkway would be primarily a transportation facility, although limited to cars and buses. The two-lane parkway, on the other hand, would be primarily a park road connecting a number of parks; only secondarily would it serve transportation.

Although the Rockville Facility was originally acquired three decades ago for a transportation route, the right-of-way today is a park-like corridor that threads through built-up neighborhoods of residences and commerce. Consequently, it is perceived as a park with its varied woods, fields, and streams. In fact, Rockville Facility connects three parks; visually, parts of the right-of-way appear to be parts of those parks.

Our study caused us to judge the two-lane parkway a more suitable and better use for the Rockville Facility than the four-lane parkway for these reasons:

1. The narrower section of the two-lane parkway (45 feet versus 100 feet) requires less clearing and grading, resulting in less disturbance to the natural features.

2. The narrower section results in a more flexible alignment, horizontally and vertically, for both the parkway and the bicycle/pedestrian paths, an alignment which fits topography and leaves ample space for securing the roadway from neighboring residences.

3. The traffic noise is significantly less due to lower volume of traffic, lower design speed, and greater area of space within the right-of-way for noise attenuation.

4. The alignment avoids the floodplain to a greater extent, leaving more of the floodplain undisturbed, and provides ample space within the right-of-way for infiltration of stormwater runoff and flow attenuation.

5. The bicycle/pedestrian path fits more effectively into the right-of-way as an independent system joining or intersecting the parkway alignment at important intersections or stream crossings.

6. The concept of a parkway as a two-lane road linking a series of three regional parks while also accommodating a major east-west traffic flow is more appropriate, given the confines of the three

hundred-foot-wide right-of-way, than a major four-lane transportation artery.

PARK CONCEPT: PUBLIC POLICY IMPLICATIONS

One policy issue studied by the MNCPPC staff was land ownership. Three types of ownership were detailed. Seventy-nine acres in the right-of-way were bought by MNCPPC's Advance Land Acquisition Revolving Fund (ALARF) for transportation purposes. If this acquired land is not used for transportation, but is used instead for a park, MNCPPC may need to reimburse ALARF. The State Highway Administration (SHA) owns 215 acres, bought for transportation purposes. Should this land not be needed for transportation, under current law, the land must be offered to the original owner for the amount originally paid by the State. The remaining 55 acres are privately owned and would be expensive to purchase, yet the cost must be evaluated against the intended use and future value.

To realize the goal of a linear park running the entire length and width of the Rockville Facility would require creative legislative action in order to use state and privately owned land for recreation purposes. One way in which the park might be considered to have a major transportation function would be to incorporate a commuter bicycle route meeting applicable county, state, and federal standards. This function might satisfy the designated transportation use of the state-owned land, while reinforcing the park concept addressed in the study, and being eligible for funding from the state and federal governments. A bikeway corridor in a park might provide a relief valve from traffic congestion at an economical cost, with minimal impacts on environmental quality.

If the state does not consider the bikeway concept viable as a transportation function, then the creation of a linear park in the entire right-of-way will require legislative changes to permit acquisition of the state-owned lands purchased for transportation purposes. The acquisition of private land would also be necessary. Although these acquisitions may be expensive, their cost should be balanced against

the permanent value of preserving valuable recreation and forest resources for future generations.

PUBLIC RELATIONS

Mounted renderings of the vegetation maps, the conceptual park plan, the two-lane and four-lane parkway plans, and related sections were presented at a public open house at a local junior high school in November, 1988. Further presentation and discussions of all the alternatives occurred at two meetings of the Montgomery County Commissioners and the transportation and Environmental Committee in December and January, 1989. The issues of impacts on wetlands and floodplains became more important as these meetings progressed, since the additional bridge structures and the loss of wetlands, even if they could be recreated in desirable locations, were so expensive. The Commissioners finally voted to recommend that the most environmentally sensitive areas of the right-of-way be set aside as parkland, and they acknowledged that a transportation use of other portions of the right-of-way, despite its costs, might still occur. This legislation was passed recently. It is difficult to imagine how a transportation use could be implemented for either end of the right-of-way, however there is not a consensus to dedicate the entire corridor as parkland.

At all meetings, public officials and citizens were surprised at the costs of either parkway option. Also, general opposition to any parkway option was voiced by most citizens in attendance, who have spent a generation living adjacent to the corridor. Even though no condemnation of housing or other existing structures was required to implement either parkway option, the strength and organization of the opposition was considerable. Legitimate concerns about costs and environmental impacts were expressed.

One can only imagine the public outcry had the right-of-way crossed through existing residential or commercial development. In Atlanta, GA, for example, a decades-long-battle has finally ended over plans now being implemented to wedge a new commuter parkway through existing residential neighborhoods, destroying many fine homes in the process. Mayor Andrew Young, elected in part because of his opposition to the parkway, became a staunch supporter of the project. It was only in 1994 that a group of planners, led by Leon Eplan, helped achieve a compromise which scaled down the scope of the project. The site includes the library and study center of former President Jimmy Carter, who as governor initially opposed the project. But years later he found the still embattled property to be a perfect site for his ambitious enterprise.

Sadly, in the case of the Rockville corridor, some issues are still in limbo. How will the remaining portions of the right-of-way not designated for park land be used? Neither the county not the state seems interested in managing additional park lands. If a transportation use, no matter how limited, is not implemented, the state, barring a change in the law, may sell the lands to the original owners, opening the way for more residential development in areas with limited and congested transportation facilities. No decisive political leadership has come forth to resolve these problems.

As a case study, the Rockville Facility has been unusual in thoroughly evaluating the proposed corridor for *both* a transportation and a recreation land use. In addition, it has been a valuable experience for both the client and the consultant to appreciate the public policy implications of evaluating a transportation land use opposed by most members of the surrounding community but favored by many planners and government officials concerned about long-term transportation issues in the region.

The reactions to this study emphasize the difficulties to be expected when transportation facilities are proposed in congested urban areas that present difficult site planning and environmental challenges. The costs will be high and there will be significant opposition by various groups affected, no matter how well-designed the planned facility is. The era is past when readily buildable land for transportation or residential use can easily be found. The first step in the placement of major transportation uses through existing rights-of-way of varied and difficult character is a time-consuming, yet necessary, study. If the results are favorable, the long, arduous process of environmental assessment can continue. The eventual outcome will be hard to predict, since the impacts, costs, and politics of the process will often be so complex.

PROJECT: *Calverton National Cemetery*
LOCATION: *Calverton, Long Island*
CLIENT: *United States Department of Veterans Affairs*
DATE: *1976–present*

In 1976, the Department of Veterans Affairs (then the Veterans Administration) engaged Clarke + Rapuano, Inc. to assist in selecting a site for a national cemetery to serve the Greater New York Region. Since Congress had not appropriated funds for the purchase of land, the agency sought federally owned land that could be transferred to cemetery use. The Department of the Navy had declared as surplus three buffer zones of its U.S. Naval Weapons Industrial Plant at Calverton (Long Island), NY.

The environmental impact statement was approved in the fall of 1977. The north- west of the three buffer sites was selected; the other two were found unacceptable due to roadways dissecting the sites, large areas of standing water and ponds, steep slopes, and poor soils. During the review of the Draft Environmental Impact Statement, concerns arose about the groundwater systems. How were the three high-yield aquifers on the site to be protected? What were the risks, if any, of potential contamination of the aquifers as a result of burial operations over many years? There were concerns identified in the Environmental Impact Statement about "pollution from surface non-point sources, such as automobiles, fertilizer, and pesticide applications, and cemetery maintenance functions," as well as "from the actual interment of embalmed human remains."

Responses were made to these questions in the Final Environmental Impact Statement. It was agreed that compliance with stringent New York State regulations to prevent the misuse of fertilizers and pesticides or the improper disposal of motor oils and greases into surface or groundwater systems would minimize the impact on water quality of the aquifers. The proposed use of a centralized interment center to service the entire cemetery operation was expected to greatly reduce on-site traffic movement and allow for the efficient control of automobile related pollution.

A thorough study of the potential of ground water pollution from interred human remains was undertaken. Consultations occurred with experts in sanitary engineering, chemistry, and cemetery operations. Comparison were made between European burial practices and American ones. In the National Cemetery System, standard concrete grave liners, which "protect against grave cave-ins, settling, and animal burrowing and nesting" are used. Caskets are chosen by the next-of-kin, and are neither air nor water tight. Although it appeared that it would be possible "for leachates from the interred remains to escape into the surrounding soil," the potential is extremely slim since the "water would first have to move down through the concrete liner, into the casket and back out," an extremely unlikely occurrence with the use of grave liners and modern day caskets. It was also found that although there are chemical residues from embalming operations, even in cases where these chemicals are misused or overused, the concentrations would be insignificantly small. "Noxious chemicals used in embalming are found in greater concentration from activities other than embalming . . . for example, in preservatives in milk and dairy products, as a common treatment to seeds prior to plantings, and formed by discharges during moderate lightning storms."

Clarke + Rapuano then proceeded with the preparation of the Master Plan. They appraised the site's accessibility within the region and examined the site's capacity to fulfill a national cemetery function. They also reviewed the relationship of cemetery use to surrounding land uses and, finally, provided a sensitive, humane and dignified solution for dealing with the magnitude of burials that would occur there.

The purpose of a national cemetery is to honor the nation's veterans in a final tribute by interment in a memorable setting where they will be remembered for their service by generations to come. Calverton National Cemetery is doing so successfully. Funeral services are conducted in a dignified setting and burials are in a park-like setting. Further, it accommodates the magnitude of funerals, already averaging close to fifty a day, in an efficient manner.

On the north shore of Long Island about a two-hour drive (60 miles) east of New York City, the site is 990 acres with state highways along its north and south borders. About 70 percent of the site is in second growth woodland, dominated by white oak (*Quercus alba*) with significant amounts of northern red oak (*Quercus borealis*) and pitch pine (*Pinus rigida*). The pines range upwards to 50 feet in height, and the oaks, 25 to 30 feet. Fires have severely impacted approximately one third of the woodlands. Many of the oaks have lost their central trunks as a result and have sprouted prolifically from their bases. The shrub and floor level plants include blueberry (*Vaccinium sp.*), huckleberry (*Gaylussacia sp.*), sweetfern (*Comptonia peregrina*), and bracken fern (*Pteridium aquilinium*). Wild flowers include lupine and yellow rocket. The gently rolling to relatively flat topography, about ninety percent of which is less than 5 percent slopes, is traversed by four principal swales. The only areas of the site with slopes greater than 15 percent are some of the edges of these swales. The elevations of the site range from 58.5 to 103.0.

Soils on the site are sandy to silty loams underlain by very deep deposits of relatively compact medium to fine sand. Topsoil varies in depth from three inches to 16 inches, averaging five inches. As each phase of work is implemented, the topsoil is stockpiled for reuse in developing the lawns for the cemetery. Due to the sandy subbase under the soils and the sporadic summer rainfalls typical of the region, an irrigation system is installed throughout the cemetery.

A severe restraint on the planning for the cemetery was the Installation Compatible Use Zone (AICUZ) Plan, which the Department of the Navy adopted as a means for assuring compatible use of the lands abutting the airfield of the Naval Weapons Industrial Reserve Plant. The AICUZ plan relates permissible land uses to zones of high noise exposure, potential accident hazards and airspace requirements. For safety reasons, AICUZ strictly controls the density of people and buildings within the flight approach areas considered the most hazardous. On approximately 60% of the site, the restrictions did not permit buildings nor more than 25 people per acre to congregate on the site. Therefore, the Cemetery's administration center, committal service center and the maintenance/service center had to be located outside hazardous

areas, within a relatively narrow 1,000 foot wide corridor along New York Route 25 on the south boundary of the site. This was accomplished successfully in the landscape architectural concept while also achieving a natural, park-like environment.

Three programmatic considerations influenced the design. Firstly, the design team, in consultation with the client, felt that a funeral party should be able to arrive at the cemetery, hold its service and depart without being required to pass through large areas of gravesites. Secondly, it seemed important for the comfort of visitors that they should be able to arrive directly at the memorial center with the least possibility of becoming lost. Thirdly, in fitting the design to the topography, it seemed appropriate to organize the cemetery as a group of smaller cemeteries, each of 15 to 20 acres, separated from one another by woodlands, in order to avoid vast expanses of gravesites.

The landscape architectural concept for the Master Plan design stems from an appreciation of the site's landscape character which is indigenous to that part of Long Is-

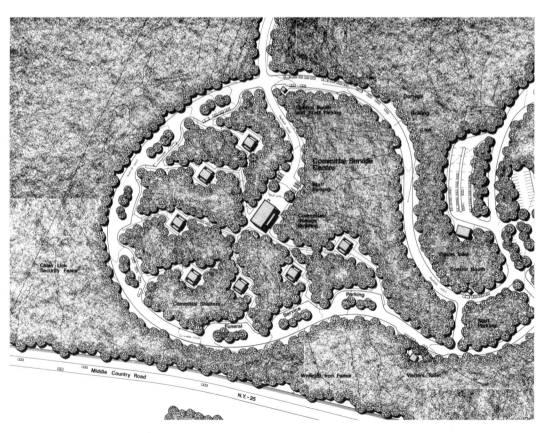

Figure 1-40: *Preliminary plan of committal service center*

PRIVATE SECTOR—LARGE FIRMS

Figure 1-41: *Aerial view of committal service center (before completion of the sixth and seventh shelters).*

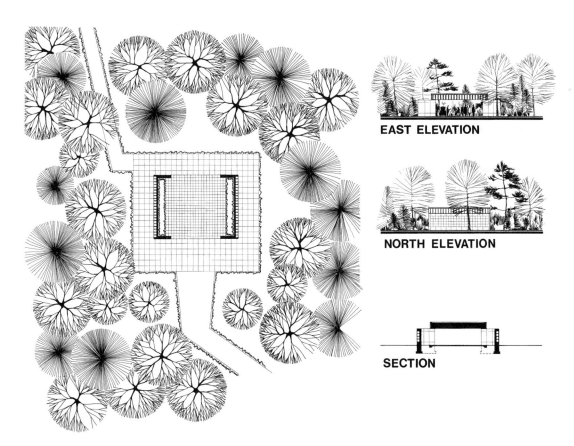

EAST ELEVATION

NORTH ELEVATION

SECTION

Figure 1-42: *Illustrative plan, elevation, and section of a committal service center*

Figure 1-43: *Committal shelter: note "floating roof." (Photo by Domenico Annese)*

Figure 1-44: *Crypts for remains in the wall of a committal shelter (Photo by Domenico Annese)*

tion that separated the functions of the funeral services from the burial operations which, given the magnitude of daily burials, take on aspects of heavy construction. This has been accomplished at Calverton National Cemetery in a solution that was unique to national cemeteries.

Clarke + Rapuano could have accepted the standard procedures for national cemeteries current at the time as the basis for a master plan. Instead, Clarke + Rapuano investigated and observed cemetery procedures at the New York National Cemetery in Farmingdale, Long Island, and at other cemeteries in the metropolitan New York region. They concluded that the current procedures for final services and interment, including private and sectarian cemeteries, could not accommodate the projected daily volumes of funerals, certainly not with dignity. Therefore, Clarke + Rapuano developed the committal service center concept which became the basis for the Master Plan.

It is a standard national cemetery practice to use portable shelters for final burial services. These are moved about as new portions of the cemetery are opened for interment. This requires funeral corteges to drive throughout the cemetery, interfering with visitor traffic and the normal cemetery operations. At Calverton National Cemetery, *permanent* committal shelters are located in a central area. Funeral corteges arrive at the committal service center along a defined roadway, with ample parking and rest rooms, without traversing the burial sections. Consequently, funeral traffic is confined to a small part of the Cemetery without interfering with visitor traffic and cemetery operations. There is also a significant aesthetic benefit: The serenity of the landscape is not broken for the visitor at a gravesite by a parade of continuous funeral corteges.

A group of seven committal shelters are located in a grove of woods in the southwest corner of the site in the AICUZ zone with the least noise exposure, separated from the burial sections. Each shelter is a

land. The design avoids monumentality in favor of preserving the natural environment to the greatest extent possible. It carves discreet burial sections from the woods, while also maintaining the natural character of the drainage swales, and providing a circulatory road system fitted to the topography. In essence, the design is park-like with pleasant drives and expansive views of open green areas framed by woods.

The practical aspects of the Master Plan design are dictated by the need to handle an ultimate peak load of approximately eighty funerals a day within a four-hour period. The planning analysis led to a solu-

Figure 1-45: *Illustrative site plan of Administration Center*

permanent structure with granite walls and open on two sides so that one is always aware of the surrounding woods. Each shelter has its own parking area. Consequently, final funeral services can be conducted with dignity in a serene atmosphere. At the departure of the mourners, the casket is taken to a central building in the committal shelter center and from there transported to a burial section for interment. The committal shelters are located far enough apart from one another along a curving loop drive so that the funeral corteges for a service at one shelter will not interfere with those of the adjoining shelters. They are permanent buildings with granite walls and flat floating roofs constructed with terne-coated stainless

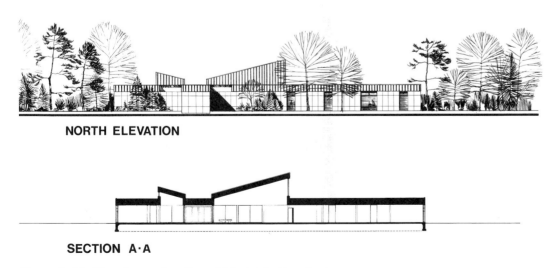

NORTH ELEVATION

SECTION A·A

Figure 1-46: *Elevation and section of Administration Center*

steel fascias. Each building is oriented north to south so that available light always washes down the inside of the wall behind the casket.

The walls of the committal shelters are designed to serve as columbaria (containers for cremated ashes), with individual niches for remains. The columbaria niches are located in the outside face of the opposing walls, each identified with a bronze memorial plaque. The bluestone floor on which each shelter rests extends outward sufficiently beyond the walls to provide a walkway wide enough to permit benches facing the columbaria niches.

A unified theme is carried out in the architecture of the administration center, the memorial building, the committal shelters, and even the maintenance buildings. The architectural inspiration is the shed roof of the salt-box, a style of architecture indigenous to eastern Long Island. The administration building and the committal shelters

are constructed of green granite with roofs of terne-coated steel with batten seams which weathers to a uniform, dull pewter color. Split face concrete blocks are used in the walls of the maintenance buildings and public toilets. The simplicity of the forms and the colors of the materials give the architecture of the site a quiet dignity.

A valley is the one major topographic feature within the gently rolling, wooded site. The major entrance road into the cemetery follows the rim of this valley, and the design of the cemetery uses this valley as a focus around which the administration center and memorial center are sited. The landscape character of meadows framed by existing woodlands creates a serene atmosphere from the moment the visitor enters the cemetery.

The Master Plan design proposed graves with flush bronze markers. The early burial sections were installed with flush markers. Since 1990, however, traditional upright

Figure 1-47: *Administration building as seen from the Meadow*

headstones have been installed in accordance with a Congressional mandate. (See Figures C-4 and C-5.) Each gravesite is six feet wide by ten feet long, enough space to permit a veteran and spouse to be buried side by side.

The Master Plan sets forth the complete needs for Calverton National Cemetery (i.e., road system, burial sections, administration center, committal service center, memorial center, commemorative gardens, maintenance/service center, public toilets, and infrastructure) and a schedule for construction in phases. The centers were all completed by 1982; about seventy-five percent of the site is now developed.

Over the 20 years since completing the Master Plan, Clarke + Rapuano has been continuously engaged in designing each phase of construction for the Department of Veterans Affairs. The firm's design responsibilities include landscape architecture, architecture and engineering, plus construction period services. The following current and former members of Clarke + Rapuano's staff served as principal designers in the development of Calverton National Cemetery from the master plan stage through each phase of construction: Current Landscape Architects: Domenico Annese, principal, Steven L. Cantor, Charles N. Gardner; Architect: Jaime A. Vasquez; Engineers: Raymond J. Heimbuch, principal, Bernd G. Lenzen, Andre P. Martecchini, William Wild; Former Landscape Architects: James Coleman, Bradford M. Greene, Ludwig Vetere; Architect: Frank C. Marcellino; Engineers: Peter F. Martecchini, Donald C. Hughes.

The construction of Calverton National Cemetery was begun in 1978; the buildings and major elements were completed by 1983. Since then, additional burial sections have been developed. A major addition to the maintenance/service center was completed in 1992. The last two committal shelters were completed and put in use in 1994.

Planting on the site reinforces the edges of existing woodlands with species of trees that are already well-established on the site. These are reinforced with additional plantings of trees and shrubs that could be expected to occur in this type of environment, in some ways like a section of the New Jersey Pine Barrens. Major trees include the following:

Acer rubrum, native red maple
Acer saccharum, sugar maple
Pinus rigida, pitch pine
Pinus sylvestris, Scotch pine
Pinus strobus, white pine
Quercus borealis, northern red oak
Quercus palustris, pin oak

Accent flowering trees include serviceberry (*Amelanchier canadensis*), dogwoods (*Cornus florida*), hawthornes (*Crataegus sp.*), and American hollies (*Ilex opaca*). Mountain laurel (*Kalmia latifolia*), inkberry (*Ilex glabra*), bayberry (*Myrica pensylvanica*), pieris (*Pieris japonica*), rhododendrons (*Rhododendron catawbiense*), and viburnums (*Viburnum sp.*) are incorporated as accent shrubs near the committal shelters. Wintergreen (*Gaultheria procumbens*) and Boston ivy (*Parthenocissus tricuspidata lowi*) are used as vines and fine textured groundcover near the committal shelters. Lowbush blueberry (*Vaccinium angustifolium laevifolium*) is planted in sods to reestablish the existing groundcover while minimizing the lawns and in areas near the committal shelters is used to integrate into the surrounding dry woodland environment. In a few drier, sandy areas bearberry (*Arctostaphylos urva-ursi*) was used.

A lawn was seeded of 30 percent Jamestown Chewing Fescue, 50 percent Baron Kentucky bluegrass and 20 percent Yorkstown 2, and is well established throughout the burial sections, and between the edge of the woods and the edges of roads and walks. In damper areas where lawn is still desired a mixture of Derby and Yorktown is established. A few areas of sod, a mixture of fescue and Kentucky bluegrass, were placed near the administration and visitor center in highly trafficked areas. Tall fescue and wildflowers mark the large meadow opposite the administration building in order to bring some color into the expanse of rolling terrain and to create a focal point. The wildflower seeding was a mixture of 30 percent by weight of sheeps fescue with the balance a mixture of bachelor's button, chicory, lance-leaved coreopsis, baby's breath, scarlet flax, Lewis flax, evening primrose, corn poppy, catch fly, and baby snapdragon. Wildflowers were also seeded in the low lying areas of the site, and succeeded well, but these areas have been allowed to follow a natural succession to field and woodland.

Prior to development, storm water runoff ran along drainage ways and collected at low areas, where it percolated into the sandy soils. Environmental regulations required that any additional runoff created as a result of cemetery construction be similarly retained on site and allowed to percolate into the underlying sand layers, thus recharging the ground water and preventing downstream erosion. Two methods of handling the increase in stormwater runoff are used. Runoff from the burial section is directed into the surrounding woods or towards roadside swales. Catchbasins along these swales intercept the runoff and discharge it underground into large leaching basins, where the collected water gradually percolates into the ground. Runoff not intercepted by the leaching basin system flows through existing, natural swales to low areas, where it eventually percolates into the sandy soils. The master plan proposed the development of two of these areas into permanent ponds, with curving contours and naturalistic paintings, to protect the recharge areas immediately below them from serious silting. However, in the execution of the work, it was found that the amount of runoff was not adequate

for this purpose, and the ponds were not necessary.

Eleven wells are planned for the Cemetery: seven for irrigation, three for domestic water supply, and one for fire control. All but two have been drilled and are operating. Domestic water needs are concentrated in the southern portion of the site where the principal buildings are located. Irrigation zones are established with automatically operated systems so that manpower requirements are minimal. Most watering occurs in the early evening hours following closing and in the early morning hours prior to opening the Cemetery to the public. Water mains are set along the road with junction boxes at each burial area. Irrigation laterals are set along the axis of the graves, with the long dimension of the 6-foot by 10-foot gravesites perpendicular to the laterals. Each lateral lies along a row of gravemarkers in a dedicated space that is not be disturbed by burial operations. Impulse sprinklers are generally used in order to cover as much areas as possible in the most efficient manner.

Calverton National Cemetery, after twenty years of continuous planning and construction, continues to meet the needs of veterans and their families from the metropolitan New York region. Currently, from 40 to 50 funerals a day occur in a simple, tranquil and dignified setting without disturbance from visitor traffic heading towards the exhibits in the memorial center or the gravesites of loved ones.

DHM, INC.

Denver, CO

In 1975 DHM, Inc., was founded in Denver, a rapidly growing metropolitan area. The firm's focus has been a broad spectrum of master planning and landscape architectural design projects. Included here are master planning for the Mount Rushmore

National Memorial and Yellowstone National Park, which both propose guidelines for future development and rehabilitation of existing facilities, and The Preserve, a residential community in the hills just outside Denver.

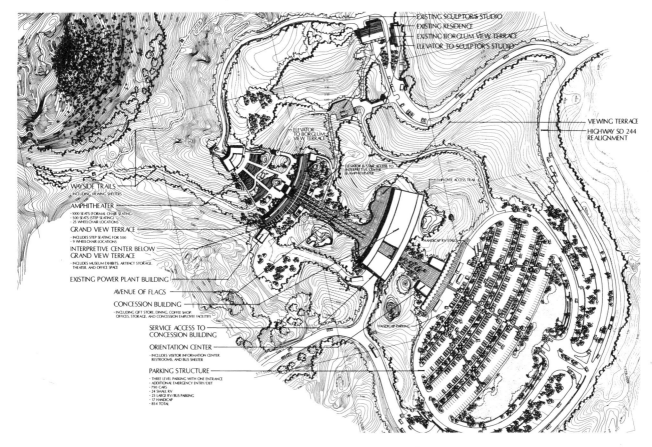

Figure 1-48: *Comprehensive design plan, Mt. Rushmore National Memorial*

EXISTING SCULPTOR'S STUDIO
EXISTING RESIDENCE
EXISTING BORGLUM VIEW TERRACE
ELEVATOR TO SCULPTOR'S STUDIO

VIEWING TERRACE
HIGHWAY SD 244
REALIGNMENT

ELEVATOR
TO BORGLUM
VIEW TERRACE

ELEVATOR & STAIR ACCESS TO
INTERPRETIVE CENTER
& AMPHITHEATER

EMPLOYEE ACCESS TRAIL

HANDICAP RV STALLS

HANDICAP PARKING

WAYSIDE TRAILS
· INCLUDING VIEWING SHELTERS

AMPHITHEATER
· 1000 SEATS (FORMAL CHAIR SEATING)
· 500 SEATS (STEP SEATING)
· 25 WHEELCHAIR LOCATIONS

GRAND VIEW TERRACE
· INCLUDES STEP SEATING FOR 500
· 9 WHEELCHAIR LOCATIONS

**INTERPRETIVE CENTER BELOW
GRAND VIEW TERRACE**
· INCLUDES MUSEUM EXHIBITS, ARTIFACT STORAGE,
THEATER, AND OFFICE SPACE

EXISTING POWER PLANT BUILDING

AVENUE OF FLAGS

CONCESSION BUILDING
· INCLUDING GIFT STORE, DINING, COFFEE SHOP,
OFFICES, STORAGE, AND CONCESSION EMPLOYEE FACILITIES

**SERVICE ACCESS TO
CONCESSION BUILDING**

ORIENTATION CENTER
· INCLUDES VISITOR INFORMATION CENTER,
RESTROOMS, AND BUS SHELTER

PARKING STRUCTURE
· THREE LEVEL PARKING WITH ONE ENTRANCE
· ADDITIONAL EMERGENCY ENTRY/EXIT
· 790 CARS
· 24 SMALL RV
· 23 LARGE RV/BUS PARKING
· 17 HANDICAP
· 854 TOTAL

Figure 1-49: *Front view of orientation center, the contact station for visitors*

PROJECT: *Mt. Rushmore National Memorial—Master Plan*
CLIENT: *United States Department of the Interior*
LOCATION: *Keystone, SD*
COST: *$35,000,000*

Like many national parks facilities, Mount Rushmore National Memorial—renowned for the busts of four Presidents carved into the face of the mountain—was experiencing an inability to support peak crowds, which were occurring with increasing frequency. The passage of the Americans With Disabilities Act had underscored the lack of accommodation for the handicapped. Finally, there were limited interpretive facilities at the park. The National Park Service hired DHM to develop a master plan for the visitor center and surrounding areas at the Mount Rushmore National Memorial.

DHM followed a five-step process in the course of developing a final master plan:

1. Evaluation of existing facilities and infrastructure.

2. Programming of needs for interior and exterior facilities.
3. Development of conceptual alternatives.
4. Evaluation of projected costs.
5. Development of a selected alternative.

The selected alternative was carefully evaluated for the visual and environmental impacts of the building program through preparation and review of an Environmental Assessment. The final program includes a $35 million reconstruction of existing facilities, with schematic plans finalized in time for review during festivities for the 50th anniversary celebration of the Memorial in 1991. Following acceptance of the Master Plan, DHM has continued to refine the site program. The work includes a more detailed analysis of site grading, building locations, program require-

Figure 1-50: *Avenue of Flags*

EXISTING GRADE
BOULDERS
PATH WITH SPECIAL PAVING
CART PATH DEFINED BY COLUMNS
STONE COLUMNS WITH FLAGS

STONE COLUMNS WITH FLAGS

PATH WITH SPECIAL PAVING
STONE COLUMNS WITH FLAGS
CART PATH DEFINED BY COLUMNS

RETAINING WALLS

Figure 1-51: *Cross sections through Avenue of Flags*

Figure 1-52: *Grand View Terrace and amphitheater*

grading, building locations, program requirements, phasing options, and costs.

The master plan addresses the entire visitor experience from arrival to departure. South Dakota Highway 244 is realigned to allow for a median in the highway at its intersection with the entrance to Rushmore and to accommodate parking. A formal axis is created, almost 1/2 mile long, from the entrance to the parking lot and terminating at the monument itself. The concept is to communicate spatially with the visitors, so that at any point in their experience with the site, a focused vista towards the monument beckons them. A three-level parking structure with two levels underground provides parking for 790 cars, 24 small recreational vehicles, 21 large recreational vehicles or buses, and 17 handicapped spaces. The primary vehicular circulation occurs around the perimeter of the parking structure, so that pedestrians focus towards the center along the primary axis on line with the monument and two secondary axes symmetrically placed in relation to the first one.

In sequence, visitors proceed from the orientation center, which includes an information center, rest rooms, and bus shelter, to a concession building providing a gift shop, restaurant, and administrative offices and storage space. The axis penetrates both of these buildings, so that the orientation towards the memorial is always clear. As the visitor leaves the concession building, he or she follows the Avenue of Flags, a broad, 40-foot wide allee and continuation of the axis. Two rows of stone columns with flags divide the width of the space into thirds. The center of the avenue is 14-feet wide to accommodate carts carrying people who are handicapped. On either side is a wide pedestrian route with special paving. The edges of either side of the Avenue of Flags transition smoothly to the existing forest of Ponderosa pine (*Pinus ponderosa*).

At the termination of the Avenue of Flags is the interpretive center, housing museum exhibits, a theater, and additional office and storage space. Again the axis interpenetrates the building and pulls the visitor through it towards the view of the Memorial. Above the interpretive center is the Grand View Terrace, which provides stepped seating for 500 people. Finally, there is an amphitheater cut into the increasingly steep slopes. It accommodates 2000 people in formal seating stepped into the mountain sides. Trails with viewing shelters at key points lead from the Grand View Terrace closer to the Memorial and loop back to the Terrace.

Some major existing buildings on the site are retained. The power plant building, for example, abuts the western corner of the interpretive center. It is as far as possible from the central axis and it is screened by plantings of Ponderosa pines, so that it is not visible to the public. A separate service access on the west is provided to the concession building and power plant. There is also a pedestrian connection from the main parking lot and the Grand View Terrace to the existing sculptor's studio and Borglum View Terrace on the eastern side of the site. A service road provides access to this facility and also to the amphitheater from its northern side. The road is depressed so that it is not visible to the public.

PROJECT: *Yellowstone National Park—Master Plan*
CLIENT: *United States Department of the Interior*

The program requirements at Yellowstone National Park are different. Again there are huge numbers of visitors to the park, but rather than concentrating all at one location, they are dispersed widely throughout the park at different landmarks and accommodations. Therefore, scattered communities provide employee housing and support facilities. The National Park Service retained DHM to undertake a comprehensive plan for ten communities within the park including the villages of Tower Junction, West Entrance, Lower Mammoth, Roosevelt Lodge, Canyon Village, and others.

DHM used a thorough inventory, analysis, and planning process to evaluate existing conditions and make recommendations on potential improvements. For each of the ten communities, the design team made a careful evaluation of man-made and natural conditions in order to identify three alternative sites for each new or renovated community. Similar to the Rushmore process, the designers produced studies for each alternative site. The Park Service selected a preferred site. It was then studied in more detail, so that a master plan with associate design guidelines, titled the Community Report, was prepared for each of the ten selected communities.

Throughout the planning process, the design team, which included a sociologist, interviewed the users of the communities—the employees—in order to determine their needs and their reactions. There were community meetings as well as individual interactions. The final plans reflect the input of the employees and establish a framework for living which is similar to that historically found in the National Parks.

Following the completion of the Community Report, DHM began the environmental assessment process, part of the public review and input phase of the project. Utilizing Yellowstone National Park's own scientists and research personnel to pre-

Figure 1-53: *Yellowstone: park employee housing at Tower Junction*

Figure 1-54: *Yellowstone: park employee housing at Madison Junction*

pare much of the baseline information and analysis for the Natural and Cultural Resources sections, DHM prepared the environmental assessment report. DHM retained an additional subconsultant to provide input on socioeconomic issues. The consequences of each of the alternatives for all ten communities were thoroughly evaluated and incorporated into the report. Yellowstone National Park required a tight time frame so that housing and associated facilities could be improved in an effective and efficient manner. Only minor changes were required to any of the preferred alternatives for each of the ten communities.

PROJECT: *The Preserve*
CLIENT: *Koelbel and Company development*
LOCATION: *Greenwood Village, CO*

In contrast to these two projects in the public sector to accommodate thousands of people, DHM worked for a private developer on a residential community. On a 522-acre site in close proximity to Denver, CO, the Preserve is set on the rolling hills of Greenwood Village. The property has several major scenic amenities, including the Highline Canal and its associated trail system and several attractive natural swales. In addition, a beautiful 45 acre natural preserve became the focus of the community's open space system. DHM was retained to design road and lot layouts, write design standards for the community, and develop landscape architectural plans for treatment of major streetscapes, entries, and naturalistic open spaces.

One of the more important priorities in development of the periphery landscape was the mitigation of noise from the nearby roadway system. In order to buffer noise without creating a series of visually intrusive barriers, the design team used extensive grading to create landforms which deflect sound away from homes while still allowing drivers selected views into the community. The landforms are enhanced with carefully controlled use of low walls to gain additional height where necessary. An extensive palette of trees, shrubs, groundcovers, grasses, annuals and perennials was added to these reshaped landforms to provide additional screening and seasonal interest. Generally, plantings are informal to complement the natural settings found within the community.

The entries to this community have been carefully designed to create a feeling of elegance and permanence. Local sandstones have been painstakingly cut and fitted to create substantial walls which embrace the entries. The entry roads themselves have been routed around an oval-shaped median, which slows down drivers as they enter the community. Concrete pavers are used extensively on the entry roadways to add color and texture and further define the entrance. As the final touches to these designs, dense plantings and discreet lights enhance evening and seasonal interest.

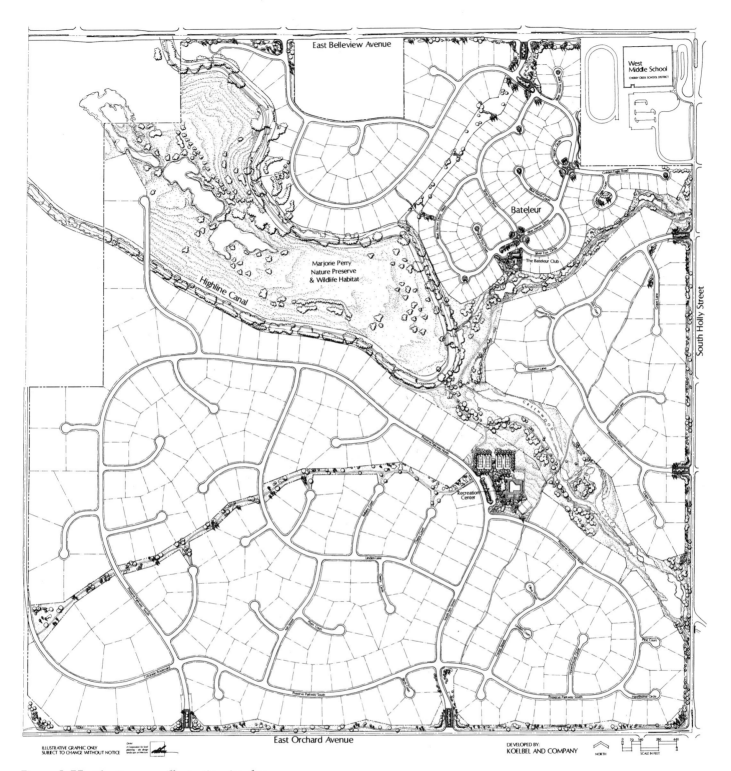

Figure 1-55: *The Preserve, illustrative site plan*

Figure 1-56: *The spectacular setting provides housing nestled against the foothills of the Rockies*

Figure 1-57: *This large duck pond serves both aesthetic and engineering functions*

Figure 1-58: *The curving walks and walks move sinuously through the richly planted landscape*

CAROL R. JOHNSON ASSOCIATES, INC.

Cambridge, MA

Founded in 1959, Carol R. Johnson Associates, Inc., is a 60-member firm in Cambridge, MA. Currently one of the largest landscape architectural firms in the United States, the firm works both as a direct consultant to private and public clients and as a subconsultant to other design professionals. The two projects featured here, the paving matrix at Logan International Airport and Charter Oak Park, represent examples of developing non-standard landscape design techniques for complex and challenging sites in which standard solutions would not be appropriate or desirable. Carol R. Johnson, Chairman of the Board and President of the firm, was educated at

Wellesley College and Harvard, and is a Fellow of the American Society of Landscape Architects and an honorary member of the Boston Society of Architects. Harry S. Fuller, the Executive Vice President of the firm, was educated at Princeton and Harvard. He has directed design efforts in urban revitalization projects, as well as corporate and institutional work. William Taylor, a vice president of the firm, was educated at North Carolina State and Harvard, and directs many of the firm's urban waterfront projects.

PROJECT: *Logan International Terminal "B" Paving Matrix*
CLIENT: *Massachusetts Port Authority*
LOCATION: *East Boston, MA*
DATE: *1982*

Carol R. Johnson Associates Inc. (CRJA) was hired by Desmond and Lord, Architects, to provide site planning services for Terminal B, the new USAir terminal. Massport, the Massachusetts Port Authority (MPA), which owns and operates Logan Airport, hired Desmond and Lord as the prime consultant. CJA was one of several major consultants for this project, and worked with architects and civil and structural engineers.

MPA provided the landscape architects with the conceptual plan of the vehicular circulation system around the new terminal. A series of roads and ramps leads visitors to the terminal under the building and into a parking garage, and provides access to and from the building. In this system of roads, some are viaducts and others are surface streets. The major challenge for CRJA was how to unify this complex transportation system, both horizontally and vertically. It was immediately obvious that to an automobile driver there would be a lot going on and he or she would have to make a series of decisions. CJA sought a way to give a simple, consistent frame of reference that would unify and simplify the driver's experience within this road system and entry complex.

The landscape architects developed a series of ground plane treatments that would make the driver's experience less hectic and less complex. They developed a plaza based on a strong grid design. The driver sees the plaza from above as he is looping into the garage and from the side as he enters the terminal. There is no pedestrian access to this plaza, so the designers had an opportunity to play with textural and vertical changes in the elements of the ground plane, giving visual interest at a distance. Portions of the grid system were not paved to accommodate planting beds. Shadow studies were done of the viaducts to determine areas where the highest light levels would be. These sites became the locations for the planting beds. The pavement is crowned upwards towards the center to facilitate drainage. A subtle but important element of the design, this site-planning detail lifts the plaza up from the ground plane so that one viewing it from above, or from the surface, notices the pavements and plantings. The gradient usually modulates from three to five percent, with two percent the absolute minimum.

Logan Airport is a compact airport, and the new terminal is no exception. There is limited space adjacent to any of the ramps, roads, or viaducts. MPA stressed the importance of having ample space for snow storage adjacent to the edges of the roadways. The plaza of grid paving comfortably accommodates snow, which, as it melts, drains back towards the curbs on either side of the plaza. The planting spaces are usually kept some distance away from the curb in order to avoid exposure to high concentrations of salt used to prevent snow and ice-buildup.

The grid was conceptualized because it had such a unifying effect on the complex geometry of the roadway system. CRJA first suggested granite as a paving material, but this was rejected as being too expen-

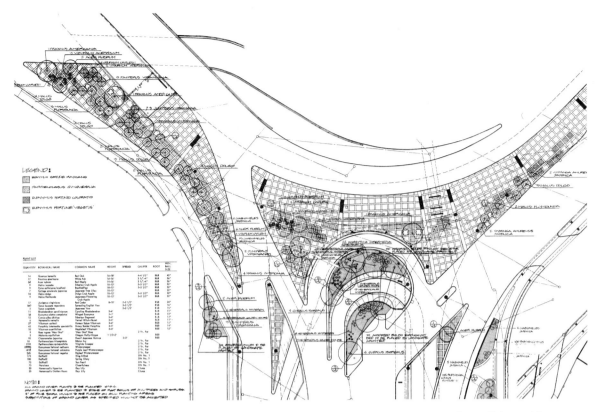

Figure 1-59: *Illustrative site plan. The ground surface at the site entrance consists of a unifying grid system in which paving is omitted where light is adequate enough to permit planting.*

sive. Different pavement materials were researched; the focus of the materials selection was on systems of unit pavers that could be adaptable to other areas of the airport. The main choices were some type of concrete or brick. Brick was rejected because it seemed inappropriate for the airport: Its texture was too fine and the color reminiscent of the city's historic areas, not the modern airport. In addition, the designers sought a warm color that would still contrast with concrete, particularly in the late fall, winter, and early spring months when the airport's landscape and much of Boston's can appear bleak. They also desired a texture that wasn't as smooth as brick and had enough variation in it to be visually appealing to passersby. They finally found a pre-cast split-faced pavement block with a warm buff color.

In order for the entire plaza not to appear too flat, the designers developed a shadow line by setting the paving blocks 1-3/4″ above the concrete ground plane. The vivid checkerboard shadow pattern ani-

mates the view. The effect of the shadow line is accentuated by the 3% to 5% gradient up towards the center of the plaza.

The pavement consists of a grid of concrete bands sixteen inches wide with infill panels 63 inches square of either these unit paving blocks or plantings. In deep shade, close to curbs, and in response to other constraints the "panels" are unit pavers; where there is more light and space these panels are planting. The unit pavers are set parallel to one another in rows, butted end to end, and swept with a sand-cement mixture.

MPA sought plant materials that would require minimal maintenance. It was decided to allow the plant materials to grow loosely and overlap the edges of the grid, softening its rigidity. CRJA concluded that in as exposed and harsh an environment as these leftover spaces between the road system, irrigation would be essential. The planting panels were backfilled with a rich loam soil mix, and a network of irrigation lines parallel and perpendicular to the grid

Figure 1-60: *As-built crown condition. The paving grid slopes gradually up from the curb line to improve drainage and to make the grid pattern more perceptible to the motorist.*

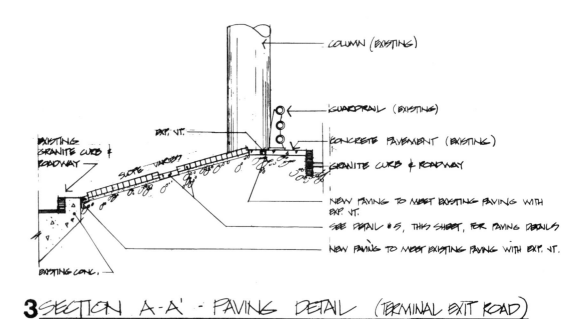

3 SECTION A-A' - PAVING DETAIL (TERMINAL EXIT ROAD)
SCALE: 1/4" : 1'-0"

Figure 1-61: *Construction detail. "Split-rib," precast concrete pavers are set into a cast-in-place concrete matrix. By setting the face of the pavers above the concrete matrix, the designers provide an interesting texture to the surface.*

Figure 1-62: *The edges of the square blocks of raised pavers cast distinct shadow lines and accentuate the textural character.*

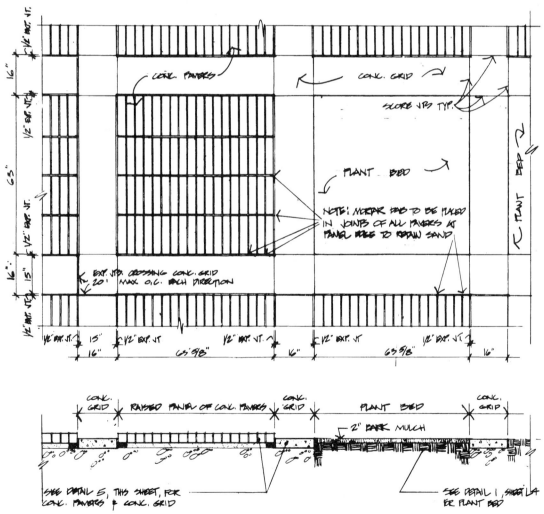

CONC. PAVERS

CONC. GRID

SCORE JTS TYP.

PLANT BED

PLANT BED

NOTE: MORTAR BED TO BE PLACED IN JOINTS OF ALL PAVERS AT PANEL EDGE TO RETAIN SAND

EXP. JTS. CROSSING CONC. GRID 20' MAX O.C. EACH DIRECTION

CONC. GRID   RAISED PANEL OF CONC. PAVERS   CONC. GRID   PLANT BED   CONC. GRID

2" BARK MULCH

SEE DETAIL 5, THIS SHEET, FOR CONC. PAVERS & CONC. GRID

SEE DETAIL 1, SHEET L4 ER PLANT BED

SECTION

6 CONCRETE GRID / CONC. PAVER PANEL DETAIL

SCALE: 1/2" = 1'-0"

Figure 1-63: *Construction detail of grid. The grid bands enclose planting pockets or paved panels approximately five feet square.*

Figure 1-64: *The grid is planted where light is sufficient. The result is a random, but geometric pattern of soft and hard surfaces.*

were provided. Since the pavement is pitched towards either curb from the center, excess water naturally drains through the plantings towards the curb.

The principal deciduous trees are the following:

Acer rubrum, native red maple
Fraxinus americana, white ash
Malus floribunda and Dolgo, crabapples
Syringa amurensis japonica, Japanese tree
lilac

Flowering quince (*Chaenomeles speciosa*) has been highly successful as a foreground shrub mass. Other shrubs include forsythia (*Forsythia intermedia spectabilis*), juniper (*Juniperus virginiana*), and two varieties of viburnum (*Viburnum carlesi* and *Viburnum acerifolium*). Euonymous (*Euonymous fortunei coloratus*) and periwinkle (*Vinca minor*) are the two ground covers. Euonymous is used in the sunnier areas while periwinkle is used primarily in the shady areas and transitional areas between deep shade and light shade.

Evergreens were planted as screening devices for particular views, but none of these plantings have been successful as they have been susceptible to the polluted environment. Particulate levels are quite high and build up on the evergreen foliage, which gradually succumbs to the pollution and withers.

This installation, in place for many years, has weathered severe winters and drought-stricken summers, and survives with minimal maintenance. The paving matrix's unified ground plane is a carpet of varying textures upon which rests the transportation framework of the air terminal. The design simplifies and organizes the complex experience of arriving, entering, parking, and leaving by automobile.

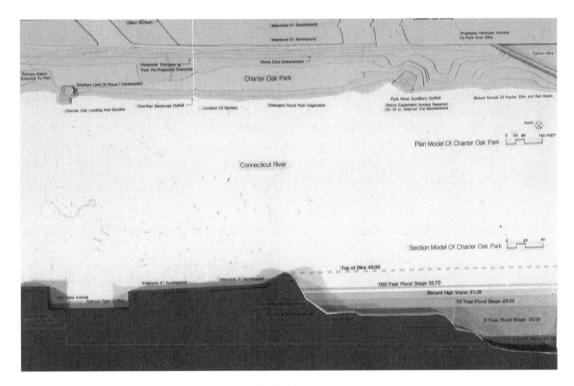

Figure 1-65: *Site plan and section showing flood elevations*

PROJECT: *Charter Oak Park*
CLIENT: *Riverfront Recapture Inc.*
LOCATION: *Connecticut River, Hartford, CT*
DATE: *1986*
CONSULTING STRUCTURAL ENGINEER: *Childs Engineering, Medfield, MA*

The most remarkable aspect of this river-front park is that it is continually accessible to the public despite being flooded as much as twelve feet deep by the waters of the Connecticut River. A series of parallel terraces, each one a few feet higher than the one below it, are designed to be inundated by rising floodwaters, yet permit access to the river's edge. The Connecticut River's flooding has a few characteristics that are factored into the design. The flood tends to rise and fall slowly without sudden or dangerous fluctuations. The river floods several times each year, but the major flooding occurs annually in the spring. Although it is seasonal, the flood also tends to occur over substantial periods of time. An-other related factor is the erosive force of ice along the river's edge during the winter.

The client, Riverfront Recapture, Inc., a non-profit group whose goal is to reclaim the

Figure 1-66: *View of parade ground with parking on the right*

river's edge for public use, was able to secure public and private funding. Carol R. Johnson Associates was faced with the daunting challenge of developing solutions to make the riverbank usable during different levels of flood. Downtown Hartford used to flood every year from the river, with sometimes devastating results. In the late 1800s a dike was built to protect the city. A railroad was located on the city side of the dike, and, more than a century later, Interstate 91 was built on top of the dike which effectively cut off the river from the city. The river edge environment became a very dangerous, crime-ridden area, abandoned for any major recreational uses, overgrown with rank vegetation, and strewn with garbage.

Figure 1-67: *View of river terraces after construction*

As part of a long-term solution to increase access to the river, CRJA is developing construction documents for a major recreational development. Their urban plaza connects downtown Hartford over the top of I-91 via a series of walks and stairways down to the river's edge, and includes replacing a major highway bridge so that it can connect to the new plaza and accommodate large volumes of pedestrians and bicyclists. The park at the riverfront, at a much lower elevation, will also be accessed via elevators. This project, and the restored Founders Bridge, is scheduled for completion in 1996. Charter Oak Park is the first of their projects along the Connecticut to increase public access to the river's edge and restore its functions as a recreational resource.

The entire park is only about 300 feet wide, but runs for nearly a mile along the river, which has flooded to a maximum elevation of 35 on several occasions. The 100-year flood elevation for this site is 29.5. Atop the dike, at approximately elevation 38, is Interstate 91, and below and parallel to it, is a frontage road linked to the highway with an underpass. The frontage road connects to a substantial parking area that can accommodate 50 cars. Adjacent to it there is a pavilion and boat dock, the access point for a river boat excursion concession. Also adjacent to the parking, at approximately elevation 24, which is above the average flooding level of the river, is a large, formal parade ground that is used for all kinds of gatherings, picnicking, informal games like frisbee, and public events and festivals.

The intent was to emphasize this man-made, formal landscape and then transition to the river's edge. A series of wide asphalt paths leads towards the river, and to the series of fishing and viewing terraces. As the paths approach the river, at approximately elevation 12, they are lined with stone seat walls and retaining walls. The walks extend in long, gently sloping gradients that do not exceed standards for people in wheelchairs. Gentle curves also prevent abrupt protrusions into the river, as they would snag trash and debris floating down the river. In-

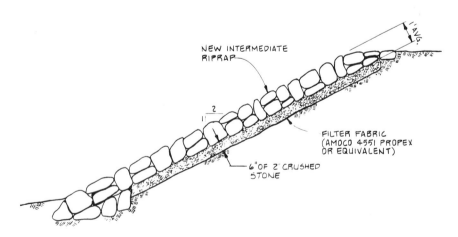

NEW INTERMEDIATE RIPRAP

FILTER FABRIC (AMOCO 4551 PROPEX OR EQUIVALENT)

6" OF 2" CRUSHED STONE

2 TYPICAL INTERMEDIATE RIPRAP DETAIL
SCALE: ½"=1'-0"

Figures 1-68 and 1-69: *Detail of riprap placement and as-built condition*

Figure 1-69: *(Cont.)*

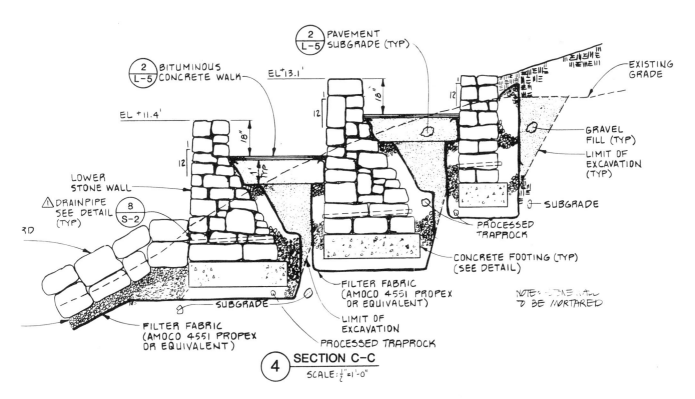

2 / L-5   PAVEMENT SUBGRADE (TYP)

2 / L-5   BITUMINOUS CONCRETE WALK

EL +13.1'

EL +11.4'

18"

12

1

1

18"

12

1

TYP

12

EXISTING GRADE

GRAVEL FILL (TYP)

LIMIT OF EXCAVATION (TYP)

SUBGRADE

LOWER STONE WALL

⚠ DRAINPIPE SEE DETAIL (TYP)

8 / S-2

3D

PROCESSED TRAPROCK

CONCRETE FOOTING (TYP) (SEE DETAIL)

SUBGRADE

FILTER FABRIC (AMOCO 4551 PROPEX OR EQUIVALENT)

FILTER FABRIC (AMOCO 4551 PROPEX OR EQUIVALENT)

LIMIT OF EXCAVATION

PROCESSED TRAPROCK

NOTE: STONE WALL TO BE MORTARED

4   **SECTION C–C**
SCALE: ½"=1'-0"

Figure 1-70: *Detail of stone walls at river terraces*

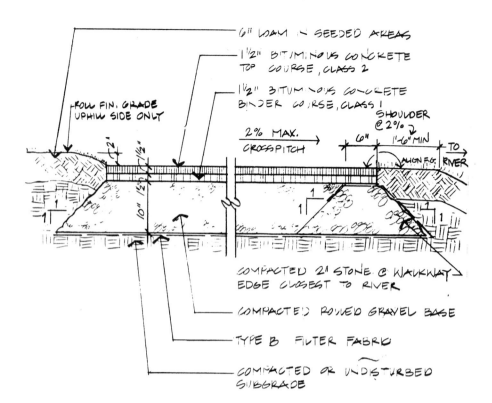

6" LOAM & SEEDED AREAS

1½" BITUMINOUS CONCRETE TOP COURSE, CLASS 2

1½" BITUMINOUS CONCRETE BINDER COURSE, CLASS 1

SHOULDER @ 2%

2% MAX. CROSSPITCH

ROLL FIN. GRADE UPHILL SIDE ONLY

6"

1'-6" MIN

TO RIVER

ALIGN F.G.

COMPACTED 2" STONE @ WALKWAY EDGE CLOSEST TO RIVER

COMPACTED ROLLED GRAVEL BASE

TYPE B FILTER FABRIC

COMPACTED OR UNDISTURBED SUBGRADE

Figure 1-71: *Detail of bituminous concrete walkway*

tegrated with the site design of the walls and walks are steeper banks, newly vegetated, that are held in place with riprap. The river typically floods up to the level of these banks, approximately elevation 7, as much as two or three times a year. Even the parking lots may be flooded annually.

CRJA researched three major problems: ice damage, flooding, and siltation. The design of the walls and paths responds to all these concerns. The size of the stones used for the retaining walls was based on calculations by the structural engineer of the minimum size stone that would be resistant to movement from ice-buildup or "plucking." Both the stone for these walls and for riprap used elsewhere are a Chelmsford granite, native to New England. The top of the walls was designed to be sittable, so they have a flat crosssection. However, rather than a standard capstone, variable size stones were used, some flatter and some rounder and bigger, so there would not be a uniform joint level at which the rising floodwaters might destroy the bond. The walls have standard footings to frost line. The subsoils are well-drained so that no additional footing depth or width was required. There are continuous footing drains.

Research on flooding revealed that during floods the constricted channel at Charter Oak Park creates more turbulence and increased abrasion due to the flow of ice debris. Since the river is controlled upstream by a series of dams, flood levels are often quite predictable, based on readily available information about the levels of the reservoirs behind these dams. Data from the National River Forecast Center guided the landscape architects in determining the elevations at which to situate the walls, walks and terraces. The amount of siltation from a flood can vary from as little as a few inches to as much as two feet, depending on the duration of the flood, the time of year, and the size of the particles. The walkways between the walls were designed to be wide enough, a minimum of eight feet, so that a front-end loader could travel over them and scrape sediment off the entire surface width of the walks. The walks also have continuous positive gradients and an exposure to normal current so that there is no puddling that would hold sediment. As a result, the walks tend to be self-washing or self-flushing: the receding floodwaters carry off considerable sediment deposited by the rising floodwaters. The walks can be easily hosed down and the sediment washed off. The walks are a 2-1/2-inch-thick layer of bituminous concrete over a crushed stone base 12 inches thick. The thickness of both layers is designed to withstand the loads of the backhoe or other vehicles driven on the walks for maintenance purposes.

A vocabulary of site furniture was developed, including benches, lighting, handrails, and scenic lookout markers. All are painted a deep blue color, which Riverfront Recapture Inc. has adopted as its standard for all of its riverfront projects being developed as a linear park system The steel handrail, modeled after an old bridge railing detail, incorporates bronze medallions at scenic points along the walk system. All of the site furniture had to be placed carefully in order not to impede the flow of floodwaters. For example, all benches line up with the flow of water in order to minimize the risk of becoming traps for the accumulation of debris as floodwaters move against them. All furniture is designed to be underwater for brief periods without damage.

Lighting was excluded from the lowest areas most prone to flooding. The telephones and lighting fixtures have sealed wiring so that, in the event of severe flooding, they can be salvaged and reinstalled with a minimum of repair after the floodwaters recede. (See Figure C–6.).

Another concern was that light levels not interfere with wildlife activities. The river supports extensive wildlife including muskrats, otters, reptiles, amphibians, and birds. The lights are programmed to turn off to coincide with the needs of some wildlife species that cannot tolerate extended light levels during breeding seasons or other critical times. Typically, the lights turn on at dusk and go off at 10 P.M.

The substantial sloping areas adjacent to the walls and walks were completely overgrown with dense vegetation, often prolific with honeysuckle and other weedy species. The weedy undergrowth was cleared out, but specimen trees were left. Clearing was done to open views towards the river from the park and the walkways. A method of stabilizing the regraded slopes was devised using a polyvinyl-chloride mesh staked and

Figure 1-72: *View of ornamental handrail*

stapled in place. Loam and seed were placed over the top of it, and some steeper areas were covered with rip rap. A seed mixture especially designed for this riverine habitat was used, consisting of a meadow mixture specially suited to a shady environment. The first year after construction, new lawns became established and the banks became stabilized despite considerable flooding. The intent was also to allow these slopes to regenerate from the seeds and sprouts that would wash over them during flooding. Indigenous species were encouraged, others were weeded. There is minimal mowing, except of the formal parade ground at the top of the park nearest the dike.

Since quite a few of the native species that seed themselves are short-lived and brittle, such as box elder (*Acer negundo*), additional trees were planted, primarily river birch (*Betula nigra*), sweetgum (*Liquidambar styriciflua*), willow (*Salix alba*), and other species native to the river's edge. Red maples (*Acer rubrum*) are also planted but do not seem to tolerate being inundated for long periods of time.

This park was the first of its kind built along the Connecticut River. It has been in place more than three years, and although it has experienced major flooding, it has held up well. The park has been scrutinized and analyzed thoroughly since it is the first in this region to be purposely designed to embrace flooding conditions. It is becoming an example for other designers to follow in developing parklands along the river. CRJA is cur-

Figure 1-73: *Riverbank stabilization, during construction*

Figure 1-74: *River bank stabilization, after planting has been established*

rently working on another phase of parkland across the Connecticut River from Charter Oak Park. However, this park site is entirely in the floodplain. The designers must research in greater detail issues about finishes: the way that insides of bench parts drain; the construction of pavement subbase to prevent silt from filling up free draining base materials; the ways that materials react to being underwater for extended periods; and the methods of anchoring such materials.

Charter Oak Park responds to the river as a living organism in which the dynamic and kinetic forces of the moving water are embraced by elements designed for being flooded. The response is not to hold back the water or push it elsewhere. Instead, the age-old pattern of flooding and siltation continues along a dynamic riverine edge which, at the same time, people can use for fishing, education, and general recreation.

JONES & JONES

Seattle, WA

Jones & Jones has established itself as one of the most prominent landscape architecture and architecture firms in the country, with a reputation for innovative designs that satisfy the expectations of clients while providing striking examples of design process, methodology and results for other designers to follow. The breadth of the firm's work includes most major subjects of landscape architecture practice: master planning—including towns, rivers corridors, botanical gardens, and zoos; urban design, historic reclamations, and park and recreation design. Located in Seattle, WA, the firm was established in 1969 by Grant Jones and Ilze Jones. Other principals include John Paul Jones, J. Thomas Atkins, W. Nikolaus Worden, Keith Larson, and Marlo Campos. The diverse staff of 37 people includes 17 landscape architects and 12 architects, many of whom are also licensed landscape architects.

PROJECT: *Nooksack River Study*
LOCATION: *Puget Sound area of Washington State*
CLIENTS: *Department of Parks and Recreation, Whatcom County, WA*
DATE: *1973*

Several of Jones & Jones projects have established and led to a new area of landscape architecture practice. The Nooksack River Plan, completed in 1973, in Whatcom County, WA, is a good example. The study involves the detailed inventory of the natural, cultural, and aesthetic resources of 96 miles of the river in northwestern Washington. The purpose is to locate and document those portions of the river which provide the highest quality of recreational experience and to evaluate the river for preservation, recreation, and conservation. The concluding section of the study makes recommendations for the best possible uses of the entire river corridor.

The Nooksack was classified into a hierarchy of spatial units according to the river channel pattern, floodplain characteristics, and adjacent physiography. Base maps at the scale of one inch to four hundred feet $(1'' = 400')$ of all of the lands adjacent to the river were used to record land use, ownership, steep slopes, soil conditions, vegetation, wildlife habitats, and dynamic river characteristics such as floodplains, channels, and dikes. Historical, archaeological, and geological sites, highways, roads, and

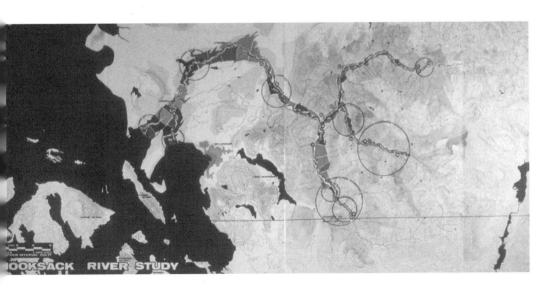

Figure 1-75: *The Nooksack River Study Management Plan for entire watershed in northwestern Washington State.*

infrastructure, and water and waste disposal sites were also recorded. The inventory and analysis was remarkably thorough.

The design team numerically totalled the resources of each river segment which exhibited desirable qualities for preservation, recreation, or conservation. Preservation was defined by the team as "limited use" relating to "high quality scenic and historic sites, unique wilderness areas, fragile plants, and fish and wildlife sanctuary." Passive recreation was defined in the study as "moderate use," such as "quiet fishing, wading and swimming, picnics, hiking, day camping, diverse areas for nature studies." Active recreation was defined as "intensive use," such as areas withstanding "concentrated activities, field sports, and intensive camping, boating and active water sports." Finally, conservation was defined as "restricted use," or "areas needing corrective attention, areas for buffering activities and land uses, wetlands coextensive with the river."

The analysis concluded that the quality of experience available at any location on the river is directly related to the intensity or magnitude of expression of its various resources and to their relative quality. The quality of the experience of the river "de-pends mainly upon how intensely the landscape expresses itself." This, in turn, is at least partly determined by a qualitative evaluation of the health of the river: Its landscape "is enhanced or diminished by the presence of certain evaluatable conditions which indicate health and determine overall landscape integrity. These indicators are defined, on the positive side, by uniqueness, diversity, fragility and seasonality, and on the negative side by encroachment from man." Matrices tabulating all natural, cultural and aesthetic aspects of different segments, or study units, of the river, gave an overall picture of that area. The design team developed a graphic notation system to tabulate the five indicators onto three matrices. For example, to summarize a river unit's evaluation for preservation, a cell value was extracted for uniqueness and fragility characteristics from separate matrices in which each was separately evaluated. This value was compared to one recorded previously for encroachment. "Since encroachment diminishes the value of that element for preservation, the encroachment totals are subtracted from the unique and fragile total, giving an adjusted total for each unit for preservation." The matrices reveal the results in terms of color intensity,

Figure 1-76: *The Nooksack River. A typical river unit.*

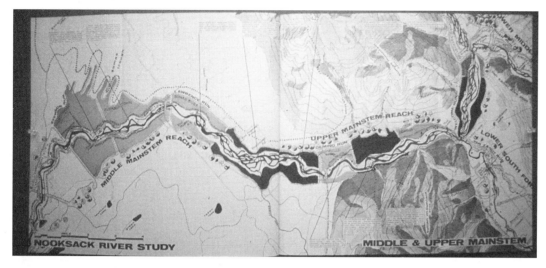

Figure 1-77: *A Nooksack River Reach and Run and unit map. The study pioneered the first use of this kind of classification as a river planning tool in America.*

but "numerical totals were used to make the final selection of units suitable for preservation." To determine suitability for passive recreation, values for uniqueness and diversity are combined and compared to values for encroachment. Finally, for active recreation, a value for fragility is factored into the matrix. Like encroachment, fragility diminished the value of a site for active recreation.

The river segments were then ranked in order of their suitability for each type of use. The team defined viewsheds, the contributing landscapes for each river segment, and depicted them graphically as a means to assess critical areas of the river corridor which should be considered scenic easements. Specific recommendations for each river segment included watershed management practices to enhance and protect the river's resources. Proposals were made for the development of design guidelines and scenic easements for the lands which form the visual setting of the river. The Whetcom County Park Board, with the help of the parks department, the planning board, and the county commissioners, persisted in trying to implement a regional recreation and open space plan. Jones & Jones was subsequently commissioned to design an interpretive center, Tennant Lake, and a recreation complex according to the recommendations of its own study.

The recommendations and management plan in the report are fundamentally ecological in nature. "Management of any part of the realm affects, and is affected by, all other parts of the realm; hence, proper management of the whole necessitates proper management of each part." Plans are first presented for each branch of the river that was studied. Recommendations for unifying corridors and easements are made, as well as specific recommendations for the best recreation, conservation, or preservation uses. This area of the report is followed by general recommendations for continuing study and evaluation of the entire Nooksack River system.

An important aspect of the recommendations is that the report is presented "as part of a continuing planning process, to stimulate interest and to make available its methods and findings openly to all." The design team sought to develop a plan so thorough in its documentation and methodology that it would "serve not only as a reference for design of park and recreation facilities, but also as a reference for future county planning and a tool for educating the public." As a result, there is at times a didactic quality about the text, perhaps, an appealing proselytization about the stewardship of a beautiful resource. For once, it does not seem inappropriate. Grant Jones, in the frontispiece, begins the report with his poem, titled "Sluice of My Eyes":

MAGNITUDE OF RIVER CHARACTERISTICS

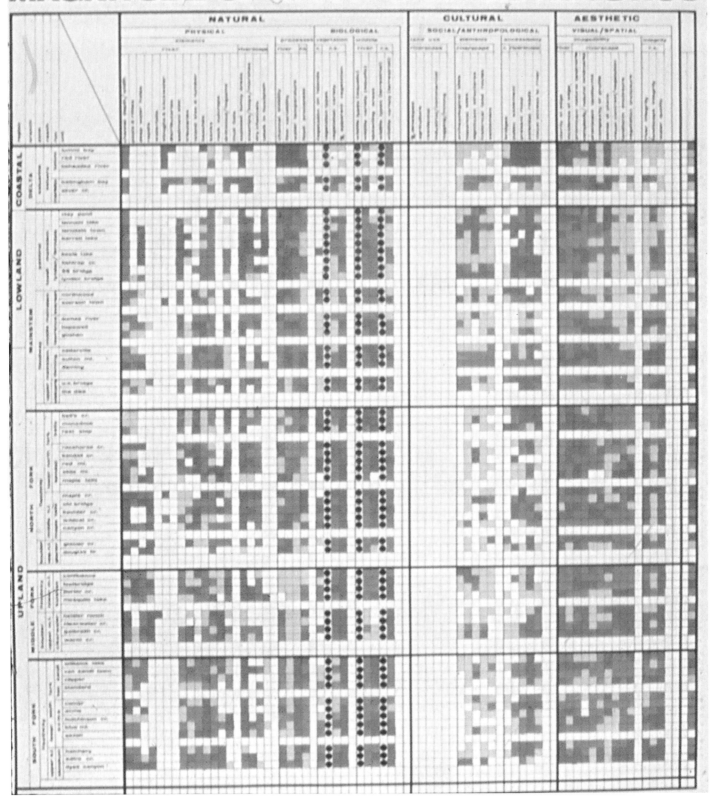

Figure 1-78: *This matrix helped document, as Grant Jones observed, "how intensely the landscape expresses itself" for each run of the river.*

My eyes have known
As slender reeds,
As rafts,
This estuary shift of life—
Slow and silting,
Eroding, twisting.
Gliding westward always—
These most immeasurable layering images,
My own:
Sluice of my eyes.

The report concludes with a glossary of terms and an annotated bibliography of 90 entries "to introduce the reader to some of the voluminous material related to water ecology, river dynamics, and to the growing number of studies attempting to assess tangible and intangible river characteristics." These two concluding sections are consistent with the spirit of educating a wide audience and setting a standard for future planning efforts.

Jones & Jones' expertise in master planning of natural resources of rivers has been sought elsewhere in the region. In 1980 the Columbia Gorge, along the border of Washington and Oregon, was proposed as a National Scenic Area by agencies, groups, and citizens concerned about the potential degradation of its visual quality by develop-

ment and land use change. The Governor of the State of Washington appointed a Select Committee to study the problem and report to the state Legislature on alternative means to conserve the scenic quality of the gorge, while preserving local or state land use control. The Committee retained Jones & Jones to identify the potential visual impacts of land use trends in the Gorge, and actions that could reduce or eliminate these impacts.

Conducted over a period of three months, this study used visual simulation techniques to assess the potential visual impacts of land use change on one of the most scenic and unique landscapes in the Northwest. Everything from suburban tract housing, to roads, to logging were simulated to arouse decision-makers into action. The study also included summaries of previous studies, contacts with more than forty public agencies and private interest groups in both Oregon and Washington, and the development of criteria which were used to designate sensitive land areas. This was a major step in reconciling the conservation of visual quality with potential land use change.

By 1986, the Columbia River Gorge National Scenic Area Act (Public Law 99-663)

Figure 1-79: *The great river of the Pacific Northwest, the Columbia drains portions of Washington, Idaho, Oregon, Montana, and British Columbia*

was passed by Congress. The law required the preparation of a Recreation Assessment, the first step consisting of providing an inventory of existing and proposed recreation resources in the Columbia River Gorge National Scenic Area. The Forest Service hired Jones & Jones for this purpose.

During the course of the inventory, the design team developed base maps which delineated the locations of recreation resources and developed matrices presenting facilities and activities at specific sites. A summary of existing studies and reports culminated in an annotated bibliography. Also included were a list of agencies and organizations to be contacted as the Recreation Assessment proceeded, and an identification of information gaps and procedures for obtaining such information. The results of the overview were presented in a final report which served as an in-house working document for use by the United State Forest Service and the Columbia River Gorge Commission staff in developing the Recreation Assessment. Jones & Jones' work in the evaluation of the Nooksack and Columbia River Gorge set standards and examples that many have used as guidelines for future planning efforts.

PROJECT: *Woodland Park Zoo—Master Plan and Elephant Forest*
LOCATION: *Seattle, WA*
CLIENT: *Woodland Park Zoological Garden*
DATE: *1976, 1982, 1987, 1993*

Another of Jones & Jones' specialties is zoos. In 1976 the firm completed the long-term Master Plan for Seattle's Woodland Park Zoo, and quietly altered the direction of zoo design in the country. Finally, animals were transformed from captives to active participants. Cages were replaced by savannas, concrete gave way to earth. The concept of habitat re-creation was thus recognized not only as the most humane, but also the most dramatic educational setting in which to display wild animals. The firm researched the field meticulously and gathered a library of information on habitat requirements; animal behavior and breeding; biological, botanical and geo-

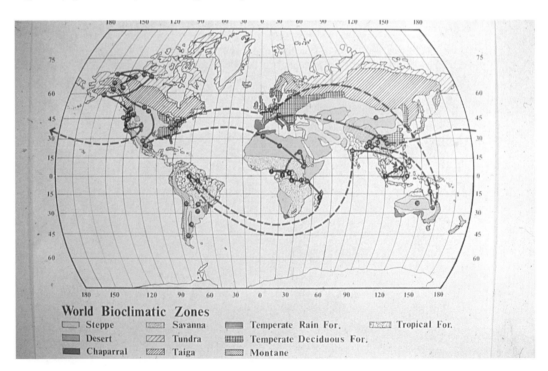

Figure 1-80: *Jones and Jones revolutionized zoo planning by grouping animals by the places they came from (bioclimatic zones) rather than by taxonomic groups*

PRIVATE SECTOR—LARGE FIRMS

Figure 1-81: *The African Savanna was designed to simulate a specific habitat in Africa. This provides animals with the best possible environment, and helps teach visitors that animals are part of a whole ecosystem.*

graphic simulation; and interpretive presentations.

As stated by Grant Jones, "The master plan provided a great range of technical solutions for reconstruction of the entire zoo, and placed the zoo in the forefront of zoological park design by proposing the innovative concepts of bioclimatic zones and social biology. A framework was created for exhibiting animals in social groupings and settings that replicate as closely as possible their original habitats, representing all ten of the world's major bioclimatic zones."

The actual location for each exhibit was determined by a site evaluation which sought the best fit between a potential bioclimatic zone and the site's existing vegetation and microclimatic conditions. Once the most suitable locations for each zone and habitat were chosen, explicit design scenarios for all exhibits were analyzed. Guidelines were developed for the proposed character of vegetation and structures, as well as noting special habitat needs for each species of animal.

In addition to being a unified plan guiding the future development of the zoo's exhibits, the resulting master plan has become a general handbook on zoo planning and design. Several exhibits—including temperate waterfowl, Asian primates, gorillas, and the African Savanna—have been completed as part of the first phase of renovation. Two are described in more detail. Two five-year updates of the long range plan were completed by Jones & Jones in 1982 and 1987.

The four-acre African Savanna Exhibit features many of the animals of the savanna, including lions, giraffes, zebras, and hippopotamuses. The natural habitat of these animals has been recreated as accurately as possible using grading, rockwork,

water barriers, and varied informal plantings. More than a half-mile of moats, walls, and fences, most of which are invisible to the visitor, separate species of animals—antelopes from lions, for example. The visitors' views of the exhibit are controlled; long and seemingly distant views are incorporated, as well as short, intimate ones. The animals are also given private spaces outside the visitors' field of vision. A major portion of the project included the modification of existing grottoes in both the feline exhibit and the bear exhibit, connecting the two into one large African Lion Exhibit. The existing holding areas in the Feline House were modified to better fit the needs of the staff.

Figure 1-82: *In designing the African savanna as well as other exhibits, Jones & Jones attempts to immerse people in the landscape of the animal. All barriers are hidden, and humans feel that they are temporary visitors.*

Figure 1-83: *Daily demonstration of traditional logging practices allow visitors to get close to the elephants (Photo by Eduardo Calderon)*

The work was "earth sculpture, basically" stated Grant Jones, "to shape a stage and coax an audience for perceiving the Serengeti." The animals of the Serengeti "survive by sight, that is, by seeing and not being seen. The design objective was just as simple—to design *for* sight by creating long-range views, 500 to 700 feet through tall grass over the backs of antelope to lions basking on granite boulders in the distance." The goal was the creation of a "domain of magnificent animals through which we may pass and appreciate." To achieve the desired effects, "a very small available area had to be maximized, by modulating space and shaping ground and by carefully calculating and studying hundreds of sight-lines." A great deal of attention was paid to the design of a sequence of visual experiences for the visitor, as well as the animals. It was important that "most structures would not be visible and that cross-views of other people would be difficult, if not impossible." One long-term goal is even to borrow, as in traditional *borrowed scenery* style Japanese gardens, "views of the Cascades which might suggest the grandeur of Kilamanjaro's snowy slopes."

Since the savanna is primarily a grassland, the design team "spent hundreds of hours in researching grasses." Since Seattle's climate is obviously not the Serengeti's, the goal was to use adaptable plant materials and grasses "to simulate grassy cousins and counterparts in Africa." Among the plants used are Beardgrass, Tall oat grass, Bermuda grass, Fountain grass, Witch grass, Weeping love grass, Reed canary grass, and Orchard grass.

The 4.6-acre Elephant Forest provides an extraordinary physical setting for the care and exhibition of Asian elephants. The exhibit houses and displays the zoo's elephants while also showing the animals' complex relationship with the people and culture of Thailand. The architecture of both the structures for visitors and for the elephants is evocative of the region.

The exhibit unfolds in three venues, each separated visually and spatially. (See Figure C–7.) Visitors move from one to the next. Graphics and exhibits emphasize that the elephants give permission and welcome humans to enter the elephants' domain and see them in their native environ-

Figure 1-84: *The Thai logging village and the elephant barn interpret traditional Thai architecture. The expression of the elephant barn as a temple expresses the elephant's central position in Thai spiritual life. (Photo by Eduardo Calderon)*

ment, not as if they are merely seeing animals on display. The first venue shows elephants in the wild, the second demonstrates the semi-domestication of elephants and their role in Southeast Asia, and the third presents the sacred role of elephants in Thai culture. The largest venue is the first, showing elephants as a keystone species in an Asian tropical forest. Plantings are integrated into the indigenous vegetation of the Seattle site.

The second venue is the re-creation of a rustic Thai logging camp, where the elephants haul and stack logs. Exhibits explain the difficulties and subtleties of train-ing elephants, and how and why they are exceptionally attuned to their tasks. A mid-nineteenth century Thai village accents the cultural backdrop.

The third major setting is Rong Chang, or House of Elephants. Again visitors are invited in as guests to the residence, and asked to be deferential and respecting toward their hosts, these magnificent animals. The shelter evokes the temple architecture of northern Thailand. It is mammoth in size and scale, and its traditional design recalls the elephants as cultural symbols over centuries of semi–domestication.

PROJECT: *Master Plan—North Carolina Botanical Garden*
LOCATION: *University of North Carolina, Chapel Hill, NC*
CLIENT: *University of North Carolina*
DATE: *1988*

Botanical gardens, as collections of plant materials for public enjoyment, research, and the study and protection of rare plants, can perhaps be considered zoos for plants. Jones & Jones has designed and evaluated many botanical gardens across the United States and in Mexico and Singapore. The master plan for the North Carolina Botanical Garden is a notable achievement. In 1903, Dr. William Chambers Coker, the University of North Carolina's first professor of botany, initiated an effort to beautify a wet meadow on the edge of the campus at the request of the University President Francis Venable. This site became what is now called the Coker Arboretum, one of three units managed today by the North Carolina Botanical Garden.

Over the remainder of this century, the garden grew as did the university. Dr. Henry Roland Totten, formerly a student of Dr. Coker's, "developed a drug garden to teach pharmacy and medical students about the plants that were the source of important medicines." A shrub collection was begun in the 1930s and 1940s, but efforts were interrupted by World War II. In 1952, the Trustees of the University designated 72 acres of the Mason Farm Woodlands for the development of a botanical garden. Also in that year, Dr. Coker gave additional property to the garden, and willed his estate to the University. In 1961 "William Lanier Hunt donated 103 acres of the dramatic Morgan Creek Gorge to protect several beautiful rhododendron bluffs and to begin a collection of southeastern woody plants." Throughout the sixties the garden continued to expand, both in land acquisitions and educational programs. In 1971, the first permanent employees were hired. Various volunteer groups became active in educating the public, and helping to establish collections of plant materials and programs. In 1976 the Totten Center opened, named after Dr. Henry Roland Totten and his wife Addie, both of whom contributed to the development of programs and funding for the Garden. It included classrooms, offices and workrooms. Finally, in 1984, the University Trustees created a unified Mason Farm Biological Reserve, covering 367 acres, which completed the present configuration of the Botanical Garden. By 1986 there was a permanent staff of 12, with 15 seasonal workers and 150 volunteers. Under the leadership of Dr. Peter S. White, the current director of the North Carolina Botanical Garden, the organization prepared "a statement of the mission, goals, and objectives of the Garden" and in 1988 it hired Jones & Jones to create "a comprehensive master plan to chart a course for the future."

The Botanical Garden has a five-fold mission: research in biological, ecological, and environmental sciences; instruction and training in these fields; conservation of biological diversity; well documented plant collections for research, instruction, conservation, public education, and enjoyment; and finally, public programs to communicate the Garden's mission and themes through a variety of activities. When Jones & Jones began work, the challenge was how to integrate all the diverse facilities, properties and collections, spread over a considerable area, into a thematically unified design that could be implemented over time.

Since the beginnings of the Garden, much had changed. For example the Coker Arboretum with its collections of major trees—once on the eastern edge of the campus—was now in a quadrangle in the center of the main campus, separated from most of the garden's other facilities and lands.

The design team developed four interpretive themes to govern their concept for the master plan: "the richness represented by the earth's biological diversity, the dependence of human quality of life on this diversity, the critical need for conservation of our natural heritage, and the importance of botanical research to human society." In communicating the master plan to the public, the staff of the Garden, and the members of the Board, the design team sought an image that would communicate these themes. "Resonance, or repetition of threads and patterns, is a central feature of this design. Centers of activity and learning are connected by threads of various lengths and intensities." They chose a tapestry as the visual image of this design: "Tapestries typically consist of threads in two dimensions, but the Garden's tapestry is multidimensional. Water weaves through the site and lends sound and texture to the tapestry . . . Tapestry threads are also represented by the garden's interpretive themes as they weave throughout the plant collections . . . In the tapestry of the Garden, the threads and images repeat throughout the landscape. Yet each place within the tapestry is unique."

As the programming and design process evolved for interpreting the Garden's mis-

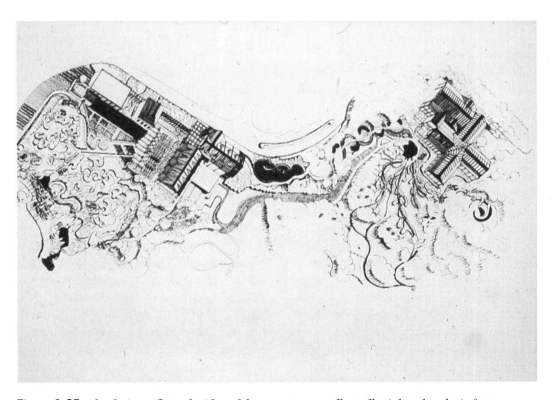

Figure 1-85: *The design reflects the idea of the tapestry as well as alluvial and geologic forms*

PRIVATE SECTOR—LARGE FIRMS

sion and applying it to the site for the future, it became clear that new facilities were needed: a research center; expansion of the Totten Center to accommodate administration, maintenance, and educational activities; and a visitor center.

Site analysis revealed that despite almost six hundred acres of land, less than ten percent was suitable for major construction. Major constraints were flooding, steep slopes, and unstable soils as well as the need to minimize impacts on existing major collections and existing forests. Eventually, the design team concluded that a central, intensively developed area could be constructed on seven acres adjacent to the Totten Center in an area of second growth forest in which old pines had been thinned by an infestation by the southern pine beetle. "Among the Garden's lands, this site has the least sensitive natural features and has a low priority for protection." There were some problems with traffic noise, soils, and access, but the advantages were compelling. The site was near the town of Chapel Hill and the university campus, there was access from the site to the rest of the Garden, and there was adequate space for central facilities and parking.

The final master plan, submitted to the client and approved unanimously in 1990, incorporates three maps at different scales. The first shows all the lands of the North Carolina Botanical Garden highlighting categories of land use and the proposed trail system. Land use is categorized by four types: natural areas; open fields and young woodlands; natural woodlands, trails, and interpretive structures; and, finally, plant collection, buildings, and research facilities, which are further designated as high and low intensity development. Three classes of pathways are proposed: simple, narrow foot paths, pathways eight feet wide and firm enough to support electric carts, and sturdier, ten-foot-wide trails and bridges to accommodate service trucks and vans. The second map presents general development for the William Lanier Hunt Arboretum and research facilities at the Mason Farm Biological Reserve. The third map, at the largest scale, shows in greatest detail the design concept for buildings, gardens, and trails of the seven acre intensively developed area of the site.

Just as some strands of a tapestry lead one's eyes to areas of visual richness, "the trail system provides access to all areas of the Garden, along routes with a variety of views, resting areas and spatial experiences." One major new trail is the Campus to Garden Trail, beginning at the Coker Arboretum and connecting to the Garden's new entrance. Through careful interpretation by means of signage and exhibits along the trail, the high visibility of the Coker Arboretum can encourage greater awareness and use of the Garden. Two hundred parking spaces are provided for visitors and 50 for staff on cleared, level areas. The parking lots will be developed in phases as budgets allow and visitor attendance increases. Since these areas will be highly used by the public, sound storm water management principles will be demonstrated and explained: There will be a minimum of pavement and impervious surfaces, and inclusion of retention ponds and recirculations systems.

Upon entering the site, whether from vehicles or by pathways, one arrives at the Heart of the Garden, an entry plaza and orientation area. (See Figures C–8, C–9 and C–10.) Equidistant between the Visitor Center and Administration Building and the Research Center for Plant Diversity, the Heart of the Garden, with its vistas overlooking many of the gardens of the developed area of the site, provides an introductory orientation to the Garden. The sequential modulation of space is a basic theme of this design, and the process begins here. The visitor experiences distant views of the piedmont landscape, such as glimpses of the Sycamore Bottom and other riparian landscapes and close views of developed gardens, such as the Habitat Gardens. The Habitat Gardens "provide sequential immersion in a series of habitats . . . to correspond with the vegetation of the physiographic provinces of the North Carolina landscape." The Coastal Plain Habitat Garden includes sand dunes with a small interpretive center, a pocosin, a pine savanna, pine flatwoods, sandhills, a cypress swamp, and coastal bottomland forest. The Piedmont Habitat Garden will include a successional pine forest, a diabase glade, a sycamore creek bottom, a piedmont bottomland forest, a beech slope, and an oak-hickory slope. The Mountain Habitat Garden, on steep, cool, north-facing slopes and incorporating some native vegetation already introduced, will provide views of the piedmont and Coastal Plain Habitat Gardens. It will include a hemlock forest, cover hardwoods, health walk, mountain stream and waterfall, and mountain bog. The Habitat Gardens are central to the identity of the Garden as they emphasize the biological diversity of North Carolina's landscape and the importance of conservation.

Specialty gardens complete the array of gardens on the site. These include a Fern Garden in a cool, steep, north facing ravine, a narrow valley with both wet and dry woods, shade slopes, sunny clearings and a variety of habitats. A Carnivorous Plant Garden is "a series of radiating terraces on a slope to allow for close-up viewing." A Native Perennial Garden will highlight the vast array of both sun-loving and shade-loving perennials in North Carolina. A Plant Families Garden will provide "information about the relationships, identification, and evolution of plants, and graphically depict the evolutionary radiation of plants in its layout." An Aquatic Garden will feature hardy aquatic and emergent plants native to the southeastern United States. A Rare Plant Garden, immediately adjacent to the Research Center of plant Diversity, will provide opportunities for viewing endangered species. The Plant Exploration Garden will be a series of thematically linked gardens that interpret botanical exploration for the visitor in a series of gardens featuring plant materials with unique historical or cultural aspects, such as a Garden of Plants the Dinosaurs Ate and a Garden of Southeastern Plants and their Southeast Asian Relatives. Two greenhouses will display a tropical rain forest and a desert environment. The rain forest "will represent an Ecuadorian forest—a place at the same longitude as North Carolina but at a tropical latitude. Similarly, the desert collection will represent a site at the same latitude as North Carolina, but at an arid longitude." A plant collection that "interprets the importance of botanical re-

search in solving environmental problems" will be the Human Impact Garden, featuring, for example, plants sensitive to air pollution and exotic species problems. An area of gardening that has seen tremendous growth in recent decades is horticultural therapy. The Horticultural Therapy Garden "stresses the importance of plants to the physical and psychological health of all people with emphasis on people with special needs." A series of gardens "dealing with medicinal, culinary, economic, shade, poison, evergreen, and ethnobotanical herbs" will be the Mercer Reeves Hubbard Herb Garden. Visitors will be able to learn about plants as sources of food, healing, and useful products. A final major theme garden will be the Children's Garden, designed to help children gain an appreciation of plants and nature.

Two other major areas of the Botanical Garden are the William Lanier Hunt Arboretum and the Mason Farm Biological Reserve. Supplemental planting within the 103 acres of the arboretum "will concentrate on specimens of southeastern woody plants not already represented in the existing vegetation." An interpretive pavilion including a lecture area, exhibits, and restrooms, will introduce visitors to the history of the collections and trails in the Arboretum. New trails, carefully "sited to take advantage of significant natural and cultural resources as well as to minimize clearing for new trail construction," will make the Arboretum's varied regions accessible for visitors.

Adjacent to the Arboretum is the Mason Farm, covering 367 acres and "containing diverse natural plant communities and protected habitats especially valuable for scientific research and teaching." Access will remain restricted to protect and preserve the areas critical for research, but new trails will provide public access and interpretation of the mission and significance of the Farm. A field research station, a caretaker's residence and additional research greenhouses are new buildings at Mason Farm.

The architectural concepts for the new buildings in the master plan follow several major themes. The buildings are designed "to serve as a frame for the gardens and as a gateway to nature." The style of the architecture conforms to a traditional North Carolina regional aesthetic. Natural materials and a modest scale are used. The buildings are all sited to follow the slope of the existing land. Since noise is one problem with the site selected for the central concentration of buildings, the proposed buildings "form a buffer and additional sound protection between the roadways and parking area and the gardens." The garden architecture, such as porches, sheds, interpretive shelters, and rain shelters, will feature heavy timber structures, "exposed for its ornamental and instructional qualities."

The proposed development of buildings and new gardens will require the installation of water, gas and electrical power, sanitary sewers and storm drainage, an irrigation system, fencing and security systems and lighting. These systems are all proposed to "be located underground to minimize disturbance of the natural landscape." Most of the new plant collections will require an irrigation system. Even for native plant materials, which adapt to drought and difficult environmental conditions, the investment of an irrigation system protects the long-term value of these plantings. A high-pressure mist system is planned for the Fern Garden and parts of the Mountain Habitat, both to maintain ideal humidity levels for plant growth and to enhance the cool and misty atmosphere of these areas.

The North Carolina Botanical Garden was founded by people "who sought to provide the appropriate setting for academic scholarship, creativity, and contemplation" in a garden. The master plan as developed by Jones & Jones provides facilities for visitor education and enjoyment, a research center to advance the University's leadership in promoting and studying strategies for biological diversity and major collections of plant materials representative of North Carolina and the southeastern United States. The plan also protects and conserves the valuable lands within the Botanical Garden while providing a blueprint for the future.

ROYSTON HANAMOTO ALLEY & ABEY

Mill Valley, CA

Royston Hanamoto Alley & Abey was founded in the San Francisco Bay area in 1958 by Robert Royston and Asa Hanamoto, two graduates of the University of California, Berkeley. The firm is now located in Mill Valley. Its key personnel are dedicated to continual involvement in the design process and continual contact with the client, as inspired by the original working philosophy articulated by the two founders: "Our purpose is to build and shape the landscape for people's use and enjoyment while protecting and preserving the beauty and substance of nature as a resource for the future. The quality of the landscape concerns us whether large or small, urban or rural, tamed or wild. We strive for a design solution which is a beautiful and responsive synthesis of human values and aspirations with the functional and economic influences affecting each project. Our desire is to continually improve our capability in the field of environmental design and to remain a constant source of human creativity in a world dominated by technology." Five principals and six associates now lead this firm, which has grown to include planning as well as landscape architecture. Testament to its high standard of service is the fact that typically more than 80 percent of current work is from repeat clients. A Minority Business Enterprise, the firm has performed considerable work in the public as well as the private sector, ranging from the rehabilitation of Glacier Point scenic vista in Yosemite National Park and the design for the National Peace Garden in Washington, D.C., to master plans for Golden Gate Park (discussed in the following section of this book), Fort Mason, and the Presidio in San Francisco.

PROJECT: *Robert Mondavi Winery Landscape Development*
LOCATION: *Yountville, CA*
CLIENT: *Robert Mondavi Winery*
LANDSCAPE ARCHITECT: *Robert N. Royston, Principal*
Barbara D. Lundburg, Principal
DATE: *1993*

Bob Royston, FASLA, graduated from the University of California, Berkeley, in 1940. With more than five decades of experience, his career has included serving as a professor, lecturer and critic at Berkeley, and a visiting lecturer and critic at more than 25 other colleges and universities. He has traveled and studied extensively in Europe, Central America, and China, and spearheaded international work that included his participation as a leading member of the team that won the International Design Competition for the Anzac Parade located in Canberra, Australia.

Royston has worked closely with the Mondavi family since the 1970s. His projects have included planning and designing for their winery operation as well as the Mondavi family residences. Over almost two decades, the firm has provided general consulting on a variety of planning issues, master planning for commercial and residential sites, development of construction documents for parking lots, walkways, gardens, wine-tasting patios, and tour areas, and most recently, the landscape design for Opus One, the Napa Valley winery jointly operated by the Mondavi and Rothschild families. Since Royston's retirement from the firm in 1993, Barbara D. Lundberg has directed efforts for the Mondavis. With a Bachelor of Arts degree in Landscape Architecture from the University of California, Berkeley, in 1970, she has almost 25 years of experience in the field. She has expert skills in public facilitation which are fundamental to her belief that "the most successful designs are a result of responsive, collaborative efforts between designers, users, owners, and builders." In addition to her work in urban design, park master plans, and community planning in the United States, she was the Principal designer of the National Arboretum in Kuala Lumpur, Malaysia, and several parks in the Republic of Singapore. She is currently involved in the design of specialized gardens for Alzheimer patients.

Since 1979, Robert Royston had proposed to implement a landscape development plan for the entrance zone of the Mondavi property. This was postponed on many occasions in order to move forward with more critical design projects, such as the olive tree promenade, the Butano Garden, and the employee garden, along with solutions to various specific site-planning problems at the visitor entrance and tour areas.

The Napa Valley, 100 miles northwest of San Francisco, is California's famous, high-quality wine region. It is 25 miles long by 1 to 5 miles wide. Many diverse conditions permit a great variety of viticulture. The soils are variable. The western side is sedimentary materials with a higher clay content. This soil retains water better than the eastern side of the valley, where there are primarily igneous materials. Grape varieties that like wet feet are planted on the western side, while those that prefer drier soils are planted on the eastern side.

Almost all rainfall occurs in the winter. In 1993 there was 44 inches, but in 1994 only 24 inches, resulting in the need for more irrigation. When rains occur near harvest time late in the summer or early in the fall, too much water is absorbed into the grapes. This destroys the ideal ratio of sugar to acid and results in a poorer vintage. The Napa Valley is an ideal area for grapes since most rain occurs in the winter; some of the best vintages have come after a winter of heavy rain. For example, after severe flooding in the winter of 1986, there was an excellent vintage. The climate is unlike that of some of the French vineyards where rains occur more regularly during the year. In France, a heavy rain before harvest is not so unusual.

PRIVATE SECTOR—LARGE FIRMS

The hot summer climate in Napa is moderated by the fogs that move up from the bay. The fog has a remarkable moisturizing effect, and does not burn off until noon. The benefit of the fog is more pronounced farther south in Napa Valley, closer to its source. Therefore, given the ranges of soil type and the effect of the fog, together with a highly suitable rainfall profile and the availability of water for irrigation, it is possible to grow a great range of grapes in this small region.

Different varieties of grapes ripen at different times. Pinot noirs and cabernet blanc, merlot, and cabernet sauvignons may be ready to harvest by mid-August, particularly if ripening is encouraged by a hot spell. When the heat is not as intense they may not ripen until early September. Sauvignon blancs and chardonnay are the last to ripen, in mid- to late-September.

The whole Napa Valley is zoned agricultural, but viticulture is an expensive industry and vineyards require intensive maintenance. Newly planted grape vines take from five to seven years to become productive and harvestable. There are legislated protections to prevent vineyards from being subdivided into housing areas. The minimum size parcel of land that can be sold is 40 acres. An acre typically sells for approximately $40,000; 40 acres is $1.6 million.

The Robert Mondavi vineyards have been quite successful. Covering an area of hundreds of acres, the vineyards feature many different types of grapes: cabernet sauvignon, pinot noir, chardonnay, sauvignon blanc, merlot, and others. The Mondavi winery offers an unusual tour to visitors. In addition to tasting wine and enjoying the comfort of an air-conditioned gift shop, visitors can actually walk in the vineyards

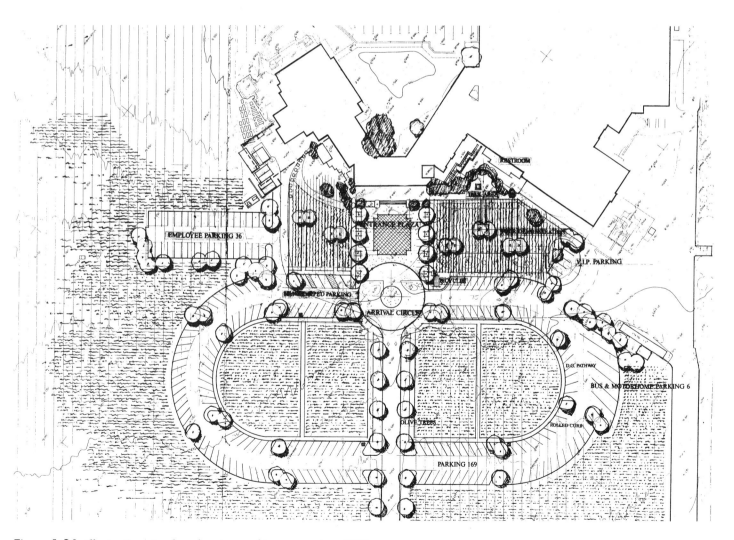

Figure 1-86: *Illustrative site plan showing parking expansion, 1993*

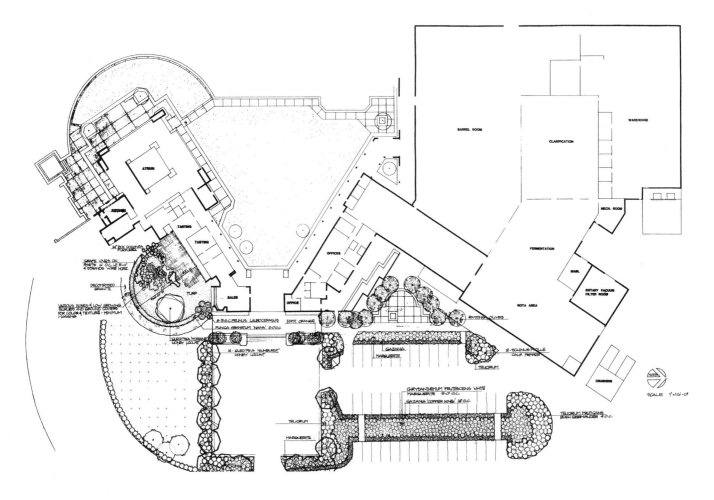

Figure 1-87: *Interim plan, summer 1982, at entrance*

and see the processing areas where the grapes are fermented and the wines mixed, aged, tasted, and packaged. Huge stainless steel vats ferment the grape mixtures at just the right temperature and humidity. A warehouse contains oak barrels, many of them decades old, for aging the wine.

Like many vineyards in the Napa Valley, acres of vines were destroyed in the 1980s by the insect phylloxera, an aphid-like animal that sucks the fluids from the vines. Entomologists had thought that the pest had been completely eradicated from the region decades earlier, but in the 1980s phylloxera reappeared, spread rapidly, and decimated the region. An unfortunate factor in the severity of the outbreak is that a very high percentage of grape vines in the region were planted on the same hybridized American and European rootstock that was thought to be highly resistant to phylloxera. The rootstock was resistant at first, but over many years the insect evolved to be able to destroy this particular rootstock. Since there was a monoculture of this particular rootstock, acres of vines were completely wiped out. Some vineyards, perhaps anticipating the dangers of a monoculture, or wanting to experiment with differ-

Figure 1-88: *A Bufano sculpture.*

ent rootstocks and vines in various types of soils and exposures, had substantial plantings of other types of vines that remained resistant.

Although Mondavi vineyards suffered significant losses, they remained productive. There were good vintages, and highly successful operations throughout the 1980s. Tourism increased, and the existing parking and visitor facilities became inadequate. The loss to phylloxera of acres of vineyards near the highway initiated the revival in 1993 of the landscape development scheme originally proposed in 1979 to accommodate the increase in visitors, but shelved due to a lack of space.

The entrance design provides a new entrance and parking plan for an area of about 7.5 acres. A formal axis centers on the existing arch, a famous landmark visible in the original vineyard building. The main loop drive is intersected by a formal allee perpendicular to the highway. The allee is lined with olive trees and terminates at an arrival circle and drop-off point. There the visitor experiences a formal entry court paved with colored concrete and terra cotta tile paving. Decomposed granite is used for paths and for the demonstration gardens, which are set in the forefront of the building on its east side. Shade trees are planted in the locations where guides talk to visitors touring the facility. Previously the demonstration gardens had been farther east of the building, where temperature conditions were often quite unpleasant—more than 100 degrees Fahrenheit during the height of the summer tourist season. Ramps and formal stairs link directly from the formal arrival court to the entrance plaza to the building. The plan calls for the expansion of the sculpture garden. Benjamino Bufano's sculptures are gaining a wider and wider audience. His most famous work is the statue of St. Francis at the entrance to the Mondavi facilities.

The parking deftly fits the site. In a long oval parallel to the highway are two concentric aisles of angle parking with one-way traffic. The traffic continues around to a one-way exit to the allee, and then to the highway. There are separate parking lots for dignitaries, buses and mobile homes, and bicycles. Some existing plantings of ivy and some trees remain in the front of the buildings. Existing olive trees were transplanted to the allee. The remaining plantings were removed.

The parking wraps around the new grape vines on variable rootstock. When the new plantings become established visitors will arrive, park, and walk through a flourishing vineyard to begin their tour of the facilities. The vineyard grades were raised to hide cars from the highway. The goal of the parking lot design was to hide cars so that visitors and those driving by would see only the remarkable, linear rhythm of rows of grape vines sweeping across the expanse between the highway and the distant building. With its formal allees, subtle pavings, and carefully engineered site lines, this modern design is truly baroque in its origins.

Changes in viticultural practice and technology have resulted in dramatic differences in the layout of the new plantings

Figure 1-93: *Plantings of new vines hide the parking areas*

Figures 1-94 and 1-95: *Tasting patio in 1979, and again in 1995. The plant materials have grown dramatically and an adjacent garden provides screening of the adjacent parking and service area.*

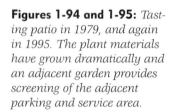

Figure 1-95: *(Cont.)*

versus the older ones. In the old vineyards, 450 vines are planted per acre in rows about twelve feet on center. Individual vines are planted about ten feet apart. In the new vineyards 2500 vines are planted per acre in rows four feet on center. The rows can be plowed and weeded using a new tractor with a 30-inch wheelbase; the layout of the older vineyards was based on a tractor that had a 10-foot wheelbase, and was later refined to about 8 feet. The new vines grow lower in height so that harvesting and maintenance is easier.

The new vines are planted inside 1-1/2-gallon orange juice containers for protection. Heavy duty wood end posts, 8″ × 8″ about 8 feet on center, support rubber hoses and steel cables that carry knee height drip irrigation lines and electronic controllers. In the same rows as the wood posts, steel posts are set in intervals of first four feet, then eight feet from the wood posts, and then at regular 16-foot intervals. The rows extend for hundreds of feet on generally flat terrain between the parking areas. The hollow steel posts support brackets to which the vines are staked. All rows are 4 feet apart. This 20-foot-square grid of support posts is established over the entire site.

An organically shaped lawn terrace extends from the rear or southern side of the processing areas and administrative offices. The visitor tasting rooms are both north and south of the lawn, which is surrounded by the building. (See Figure C–11.) The terrace terminates with a low curving wall, a few feet high, above which are extensive vineyards. They are set on a plateau that slopes up gently towards the hills on the western slopes of Napa Valley. Several sculptures by Benjamin Bufano decorate the lawn. This provides a spacious and graceful setting. The intersection of the rigidly straight rows of vines with the curving alignment of the low wall creates an interesting and pleasing pattern on this landscape, the form and character of which have been shaped for almost twenty years by skillful and fortuitous design by landscape architects.

PROJECT: *Golden Gate Park Master Plan and Reforestation San Francisco, CA*
CLIENT: *San Francisco Recreation and Park Department*
LANDSCAPE ARCHITECTS: *Royston Hanamoto Alley & Abey*
   Asa Hanamoto, Principal in Charge
   Douglas Nelson, Project Manager
URBAN FORESTERS: *Guido Ciardi and Jane Herman*
PARK PLANNER: *Deborah Learner*

The creation of a viable master plan document for Golden Gate Park and the beginning of its implementation have involved many key people. Deborah Learner, the park planner who hired Royston, Hanamoto, Alley & Abey to prepare the master plan, has been fully involved in both the master planning effort and coordination with the park staff. Since becoming the park planner in 1978, she has written or directed many of the documents that were reviewed and updated for the final master plan such as the Statement of Objectives and Policies (1979), the Forest Management Plan (1980), the Transportation Management Plan (1985), and the Kezar Corners Plan (1987). As the client she defined the scope of work for Royston Hanamoto Alley & Abey, approved all expenditures, administered the contract, represented the San Francisco Recreation and Park Department at all community meetings, brought matters for resolution to the Park Commission, and edited the text of the master plan report.

Landscape architect Douglas Nelson, the project manager for Royston Hanamoto Alley & Abey, has extensive experience in large scale site planning. During the work on the master plan, Ms. Learner and Mr. Nelson conferred on a daily basis and developed a close collaborative relationship. For example, for sensitive topics, it was necessary to craft and revise the wordings of the text, and the client and consultant discussed such matters regularly. He wrote the master plan document and directed all the work by his firm, including the inventory, analysis, and design drawings. At the public meetings, which Ms. Learner chaired, Mr. Nelson and other staff from his firm provided technical expertise and facilitated discussion. Under her direction, they also implemented public participation in the master plan process. This included coordination with the various groups who all

had a vital concern about what would happen to their park.

Guido Ciardi is the Urban Forester in charge of all arboriculture and forest management in San Francisco parks. His department has been responsible for the reforestation program since the beginning of its implementation in 1980. Working closely with Ms. Learner, he has translated the general and comprehensive planning goals into specific policy actions. Jane Herman is the acting supervisor for Golden Gate Park's reforestation crew. She notes that "although the relationship between humans and trees is ancient, I think it is very exciting to be involved in the field of urban forestry, which is an area of interest which is relatively new, and not yet thoroughly explored." This narrative will focus on the history of the park and the master plan, and how it has given direction to and enhanced one specific long-term project in the park: the reforestation program.

In 1866 Frederic Law Olmsted proposed a series of public parks for San Francisco, including a promenade across the city to the bay and a sheltered inland park in Hayes Valley. The city and state government rejected his plans since the cost of the land was already quite high, compared to much less expensive land on the western side of the city, called the "Outside Lands." The federal government ruled that these lands, often occupied by squatters, were under the jurisdiction of the city. Intense speculation by real estate interests encour-

Figure 1-96: *Prior to the development of the park, the site was an expanse of sand dunes. (Photo courtesy of Wells Fargo Bank Historical Services)*

aged development of the city westward into these areas. In 1870 the state legislature authorized the development of public parks in San Francisco and the planning for Golden Gate Park moved forward. Squatters agreed to donate portions of their claims for this public park in exchange for having clear title to the remainder.

William Hammond Hall, the surveyor and engineer turned park designer, directed the development of the park. Especially since the two men corresponded, Hall's concept of park experience was similar to what Olmsted would have envisioned: "A park should be an agglomeration of hill and dale, meadow, lawn, wood, and coppice presenting a series of sylvan and pastoral views, calculated to banish all thoughts of urban objects, and lead the imagination to picture space beyond a continued succession of rural scenes and incidents." Of a similar rectangular shape to Olmsted's Central Park, Golden Gate Park is 1017 acres; its main body is 3-1/2 miles long by 1/2 mile wide with a narrower panhandle at its eastern end.

Early maps of the city, dating from the Gold Rush days and extending into the 1920s and 1930s show the western region as a great, uninhabitable sand waste. Golden Gate Park was originally a site of drifting sand dunes with some pockets of native vegetation, primarily willows and oaks. As part of the development of a park on the site, trees were planted about 85–120 years ago. Starting about 1872, 22,000 trees of diverse and quick growing species were planted. The three that did the best are Monterey pine (*Pinus radiata*), Monterey cypress (*Cupressus macrocarpa*), and a particular species of eucalyptus, (*Eucalyptus globulus*). Many dunes were stabilized with a mixture of barley and lupine—the faster growing barley sheltered the lupine while it was becoming established.

Various facilities were sited in the park, primarily in its more protected eastern side, during the next few decades in order to meet growing demands for recreation. A conservatory was erected in 1877, a music

stand in 1882, and children's quarters and playground in 1888. In 1886 Olmsted, who had not thought a park could be established on sand dunes, acknowledged how far the work had progressed and how impressive the results.

Hall constantly fought to guide development in a sensible manner and to resist corrupt politicians. Hall resigned under pressure in 1876, but was reinstated a decade later as a consultant to the commission, after a change in the political climate. John McLaren was appointed park superintendent in 1890 and held this post for more than 50 years, until his death in 1943. During the course of his career many park facilities were added, and his challenge was to site these structures, to the extent that he was given authority, in a way that would minimize conflicts and allow ongoing recreational use by the public. He also continued extensive tree plantings. Several park features that were constructed as part of the California Midwinter International Exposition in 1894 became permanent facilities. The most notable are the Japanese Tea garden and the De Young Museum, both of which are still used. The Fine Arts Building, also constructed during this period, was demolished. McLaren Lodge was constructed in 1896 as the Park headquarters. A series of lakes, additional drives, and two windmills were added at the turn of the century. A structure, Portals of the Past,

Figure 1-97: *View of the Golden Gate Park Conservatory built in 1877.*

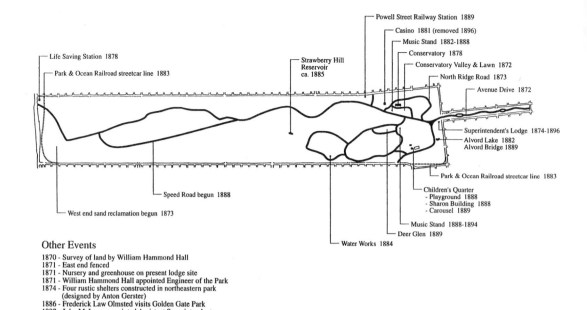

Life Saving Station 1878

Park & Ocean Railroad streetcar line 1883

Strawberry Hill
Reservoir
ca. 1885

Powell Street Railway Station 1889
Casino 1881 (removed 1896)
Music Stand 1882-1888
Conservatory 1878
Conservatory Valley & Lawn 1872
North Ridge Road 1873
Avenue Drive 1872

Superintendent's Lodge 1874-1896
Alvord Lake 1882
Alvord Bridge 1889

Park & Ocean Railroad streetcar line 1883

Children's Quarter
- Playground 1888
- Sharon Building 1888
- Carousel 1889

Music Stand 1888-1894
Deer Glen 1889

Speed Road begun 1888

West end sand reclamation begun 1873

Water Works 1884

Other Events

1870 - Survey of land by William Hammond Hall
1871 - East end fenced
1871 - Nursery and greenhouse on present lodge site
1871 - William Hammond Hall appointed Engineer of the Park
1874 - Four rustic shelters constructed in northeastern park
          (designed by Anton Gerster)
1886 - Frederick Law Olmsted visits Golden Gate Park
1887 - John McLaren appointed Assistant Superintendent

The Development of Golden Gate Park
1870-1889

Stow Lake Boat House rebuilt 1946

Redwood Memorial Grove 1948

Rose Garden 1961

Asian Art Museum 1969

Rhododendron Dell 1942

6th Avenue pedestrian entrance 1987

Queen Wilhelmina Tulip Garden 1962

Golf Course 1951

Senior Center 1980

Fuchsia Garden 1940

Lodge Annex 1950

Kezar Stadium rebuilt 1990

Existing Tennis Clubhouse 1950

Morrison Planetarium 1951

Victory Garden 1942

Hall of Flowers 1961

Chinese Pavilion 1981

Huntington Falls reconstructed 1984
(collapsed 1962)

McQueens Plant deactivated 1982

Other Events

1969 - JFK Drive Sunday closure
1979 - Objectives and Policies for park adopted
1980 - Reforestation program started
1981 - Marx Meadow Drive removed
1981 - 6th Avenue entrance closed to vehicles
1985 - Transportation Management Plan adopted
1993 - Sunset Richmond Sewage Plant closed

The Development of Golden Gate Park
1940-Present

Figures 1-98 and 1-99: *The Development of Golden Gate, 1870–89 and 1940–Present. (From the Master Plan)*

was erected to commemorate the great earthquake of 1906 when the park became a refuge for thousands of citizens who lived throughout it in temporary tent camps. The Academy of Science was relocated to the park after the earthquake wrecked its

downtown facility. A polo field was added in 1911. Several major facilities were constructed in the 1920s including Kezar Stadium, the Shakespeare Garden, and the North American Hall and Steinhart Aquarium. Major facilities, including police stables, a yacht club, comfort stations and a water reclamation plant were added in the 1930s. These projects were implemented by the Civilian Conservation Corps of the New Deal. After World War II a golf course was added and an additional building, the Annex, to house the Recreation Division and administrative services of the San Francisco Recreation and Park Department.

Sadly, like many other cities, San Francisco's ability to raise enough taxes to support public services, including maintenance of the park, is limited. The park was neglected in the decades following World War II. The neglect intensified in the 1970s as city funds were often allocated to more prestigious programs than park maintenance. However, rededication of the children's playground, restoration of the park carousel, and renovation of the music concourse occurred, and park reforestation began. In 1979 a study of the park was undertaken, some objectives were established, and some road closures occurred. Finally, in 1992, after the deterioration of the park had been widely publicized, a bond issue was passed by the voters to

fund the repair and updating of the park's infrastructure. Trees were considered a part of the "living infrastructure," along with irrigation, sewage, lighting, and walk systems. Approximately $78 million was provided for the next decade, including $6 million for forestry. In 1993, the work included a new survey and new inventory of the park as part of a new forest management plan.

The firm of Royston Hanamoto Alley & Abey was hired to develop a comprehensive master plan, a study of how to make the best use of all the park's resources and to update the 1979 master plan. The challenge for the master planners was to "provide a framework and guidelines to ensure responsible and enlightened stewardship of the park," to balance the uses of a 19th-century pleasure ground with those of a modern urban park. The master planning process began in late 1992 and is being completed in 1995. The process has involved careful consultation with the staffs of the San Francisco Recreation and Park Department and other departments, a task force composed of representatives from

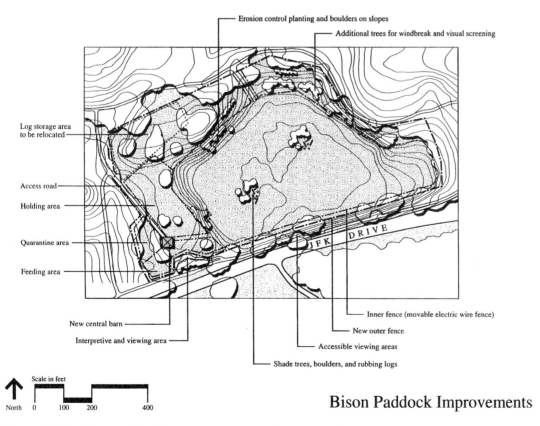

Bison Paddock Improvements

Figure 1-100: *Bison paddock improvements (From the Master Plan)*

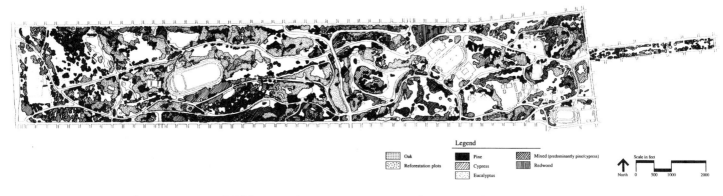

Figure 1-101: *Map of Forest Canopy (From the Master Plan)*

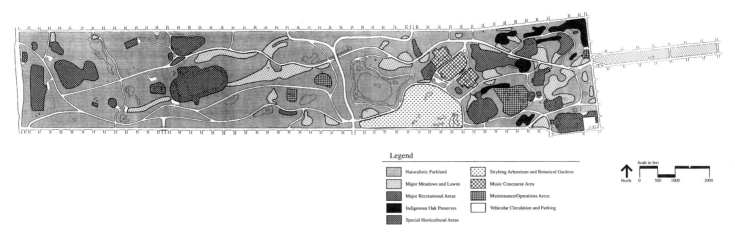

Figure 1-102: *Map of Land Use Zones (From the Master Plan)*

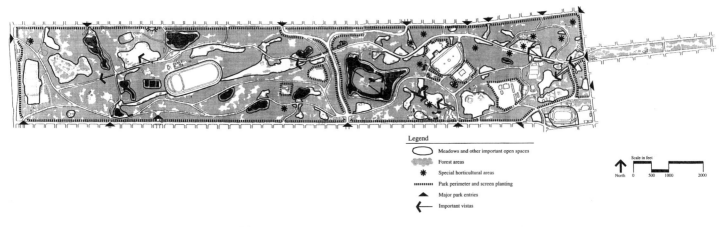

Figure 1-103: *Landscape Design Framework (From the Master Plan)*

various neighborhood and user groups, and the general public. Incredibly diverse interests and types of groups all use the park. Efforts were made to communicate and listen to representatives of all such groups. Perhaps the only group that did not speak for themselves was the bison herd.

The importance of the master plan cannot be understated. As Mr. Nelson notes, "It is the first document that has looked at everything in the park." There are five phases to the master plan: 1) issues identification, 2) assessment of existing conditions and needs, 3) assessment and revision of

Figure 1-104: *The relationship between forest and meadow creates the park's spaces. This relationship must be preserved as the park's forest is replanted. The park's forest provides unique opportunities for recreation and relaxation within the city (Photo by Douglas Nelson)*

the existing objectives and policies of 1979, 4) recommendations and action plans, and finally 5) implementation. Meetings with all interested groups and questionnaires were used to identify major issues and concerns in order to determine both areas of consensus and divergent opinions requiring further study. A thorough assessment of all park elements was undertaken to identify deficiencies and to determine which elements in the park merited special attention in the master plan. This analysis summarizes and distills the results of separate investigations of major park issues and elements. The Objectives and Policies, first developed through an extensive public process in 1979, have been revised to reflect current conditions and issues. The objectives for the park are now summarized in a mission statement and seven elegant goals, each of which is further explained by a series of explicit policy guidelines. The fourth phase of the master plan "includes specific recommendation and action plans to correct deficiencies and address problems identified during the master plan process. These are both parkwide recommendations and recommendations for selected areas within the park." The implementation of the master plan will occur over a period of several years. Cost estimates and a priority rating are given for all proposed actions and recommendations of the master plan. Strategies are proposed for developing new sources of public funding for the park.

The Draft Master Plan notes that although the design remains true in many respects to the original design of the 1870s, the "forest and landscape is not regenerating as a natural landscape would. The problems are much greater than appearances would indicate. The forest is green, but in serious decline." The master plan takes note of the special relationships be-

tween "forest and meadow, the convoluted edges of the forest, and the vistas they create," that result in visual interest in the park. "The mature pine and cypress trees create the park's unique skyline of dark green horizontal silhouettes. The tall eucalyptus trees, which were planted primarily on the park's ridges and hilltops, exaggerate the topographic relationship with meadows. The park's evergreen forest may be more the result of the high survival rates of pine, cypress and eucalyptus than design intent but the result is a park landscape that is unique to San Francisco." (See Figure C–12.) Currently, the park's diverse landscapes include "approximately 680 acres of forested area, 130 acres of meadows, fields and open areas, 33 acres of lakes and 15 miles of roads."

The new master plan embraces the goals of the Forest Management Plan of 1980 (FMP) and points out its implementation has been limited primarily by reductions in the numbers of park staff, the redirection of some staff to other functions, and lack of funds. For example, "the reforestation program is operating at a 50-year replacement cycle, instead of the originally intended 25- to 30-year cycle outlined in the 1980 FMP." Continued efforts in park reforestation are recommended in order to provide windbreaks from the severe winds addressing the site from the bay, habitat and food source for birds and other ani-

Figure 1-105: *Downed trees have become an increasingly common sight in recent years (Photo by Douglas Nelson)*

mals, screening of buildings and maintenance facilities, and aesthetic functions.

In 1980 efforts for redevelopment and conservation of the park proceeded according to the Forest Management Plan. A joint inventory by state and city urban foresters counted a total of 33,000 trees, of which 17 percent were found to be dead or dying. Under the direction of Deborah Learner, a Practices and Procedures Manual was prepared that applied the goals of the FMP to specific management units throughout the park. The consulting forester and Ms. Learner's staff divided the park into 45 management units, based on geographic factors and the ease of assessment rather than the species of plant materials or specific microclimatic conditions. For each inventoried management unit the team developed a prescription based on the use of the area for wildlife and/or recreation functions. (An effort is being made in 1995 to re-evaluate each management unit.)

Coincidentally, severe storms, marked by high winds and rain, struck San Francisco in 1982. City-wide between 2500 and 4000 trees were blown down. A state of emergency was realized, with conditions reminiscent of southeastern regions of the country after a hurricane. City tree crews were expanded from five arborists to 15 climbers and a staff of 40–50 clean up people. Concomitant to all of this activity,

there was an increased awareness of urban forestry by the public. Sadly, devastating winds and torrential rains again struck the park in the winter of 1995. The damage is still being assessed; nevertheless, it is clear that future severe weather will make the configurations of the forest, particularly on the western side of the park, more vulnerable to major damage. Parts of the park were closed due to the severity of the damage and the risk to the public from potential falling trees and limbs.

Based on the inventory of 1980 a reforestation program started and progressed at a good rate. Generally, the goal was to restore Golden Gate Park to the character it had fifty years ago. Aerial photographs from 1935 showing vegetation patterns in the park, were used as aids to restoration. When a species was removed from an area due to death or weakness, generally the practice has been to try to replant the same species. Studies in 1980 noted that the Monterey pine has the shortest life span of the three principal species, and that they are failing at the fastest rate. A re-inventory of the park forest in 1993 revealed that Monterey pine comprises only 17 percent of all trees, compared to 22 percent in 1980. More than six thousand trees were lost between 1980 and 1993, a mortality rate of 18.5 percent. During the same period more than 12,000 trees have been planted. Nevertheless, approximately 23 percent of the trees inventoried in 1993 were found to be in good or excellent condition, "a marked decline from the 41 percent that was measured in the 1980 inventory and represents the trend for an overmature forest. Consistent with this trend is the finding that 14 percent of the forest trees are in poor condition, a slight increase (two percent) over 1980. It is apparent from these data that proportionally more trees are now in fair condition." However, the master plan notes that "the number of trees in areas where reforestation has occurred has greatly increased and most of these trees are in good to excellent condition—a clear reversal of

Figure 1-106: *Reforestation plot with trees planted approximately six years earlier. (Photo by Douglas Nelson)*

conditions observed in 1979 . . . The inventory data confirm that reforestation should continue to be concentrated in the west end of the park, but that it is also needed in the other forest areas." The master plan makes the following general recommendation for preserving Golden Gate Park's forests:

- Extend reforestation to all parts of the park
- Identify, monitor, and remove structurally weak trees that pose a significant risk to the public
- Preserve eucalyptus forest, but contain it within designated areas
- Preserve remnant native plants, predominantly oaks, in designated oak preserves
- Replace previous trees in kind using the 1935 aerial photographs as guidelines
- Replace individual large trees with similar species of specimen size
- Reforest high use and high visibility areas in the eastern park with larger trees rather than seedlings
- Increase the efficiency of wood and brush recycling
- Use the dedicated tree program as a means of replacing specimen trees

The Division of Urban Forestry has directed the reforestation program and many, but not all, of its policies follow those of Royston Hanamoto Alley & Abey's updated master plan. In 1980–1988 most of reforestation effort occurred in the western half of the park, which is the least used but in the worst condition, because it is closest to the ocean and subjected to the fiercest winds. Without the windbreak provided by these existing trees at the western end, "the front door to the park," it would not function, and would begin to revert to sand dunes. The urban forester directs crews of reforestation workers and tree removal crews. Hazardous trees are removed and failing trees are identified. Only about 1 percent of the trees have been found to be

dead, but the percentage of trees that are hazardous or failing is much higher.

Public safety is a primary concern: Typically, with all three species, massive limbs may break and fall. High winds cause trunk failures as well. Although 1994 and 1995 were very wet years, drought conditions from 1987–1993 weakened the trees so that it might take at least a decade for them to recover. Trees weakened by the drought are more susceptible to disease and insects attacks. San Francisco's climate is not ideal for insects such as bark beetles, since the summers tend to be quite mild, rather than the hot, humid conditions in which many insects thrive. Still, a significant increase in insect-infested trees was noted throughout the 1980s.

Interestingly, there has been only one finding of Dutch Elm disease in San Francisco, a solitary tree on Page Street in 1980. The disease was contained and did not spread. The state imposed a quarantine against all elm plantings in nine bay area counties. Agronomists and entomologists were worried that the beetle could spread. In the last decade, disease-resistant elms have been planted, such as Chinese elms and special cultivars, but elms in general are still not widely planted.

In the last decade there have been unanticipated complications. There has been an increase in fires in the park, a few of which have been caused by homeless encampments. The Australian tea tree (*Lep-*

tospermum laevigatum) was one of the park's foundation plantings. With a twisting ribbony bark and dense foliage, it is quite attractive and is also an important, drought-tolerant understory species. Unfortunately, it forms a good thicket for protective encampments of homeless people living in the park. Some have chopped it for fuel. It burns at a tremendously high temperature, with a very high BTU output. It is not recommended as fuel for woodburning stoves as it has the potential to burn out the stove bottom. In the park the intense heat and energy of fires in tea trees has spread on several occasions to the upperstory trees. The *eucalyptus globulus* is the most susceptible of these trees to fire, as it has a highly flammable resin within its bark and also tends to hold onto lower, tinder dry branches for extended periods.

Ironically, the Monterey pines and Monterey cypress are species that normally depend on fires to regenerate. The cones pop open, like the southeastern pine species of the coastal timberlands of Georgia, only when exposed to the intense heat of a forest fire. Since fires have been minimal in Golden Gate Park, there has been a lack of regeneration. Another impediment to natural regeneration has been severe soil compaction problems as a result of the park's ten to fifteen million annual visitors. In areas that are chipped to displace compaction there has been significant regeneration of all three major species. More often than not, naturally sprouted tree seedlings that are not given follow-up maintenance and deep watering are pulled up by people or animals or blown over since they are not deeply rooted.

Eucalyptus globulus is now no longer planted. The percentage of eucalyptus had increased 2 percent from 1980 to the 1993 re-inventory. With the added fire hazard these trees present, as well as their dominance in the forest canopy, it was decided not to continue planting them.

The reforestation teams have developed a complete program to insure the best results:

1. *Assessment*: The first step is to make an assessment of a plot that is designated by the master plan for evaluation. A team consisting of an urban forester, a park planner, an arborist, tree climbers, supervisors, and, sometimes, representatives from the community all participate. The existing conditions of all trees are determined. Those that are dead or deemed in too dangerous a state of decline are removed from the site. Felled wood is recycled as possible.

2. *Planting strategy*: Simultaneously, a plan is developed focusing on what species will work best for that particular site. Factors that are considered include the proximity to the ocean and, therefore, exposure to winds, the anticipated pedestrian traffic and use of the site, proximity to major roadways, the formality of the existing design treatment, and whether the site is part of one of the notable collections within the eastern part of the park such as the rose gardens, the rhododendron dell, the Shakespeare Garden, the De Laveaga Dell's AIDS Memorial Grove, and the Strybing Arboretum and Botanical Gardens.

3. *Nursery development*: The Park now grows its own trees in order to insure the development of the best root systems and genetic conditions. The staff is working with a forester from Monterey in collecting seed from native stands. Previously, they had ordered seeds from reputable catalogs. However, those seeds had been collected from trees in the Monterey peninsula that had blown down, exactly the opposite characteristic to breed for in new generations of trees. At one time seedlings were grown in standard one-gallon containers, but these tended to encourage circling root development. When the seedlings were transplanted, the root systems did not always develop normally and shallow and girdling roots were a problem. Now tree pots are used, measuring $4'' \times 4'' \times 18''$ deep with ribs for structural support. A substantial root mass develops in these containers.

4. *Use and removal of old trees*: Mobile chippers, both disk and drum type, are used. Logs are stockpiled, as some are quite long, from trees as large as 20 inches to 50

inches in diameter. Many logs are rotted and infested with termites, all indicators of why the trees were removed in the first place. However, as lumber becomes more scarce, the urban foresters are investigating uses of this wood that once would have been discarded. For example, there is ongoing research into the use of chips for particle board and several local lumber mills have been testing the suitability of Monterey cypress as a substitute for redwood in non-structural applications in furniture. Between 1980 and 1994, more than 6,100 major trees were removed from the park, so that the volume of available sizeable logs for furniture or chipping has been quite significant.

5. *Intensive labor process:* Removals, cleanup, and planting are carried out by a crew of six to ten full-time employees, with an average of seven. Reforestation gardeners are assigned to specific areas in the park so that they become more efficient and more informed about conditions in that area. After the removal of dead trees and dead branches from other trees, the site is prepared. Rather than prepare individual holes one at a time, the entire site is sometimes amended with soil additives. Small seedlings are typically planted. In the park staff's experience, the smaller the size the better. A 6-inch to 12-inch-tall seedling grown in a tree pot, by its seventh to tenth year, will outgrow a much more expensive tree grown in a 15-gallon container. The one disadvantage is that there are some losses of smaller seedlings due to vandalism. Trees are typically planted 10′ to 15′ on center. The density of planting is increased nearer the ocean or adjacent to other reforestation plots, where winds are typically higher. The crew individually prunes existing specimens and thins forest plots over time.

6. *Soil amendments:* 75 percent of the existing soil in the park is basic beach sand. Over the 100-year life of the park, depending on forest type, there has been some change in profiles with some accumulation of humus and organic materials. A few areas have evolved into a sandy soil. At Strawberry Hill there are rocky chert (flinty quartz) soils, quite different from the sand dune soils. In a few areas sewage sludge has been used as an additive, and is being studied. Typical soil amendments used are a composted mixture of sand, straw, and manure from horse stables in the park and from the stables of the San Francisco Mounted Police. The Recreation and Park Department makes its own compost. The composting operation is supervised by the urban forester.

7. *Planting techniques:* Small bamboo stakes are used to stabilize the seedlings in very windy areas. A mulch of wood chips is used to suppress weeds and hold in water. There has been considerable experimentation to determine at what depth the trees should be planted. Seedlings planted low with basins of soil around them often develop root crown decay and are subject to insects and disease. The survival rate of seedlings planted above the predominant existing grade is more favorable. On slopes, the most success occurs with trees planted high, but with basins to trap water. In flatter areas, the most success occurs with trees planted slightly depressed but without saucers. The growth rates of all tree seedlings have been observed, and

the staff has found that the Monterey pines grow the fastest of the three major species. An important factor affecting the rate of growth is the amount of sunlight reaching each stand of seedlings, along with the amount of watering and soil type. Thinning of plots is carried out periodically to allow penetration of sunlight. The shapes of the plots are arranged in order to maximize the penetration of sunlight. After initial planting, the staff anticipates the removal of other dead or dying trees in 10–15 years. However, due to the extensive planting that has been performed in the last 14 years, reforestation efforts are moving towards the developed areas, away from the interior to more visible parts of the park. Generally, planting of trees is scheduled in the winter. After November is best, after some rainfall. But often planting must occur out of season due to the location of particular plots and the existing conditions of the site.

8. *Watering*: The forestry staff has found that individual hand-watering on trees has worked better than wide watering with sprinklers, because deep rooting is encouraged. The sources of water are available water lines with quick coupling valves. Water trucks with a capacity of 400 gallons drive into the sites along existing park roads, and use hoses to fill the tanks. Ten gallons per tree per three weeks is the usual amount required for deep watering.

9. *Water supply*: Golden Gate Park is in the unique position of being above a major aquifer, under San Francisco and northern San Mateo County, that flows into the Pacific Ocean. Lake Merced, in the city, is an expression of the aquifer. Its water level has been going down steadily as more water has been drawn from it in response to drought conditions. In Golden Gate Park water from the aquifer has always been blended with San Francisco's water supply. However, a plant for drawing reclaimed water from the aquifer has not been used since the early 1980s.

Wells to provide water from the aquifer for park use were part of the original plan. A pair of windmills near the western end of the park pumped water for a short time. A secondary treatment facility was located in the park many years ago so that the park could use reclaimed water. That process stopped in the early 1980s as public health officials became concerned that there was too much risk of park users, particularly children, being exposed to potential contaminants. In response to the drought and as a result of a new landscape conservation ordinance, this former method will be re-introduced. The recycled water will be used for irrigation in a lot of areas of the park that have limited use. Currently, there are test plots for recycled water in two areas. A plant to provide tertiary treatment of reclaimed water may be built in the next decade, which would greatly increase the available water for use in the park. There is an extensive, but very old, system of existing irrigation lines featuring quick couplers. Most of the water distribution system and the older irrigation system will be replaced as part of the work covered by the 1992 Park bond. New mains will carry groundwater and reclaimed water. A separate well line will feed the lakes and sensitive plant collections.

10. *Specimen tree replacements*: The park foresters have implemented an individual tree replacement program for specimen trees, which, due to their uniqueness, are usually replaced by the same or similar species when they die. The urban forestry staff has developed a tree dedication program. A donor who agrees to contribute at least $500 for the purchase and planting of a replacement tree selects an individual to be honored or memorialized. The donor receives a certificate acknowledging his or her commitment to the restoration of the park. Many donors choose to be on hand when the planting occurs. Typically 15-gallon trees have been planted. Now trees no smaller than four feet to six feet in height are selected. Public interest in the program has been increasing each year. Originally three to four specimen trees were planted

monthly, but that number has risen to as many as seven to ten per month. One staff member is fully occupied all year with the program. The program is not money-making, but it does hold its own. The park planning staff determines the species of trees to be dedicated well ahead of time in order to avoid selections incompatible with existing plantings. The arboretum in the eastern part of the park has its own program. The park staff has enlisted volunteers as planters of specimen trees. The coordinator has involved school children and various employee groups from corporations such as the Pacific Gas and Electric Company. Ceremonies are held on Arbor Day and Earth Day. It is generally felt that the more the public knows about issues involved in the conservation of the trees of the park, the more successful the process will be.

11. *Vandalism and destruction*: Sadly, at least some mature trees now in the park will not be in place in 15 years due to storm damage, natural aging, and vandalism. It is important to remember that trees are not static elements in the park landscape. There is a limited amount of vandalism and theft. Dedicated trees are staked to help prevent theft. Amid the vastness of the forces at play in the city and the sheer numbers of park users, it is easy to forget how seriously just one individual can inpact the program. Last year a group of skinheads devastated

one reforestation site before they were apprehended, but this was an isolated incident. Aside from accidental vandalism, it has been estimated that 90 percent of the vandalism of the trees has been done by as few as 80 people. When vandals are apprehended and held accountable, the park staff follows the guidelines of the International Society of Arboriculture in setting the value of trees that were lost so that appropriate reparations can be demanded.

The reforestation program is, of course, only one part of many projects underway as directed by the master plan. Others include mapping of the park landscape design, an upgrading of the park infrastructure, erosion control, lake restoration, accessibility/ADA path improvements, and bike trails, most of which are at least partially being funded by the 1992 Golden Gate Park Infrastructure Bond. These funds however, provided only for construction or restoration of park facilities, not their ongoing operation or maintenance. The reforestation program has been authorized $600,000 per year from the bond proceeds for each of the next ten years.

The master plan sets priorities and phasing, so that tasks such as mapping and survey assessments come first. Capital improvements estimated to cost approximately $85,000,000 are itemized in the master plan, plus another $2,900,000 for additional annual maintenance needs and

Figure 1-107: *Proposed irrigation and lake water supply system (From the Master Plan)*

Proposed Irrigation and Lake Water Supply System

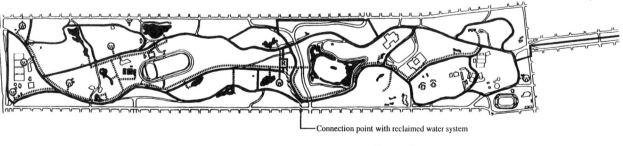

Connection point with reclaimed water system

Legend

⠿⠿⠿⠿⠿⠿	Non-potable irrigation (well water only)
———————	Non-potable irrigation (well water and/or reclaimed water)
∿∿∿∿∿∿	Reclaimed water
Ⓦ	New or existing well
Ⓡ	Central pumping plant and new reservoir

$535,000 for additional maintenance equipment. The tasks ahead are daunting. For example, the amount of water lost into the sandy soil below the deteriorating clay liners of the lake system has been measured at 560,000 gallons per day. Fortunately, "the water loss recharges the aquifer under the park, which supplies the park's wells," but this is just one problem with the lakes. Others include the deterioration of the lake edge, poor water quality, and significant sedimentation.

Specific recommendations of the master plan address vehicular and pedestrian circulation, recreation, visitor facilities, buildings and monuments, utilities and infrastructure, and maintenance and operations. A non-profit conservancy organization is proposed, modeled after those of Central Park in New York City and some local organizations such as the San Francisco Zoological Society, the Golden Gate National Park Association, and the Strybing Arboretum Society, to raise funds for park improvements and maintenance. As the Master Plan report states, "The park is as vital today as it was a hundred years ago . . . It is intended that the Master Plan will provide the impetus to raise the necessary funds, both public and private, to maintain Golden Gate Park as the world-class urban park that it is."

CHAPTER TWO

THE PRIVATE SECTOR: SMALL AND INTERMEDIATE FIRMS

Firms with fewer than 25 employees are highlighted in the following sections. Again, their work is diverse, ranging from environmental mitigation to residential design, from gardens without plants to gardens with an abundance of horticultural delights. The seven firms presented, are geographically dispersed. Four are located in California: Jack Chandler & Associates in Yountville, George Hargreaves Associates in San Francisco, and Schmidt Design Group and SPURLOCK/POIRIER in San Diego. Two are in Massachusetts: Elena Saporta and Martha Schwartz, both in Cambridge. Jacobs/Ryan Associates is in

Chicago, IL. The longevity of the firms is also quite variable, from Jack Chandler, who has been in practice for more than 35 years, to Elena Saporta, who started her own firm just a few years ago. The size of the firms varies as well. With only occasional part-time staff support, landscape architect Elena Saporta and John Taguiri, sculptor and artist, have conceived some remarkably creative projects. All of the other firms are significantly larger. In order to give a broad sense of the type and character of work, at least two projects by each firm are presented.

JACK CHANDLER & ASSOCIATES

Yountville, CA

Jack Chandler has more than 35 years experience in landscape architecture, with a practice ranging from intimate city courtyards to large estates in Napa Valley. His firm features hands-on design with great attention to detail. Installations tend to be by contractors with whom he has established long working relationships, so that initial development of preliminary sketches to the

completion of work can occur in as little as 18 months. Some clients are much more trusting and accepting than others. "We had one client for whom we designed a large residential garden, and she was on the site only four times during the entire process. And we did it all. It's fun when the client gives you so much trust, but it's also a big responsibility. Even though I knew the garden was very good, she couldn't see from the plans. So she would come out, and say, 'Oh this is what that material is, that's OK; or 'oh, so that's what you were talking about, that's wonderful.'"

Chandler graduated in 1962 from the California Polytechnic Institute, in landscape architecture and started a design-build practice in Orange County. He acquired expertise in plants from his love of the materials and the necessities of business: "If you have to pay for its replacement because you planted it where it shouldn't have been planted, where it doesn't grow, you learn in a hurry. I like plants anyway. It's a situation where I am always keeping my eyes out for new guys, but then I have my old friends that I can take along with me; that's my palette, that's how I create a canvas." Among the old reliables that he regularly uses are the perennials gaura (*Gaura lindheimerii*), day lilies (*Hemerocallis speciosa*), lavender (*Lavendula vera*), Russian sage (*perovskia atriplicifolia*), for its looseness, and wall germander, (*Teucrium chamaedrys*). For shrubs he finds the whole range of shrub forms of Cherry laurel (*Prunus laurocerasus*) very satisfying: *Prunus Bright n Tight*, 'Otto Luyken,' and 'Zabeliana.' He also prefers Xylosma (*Xylosma congestum*), which doesn't grow in the east, for its looseness. These materials are often used in his residential gardens, and are supplemented with additional materials.

The three projects discussed here are typical of the range of his work. The Isgur Residence represented a challenge of how to create a series of garden spaces around a modern house on a rough site in Woodside, CA. The Danforth Estate illustrates the design challenges of integrating the outdoor environment of a wine country estate into the rigid geometry of the surrounding vineyards. Finally, the visitor center for the Cakebread Winery in Oakville, CA, illustrates his artful use of landscape architecture techniques to accommodate large numbers of visitors, create flexible spaces for entertaining, and mask the sounds of the highway.

PROJECT: *Isgur Residence*
CLIENT: *The owners*
LOCATION: *Woodside, CA*

The town of Woodside is located on a peninsula south of San Francisco and Stanford University. The owners, a sophisticated couple who have traveled extensively, hired Jack Chandler to evaluate their post-modern house. The Isgars interviewed four to six firms and chose Mr. Chandler on the strength of his residential experience.

Batey Mack Architects had designed three or four contemporary homes in the area and conceived of an addition to the original home, a ranch style, for the previous owner. The architecture added was a post-modern, square plaster box with a plaster facade in a stark contemporary style. It was a two story structure in the center of the one story ranch house. There was also a garage. Mr. Chandler found the two parts of the house expressive of the marriage of country to contemporary style. Given this eclectic architectural vocabulary, the garden "called out for stylized presentations, more philosophical than what I normally get into." The challenge was to unify the front and back gardens while acknowledging the contemporary style of the architecture. By its end the project included the renovation of the existing swimming pool, reconfiguration of driveways and parking areas, the creation of several water elements, and related pavements and plantings.

There were some dramatic and troublesome existing features on the two-acre site. Mr. Chandler inherited a swimming pool near some large trees, mainly Deodar cedars from 75 to 125 years old. Quite mature, they regularly lost limbs as thick as 12-14" in diameter. Although these trees were attractive, their needles were "user-unfriendly"—quite sharp and capable of puncturing fingers or toes—not at all suitable for people wishing to walk around barefoot. Therefore, the trees near the pool were removed, even though this location was where the challenge was to marry the house to the pool site. Some of the trees removed were found to have significantly decayed interiors and might not have survived much longer. They posed a significant hazard to the house. Those that remained were limbed up to 40 feet high.

Situated on one of the busiest corners in the town, the site is subjected to a lot of road noise. There was also a circular drive from the main road that invited drivers to use it as a turnaround. Mr. Chandler eliminated this nuisance by transforming the driveway into a smaller autocourt in the front with only one entrance. The garage was not moved, but access from the other street was eliminated, thus freeing space for a garden.

Playing off the geometry and forms of Mark Mack's plaster box, the landscape ar-

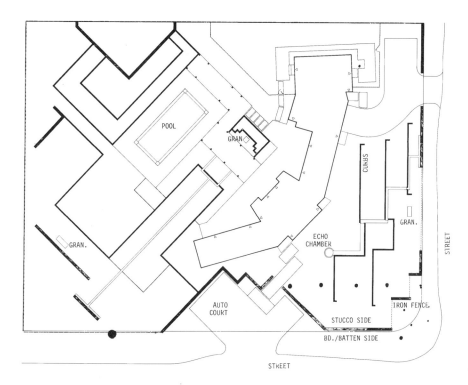

Figure 2-1: *Illustrative site plan*

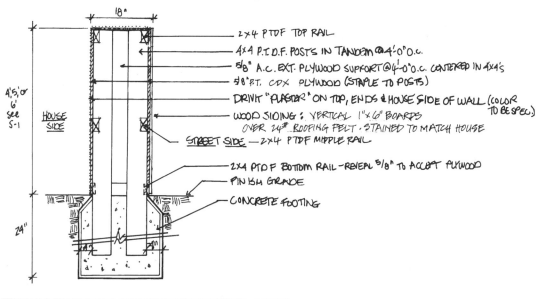

Figure 2-2: *Construction detail of wood/plaster wall stuccoed with Drivit "plaster"*

chitect first designed six-foot sound walls, plastered to match the architecture. However, the city's zoning requirements dictated that these property line walls not exceed four feet in height and could not be plastered on the street side, as this would not be in keeping with the rural character of the neighborhood. Mr. Chandler redesigned the walls in wood about one foot thick to match the required board and batten street vocabulary. They were plastered on the inside. On the street side, the walls were painted gray to form a backdrop to a hedge of cherry laurel (*Prunus laurocerasus*) and pittosporum (*Pittosporum tenuifolium*).

A love–hate relationship persisted between Mr. Chandler and the city reviewers throughout this project. The city initially objected to the choice of color for the plaster finish, an orangy persimmon the same as that used for the addition by Mack. But the city bureaucrats were eventually convinced.

Since the house site was basically flat Mr. Chandler sought a way to create some visual interest. He used granite curbs, 6″ × 6″ in the front yard and 6″ × 8″ in the back yard, to accentuate grade changes and create a sequence of very small terraces. The total elevation change is only 16 inches in the front and 24 inches in the back, but the repetitive treatment with the curbs dramatizes the changes. In the front of the house, he specified a ground plane material of de-

composed granite that extends into the auto court and into the driveway. Decomposed granite, indigenous to California, is a raw product that is coarser than sand and finer than gravel. It is easily compacted. Geologically, it has not been subject to compressive forces to the extent of the granites in the eastern United States. It also has much rounder edges than crusher-run stone, so that it makes a comfortable walking surface when compacted. It has the advantage of appearing to be a natural soil so that it does not stand out. A similar material is commonly used in Europe. Mr. Chandler specified that for the driveway and autocourt the decomposed granite be mixed with cement in the ratio of one bag of dry cement to ten square feet of decomposed granite four inches thick. It was then wetted down and vibrator compacted. It hardened into "a very successful soil cement. It grows moss on it to this day." The area withstands heavy pedestrian traffic and is hard enough so that no footprints are left. Used as the major base plane element in the front yard, it is nevertheless quite recessive in appearance. In the garden areas, the material was *slightly* compacted so that water percolates through it like any gravel surface. By contrast, water drains to the edge of the driveway and autocourt, where it percolates through the uncemented materials. The driveway and autocourt appear to be part of the landscape, rather than the garden appearing to be part of them. Pockets for plantings, including olives, lavender, sages, grasses, and Mediterranean plantings, were created within the decomposed granite.

Chandler sought to achieve "a visual from the house outward from the front part of house since it was street-oriented on both sides." Again, faced with restraints about the street-facing side of any structure, he designed a Luis Barragan-style picket fence that tied together different lengths of the sound walls where they could not penetrate because there was not adequate room. Steel bars, 1-1/2″ × 4″, were set four inches on center into a concrete base one foot thick. They were allowed to rust, resulting in a color that dovetailed beautifully with the persimmon color of the plaster.

Figure 2-3: *The small change in the vertical grade is accentuated by these low linear elements. (Photo by Jennifer Chandler)*

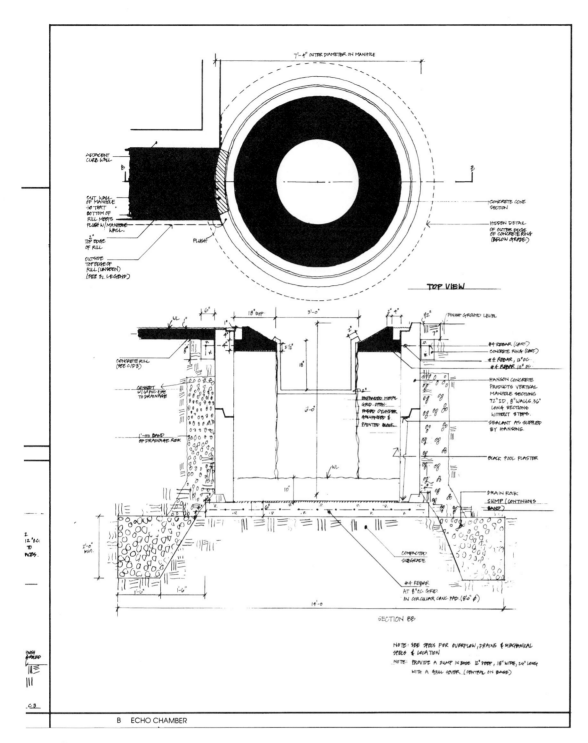

Figure 2-4: *Construction detail, plan, and section, of echo chamber*

Another dramatic feature of the site begins in the front yard. A playful water course emerges from the ground in the form of three bubblers spouting water 12 inches high against a persimmon-colored plaster wall. The water flows through dry courses of decomposed granite, gradually widens, and collects into an echo chamber. It flows around the edge of this chamber and falls into its center. The drops and echoes mask road noise that comes over the walls. Constructed of a round pipe with an outside diameter of approximately five feet, the inside hole through which water falls is about three feet wide and six feet deep. Also incorporated are a leaf catcher and varmint catcher, which can be lifted up and removed for easy cleaning.

Figure 2-5: *As-built view of echo chamber (Photo by Jared Chandler)*

The echo chamber has a shoulder all around it with a small trough around the perimeter. The four inch deep formed cement trough slowly fills up with water, which falls over the lip of the pipe into the center. A recirculating pump powers the stream of water, which flows at the rate of 20 gallons per minute. The stream trough, at first 8 inches wide, widens to 24 inches as it approaches the echo chamber. The concrete trough is tinted a sand color which matches the decomposed granite.

In the back of the property, the water appears to reemerge, but is in fact a separate system. The site has been sculpted slightly more in the back. The two-foot elevation change is limited by the edge of the pool. A planter wall serves as a backdrop to accentuate the pool. A much larger granite block is set in a shallow pool in front of the planter where the water appears to reemerge. The granite in front of the persimmon stucco wall creates quite a dramatic contrast: the uniform, sun-washed stucco color of the wall is offset by the angular shape and varied grain and color of the granite. A fog machine mists water around the face of the granite, an effect which adds mystery and accentuates the range of color in the stone. The water flows through two narrow rills underneath the cement terrace connecting to the swimming pool. The terrace was elevated during the redesign of the pool. The two rills converge and form one very long rill that terminates in a semi-echo chamber against a six-foot-high wall, also treated with the persimmon stucco finish. In the summer the flow is kept to a trickle, yet the sound is quite audible. For the winter, Chandler designed a steam effect produced by a water heater placed near the pool equipment. However the water heater specified by the project engineer could not get the water hot enough to create a steam effect. This was changed to a simple fog emitter, consisting of high pressure, small orifice nozzles. It gives the de-

Figure 2-6: *The color and form of the principal elements, gray and massive granite, thinner persimmon wall, and the delicate tracery of the water plants, contrast remarkably with one another. (Photo by Jared Chandler)*

signer the result he sought: a misty fog effect in winter. In the summer the water gurgles through the crack in the granite block. At each change in grade along the channels is a stainless steel weir, set flush with the concrete curbs that accentuate the grade changes.

The granite block from which the water appears to emanate in the back yard is a spectacular sculpture. Mr. Chandler has worked with granite in the past. The source is a granite quarry in Cold Springs, near Fresno, CA. The granite's rich grain and warm color contrasts remarkably with the persimmon stucco. The massive granite is tool-split all the way to its base, and then re-confiigured squarely on a concrete plinth with a very strong, quick-setting epoxy at the base, where the water pipe is attached. The granite block is anchored on the plinth just below the surface of the water. The beauty of the large granite block, about 3′ × 5′ × 2′, is the irregular split within the clear geometric form. This granite weighs 180 pounds per cubic foot, and the larger cube, in the back yard, weighs approximately 5500 pounds. The one in the front yard is much smaller, about an 18-inch cube sitting to the side of the water bubblers. (See Figure C–13.)

The front yard of this residence had once been part of a walnut grove. Taking an orchard as a theme, Chandler planted a grove of about 15 olive trees (*Olea europea*) in a 20-foot grid in the front yard, through which the rills flow. The regular geometry of the grove helps emphasize the fall in elevation of the rills. The olive grove masks some of the mass of the house, creates more intimacy, and also helps to create a composition that can be viewed either from the house or from the street. Since there is a lot of traffic noise, it is important that the front yard serve as a visual element rather than a space to be used by the owners.

In the back yard Mr. Chandler designed a border garden. There is no decomposed granite, but instead a softer treatment with lawn and roses—particularly tea roses. He selected the "Iceberg" variety because it blends well with perennials, doesn't suffer from mildew or rusts, and blooms freely all

Figures 2-7 and 2-8: *The wall, the granite block, stabilized gravel, and the steel fence form a striking sculptural composition with softening hints of planting. (Photos by Jared Chandler)*

summer. The lawn is a standard sod mix for that area. There are a number of varieties of Beardstongue (*Penstemon speciosa*), lavender, and other perennials. Reliable shrubs include sasanqua (*Camellia sasanqua 'White Doves'*), *Prunus 'Otto Luyken'* and *Xylosma congestum*. Two thousand Narcissus bulbs were scattered in drifts in the rear borders. Trees in the back yard are Japanese flowering crabapples (*Malus floribunda*) and Bradford pear (*Pyrus calleryana 'Bradford'*) as accents. A few redwoods (*Sequoia sempervirens*) were planted to screen neighbors, although the remaining Deodar cedars accomplish most of that function.

To screen the board and batten side of the wall on the street side, a hedge is established of *Prunus 'Bright n Tight,'* which is dense, upright, and compact, and contrasts with the coarser English cherry laurel (*Prunus laurocerasus*) that is planted more informally. *Pittosporum tenuifolium* is included for some color change.

The clients have been satisfied. The only complication was a contractor who went bankrupt during the middle of construction. Mr. Chandler quickly replaced him with three other contractors and did some of the work with his own crew. Because of the unusual nature of the work, he exerted extra effort to get the job done. He is grateful for the client's faith in him to create a garden. The garden "was very successful philosophically. It will become her garden as she makes minor tuneups to it, and adds some more goodies. She put her faith in me to create the garden. She is now moving into it, and adding her touches." Some of the client's personal favorites in plant materials are particular varieties of sage and lavendar.

PROJECT: *Cakebread Winery*
CLIENT: *The owners*
LOCATION: *Yountville, CA*

This small Napa Valley winery, near the Robert Mondavi vineyards in Yountville, called on Mr. Chandler to help create a more comfortable and expansive space for wine tasting and entertaining. Another concern was to mask the heavy traffic noise from Highway 29. Finally, it was important that the spaces be planned flexibly so that small or large groups could be accommodated and additional facilities could be added. Originally, a network of soft pavements connected the various spaces around the old farmhouse, but as the winery was established, these walks and spaces became impractical. Besides the buildings, a few other prominent existing elements were some magnificent pecan trees, some old valley oaks, and an old, circular stone fountain.

To define the visitor parking and the property, Mr. Chandler designed a series of stone walls and split-cedar fences. The stone walls played off the materials of the stone fountain so that it gained in importance as a centerpiece in a terrace for wine tasting. The stone, referred to locally as engineer's stone, is often used as riprap. The local labor force includes some skilled Mexican masons who produce beautiful stone work at reasonable costs. Mr. Chandler's design took advantage of this valuable resource. Adjacent to the terrace is a professional kitchen, as the winery has a catering program and brings in chefs to prepare meals for large gatherings.

Parallel to the edge of the highway right-of-way a dramatic brick fountain and stone water wall were created to mask the highway noise. There was some discussion of building a stone wall for sound mediation, but massive construction would have been required in order to be even marginally effective. Instead this water feature recalls the little stone fountain near the food service area. The water wall is constructed with two pool levels. Two pumps provide constant water circulation: One brings water from the middle level to the top and releases it through six spouts at the upper level, and the other pump takes water from

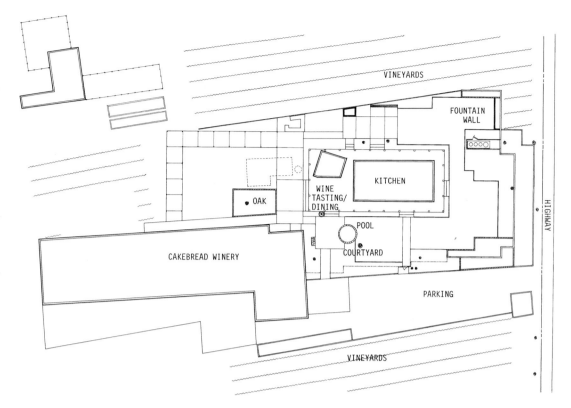

Figure 2-9: *Illustrative site plan. The fountain is in the upper right hand corner of the drawing. The parallel lines are vineyards.*

Figure 2-10: *Sketch of fountain*

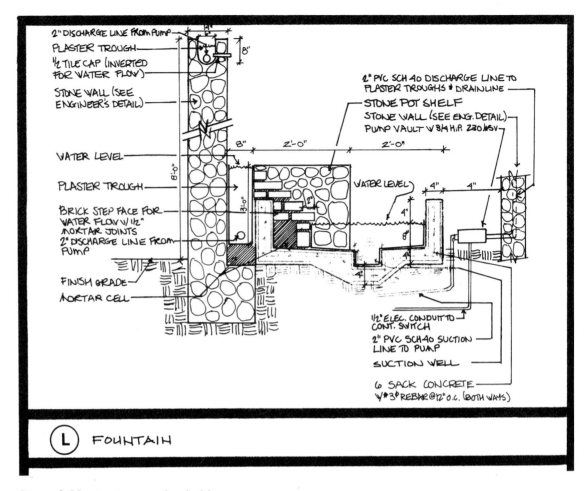

Figure 2-11: *Construction detail of fountain*

the bottom and recirculates it to the center pool. This two-pump method creates a maximum volume of water. The southeastern exposure of the water wall insures the play of sunlight on the water. Dark field stone is used for the upper level of the water wall, and dark brick for its lower level. The water coursing over the darker materials sparkles more than it would on a lighter colored brick. Little brick steps offset in the brick face of the wall catch the sunlight and create an additional sparkling effect against the generally dark background. The total height of the water wall is about eight feet, with the middle tier three feet up.

On the other side of the professional kitchen are a quiet space and a barbecue area. In general, the edges have been cleaned

Figure 2-12: *The spare furnishing of this outdoor room, formed by the fountain wall and decorative vase, frames a view across the valley while screening the highway and masking its noise. (Photo by Jennifer Chandler)*

up; instead of what Mr. Chandler described as a "rustic and woolly" environment there are a series of sunlit, dappled terraces. Additional trees planted included sweetgums and pistachios to complement the old pecans, and a new arbor planted with vines. The few valley oaks that require drier soil conditions are kept isolated from these other plantings.

The tables created for winery events exemplify the flexibility of the space. They are made with redwood tops set on welded steel frames. The redwood tops lift off easily. Designed like an old parsons table, they can be set individually—a standard 4' × 4' table top will seat eight people—or they can be grouped to form long tables for seating or winetasting.

Figure 2-13: *Sturdy table designed for the space. (Photo by Jennifer Chandler)*

PROJECT: *Danforth Residence*
CLIENT: *The owners*
LOCATION: *Yountville, CA*

The Danforth Residence is not far from the Cakebread Winery, and takes advantage of views towards the vineyards, although the Danforths do not own them. Mr. Chandler concentrated on creating a sense of entry to the existing Italianate residence and providing for the phased expansion of the outdoor spaces. It was also important to link the house with the vineyards, which were being expanded towards it.

The existing building had a small walk to the front door that lacked a sense of entry. Mr. Chandler designed a short, thick wall perpendicular to the main body of the house. This wall is backed by a larger intermediate wall that forms the back of the entrance space. The walks are poured concrete cut the next morning with a saw blade to give a cut stone look. To entice all the senses, a fountain was included in the original design, but the client did not want it. Instead, the landscape architect concentrated on planting with fragrances: star jasmine (*Trachelospermum jasminoides*), citrus, and *Osmanthus*.

The garden spaces feature a straight line design. "I tend to like my straight lines. They perhaps look harsh from plan view or helicopter. But at people elevation, you lose some of the harshness, and the plant material takes over. You get a nice crisp-reading garden. With a Thomas Church line, a curvy line, you might lose a sense of depth." (See Figure C–14.)

The site is very flat. Similar to the Isgur Residence, Mr. Chandler created interest with some vertical elements. In this case, major features adjacent to the pool are two pergolas. Their unusual roof lines recall old hop towers that he observed in the Healdsburg area of California. The pergolas, constructed of painted redwood, frame a view into the vineyards. (See Figure C–15.) He chose to use the same vocabulary of wood construction as is used in the architecture: a finely tailored appearance, with nothing rustic. The plantings are the exception.

A grove of olives on one side of the pool frames a view towards the vineyards as well. Pink coral bells (*Henchera sanguinea*), jasmine (*Jasminum polyanthum*), cat mint (*Nepeta faafennini*), oleander (*Nerium oleander*), Iceberg roses, and Russian sage are all featured plantings. The straight lines of the design tend to create precise edges with clean transitions. However, the plantings tend to be massed in large groupings, almost like overlapping paint splotches on a palette. "Instead of one, two; or one, two, three, four; I use 25, 50, or 110 plants to form a sweep of color, like a painting. It's not an arboretum, it's a painting. I wish I could sell my fees like a painting." As the plantings grow, the straight edges of the design are softened and the forms merge and dissolve into the expansive vineyard landscape.

Mr. Chandler changed the existing white-bottomed pool to a dark gray plaster that contrasts remarkably with the cobalt blue of the new coping tiles. A low seat wall parallel to the length of the pool at its rear is used visually to hold one's view in the garden. Since one can easily look over the wall into the vineyards, the seat wall acts as a pivoting element, demarcating a psychological boundary between the garden and the vineyard. Mr. Chandler wishes to punctuate it with some large Santa Barbara beach umbrellas and chairs. For evening use, the outdoor spaces are lit with small bronze lights manufactured by Coe.

Phase I has been constructed. Ultimately, the sidewalk by the pool will be extended and there will be additional guest parking. The existing driveway will be removed and a new driveway will enter the garage from its far side. A new garden will be built on the former driveway site.

Mr. Chandler maintains an ongoing relationship with most of his clients. As gardens are for living, it is often the case that clients want to expand in a particular direction or adjust features as the uses of the site change. As a family ages, or a business grows, different programmatic needs evolve. There is both an inherent flexibility and a strong figurative design that unifies his gardens while simultaneously inviting change.

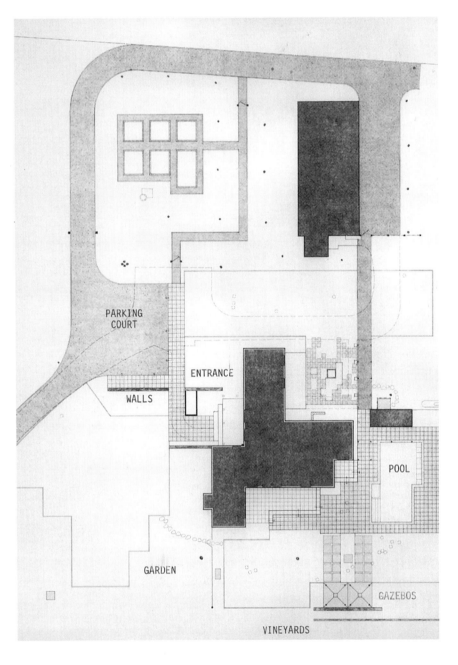

Figure 2-14: *Illustrative site plan*

Figure 2-15: *View of entrance before landscape development. (Photo by Jennifer Chandler)*

HARGREAVES ASSOCIATES

San Francisco, CA

Hargreaves Associates office was established in San Francisco in 1983. Currently it has 15 employees and three principals, George Hargreaves, Mary Margaret Jones, and Glenn Allen. The firm specializes in public work and waterfront projects, including many that require public participation in meetings and hearings and multiple agency reviews. George Hargreaves earned a BLA from the University of Georgia in 1977 and subsequently a MLA from Harvard in 1977. Prior to founding Hargreaves Associates, he worked for SWA in Sausalito, CA and the Cheshire Design Group in Chester, England. He lectures widely on landscape architecture, has been a visiting professor or critic at numerous universities, and has served on many national design juries. Glenn Allen earned a BLA from the University of Virginia in 1973, and a MLA from Lousiana State University in 1977. He worked previously for Reich Verson, Landscape Architects in Baton Rouge, LA; Myrick Newman Dahlberg, in Dallas, TX; and the SWA Group in Sausalito before joining Hargreaves Associates. Mary Margaret Jones earned a BLA degree from Texas A&M University in 1979 and was hired by Johnson, Johnson and Roy (JJR), of Ann Arbor, MI, after one of the principals interviewed her while in Texas lecturing to the landscape architecture students. She worked for JJR for five years until she moved to San Francisco to join Hargreaves Associates. She has lectured widely at universities in California.

The three established an office on Folsom Street in a stretch of the city built on bay mud. The office suffered severe damage on October 17, 1989, during the earthquake that struck as the third game of the World Series between the San Francisco Giants and the Oakland Athletics was about to begin. Immediately after the quake had subsided, the landscape architects discovered that their building had separated into two buildings. Legend has it that Mr. Hargreaves, antithetical to Samson, singlehandedly, with his bare hands, held the building together long enough to allow others to remove critical drawings, records, and #314 drafting pencils. It took several months to relocate the office to its present location on Mission Street. During the transition, some projects were finished by a group that regularly worked at his house.

PROJECT: *The Byxbee Landfill*
LOCATION: *Palo Alto, CA*
CLIENT: *Palo Alto Department of Public Works*
DATE: *1988–1990*
CONSTRUCTION COST: *$1.25 million*

PROJECT: *Candlestick Park Landfill*
LOCATION: *San Francisco, CA*
CLIENT: *California State Parks and Recreation Department*
DATE: *1985–1991*
CONSTRUCTION COST: *$1.2 million*

These two innovative landfill projects are both as similar in concept and as distinctly different in execution as two projects of the same type in the same region could possibly be. Both feature the sculpting of landforms to emphasize the views towards the bay and integrate the edge of the water with the land. Both sites are severely impacted by winds and require a refuge from its unrelenting force. Both designs introduce elements on the human scale in an otherwise overpowering landscape. Finally, artists and engineers were principal collaborators in a structured team approach that involved breaking down barriers between the various professions: landscape architecture, civil and structural engineering, architecture, and art.

For Candlestick Park the client was the State of California, whereas the Palo Alto Department of Public Works was in charge of Byxbee. The chronologies for the two projects are revealing. Although the design for Candlestick began well in advance of Byxbee, Byxbee was constructed first as the process of reviews and approvals on the state level was far slower for Candlestick.

Byxbee had been extensively studied when Hargreaves began work. A first phase had already been executed according to a master plan prepared in 1981 by Eckbo-Kay, a landscape architecture firm, and a one-foot clay cap had already been placed over mounds of garbage.[1] There was no such phasing or preliminary planning for Candlestick, only a schematic regional land-use plan prepared by the state.

The consultants selection process was quite different on the two projects. For Candlestick, Hargreaves Associates responded to a request for a proposal. The State Parks Department's design office saw an opportunity to combine different fields, such as large-scale landscape architecture, environmental art, environmental assessment, and interpretation in developing a final design for the use of the site. The state interviewed and hired the team of Hargreaves Associates, landscape architecture, Mark Mack, architecture, and Douglas Hollis, artist.

Byxbee Park was funded as a public works project by the city of Palo Alto, as influenced by the Office of Cultural Affairs and the Art Commission, who encouraged Public Works to take the lead in conceiving an arts project rather than merely engineering a landfill closing. The artist was therefore selected first. The Palo Alto Department of Public Works chose Peter Richards as the prime. He was in charge of the artist-in-residence program at the Exploratorium, San Francisco's marvelous wild and crazy science museum. Richards invited Michael Oppenheimer, now at the Children's Museum in San Jose, to join him

---

1 See also Rainey, Reuben M., "From Refuge Dump to Public Park, the Alchemy of Byxbee Park," Paysages, Vol. 4, 1992–3, p. 198–207.

as a second artist. This pair of artists was involved in selecting Hargreaves Associates as landscape architect.

The Candlestick Park landfill material, whose renovation into a park was completed in 1991, consists of construction rubble, concrete, street curbs, and related debris that accumulated over 115 years of use. Filling of the landfill ceased in 1965, and a parking lot was established on top of it. As education and knowledge of environmental issues increased in recent decades, it was found that the bay was shrinking and any additional filling on the 22-acre site was outlawed. Byxbee is much larger, about 180 acres. The site was a repository for garbage for many years, with the demand for additional disposal increasing annually.

At Candlestick, Hargreaves Associates began with a generic master plan done by the California State Parks Department, and evaluated it according to a thorough reconnaissance of the site. The design team's analysis showed the site to be influenced heavily by the wind. The infamous, wind-swept Candlestick Park, home of professional football and baseball teams, is the major land use adjacent to the landfill site. Wind became the defining and causative force behind the design: wind direction and shelter were key. The dramatically bold, large landforms, achieved through large scale grading that approximately balanced cut and fill, appears to be a result of the impact of winds on the site enhanced by an environmental artist. Constantly evolving as wind and weather affect it, the entire site reads as an artwork in three dimensions.

By contrast, at the Byxbee site there could be no excavation, only filling, because the site was filled with garbage. The whole sculpting process was additive. The designers had to deal with 40–60' high-clay-capped mounds of garbage that were already in place based on the master plan developed by Eckbo-Kay. Taking the Phase II and III concepts for the site, Hargreaves Associates was able to develop and enhance the design. The landfill was still in use, and garbage was still being added in some portions of the site,

Figure 2-16: *Illustrative site plan*

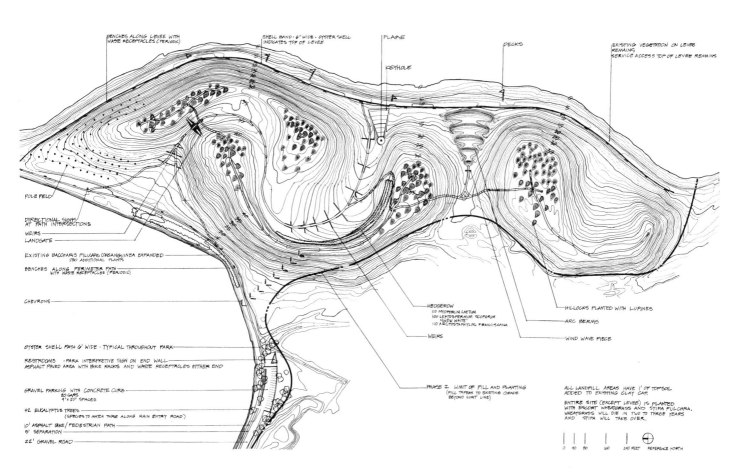

so that additional phasing was required. The amount of garbage being disposed of was significantly greater than in Phase I. "If anything, it was tougher than Phase I, because the Department of Public Works wanted to deposit more garbage. We talked about it as if you inflated a balloon—the mounds became more balloon-like." The challenges were daunting. "We couldn't irrigate, we couldn't puncture the clay cap because of the danger of escaping methane gases, we couldn't plant trees. Everything had to be additive." The technical requirements of the landfilling operation were paramount in dictating its adaptation into a park. "We had to deal with the shape of garbage hills that were already in place. We could not move the fill material around, because it was garbage. Instead, these landforms created much of the basic structure of the site, which we further molded and sculpted as an additive process."

At public meetings for Byxbee Park, half of the people wanted a replica of Storm King West: a romantic landscape park for sculpture, and half wanted nature. Among those attending were members of the Sierra Club, the Audubon Society, art clubs, and many birdwatchers. "We were stuck in the middle, saying, 'Now realize that it's not nature, it's 40–60-foot-high hills of garbage; we can't recreate nature. Perhaps we don't want to recreate Storm King West either, perhaps we want to do something that makes the site art, rather than a place for supporting art.'" The design team decided to make art, rather than a place for art. How could the prospect of the bay and the bay's edge be magnified and emphasized as a man-touched environment? Again, there was the powerful presence of wind: to both emphasize its presence and also provide refuge from it became the operating logic of the design. Another major constraint, or potential, was that the major landing zone for the adjacent municipal airport crossed the site and could not be obstructed.

"How do we magnify man-touched, man-created nature? With Michael Oppenheimer and Peter Richards, we would go to the site for an afternoon, a Saturday picnic. We realized there was an issue of wind, an issue of prospect, affording wonderful views, and an issue of refuge, to be out of the wind. Also we were in the landing zone for the municipal airport, with small planes

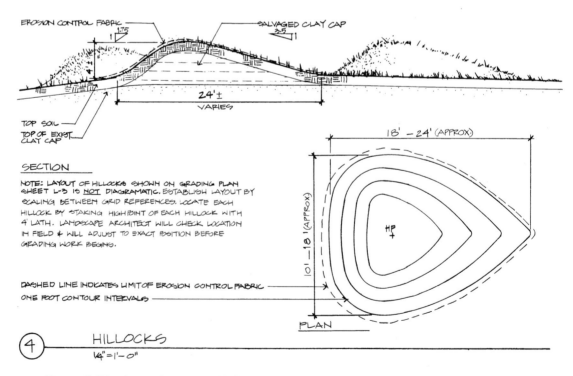

Figure 2-17: *Plan and sections of hillocks*

coming in right over your head. The idea of being on top of these hills gave you both the prospect, but the need for refuge. Then we came up with the idea of the hillocks, the aerodynamically shaped mounds where you can get in front of them and be out of the wind but still have the prospect. It became an open composition, a picturesque landscape, rather than a formal or composed style, driven by the forces of the site, the views and the wind and the shape of the garbage below." The Byxbee site's final configuration is punctuated by a series of these hillocks. They create human scale, as they do not exceed 3-1/2 to 4 feet, are below eye level, and are usually no longer than 8 feet. A few are as much as 5 feet high and 12 feet long. Even as they shelter from the winds sweeping off the bay, their diminutive scale, a series of dimples on a large landscape, contrasts to and magnifies the presence of the bay and the bay's edge. Picnicking areas are nestled in the leeward side of the hillocks in diminuitive, individually scaled spaces inviting visitors to "bring your own blanket."

Despite all of the dumping of waste on the site, and subsequent filling, much of it without supervision or compliance with standards, a natural marsh persists on one point of land. The Army Corps of Engineers constructed a slough, or channel, through it. The water level is controlled by a series of sluice gates surrounded by dikes. The design team sought a way to suggest the marine origins of the field created by the earlier grading operations. They were drawn to the rickety, weathered, remnants of old piers and related structures that often occur at the edge of the bay. A field of poles, first conceived as old pier pilings, is installed in a flexible rhythm over the site. For durability, new poles were used: eight inches in diameter, they are set in a grid that is 30 by 20 feet. They have a clear stain treatment that will allow natural weathering of the wood, yet protect it from rotting. On the side of the site where the marsh is naturally filling in, the spacing and heights of the poles are irregular, as if to express the powerful forces at play that result in the land consuming the marsh. In this location,

the poles are also shorter and set farther apart, accentuating the effect of the land swallowing up the marsh. The Palo Alto community was environmentally enlightened, and the locality approved the plan allowing the dynamic edge of the site to "do its thing." The pole fields also express more subtly the hidden forces that created the seemingly benign site on which they are set. The landfill will settle irregularly over time, particularly since the layers of garbage are so variable. The poles will sink slightly or sway, thereby expressing the quixotic nature of the natural forces that shaped the site.

Figure 2-18: *Hillocks*

Figure 2-19: *Pole field layout and grading*

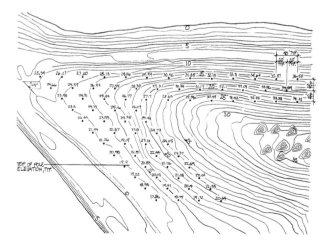

POLE FIELD LAYOUT AND GRADING PLAN
1" = 50'-0"

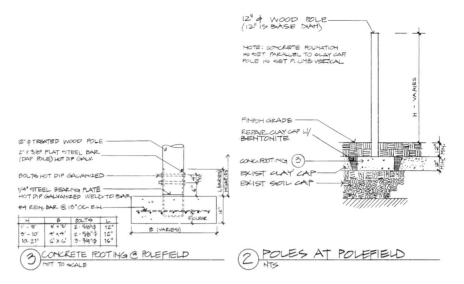

Figure 2-20: *Pole field footing plan*

Figure 2-21: *Pole field*

The poles are expressive of the site in still another way: They serve as bird perches. Alit atop the poles, gulls and other birds always face towards the wind, as this position enables them to quickly fly aloft should danger confront them. Amidst this forest of poles a visitor to Byxbee Park will always be aware of the wind, no matter how gentle or fierce.

The waste areas on the site are consistently capped with a layer of clay. The reviewing engineer for the City of Palo Alto was concerned about puncturing this cap,

so the designers engineered a spread footing for each pole. The bottom of the footing is still several inches above the top of the clay cap. The consulting engineers for the project, Encon Associates, experts in landfills, devised the design and assisted with the approvals and permits.

Underneath the cap is an extensive system of methane collection pipes designed by Encon Associates for the California Department of Public Works. The pipes connect to a methane gas generating system that converts the gas to electricity. Hargreaves Associates was involved in siting the system, developing landforms around it, and suggesting materials and finishes for the engineering elements.

The methane release tower features a potentially dramatic element: a safety gap release flame. It burns when the quantity of methane builds up to a critical level. By being visible, it helps educate the public about the processes and forces that have shaped the history and use of the site. Hargreaves Associates proposed to make the tower a sculpture of light. At its base is white gravel, which captures the evanescent shadows cast by the sun. It is proposed that the stack be painted white and encased in metal screens that would create a shimmering quality. Two contrasting grids, one superimposed over the other, would create what is called a moiré effect, named after a French physicist. A moire is a shimmering pattern created when two geometrically regular paterns are overlayed, especially at an acute angle. As the park visitor moves around the screens, the patterns of the overlayed grids will seem to shimmer.

Another major design element is the earthen dam, or land gate, at the entrance

to the site. Located between two hills of garbage that suggest a doorway, the land gate occurs at a natural opening. Through regrading, the sides of the existing landforms were made steeper. The inside faces that actually create the doorway are graded at 1: 1. Other slopes are more traditional: 4, 3 or 2:1. A polyester fabric honeycomb system supports the slope. The "door" is six

Figure 2-22: *Pole field*

Figure 2-23: *Grading plan and section of Landgate*

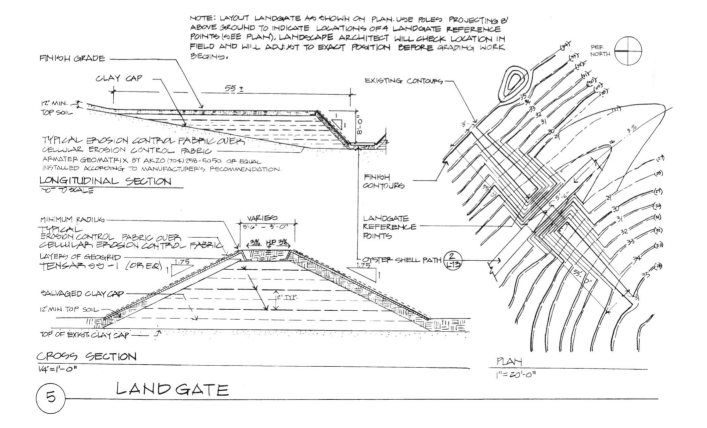

Figure 2-24: *Landgate*

Figure 2-25: *Chevrons appear to march towards the Landgate*

the hills of garbage. In aeronautical symbology, the chevron means "don't land here," so the rows of chevrons lead off the site towards the airport and serve as an aid to navigation. A delightful touch to the many ways of interpreting the chevrons is that their shape approximates the shadows of planes on the ground.

In the original design, the chevrons extended into the marsh at the edge of the bay in order "to make a greater connection between land and non-land. It would be a gesture towards the integration of the edge of the bay, which is becoming blurred." However, at public meetings, there were considerable objections from people who felt that the chevrons were too similar to the "junk" that was being removed from the landfill and disposed of off-site. These people did not want to be reminded of the concrete rubble excavated from the landfill, no matter how sculptural or symbolic the chevrons' appearance would be in an industrial landscape park. The chevrons were deleted as an element in the marsh, stopping at the water's edge. (See Figure C–16.)

For the path system, oyster shells, another material indigenous to the site, was chosen. The Ohlone Indians of the Pacific coast used garbage mounds covered with oyster shells as their landfills. The designers did not want impervious surfaces that would concentrate runoff and potentially increase erosion. They added crushed and cementitious material watered in as a stabilizer. The paths are uniformly six feet wide. Landfill vehicles bringing truckloads of garbage and cover materials and small vehicles, such as the ones that routinely check the flares from the methane generator, use a separate route eight feet wide.

When Hargreaves Associates began work on the site, the cap that was being placed consisted of a foot of clay. As the structural requirements for supporting the wood posts and concrete chevrons became evident, a second foot of clay was added in those areas, and a final layer of a foot of topsoil. When work began there could be no irrigation as local government officials

feet wide at the bottom, 22 feet at top, and the landforms are about 8 feet high, enough to block views. The visitor walks through the opening and the whole site is suddenly revealed.

To acknowledge the airport flypaths, the designers used a common element, concrete chevrons made from the famous Jersey barriers used in traffic control projects. The design team was "interested in using material that might be in the landfill itself," and something that would "play up the size of the hills." A row of the chevrons comes down the hill in a v-shape. Each is embedded into the topsoil and clay layers that cap

Figure 2-26: *Approach to the park along the wetland edge*

were wary of any water percolating through the waste material and releasing leachate. However, there are monitoring wells to detect any potential contamination of the ground water. Over recent years, fears have been assuaged as it is apparent that the great bulk of the refuse deposited in the landfill was residential waste, rarely of a toxic nature. Meanwhile, keeping the clay cap completely dry has resulted in some cracking. Encom pointed out that the clay cap needs repairing from time to time, and that cracking is difficult to anticipate or control. Therefore, future phases may be irrigated lightly.

Given the irrigation restriction, the designers adapted a plant vocabulary of native grass, primarily a lawn of *Stipa pulchra*. It is hardy, drought tolerant, and adaptable to the varying conditions of the site: withstanding winds, pedestrian traffic, and intense heat. The hillocks are planted with lupine, a blue wildflower. The hedgerows consist of four plant materials:

Arctostaphylos franciscana, manzanita
Bacharis pilularis 'consanguinea,' coyote
 brush
Heteromeles arbutifolia, toyon
Leptospermum scoparum 'Ruby Glow,' New
 Zealand tea tree

The restroom and parking areas, not on the landfill, feature eucalyptus trees (*Eucalyptus rudis*).

Phase I has been completed for a cost of $1,250,000. The major costs were the clay cap, the topsoil, and grading. Phases II and III are being implemented currently. They will feature larger, more inflated landforms of garbage. They repeat the vocabulary of hillocks established in Phase I. At the highest point of elevation on the site there will be an observatory with a circle of paving. That part of the landform will be graded to be the darkest place on the site, and therefore the best place to view the stars.

Figure 2-27: *Detail of oyster shells path*

Hargreaves Associates, once selected by the team of artists, became the project managers, creating all construction documents, coordinating all review and approvals with the client, and performing site inspections and observations. There was a wonderful collaboration of many creative

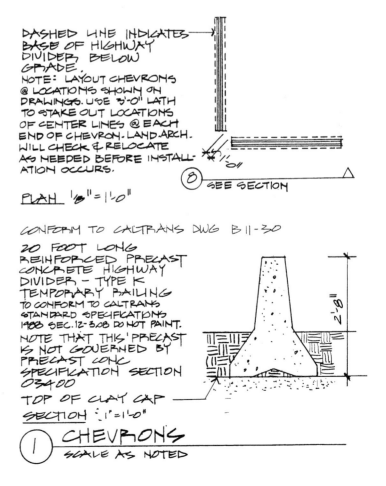

minds. The main reviewing agency for Byxbee Park was the local government of Palo Alto. An enlightened bureaucracy approved and expedited the review and approvals process. There were rarely any delays. Even the Army Corps of Engineers had no objections.

Hargreaves Associates proposed as part of the program for the Byxbee site that people would take advantage of the wind to enjoy activities like frisbee and kite-flying. FAA regulators worried about kites interfering with aircraft landings, but did not express similar concerns about supersonic, high altitude frisbees. The Palo Alto Department of Public Works pointed out that kites would not be able to achieve adequate altitude to pose a danger to aircraft. The site was rescued for kite flying!

When work began on the Candlestick site, it was much rawer, but with fewer limitations than the Byxbee site. It was determined early on that the rubble debris could be moved around, so the major constraint of the Byxbee site did not apply. The Candlestick Park stadium abuts the site on the inland side. It was fortuitous that at least one member of the design team was a sports fan, as it ensured that spectacular views of the site were afforded from the central escalator in the ball park. On the northeast side of the site is a rubble art park, and to the east a state park, primarily for picnicking. The majestic San Bruno mountains loom in the background. Across the bay are views of container shipyards.

The initial impression of the design team was of there being a ridge line that blocked views from the site to the bay. One immediate challenge was to develop a design that would enhance access to the water. How could people be moved to the edge of the spectacular bay, which seemed so isolated from the site? There was also the challenge of how a diverse team of professionals could break down barriers between their professions in order to implement a creative solution. "One of the things that we like about collaborating with artists is that it frees up people's minds about what you're going to do and allows us more freedom."

The process of working together as a team and understanding the site "involved going to the site, hanging around the site, and talking about our impressions initially." Ideas began to be formulated, particularly when it was determined that they were free to move the earth, rubble and all, and create new landforms. One way that the designers broke the ice was to build as an experiment a model of the site in a sandbox in the middle of Hargreaves Associates' office. "We built a sand box in our office, so that whenever we had team meetings—and we only had team meetings, we never played with it ourselves in our corners and then came together to talk about what we were doing—everyone could see the landforms. We used the sand as a means to sculpt the form of the park. It gave us a lot of freedom, to shove things around and grade things immediately. The design of the park really took shape right there." By hand-sculpting the landforms, experimenting with orientations, and calculating rough volumes of cuts and fills, the designers soon energized one another. The team that plays well together works well together.

Other concerns were similar to those at Byxbee. There were aircraft flight lanes, and the Federal Aviation Administration forbade any obstruction that could interfere with aviation. There were water concerns: It was imperative that any filling not impact water quality. Finally, fierce winds were the rule, rather than the exception, on most days.

The final design solution is dramatic and spectacular. The ridge line was pulled back and the entrance moved back to penetrate it. "I think the wind was the key. It was almost as if we allowed the wind to sculpt the site. We pulled the ridge line from the edge of the bay back into the beginning of the site. You entered the park at the top of the site and the view opens in front of you and the wind blows you into the park. The sculpting of the landform was very aerodynamic, and created pockets of wind shadow which could give us really beautiful places out there." Picnicking areas are designed to fit within the wind shadows of the new landforms. Com-

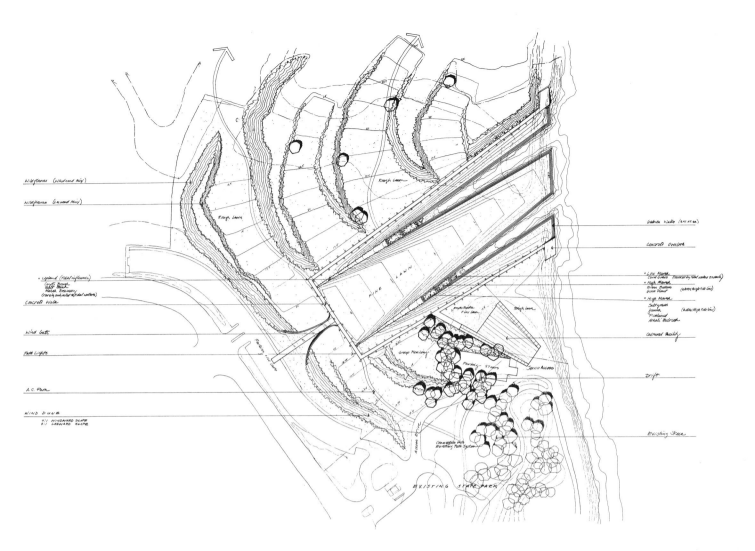

Wildflowers (Windward Mix)

Wildflowers (Leeward Mix)

Rough Lawn

Rough Lawn

PINE LAWN

• Upland (Tidal influence)
  Soft Brush
  Marsh Rosemary
  (Rarely inundated w/tidal waters)

Concrete Walk

Wind Gusts

Path Lights

A.C. Park

WIND DUNE
4:1 Windward Slope
2:1 Leeward Slope

Gabion Walls (approx. ht. ea.)

Concrete Overlook

• Low Marsh
  Cord Grass (covered by tidal water 2x each)
• High Marsh
  Bran Buttons (above mean tide line)
  Yerba Mant
• High Marsh
  Salt grass
  Jaumia (below high tide line)
  Pickleweed
  Alkali Bulrush

Cultural Facility

Drift

Existing Green

EXISTING STATE PARK

pared to Byxbee, the scale is larger with rubble found during construction used as furniture. Finger-like dunes connect to surrounding parklands and provide wind shadows as protection for park visitors. Once entering, people are led to the edge of the bay via a central, formal green plateau, four football fields long, that tapers and slopes towards the bay. The escalator in the Candlestick Park is aligned with the axis of this giant, kinetic landform that draws one's view towards the edge of the bay, now spectacularly evident. Since the central green tapers and slopes down, it distorts perspective, making the distance seem longer, even infinite, as if the plateau "is reaching out to the water forever. The experience of progressing

Figures 2-28 and 2-29: *Illustrative plan and model*

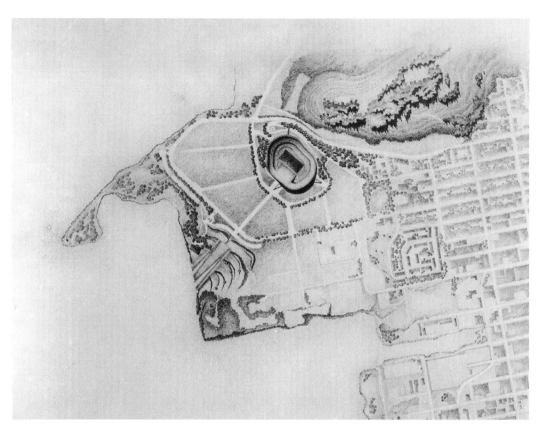

Figure 2-30: *Aerial perspective of the completed park*

and experiencing the prospect along the central green magnifies the feeling of being on the edge of the bay, it takes it and makes it more." The intensity of the experience can be compared to the feeling of telescoping that occurs in traditional Japanese gardens in which larger trees in the foreground are planted against a background of a thicket of smaller trees. The irrigated plateau is planted with native red molate fescue and is mown regularly. (See Figure C–17.)

Two sides of the plateau were originally proposed to be water-filled canals with set water elevations, as a means of drawing the water into the park and integrating the land with the water. But concerns were raised that the wind would sweep debris and paper into the canals, making them appear as giant trash collectors, rather than pristine still blue waters. Instead, these edges were developed as tidal marshes with zones of native vegetation being established to reflect the varying brackishness and hydrological characteristics of each area. Weirs were designed and engineered to capture rainwater runoff and mitigate erosion. The mini-watersheds behind the weirs each have unique hydrological characteristics.

The landscape architects were able to begin to establish varied plant communities that would adapt to each set of conditions, based on the soil horizons, hydrological characteristics, and sun/shade exposures that evolved. Some examples are the following:

Elevations 1 to 2.0 NGVD: cordgrass (*Spartina foloiosa*)

Elevations 2.0 to 3.5: pickleweed (*Walicornia virginica*)

Elevations 3.5 to 5.0: saltbush (*Atriplex patula*), saltgrass (*Distichlis spicata*), alkali heath (*Frankenia salina*), marsh gumplant (*Grindelia stricta var. augustifilia*), fleshy jaumea (*Jaumea carnosa*), and marsh rosemary (*Limonium californicum*).

Elevations > 5.5: coyote brush (*Baccharis pilularis*), blue blossom (*Ceanothus thyrsiflorus*), California poppy (*Eschscholzia californica*), toyon (*Heteromeles arbutifo-*

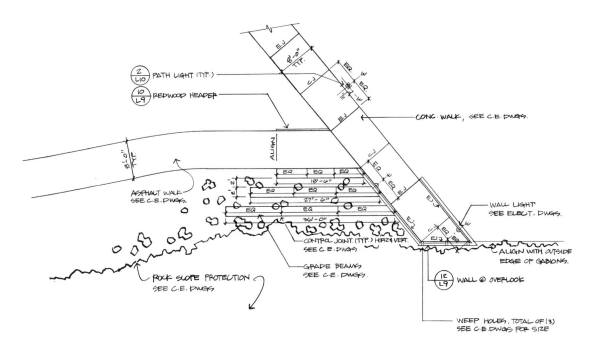

3 / — | SOUTH OVERLOOK LAYOUT PLAN
1/8" = 1'-0"

lia), beardless wildrye (*Leymus triti-coides*), arroyo willow (*Salix lasiolepis*), and fescue (*Vulpia microstachys var. pau-ciflora*).

Some materials were planted as plugs, such as the cordgrass and pickleweed; others were seeded such as the California poppy. The willow was planted as cuttings, and many materials were planted in six-inch leach tubes (liners). The only soil amendments were lime and organic materials for the 3.5–5.0 zone and organic material only in the zone >5.5.

Walks at the base of the formal plateau traverse an alluvial landform. The walks flare in contrast to the taper of the plateau. The walks are a uniform width and held level with the central plain which falls towards the water at three percent. As the walks approach the water, they are built on more fill. A guardrail, consisting of a con-

crete wall wrapping around each walk on three sides, gives a secure enclosure and exclamation point to the end of the pedestrian route.

Just as the wind appears to have sculpted the park, the wind is the activating force on one of its imaginative features, a wind gate at the pair of walls forming the

Figure 2-31: *South overlook layout plan*

Figure 2-32: *The overlook, a dramatic feature in itself, affords visitors a dynamic view of the surroundings*

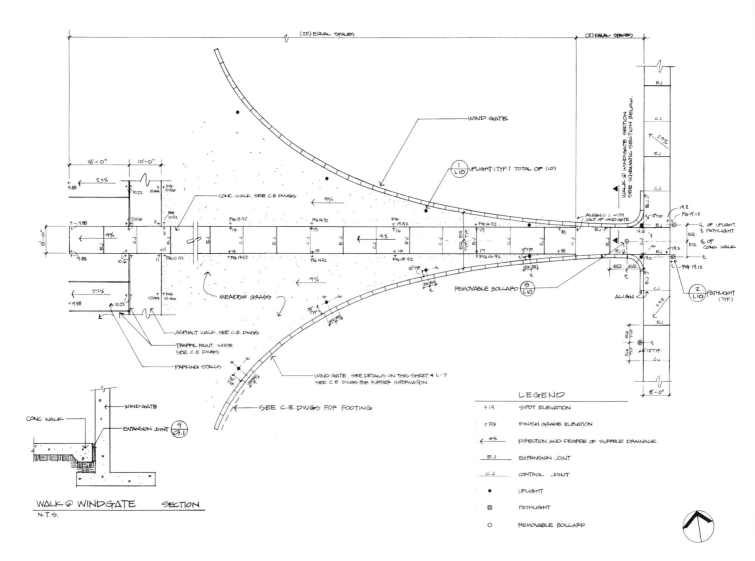

Figure 2-33: *Construction plan of Windgate*

Figure 2-34: *Windgate as built*

park's entrance. The walls are aerodynamically shaped to accentuate wind flow and contain pipes that are wind activated. This wind "organ" gives visitors a constantly changing concert.

An innovative building is sited recessively to yield to the forces of the winds. Flexibly designed, the building can be primarily an indoor, protected space for lectures or concerts, or one whole end wall can be raised like a giant garage door. This creates a backdrop and stage for an adjacent, informal amphitheater space. The rear wall of the building can be a backdrop to this stage, or if weather permits this wall can also be raised, opening up a spectacular view of the bay.

Compared to Byxbee Park, there was extensive grading at Candlestick. After construction debris was properly removed, stabilized, or covered, there was considerable excavation and filling to create an integrated network of landforms. In contrast to Byxbee, where there are substantial garbage deposits, the Candlestick site is fairly stable, with considerably more dirt than rubble. Over the finish grade, a final cap of two feet of clay and one foot of topsoil was placed. Except for the clay and topsoil, albeit significant volumes, there was a balance of cut and fill on the site. Some unsuitable materials, such as a substantial amount of an old rotting pier, had to be removed and hauled off the site to an operating landfill. This pier inspired the use of the forest of poles on the Byxbee site.

The establishment of grass is a process requiring several years. First, annual grasses were planted, which germinate and grow quickly and protect the newly graded slopes and fills from erosion. Perennial grasses were then seeded, which gradually take over from annuals. Careful cutting and mowing schedules maximize the survival of the desired species.

The exterior edges of the park were seeded in the first year of construction, 1989.

Then there was a halt to construction as the contractor waited for the end of the rainy season in the winter. Unfortunately, the notorious drought that only now is showing signs of abating struck the region. Hydroseeding with irrigation had been planned, but to comply with drought requirements there could be no irrigation, so the seeding was postponed. A considerable amount of erosion occurred that had to be repaired. The seeding operations resumed in 1990.

Elsewhere on the site are informal drifts of pines. These embrace the central bowl of the site and other major landforms. The native fescue and red millet planted on the formal, raised plateau is not used anywhere else on the site. There is therefore significant contrast between the fine, uniform texture and landscape character of the vast plane of the formal plateau and the undulating grading, informal plantings, and diverse textures of the adjacent grasslands. The windward and leeward side of the formal landform are planted with different mixtures of wildflowers adaptable to the contrasting conditions. Additional plantings are dwarf coyote bush, myoporum, and other native materials.

To stabilize yet naturalize the water's edge, rock-filled gabions are built at the

Figure 2-35: *The gabions and overlook are evident in this view*

Figure 2-36: *At the ground level, the edge of the gabions, which contain the fine lawn, transitions to the rocky shore, with the pair of concrete overlooks like giant battlements*

most turbulent locations. Undulating riprap treatment is used in more stable areas. The areas are massive in scope, yet the undulations reflect the dynamic state of the water's edge and soften it.

Both of these projects underscore the fruits of collaboration among dedicated professionals and public servants. It is a signpost of Hargreaves Associates work that their efforts are never cosmetic approaches, but a usually successful process of understanding, harnessing, and using the vital forces of a site to create a design. They are the geomancers of our age, interpreting the nature of humanity in our industrialized urban settings. The concepts are clear: dramatic landscapes, bold forms, and simple and elegant details, and clear meanings result. The public responds and welcomes.

JACOBS/RYAN ASSOCIATES

Chicago, IL

Jacobs/Ryan Associates was founded by Bernard Jacobs in 1976, and includes two other partners, Terry Warriner Ryan and Jacqueline A. Kotz. Their work is diverse, ranging from residences, campuses, and office parks, to unusual projects such as the telephone switching stations discussed here, town and city centers, such as the Buffalo Grove Town Center near Chicago and Chicago's Cityfront Center, and the renovation of Chicago's Navy Pier on Lake Michigan. Perhaps, because of the diversity of their work as well as their commitment to design excellence, each project is treated as a unique opportunity to create a rich design vocabulary, rather than stylistic tendencies that will repeat from project to project. The firm insists on a major role in the design process from the beginning of a project and a studied exploration of the details of construction.

Originally from New York City, Jacobs worked for the prominent New York City landscape architect Paul Friedberg before moving to Chicago in 1973 to work for C.F. Murphy & Associates, and starting his own firm in 1976. Ryan studied landscape architectural design at UCLA and joined the firm in 1979. Kotz is a native midwesterner and started work at the firm in 1983. Occupying two adjacent townhouses near the Loop, the firm of six employees has an intense, intimate environment. All the professional staff design, rather than merely draft for the principals. An advantage in winning contracts has been the firm's status as a Women-owned Business Enterprise (WBE). Federal law requires that a portion of funds for public projects go to WBE's or MBE's (Minority Business Enterprise).[1]

PROJECT: *Vernon Hills Switching Facility*
LOCATION: *Vernon Hills, suburb of Chicago, IL*
CLIENT: *Illinois Bell Telephone Company/ Ameritech*
        Vernon Hills: Terry Ryan, design principal
        Daniel Heuser, project manager
ARCHITECT: *Ross Barney + Jankowski*
CIVIL ENGINEER: *Teng & Associates*
DATES: *1989–1990*

The two switching facilities were designed for the same client, the Illinois Bell Telephone Company. Unmanned installations, each switching facility contains a building housing sensitive equipment generators and cables. However, both the design of each building and its landscape reflect the visual qualities of two starkly different sites. The contrast underscores the designers' depth of vision in responding to the needs of the client and the qualities and conditions of the two sites.[2]

The 2-1/2-acre Vernon Hills site is located within a new industrial park. Formerly a farm, the site was flat and had no remaining vegetation. The rear property line had a perimeter berm planted with evergreen trees intended to soften the rear of a retail shopping center. The Vernon Hills Community and the industrial park developer had design criteria—which needed to be applied to the final design—calling for traditional landscape treatments in the front and side yards. The client wished to minimize maintenance, particularly because the site was larger than was needed for the requirements of the building and its parking. However, the client indicated that expansion of both the building and parking lot might occur.

Initial design concepts by the architect showed a brick prairie-style building with broad horizontal lines. The architect's rendering of the building featured vines spilling over the horizontal walls and large poplar-like trees forming a backdrop, with the powerfully evocative style of a Frank Lloyd Wright design drawing. The strength of these initial studies inspired the form and content of the landscape design. The building schematics hinted at a kind of timelessness, a modern building with an ultimately technological use in the shape of something old and familiar. The project evoked technological process, evolution, succession, and also return.

During the conceptual design of the building, the architect and the landscape architect met to share ideas for the project. At the time, two points were stressed: first, that the project must conform to Village code and development standards for the industrial campus; and second, that the project must be easy to maintain. The architect wanted a design which would complement the prairie-style structure which was taking

1 Manheimer, S., "Their Kind of Town," *Landscape Architecture Magazine,* Vol, 81, #5, May, 1991, p. 66–67.

2 Hauer, B., "Profit of the Prairie," *Landscape Architecture Magazine,* Vol, 82, #4, April, 1992, p. 56–57.

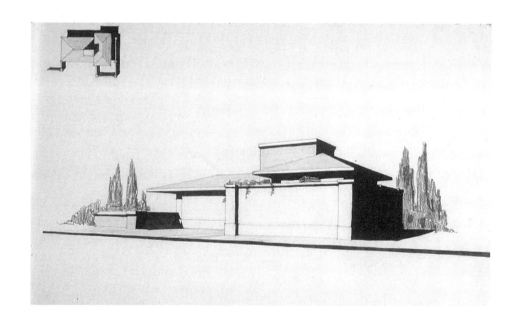

shape. As it turned out, the industrial campus had established a theme of perennials and grasses on berms in the campus parkways. Although these materials were not strictly native, the campus beds would harmonize well with a prairie planting. The client was more interested in the low maintenance aspects of the plan, but became more enthusiastic when it became clear that local area planners warmly greeted the plan and its ecological approach.

To achieve the architect's vision, the landscape architects planted a backdrop of poplars (*Populus x robusta*) in many groves of various sizes. They provide a quick-grow-

ing, scale-defining mass so that the building is not dwarfed by the wide open character of the industrial park. The short-lived poplars also provide an important landscape succession function by providing some shade and shelter to nurse along baby burr oaks (*Quercus macrocarpa*), 6–7′ high, planted about 50 feet apart. As the poplars age and eventually die, the native burr oaks, which are very slow to establish, will grow and take over in a "natural" succession, ultimately forming a more appropriate backdrop.

The front and side yards of the project have a standard midwest corporate appearance. They are sodded with Kentucky bluegrass sod, and planted with Norway maples (*Acer platanoides* 'Emerald Queen'), native hawthornes (*Crataegus phaenopyrum*), and Scotch pines (*Pinus sylvestris*). The village requirements and practical consideration of climate and soil conditions factored into the selection of plant materials. Sodded areas are irrigated and all ornamental plantings include soil amendments. To accentuate the building's entry, improved varieties of mixed day lilies (*Hemerocallis species*), which naturalize in Illinois, and native hawthornes were planted. Boston ivy (*Parthenocissus tricuspidata*) plants, planted behind architectural walls which screen the equipment, climb over the wall and hang down the other side. The designers selected a cold dark gray

Figure 2-39: *The finished building, shown here in its western side elevation, exhibits the horizontal lines which define the prairie school style of architecture. (Photo by Sandra Kuffer, Vernon Hills Remote Switching Facility)*

aggregate for the drip strips designed to catch the overhang runoff which can damage sod underneath the roofline of the building. It was designed without gutters, in keeping with the prairie style.

By contrast, the rear yard, about an acre, is planted to develop a short grass prairie. There is a gentle gradient from the back of the site to the front, creating drier, upland conditions in the rear with moister areas to the front. The seed mix includes little bluestem, blue gramma, sideoats gramma, and junegrass, with a temporary matrix of timothy grass, oats, and wild rye. Sprinkled within the grass mix is a smattering of yellow and purple coneflowers. The prairie grasses require neither soil amendments nor any permanent irrigation system.

To make the prairie grasses more visually palpable to those unfamiliar with prairie landscapes, the design punctuates the edges of the short grass prairie with intervals of prairie forbs planted as perennial plants. Forbs, a term usually applied to native materials, are herbaceous flowering plants. These showy forbs include New England aster, goldenrod, loosestrife, nodding onion, rattlesnake master, purple prairie clovers, tick-

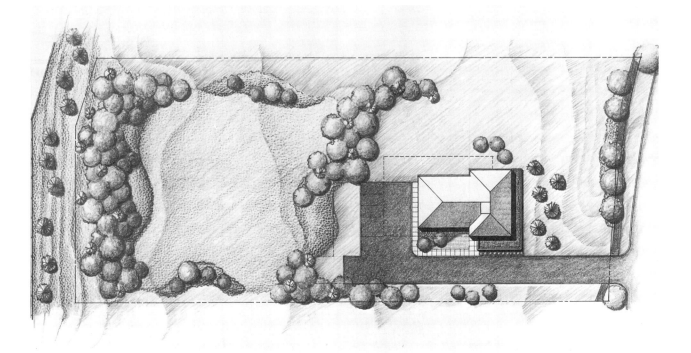

Figure 2-40: *Illustrative site plan. The site is a very narrow strip of land which faces south to a curved road within an industrial campus. There are parcels for other buildings to the east and west, and a buffer berm which separates the campus from the rear of a retail shopping center.*

Figure 2-41a: *Poplars were planted for quick growth to offset the scale of the building while slower-growing species such as the burr oak become established.*

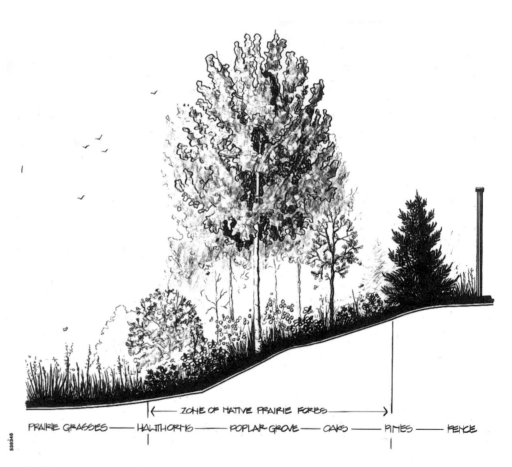

ZONE OF NATIVE PRAIRIE FORBS

PRAIRIE GRASSES — HAWTHORNS — POPLAR GROVE — OAKS — PINES — FENCE

Figure 2-41b: *Construction detail: A design section through the rear berm shows the transition from shortgrass prairie to the hawthorns and forbs, up the slope through the poplars and burr oaks to the pines and fence which were provided to screen the retail strip behind the project.*

seed, false dragonhead, prairie buttercups, and purple coneflowers.

The prairie cannot be maintained through the preferred management technique of controlled burning because the building houses electronics equipment which is highly smoke-sensitive. A three year period of mow-management and weed-wicking has just concluded. The prairie grasses have been high-mown in the early spring, and all of the litter has been raked off so that light can penetrate and warm the soil to encourage further germination. The prairie grasses are beginning to squeeze out the timothy and rye. Since the prairie roots penetrate much deeper, the prairie plants simply out-compete the other temporary grasses. Aggressive foreign weeds (both native and non-native) are wicked, or painted, with herbicide to suppress them while the prairie grasses develop. As the prairie becomes fully established there will be no need for irrigation, fertilization, or other chemicals, only an annual mowing if desired by the client to control the height of the growth.

The Jacobs/Ryan design team carefully documented and monitored the establishment of the prairie. The project was planted early in the summer of 1990. By the following autumn, the perennial asters were particularly spectacular, but the balance of the prairie appeared barren. During the summer of 1991, timothy grass, a temporary perennial species, became the dominant grass species, rather than one of the permanent prairie grasses. Yellow coneflowers became dispersed throughout the timothy grass during the summer of 1991. By the autumn of 1991, some side-oats gramma were found, which turned a beautiful blood red with the onset of cold weather. The perennial forbs were breathtaking during the summer of 1991. Particularly profuse were the asters, goldenrod and loosestrife. The asters have seeded themselves into the grasses. The designers expect that eventually the hard edge between the forbs versus grasses will vanish, as the species blend and merge. The plants and grasses which prefer moister soils will migrate to the bottom areas, and those which prefer dry soils will seed themselves in the upland areas of the site. A community of birds, bees, butterflies, and small animals inhabits the site. Hawthorns (*Crataegus viridis 'Winter King'*) provide cover for the birds.

Today the Vernon Hills switching station stands among many other buildings in the campus complex. Along the curbed roadway, its sodded front presents a neat and trim corporate appearance. The poplars give the buildings its intended backdrop, despite a couple of losses due to lack of care. In recompense, several poplar seedlings have sprung up and are already five or six feet tall. By the winter of 1995, one of the oak trees had reached ten feet in height. The other oaks are healthy, although they are still small. In the prairie, character-defining small hummocks of grass dominate and the winter russet tones of little bluestem grasses infuse the otherwise blond grassland. At its edges, the asters, coneflowers and rattlesnake masters are abundant. (See Figure C–18.)

PROJECT: *Gurnee Switching Facility*
LOCATION: *Gurnee, suburb of Chicago, IL*
                    Terry Ryan, design principal
                    Scott Mehaffey, project manager
CLIENT, ARCHITECT, CIVIL ENGINEER, DATE: *same as Vernon Hills*

The Gurnee site, although similar in size to the Vernon Hills development, is located at one of the main entries of a new, 2.2-million-square-foot regional discount shopping mall. (See Figure C–19.) The site is bordered on three sides by roads: a busy exterior road sheltered from the site by a berm and a large silver maple; a tree-lined boulevard entrance to the shopping mall; and the mall's interior ring road which separates the site from an enormous parking lot. Therefore, it was clear from the beginning that although the switching unit would be entered by only an occasional technician, the site would be seen by thousands of people. The side yard on the north contains a narrow planted strip. The Gurnee community and the shopping center developer had design criteria calling for particular landscape treatments, such as double and single-row street tree plantings in the front yards, which needed to be incorporated into the final design solution. The client wanted to minimize expense and maintenance, but also wanted a result appropriate to the fun, razzle-dazzle character of the mall's entry. It was also necessary to accommodate future expansion.

The unusual program for this project led to its unique design. Since the building is not permanently staffed and occupies such a festive context and prominent location, the project's principal design criteria were visual. The design solution is the result of the merging and application of unusual programmatic elements, design guidelines, site location, building function, architectural creativity, and client receptivity. The role of the landscape architect was to collaborate with the architect in creating a sculptural quality to the landscape design and to produce biddable and buildable contract documents. Her responsibilities included hand-selecting specimen rocks from a quarry in Wisconsin, tagging specimen trees at nurseries, assisting the client in obtaining a responsible contractor, and performing site reviews to insure the success of the project.

The architect created a modern sculpture, a box building that is set askew as if it crash-landed and its triangular roof rotated to a weird angle. Pipe columns, which support the roof, are actually vents, but look as if they could catch lightning or some other form of electrical or wave transmission. This wave-like element is repeated along the building's facade in subtle graduated bands of shiny and dull brick. The brick at the bottom of the building is in earth tones with a rough finish, and gradually transitions to a smooth, uniformly glazed finish. Other sculptural elements include triangular louvers forming exhaust openings, a canopy of steel decking and pipes over the equipment door,

and a corrugated metal deck that covers roof-top air dampers.

The landscape architecture and the architecture are integral to each other. Materials and colors are selected to underscore the tension between the building and the landscape. Responding to the site's high visibility, the landscape architects and the architect sought to create sculpture from the building and its landscape. Essentially minimalist, the design includes a few simple materials: a couple of maples to mark the site's boundaries, one specimen Scotch pine (*Pinus sylvestris*) as an accent, and a row of three hornbeams (*Carpinus fastigata*). The minimalist approach to this modern landscape demanded the highest quality materials and craftsmanship. The imaginative use of a few materials accomplished what might otherwise have been more costly. The execution of the design has achieved its functional intention: an eye-catching visual creation.

Plantings are square-spaced and geometric to accentuate the effect of geometry and rhythm, two recurrent themes in the design. Masses of Kallay juniper (*Juniperus chinensis compacta "Kallay"*) screen parked vehicles, and massed tufted hair grass underplanted with dwarf narcissus anchors the building in the landscape. The balance of the ground plane is a native bluegrass sod, as required by the design guidelines. The turf forms a neutral matte-finish upon which the design elements rest. The foliage of the plant materials presents soft textures which strongly contrast with the hard architecture and other elements of the site design.

The principal feature of the garden is not its plants, however, but its rock. The landscape architect selected seven boulders of rough-hewn Valders stone from a quarry in mid-Wisconsin. The deconstructivist building with its roof tipped and askew appears to have collided with the earth. The boulders similarly evoke a larger power, like a more ancient glacial or seismic force. While the building may have fallen from the sky, the boulders lift from the earth. They are placed along a specific line, diagonal to the building's orthogonally oriented

walls, in line with one of the sides of the canted roof, significantly pointing towards true north.

The stone menhirs have an average size of three by five feet, and weigh 165 pounds per cubic foot, or an average weight of 1-1/4 tons each. The landscape architect staked locations for the boulders, but there was some controversy about their placement. The original plan called for the stones to be notched into the walkway, but the client objected and in the end they were placed offset from the walk. Concrete curbs and walks were planked and ramped to avoid damaging them during installation. With the landscape architect present and using a bobcat and several crew members, the contractor installed the boulders on gravel bases.

As a whole, the boulders form a metaphor of cosmic transmission of energy, and embody some form of larger and more universal communication. On the south side of the building, the boulders lean towards the pipe columns, as though mysteriously lifted from the earth and drawn towards the structure by some larger, perhaps magnetic force. On the north side, the boulders rest more comfortably, as if the counterbalance of magnetic north offsets the attraction towards the pipe columns. A sense of mystery pervades the site, as if unexplainable and ethereal forces are at play. (See Figure C–20.)

Exterior equipment and trash are screened according to the developer's requirements with permanent cast-in-place concrete walls. These are geometrically shaped with triangular sides which rise gently from the earth and are painted a teal green, but not quite within the green palette of nature. These planters contrast beautifully with the architectural brick of the building. The stark-white boulders contrast dramatically against the walls, which also receive the silhouettes of clump form maples.

Underneath the canted roofs, steel edging holds in place drip strips of the same Valders stone chips. The lines of these drip strips mark on the ground plane the projection from the overhang above. The band of material also ties the southern screen wall to the building. A visually arresting composition presents itself, of materials of contrasting colors and textures, the brick screen wall, the granite boulders, the chipped stone drip strips, the pipe columns, and the grass. Little mounds of soft tufted hair grass form the foundation planting, punctuated by the boulders. Dramatic lighting heightens the contrast at night. Uplights graze the backs of the boulders to reveal an otherworldly, eerie presence, while the pipe columns are

Figure 2-43: *The contrasting textures of materials create visual excitement in a simple and straightforward minimalist design. (Photo by Hedrich Blessing and Nick Merrick, Gurnee Remote Switching Facility)*

brilliantly illuminated in a dominant character.

Although many parameters were set by design guidelines for the site, the resulting design has elements of environmental stewardship. Many native plants are featured. The site is graded gently. A shade tree on the south side of the building assists summer cooling. Drought-tolerant plants are used so that there is no need for an irrigation system, although water supply is provided. In drought years, the client permits the bluegrass lawn to go dormant, which, according to turf specialists, can actually be healthier for the native turf than artificial, irrigated growth cycles which encourage disease. The resulting straw-colored summer ground plane presents an interest-

Figure 2-44: *Construction detail: the standing stones are set on a gravel and sand base, recessed in the earth*

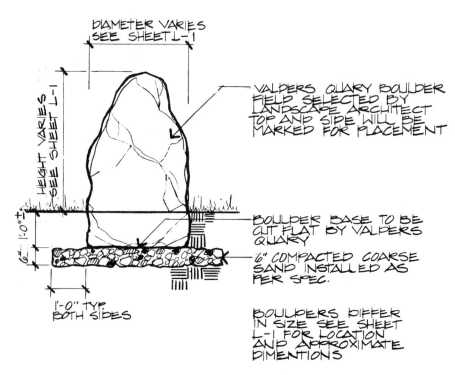

Figure 2-45: *The sun creates a silhouette of clump maple on the teal screen wall*

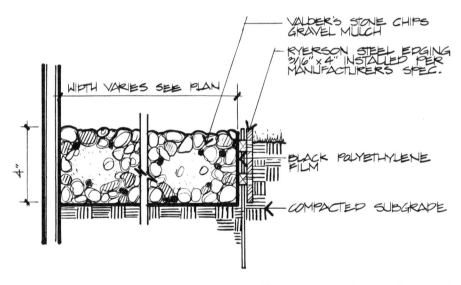

VALDER'S STONE CHIPS GRAVEL MULCH

RYERSON STEEL EDGING 3/16" x 4" INSTALLED PER MANUFACTURERS SPEC.

WIDTH VARIES SEE PLAN

4"

BLACK POLYETHYLENE FILM

COMPACTED SUBGRADE

Figure 2-46: *Construction detail: a drip strip of gravel held in place with steel edging catches rain runoff from the roof line*

ing alternative appearance, and transforms the landscape architect's sensitivity to environmental management and the client's program into a design asset.

The relevance of this project is not cosmic. Within a small site it is a sculptural statement about the contrast between the forces of nature and the forces of technology. The resulting work "challenges the public to meditate and interpret the mysterious nature of life and the universe," says Ms. Ryan, waxing philosophically.

ELENA SAPORTA
Landscape Architect and
JOHN TAGIURI
Sculptor, Fabricator

Cambridge, MA

Elena Saporta, Landscape Architect, and John Tagiuri, Sculptor, have evolved a partnership as a design-build team. Most recently, they collaborated on the Lafayette Park, Salem Walkways, and Re-Vision House projects. Elena Saporta started her own firm in 1992, after working in public and private practice for more than 15 years in both New England and the Southeast. Ms. Saporta's firm provides urban design, waterfront design, and environmental planning services for a broad variety of both public and private sector clients. Two of her office's most recent projects are the design of the Waterfront Project Park for the Chilren's Museum Wharf in Boston, and landscape development for the New View Cohousing Development in Acton, MA. John Tagiuri is a sculptor with almost twenty years' experience in New York City and Boston. He is also highly respected as an art fabricator, capable of working in a wide variety of media. Mr. Tagiuri's experience has been primarily in the area of designing and building large scale public art pieces. He is currently building several pieces for several public parks in Roxbury, MA as well as a public school in Somerville, MA. Much of the work of both Ms. Saporta and Mr. Tagiuri involves the integration of an extensive community-driven participation process.

PROJECT: *Lafayette Park*
CLIENT: *City of Salem, MA*
LOCATION: *Salem, MA*
CONSTRUCTION BUDGET: *$50,000*
DATE: *1992–1993*

Ms. Saporta's and Mr. Tagiuri's first joint project was the winning competition entry for a redesign of Lafayette Park in downtown Salem, MA for the City of Salem. Lafayette Park was originally dedicated in 1915 to commemorate the Great Salem Fire of 1914. The park is located in the virtual center of the two-square mile area of the city which was devastated by the fire. "You can see the extent of the fire as you drive through Salem now, because there are areas where everything was built after 1913. The contrast is very abrupt, you go from 17th, 18th and 19th century buildings and then there is a line." After the fire the city purchased the block and created a park. It is, ironically, the site of former Firehouse #5, a stately Victorian structure destroyed in the fire. While researching the history of Salem, the collaborators were struck by the significance of this event. They learned that the fire had started in a tannery and during the course of a day had leveled half the city and left approximately fifteen thousand people homeless. The Great Salem Fire of 1914 has been overshadowed by Salem's earlier history. Most of the attention on the city revolves around the Salem witch trials and Salem's eighteenth and nineteenth century maritime trade with the Orient.

Ms. Saporta and Mr. Tagiuri initially explored the possibility of recalling the park's namesake, the Marquis de Lafayette, in their design. They dismissed this notion when they discovered that Lafayette, a dandy and close friend of George Washington, had nothing to do with the park. His only contact with Salem was an open carriage ride through the streets of the city. The designers changed course and decided to focus on the Great Salem Fire of 1914 instead.

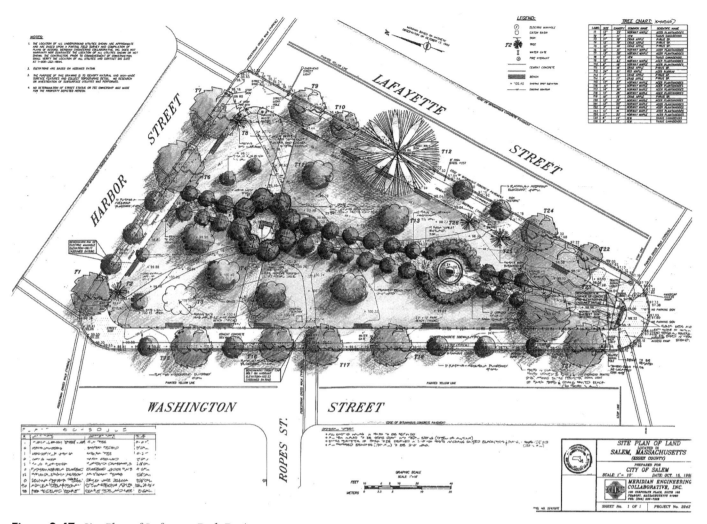

Figure 2-47: *Site Plan of Lafayette Park Design*

When the designers began researching the cultural history of the fire, they realized "that when people go to Salem, all they talk about are witches, shipping, and whaling. No one even talks about this fire and that there are people still alive who remember it. So we thought this was a priceless piece of history that we really ought to uncover and dust off and get people to know about. We decided originally to build a play structure that was a firehouse, but the City objected to the playhouse because they didn't want kids to play in the park because there was too much surrounding traffic making the site dangerous. Then we did more research at the Essex Institute and found more information about the fire, poems written by kids after the fire, letters back and forth to a doctor in New York City who was going to buy a flagpole for the park to commemorate the fire."

Lafayette Park is on a roughly one-acre triangular parcel of land bounded by Salem's largest street, Lafayette Street, which links downtown Salem to Salem State College and Marblehead. It serves as a gateway to the city from the south. The apex of the park is dominated by a 40-foot-high World War I memorial floating in the middle of a lawn. The designers decided to embrace this forbidding structure in their design by bisecting the triangle of the park with a tree and bench-lined pedestrian spine. The existing park also had a memorial lamp structure in the middle that looked like a flying saucer with a sign that said, "no playing golf." "Everyone who entered the competition wanted to get rid of the memorial but we wanted to embrace it. It's 40 feet up in the air. It's always been a gateway, literally a gateway." The war memor-

Figure 2-48: *Lafayette Park prior to renovation*

ial serves as the focal point at the southern end of the spine with a memorial to the fire as another focal point toward the northern end of the axis.

The proposed memorial to the fire is a 1:10 scale cast-iron replica of the Victorian Fire Station and hose tower which previously occupied the site. The structure is sand-cast, in modular pieces which are bolted together, much like a Franklin stove. The roof peak of the fire house memorial is 3-1/2′ high. The roof is constructed of granite slabs which have been sandblasted with explanatory text, poems written by children about the fire as well as a map showing the extent of the fire. Part of the roof is polished granite, part is carved, and part is a honed finish. The structure therefore functions as a stand-up reading desk. The firehouse memorial sits in a small plaza ringed by zelkova trees with seating and shrub planting under the trees. For a while, Mr. Tagiuri was tempted by the idea of casting the sides of the "building" in aluminum because it is a material that can easily be painted. However, it was decided that for long term maintenance reasons it would be better to specify unpainted cast iron.

Figure C-1: *Anshen + Allen, Inc. The stepping-stones across the pool at the residential studio are illuminated at night with evocative effect. (Photo by Anne Gummerson)*

Figure C-2: *Clarke + Rapuano, Inc., Merck International Headquarters. Native plantings of shade trees from the on-site nursery are underplanted with redbud, dogwood, mountain laurel, azalea, ferns, and wildflowers sited by Edmund Hollander and Maryanne Connelly to soften the transition from the finished "farm" retainings walls to the building. (Photo by Edmund Hollander Design P.C.)*

Figure C-3: *Clarke + Rapuano, Inc., Rockville Facility Right-of-Way. Many alternate alignments were studied for the two-lane parkway with an independent bikeway. This study terminated the parkway at Rock Creek Park and traffic was directed to Gaynor Road. Only the bicycle path proceeded through the more difficult terrain along Turkey Branch Creek, which was proposed for recreational use.*

Figure C-4: *Clarke + Rapuano, Inc., Calverton. An early burial section with flush grave markers. (Photo by Domenico Annese)*

Figure C-5: *Clarke + Rapuano, Inc., Calverton. A later burial section with grave headstones. (Photo by Domenico Annese)*

Figure C-6: *Carol Johnson & Associates. The light standards at Charter Oak Park include fixtures which can be removed in the event of flooding. Together with the ornamental fencing along one edge of the plateau within the river park, the light standards and site furnishings reinforce the linearity of the park.*

Figure C-7: *Jones & Jones, Woodland Park Zoo. The Thai Elephant Forest depicts the position of elephants in human culture as well as their natural environment in southeast Asia.*

THAI ELEPHANT FOREST

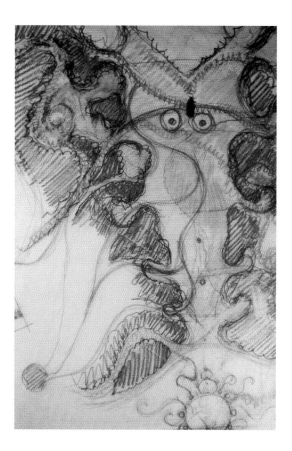

Figure C-8: *Jones & Jones. The evolution of the design form of the Master Plan for the North Carolina Botanical Garden.*

Figure C-9: *Jones & Jones. At the North Carolina Botanical Garden, near the display greenhouse are proposed gardens demonstrating the cultural uses and attributes of plants including an ethnobotanical trail, a garden maze, and medicinal herb and carnivorous plant gardens. Adjacent, the arboretum displays native plant associations of North Carolina.*

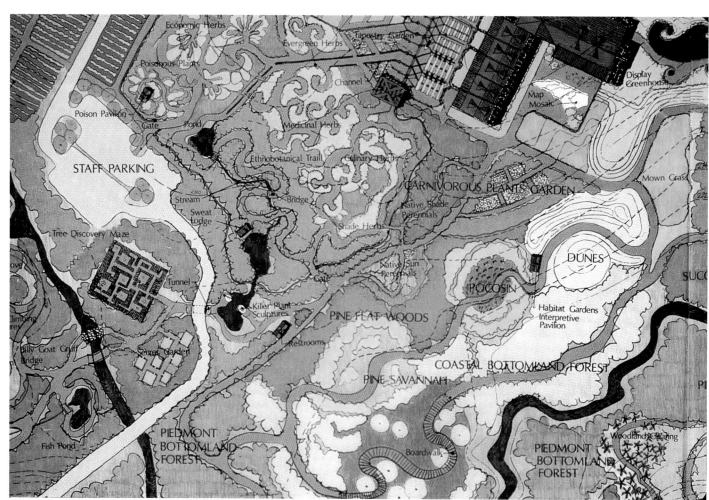

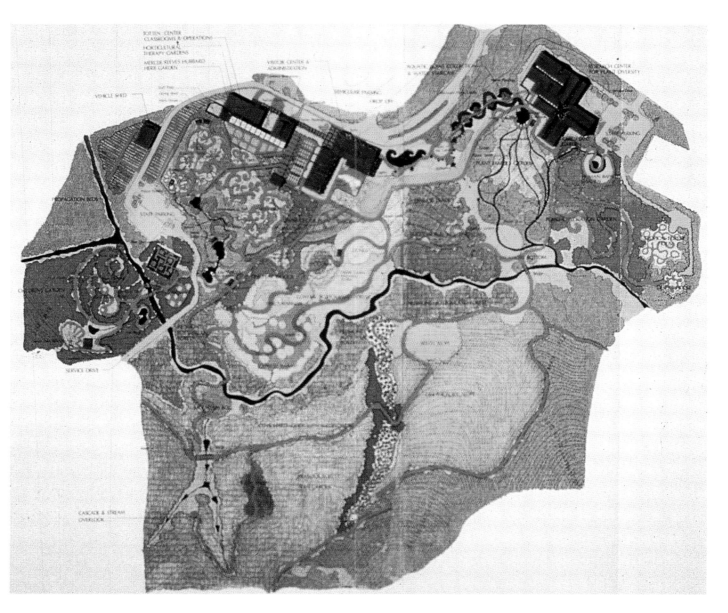

Figure C-10: *Jones & Jones. The overall scheme interprets human uses of plants near the Visitor's Center and Research Center, and moves outward through re-created regional plant communities to the existing natural landscape of North Carolina.*

Figure C-11: *Royston Hanamoto Alley & Abey. The tasting patio at the Robert Mondavi Winery in the Napa Valley provides a quiet, secluded yet colorful setting in which to relish the fruits of viticulture. (Photo by Barbara Lundburg)*

Figure C-12: *Royston Hanamoto Alley & Abey. Golden Gate State Park features expanses of lawn punctuated by mature, usually evergreen trees, many of which have reached their old age, are declining, and need to be replaced in an appropriate manner. (Photo by Douglas Nelson)*

Figure C-13: *The modernist pallette of landscape architect Jack Chandler for the Isgur Residence includes persimmon colored stucco walls, giant granite blocks, and delicate movement of water. (Photo by Jared Chandler)*

Figure C-14: *Jack Chandler & Associates. The redesign of the entrance to the Danforth Residence creates a sense of privacy and an arrival at the front door. Fragrances of the plant materials waft into the foyer of the residence. (Photo by Jennifer Chandler)*

Figure C-15: *Jack Chandler & Associates. At the Danforth Residence twin pergolas with fence anchor the pool and frame a view towards the vineyards and the mountains. (Photo by Jennifer Chandler)*

Figure C-16: *Hargreaves Associates. This view of the edge of Byxbee Park shows the curving edge of the wetland with the field of poles in the distance.*

Figure C-17: *Hargreaves Associates. This aerial view of the completed Candlestick Point Cultural Park clearly shows the alignment of the existing stadium with the axis of the formal plateau of the park.*

Figure C-18: *At the Vernon Hills Switching Station, edges of the prairie landscape, designed by the firm Jacobs/Ryan Associates, were planted with pots of perennial forbs. The wide variety of flowering plant materials easily embraces the parking demands of suburbia. Shown here are white prairie asters, purple prairie coneflowers, and the round heads of rattlesnake masters.*

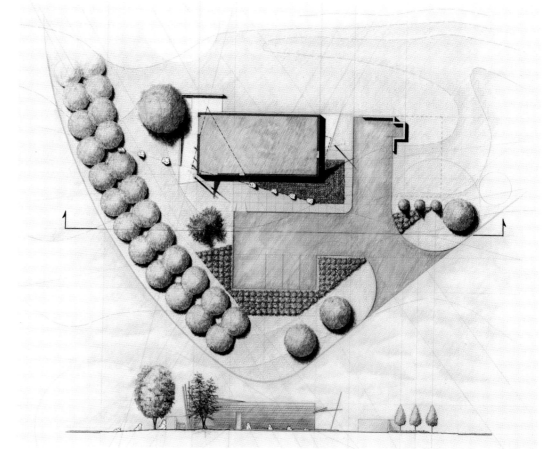

Figure C-19: *Jacobs/Ryan Associates. The site plan of the Gurnee Switching Station shows the triangular nature of the site and the various important lines and angles upon which the design hinges.*

Figure C-20: *"This project appeals to the part of me that was once a 'San Francisco hippie,'" says landscape architect Terry Warriner Ryan about the Gurnee Remote Switching Station. The massive stone megaliths align with true north and lean towards the building's pipe columns. (Photo by Hedrich Blessing, Nick Merrick)*

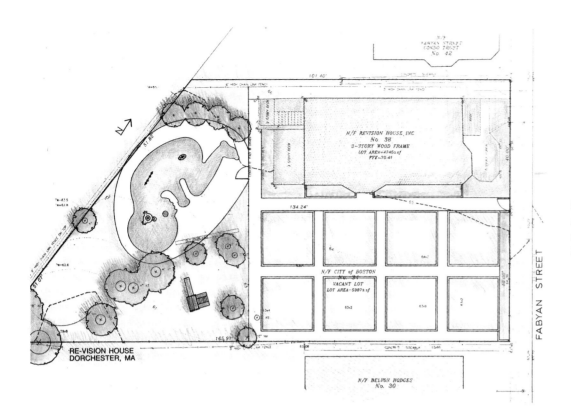

Figure C-21: *Elena Saporta and John Taguiri. The illustrative site plan for Re-Vision House.*

Figure C-22: *Tagiuri's Chessmen painted Ferrari red and electric blue.*

Figure C-23: *The Schmidt Design Group, Inc. The completed Swami's Beach Access stairs and landing harmonize with the pastel colors of the limestone cliffs and seascape.*

Figure C-24: *Martha Schwartz, Inc. The brilliant colors of the tiles, which sweep up the walls of the Jailhouse building, give structure and form to this garden.*

Figure C-25: *Martha Schwartz, Inc. Illuminated at night, one courtyard of the Dickenson Residence revels in exotic colors and Moorish elements.*

Figure C-26: *SPURLOCK/ POIRIER, Snake Path. The complete installation as viewed from the entrance to the library building at the University of California at San Diego. (Photo by Phillipp Scholz Rittermann)*

Figure C-27: *SPURLOCK/ POIRIER, J Street Inn. The thrust block, which can be seen from the hotel lobby, supports the linear sculpture that runs the length of the courtyard. (Photo by David Hewitt/Anne Garrison)*

Figure C-28: *The illustrative site plan for the Harlem Meer by the Central Park Conservancy.*

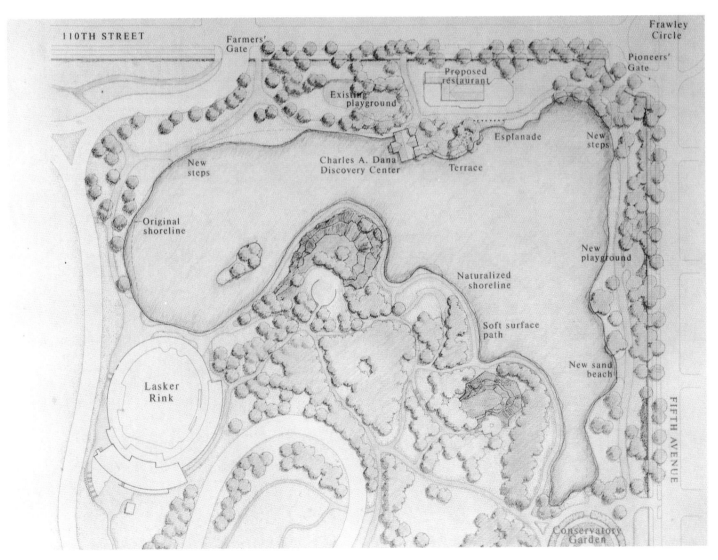

Figure C-29: *The Central Park Conservancy and Clarke + Rapuano, Inc., Concert Ground at Central Park. The bluestone patio at the flagpole consists of a pattern of rectilinear and trapezoidal forms that repeats eight times. The serenity of the landscape belies the fact that hundreds, sometimes thousands, of people walk past the lush lawn as they proceed through the paved allees of the concert ground from the mall to Bethesda Terrace and Fountain. (Photo by Steven L. Cantor)*

Figure C-30: *Central Park Conservancy. The euonymous groundcover gives a reddish tint that complements the rich browns of the new benches that surround each of the elm islands at the Concert Ground. (Photo by Sara Cedar Miller)*

Figure C-31: *Snow fencing protects new plantings of understory trees beneath the mature canopy of some of Prospect Park's original plantings of horsechestnuts, oaks, lindens, and maples at the woodland edges near the Vanderbilt Playground. A newly planted tree left unprotected has been destroyed by vandals. (Photo by Steven L. Cantor)*

Figure C-32: *Mira Engler and Gina Crandell's Interior Garden at Iowa State University jars the senses and challenges visitors to think about the impacts on people of the processes which occur in the adjacent buildings.*

Figure 2-49: *Lafayette Park after completion*

Prior to the design competition, the park had fallen into a state of neglect and disrepair. The site was "terribly compacted and nothing was growing. It was unusable and we were trying to provide a place where people would be able to go in and sit in the park and enjoy it." Surrounded by parallel parking and busy city streets, the site functioned as little more than a giant traffic island. Seating and pedestrian circulation were limited to the perimeter of the park. All benches faced out towards traffic. The new design, with its central pedestrian spine, attracts more people than before as it encourages activity inside the park as well as along its edges.

Even for a small park, the designers skillfully used diverse new plantings to harmonize with existing ones and to avoid monopolizing with one species. Some existing crabapple trees were saved and two new ones were added to define a broad arc. Existing street tree plantings consisted of Norway maples. The designers selected another coarse-textured tree, the London Plane, to fill in gaps.

To unify the park, the designers decided to play up the fire imagery by using the color red throughout. Plant materials include dogwoods with red berries and fall foliage, Callery pears with red autumn color, continuously blooming Scarlet Meideland roses, bright red azaleas, and burning bush, as well as seasonal plantings of red annuals. Paths are steel edged and surfaced with reddish stone dust. Benches, because of the very limited budget, were the standard city-built, green and white wood slat/concrete end design. Ms. Saporta and Mr. Tagiuri used the simple device of painting them a high gloss fire engine red to give them a life of their own.

PROJECT: *Salem Walkways*
CLIENT: *The Salem Partnership with funding by the National Park Service*
LOCATION: *Salem, MA*
CONSTRUCTION BUDGET: *$50,000*
DATE: *1994–1995*

As a result of having worked with the City of Salem in designing and overseeing the construction of Lafayette Park, Ms. Saporta and Mr. Tagiuri were asked to submit a proposal to the National Park Service to design and fabricate prototypical marking systems for two self-guided walking tours for the city. These walking tours represented the first phase in a pedestrian master plan developed by the Walkways Committee of the Salem Partnership, Inc., the organization which serves as the local liaison with the National Park Service. The National Park Service and the Salem Partnership confidently trusted both the instincts and talents of these designers to tackle a different project: the interpretation of the cultural history of Salem. Ms. Saporta's and Mr. Tagiuri's proposal was accepted.

The designers discovered that most visitors to Salem go just to the center of town. The tendency is for people to visit the witch house, Hawthorne's House of the Seven Gables, and the Peabody Essex Museum—all on Salem's Heritage Trail—and then leave. However, Salem is a beautiful town with much more to offer. The Partnership sought ways to develop five new pedestrian loops that would extend the Heritage Trail and draw interest to the outlying neighborhoods.

The Peabody-Essex Museum and the National Park Service Visitor Center are located on the Essex Street Mall. This pedestrian street is the center of tourist and commercial activity in Salem. The Mall forms the first segment of the Heritage Trail, which is defined by a wide red line painted on the sidewalk. The Salem Partnership developed the five new pedestrian loops to extend the Heritage Trail and to encourage exploration beyond the center.

"We walked around with people dozens of times, talked with them, looked at signs, got lost with people and realized why they got lost. We realized that people were offended by the red lines because they seemed too chintzy." Salem hosts several million tourists a year and is trying to enhance and beautify its image. The city planted thousands of trees last year. "They are really trying, they are ripping up blacktop and putting down grass like mad. They are restoring parks and they didn't feel that the painted line was an image that they wanted to perpetuate. They wanted something permanent that would actually be beautiful."

The first marking system conceived and fabricated by Ms. Saporta and Mr. Tagiuri was for the McIntire District, a walking tour spur off the Essex Street Mall. The McIntire district, an area where many sea captains built their homes, is an affluent, established residential area with numerous eighteenth-century mansions. Local residents, leery of extending the red line into their neighborhood, desired a more discreet and elegant, yet permanent, marking system.

The McIntire District was named after Salem's premier architect and wood-carver,

Samuel McIntire (1757–1811). There are numerous examples of his work along this mile-long walking tour. He was the architect for the nearby Benjamin Hawkes Mansion, originally built for the family of Elias Hasket Derby. Derby, the first millionaire in the United States, made his fortune as a merchant when Salem was a prosperous center of trade with the Far East.

For the McIntire tour logo, Ms. Saporta and Mr. Tagiuri selected a bound sheaf of wheat, one of the architect's favorite motifs. To him it symbolized Salem's bounty and prosperity. A rubber mold of one of McIntire's sheaf-of-wheat carvings taken from one of his mantel pieces was used in the fabrication of the trail markers.

The Salem Partnership gave the designers an established route for the McIntire Trail. Having researched the locations of McIntire buildings nearby, they proposed changing the route in a few areas to include additional buildings, but that idea was rejected. The client felt that certain streets were less savory and should be avoided by tourists. It was better to present the city's best face.

The trailhead of the McIntire Walking tour is located in front of the Salem Witch Museum at the terminus of the Essex Street Mall. The trailhead relates the history of the McIntire District, discusses the work of Samuel McIntire, and provides a map and description of the self-guided walking tour. The designers felt that a fiberglass sign would not be in character in the historic district, so the trail head text and images are silkscreened onto aluminum. The sign is encased in a cast iron peaked structure, painted black with a slate shingle roof and a cast iron base. On the pediment of the structure is an inlaid brass emblem with McIntire's sheaf of wheat motif. The designers also wanted something that was abstract and easy to recognize, and a system in which the motif could be changed for each walking tour.

The rest of the marking system consists of a series of fluted cast iron bollards with brass caps, and brass sidewalk plaques, located at key intersections. These markers allow visitors to "connect the dots" on the tour. The brass bollard caps are dome-shaped with a relief of the sheaf of wheat motif in the center and painted directional arrows along the sides. Many of the McIntire District's north-south streets are small, with sidewalks as narrow as four feet. On these streets there was insufficient space for the bollard markers, so brass plaques set flush with the sidewalk were used. The sidewalk plaques, like the bollard markers, have the raised sheaf of wheat motif flanked by directional arrows. Bollards are anchor-bolted into 1'-0" by 3'-0" pre-cast concrete footings. Existing bricks are re-laid around the bollards. Sidewalk plaques are

Figure 2-50: *Cast iron bollard, brass cap trail marker*

Figure 2-51: *Cast brass McIntire District side-walk plaque*

was also the most respected wood carver in the US at the time so he is really known as much for his wood-carving as for the architecture. We met the head of the Essex Institute (an organization affiliated with the Peabody Museum, Harvard University, that catalogs information about Essex County) who said that they actually had a rubber mold that they had taken from a detail of a sheaf of wheat from one of his fireplaces, and he gave us the rubber mold. We were able use the rubber mold to make a plaster mold. From that we made an aluminum mold, which was used to produce the bronze casting. The rubber mold was made about ten years ago. We are excited about the idea that this ornament is not fake, but a genuine art object based on a design by McIntire himself. The tourist touches the actual thing."

The casting process is complex. The Essex Institute had found a McIntire fireplace decorated with a carved sheaf of wheat. Craftsmen built a little box to encapsulate the carving, then poured in latex rubber, a waxy, honey-like substance. Hardened latex bends, so that even with intricate designs, it can be easily pulled from the object being molded. A plaster cast would just get stuck. Mr. Tagiuri "can pour plaster into the latex mold and make a positive, which will be exactly the same size as the original. The original had 50 coats of paint on it and the positive looked like the original with 50 coats of paint. Then we cast in aluminum because aluminum is not fragile, compared to the plaster which is a very difficult material to work with. Aluminum can be sanded smooth and worked very easily." Air bubbles in the aluminum can be filled in without breaking the mold.

Mr. Tagiuri had a cast-iron bollard from the factory. In his workshop he bolted a curved aluminum sheaf of wheat to the bollard. Then he glued lead letters that said, "McIntire District-Salem Walkways" onto the bollard with epoxy cement. Mr. Tagiuri took the assembled bollard to the foundry,

Figure 2-52: *Installation of cast brass plaque into antique brick*

cast with anchor bolts which insert directly into 1'-0" by 3'-0" concrete footings with lifting points. Plaques are dimensioned to fit into the module of historic brick pavers. Both the brass bollard caps and brass plaques were sand-cast at an industrial foundry.

"One of the interesting things that happened was that when we were doing research at the Essex Institute to come up with the appropriate logo for the district we spent days looking through books on McIntire. He used funerary urns a lot, he used baskets of fruit, garlands of flowers, cornucopia, all sorts of symbols of wealth, but the sheaf of wheat is what really struck us. He

where the workers stuck the aluminum and wood mold in the sand making two halves. Then the first bollard was cast. The foundry workers used the first casting, in two halves, to make the sand impressions for the 15 bollards required for the trail.

"When you push the form in the sand it is like stepping in the sand with your foot. You leave an impression, and the sand has a binder in it just like wet sand at the beach leaves a perfect impression; dry sand doesn't. Anything you stick in has to be a little bit tapered so that the mold comes out easily, without tearing away at the sand, and there can't be any overhangs at all, so the perfect things to cast would be half a ball, or a pyramid upside down, or a wedge, a footprint. I wanted to use sand casting because it is an old technique and was used around McIntire's time," Mr. Tagiuri explains.

Any three-dimensional form can be used to make a mold. For example, Mr. Tagiuri used a finial form, split through the center. It was pressed into the moist sand, and the sand impression became the mold. "So we have the finial form which you stick into the sand and the sand itself is the mold. So the form just has to look like what you want your finished product to look like, not the mold." The forger pours molten bronze (or cast iron, or other metal) into the sand mold. "In order to get the bronze out they just knock the sand off and use the aluminum and lead mold to make another sand mold or impression. The plaque is easier to understand in that it is much flatter."

Although the designers sought a traditional historic style three-dimensional lettering, their choices were few. "At this point we were limited to a couple of styles. Lead letters only come in three styles; we couldn't even get the manufacturer to copy anything, so we chose an old blocky style." The letters are 7/8″ high, by 1/2″ wide, by 3/32″ thick.

The distance between consecutive markers is about a block for short blocks. In the longer blocks, there is also a mid-block marker. As Ms. Saporta explains the design considerations, "We found that we needed ample markings, because visitors might get nervous that they might be off the trail, so we planned for the minimum number necessary to clearly mark the trail route. There are also many trees so it can be difficult to see the bollards. Whenever there was a decision point, such as an intersection, we were very clear about markings. The large trees and uneven sidewalks make the potential for missing a bollard very real. You could even miss a mailbox because the trees are so big. What a wonderful problem for us to have to work with—large, beautiful, stately trees."

The designers originally proposed a third marker top to be set in front of each McIntire house that would have the name of the house and the date. The Salem Partnership, ever encouraging New England independence and ingenuity, felt that "it was the responsibility of the people who owned the houses to come up with their own system." Also, many of the McIntire houses are owned by an organization called the Essex Institute and already had historic markers.

The second marking system for Salem Walkways developed by Ms. Saporta and Mr. Tagiuri, was for the Forest River Conservation Area in the southern part of the city. Located in a non-urban setting, the marking system for this trail involved a completely different set of design parameters than those of the McIntire District. The Forest River Conservation area consists of two distinct ecosystems, a river/marsh ecosystem and an upland forest ecosystem. Interpretive signs were developed for each area as well as a trailhead describing the entire park and directional signs leading to the park. In addition, four hundred trail blazes were mounted to trees, guiding visitors throughout the conservation area. These three-color blazes were silk-screened onto four inch square aluminum signs. Inspired by an Audubon painting, the designers chose the red-winged blackbird as the motif for the Forest River Conservation Area trail blazes and interpretive signs. The designers sought to create a "two-color image that could be printed on a third color that would be seductive, directional, easy to see, upbeat, and topical."

A plexiglass cover protects the aluminum trailhead sign. The total cost of the alu-

Figure 2-53: *Red wing blackbird trail marker, Forest River Conservation Area Trail*

minum panel is several hundred dollars and the plexiglass is only forty dollars. Anticipating that vandalism is a strong possibility, the designers used affordable, practical materials that can be easily replaced. This same technique was used on the McIntire trailhead.

Another walking tour is proposed, the Lafayette Trail, which will go by Lafayette Park. Three other tours are in preliminary planning stages.

Both Lafayette Park and the Salem Walkways Signage are projects about the interpretation of the cultural history of a community. The subjects are different but the approach has been the same. In the former case, the designers redesigned Lafayette Park in a modern context of bright red themes while emphasizing its historical ties to the site of a devastating fire that roared through much of Salem. In the signage project, they developed design vocabulary for trail markers for two entirely different settings, one historical and one ecological. In each case the interpretive signage dovetailed with the architectural vocabulary of historic Salem on the one hand and the National Park Service's standards for trails on the other.

PROJECT: *Re-Vision House*
CLIENT: *Re-Vision House, Inc., Dorchester, MA*
LOCATION: *Dorchester, MA*
CONSTRUCTION BUDGET: *$95,000*
DATE: *1994–1995*

Re-Vision House is a minority and woman-owned organization serving pregnant and parenting teens from Boston's inner city neighborhoods. Its transitional living program evolved from a citizen's mobilization effort to address the problems of homelessness among pregnant and parenting youth in the Dorchester, Roxbury, and Mattapan neighborhoods. Since 1991, Re-Vision House has served approximately 165 homeless, pregnant, and parenting teenage and young-adult mothers and their small children, providing them with emotional support and a structured educational environment. One of the organization's goals is to become progressively more self-sufficient, introducing energy-efficient systems for the building, as well as year-round food production on site. Ms. Saporta, working with Boston Urban Gardeners, with funding from the City of Boston, was asked to develop a landscape master plan for the property. The program included the siting of a greenhouse structure, a play area for children under the age of five, and community garden plots for up to fifteen people on approximately fourteen thousand square feet of land.

Several greenhouse schemes were proposed; the scheme which was selected consists of a three-story structure on the south side of the house. The proposed greenhouse encloses the building's existing rear porches. This placement allows for ease of construction, ease of operation, and efficient vertical gardening systems accessible from each floor of the house.

The community garden plots are raised beds, constructed of granite curbing which was selected over pressure-treated lumber because it is non-toxic and completely permanent. All soil for the garden plots consists of a mixture of compost and clean, lead-free fill.

The play area took the form of a fifty-five-foot-long fetus in utero. (See Figure C–21.) The fetus itself is a giant sandbox with Kompan play equipment placed in the position of the eye, ear, and backbone of the figure. The amniotic sac, which gives the fetus its outline, is constructed of poured concrete. The concrete perimeter serves as a restraint for the sand and provides a surface for young children to ride their tricycles. The sand box is shaded by existing black walnut trees to the south. A toddler's den and slide are nestled among the trees. Along the northern edge of the play area are four mature apple trees transplanted from an established orchard. Seating is provided along the perimeter of the area and a spray feature off to the side provides relief on hot days.

Two different wood forms for the concrete had to be constructed, an exterior oval and an interior fetus shape. The exterior womb form was made up on the site and consisted of three layers of 1/4″ Luan plywood, 5″ high, staked every foot. The interior "fetus" shape was pre-fabricated in 8′-0″ sections in Mr. Tagiuri's studio and was assembled on site just prior to the pour. This form was built using 3/8″ AC Fir plywood; where the curves were too sharp, a bending plywood was used to make the tight turns. The 3/8″ plywood skin was screwed to a framework that took the shape of the fetus. The form was staked every two feet and braced diagonally to the earth at all joints. The concrete slab is a minimum of 5″ deep except at the inner fetus edge where it is increased to a depth of 12″. This thickened edge is to help prevent children from digging in the slab's sub-base.

Figure 2-54: *Concrete pour at play area*

Figure 2-55: *Re-Vision House completed play area*

PROJECT: *Chess Set*
CLIENT: *Boston Society of Architects*
LOCATION: *Boston, MA*
CONSTRUCTION BUDGET: *$1,000*
DATE: *1993*

Mr. Tagiuri, a sculptor with varied experience in public projects, won a design competition sponsored by the Boston Society of Architects to develop a set of child-height chess pieces that children could easily pick up and move. The cost of materials and labor could not exceed $1000. The pieces had to average 2-1/2 feet in height and had to be assembled using unskilled laborers, so that the *average* cost per piece would not exceed $30.00. His solution was to design chess pieces of galvanized sheet metal duct work components. These materials are readily available throughout the United States, are "inexpensive, weatherproof, lightweight, stable, and easy to assemble." They are available in a large range of standard shapes and sizes. The galvanized finish allows the finished chess pieces to withstand all weather conditions without rusting or staining. They can be spray-painted any color. Using a drill, screw-driver, measuring tape and a file, a crew of four people can assemble the entire set in an afternoon. Students in a vocational education school in Somerville, Massachusetts assembled the first set. Using car paint manufactured for Ferrari, body shop students painted the chessmen Ferrari red and electric blue. (See Figure C–22.) The cost of the entire set is $980.

The heaviest piece, the king, stands 49" tall, and weighs only 12 pounds. His crowned head is formed by a roof vent and a storm collar, while the queen's is a gas vent and storm collar. Reducers typically join the components and act as pedestals and necks. The shortest piece is the pawn, 21" high, with a chimney cap as its head. Ovals, rounds, and angles form the knight's head, while a register boot is the pointed head of the bishop. A tee cap

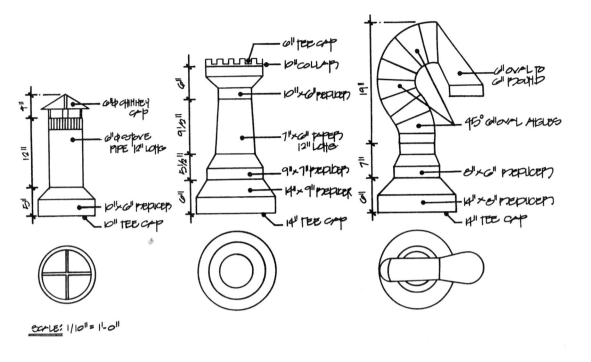

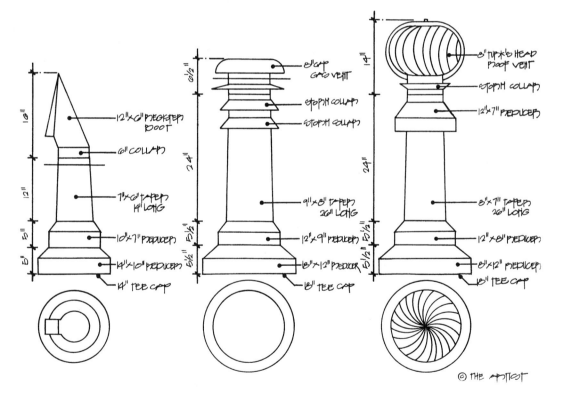

Figure 2-56 and 2-57: *Drawings of entire set of figures*

forms the typical serrated edge on the top of the castle. The whole set's dimensions are proportional to the sizes of a traditional chess set.

This set has been used in Boston area parks and arts festivals. Children delight in chess pieces of their own size that they can grasp, pick-up, move, and hug.

Figure 2-58: *Photo of entire set with a young chess player*

SCHMIDT DESIGN GROUP, INC.

San Diego, CA

Located in San Diego, the Schmidt Design Group, Inc. is a full-service design firm specializing in art installations, landscape architecture, and planning services for clients throughout the western United States. Four licensed landscape architects make up the professional staff of six. Joel Harms, Senior Associate for the firm, acts as Director of Design. He received a BS degree in Landscape Architecture in 1981 from California Polytechnic State University, San Luis Obispo and has worked continuously in planning and landscape architecture, with a particular interest in coastal issues. Landscape Architect Glen Schmidt earned a BS in Environmental Planning and Management in 1977 from the University of California at Davis. He founded the firm in 1983, and has directed its commitment to technical expertise in environmental issues, such as mitigation projects, revegetation and restoration of native habitats, and landscape management.

PROJECT: *Swami's Beach Access and Bluff Stabilization*
CLIENT: *City of Encinitas*
LOCATION: *Encinitas, CA*
DATE: *1991*
CONSTRUCTION COST: *$435,000*

At Swami's Beach, named after a privately owned, "self-realization" fellowship temple on an adjacent property, the firm performed a geological analysis of beach and bluff erosion, an analysis of potential wave action at the base of the bluff, the design of a wooden and concrete stairway structure connecting to the beach, and the processing of the coastal permit.[1] In order to stabilize the bluff, the design team

---

1 See also, "New," *Landscape Architecture Magazine,* Vol. 83, No. 6, June 1993, p. 26.

developed an extensive horizontal drain system, and a method of bolting rock directly into the sandstone bluff. In order to bridge over the most sensitive part of the delicate sandstone bluff, the landscape architects designed a unique 50-foot span using glue-laminated beams.

In analyzing the site, the team benefitted from interviews of local surfers who pointed out the area of the most powerful waves. The site of the staircase was shifted to a less severely impacted location. The graceful curve of the stairs is in response to the concerns of the surfers. Instead of a more standard rectilinear or straight form, the curving form accommodates long surfboards so that they do not bump the sidewalls of the stairs.

Encinitas was originally a part of San Diego County, but became incorporated as a city in its own right in October, 1986. The new city government undertook restoration of the beach access, which was dilapidated and dangerous and so badly deteriorated that it could not be reasonably repaired. A private organization, the Coastal Conservancy, provided partial funding for the project. During the public approvals process that was jointly required by both the city and the sponsor, local citizens expressed concerns. Among the groups turning out in appreciable numbers were members of the Swami Surfrider Association. As a result of their input, Schmidt Design Group moved the location of the new beach access farther back and tucked it in where there was less wave action at high tides.

Research revealed that as much as two inches of erosion can occur annually from the sandstone bluffs as water dissolves the delicate sandstone particles. To retard the process, the landscape architects designed a system of 40 drainage pipes, each of which removes as much as three gallons of water per minute. A chain-link fence further stabilizes the face of the bluff.

A special technique was used to hold it in place with 80 rock-bolt anchors drilled into the sandstone. To stabilize the bluff, holes four to six inches in diameter on a grid about five feet on center were drilled into the bluff. Most of the holes, extending into the sandstone as much as 20 feet to 30

feet, were filled with a high-quality grout cement. Pre-stressed steel bolts, similar to concrete reinforcing bars, were driven into the holes, and anchor the front face of the bluff into the deeper, more stable rock face. Holes that were not grouted were filled with perforated plastic pipe to act as drains.

At the base of the bluff, the erosion was exacerbated by the undermining action of the ocean waves. Starting from the base of the bluff, a gunite mixture was sprayed over a reinforced steel mesh attached to the face of the bluff. The cured concrete was treated with resins and sculpted to match the color and texture of the adjacent bluff.

Another significant challenge to the landscape architects was how to descend from the bluff 78 feet to the beach with a structure that would not overpower the site. The entire concrete and wood construction is tucked into the hillside area. From the plateau above the bluff, the visitor looks over the edge of the concrete stairway and is drawn towards the ocean without any visual interference from the structure. The upper portion of the stairs is a curving S-shape of poured-in-place concrete, set upon two- to three-foot diameter friction piers embedded as much as 15 feet deep. The friction piers, constructed from sono tubes filled with reinforced concrete, support the structure. The two entrance piers are decorated with a raised relief design of a headdress or minaret, adapted from a decorative motif used at the temple at the adjacent fellowship property.

The lower wooden portion of the stairway, which clears the surface of the bluff without touching it, is spanned with glue-laminated beams and supported by wood pilings, that, in turn, rest on beach level concrete pilings. Alaskan yellow cedar was chosen as the wood for the 8″ × 4′ × 50′ long beams because this species is inherently resistant to insects and decay. The beams support a five-foot-wide staircase with a total drop in elevation of 24 feet. Two sections of stairs, each with a drop of twelve feet, are separated by an intermediate landing. The two beams support the staircase. Wood for all the decking, stairs, and guardrail is pressure treated Douglas fir with an additional treatment of a preserva-

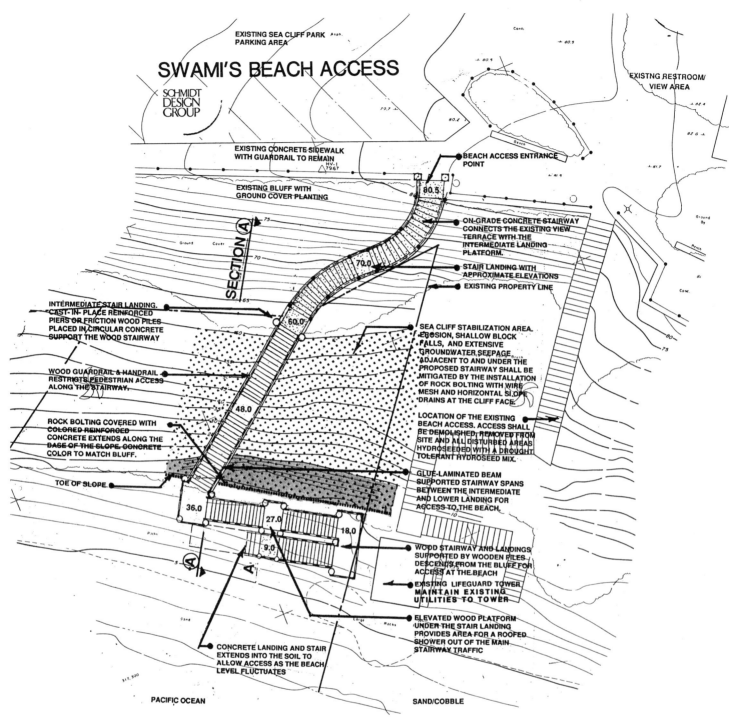

SWAMI'S BEACH ACCESS

SCHMIDT DESIGN GROUP

EXISTING SEA CLIFF PARK PARKING AREA

EXISTNG RESTROOM/ VIEW AREA

EXISTING CONCRETE SIDEWALK WITH GUARDRAIL TO REMAIN

BEACH ACCESS ENTRANCE POINT

EXISTING BLUFF WITH GROUND COVER PLANTING

ON-GRADE CONCRETE STAIRWAY CONNECTS THE EXISTING VIEW TERRACE WITH THE INTERMEDIATE LANDING PLATFORM.

STAIR LANDING WITH APPROXIMATE ELEVATIONS

EXISTING PROPERTY LINE

INTERMEDIATE STAIR LANDING. CAST-IN-PLACE REINFORCED PIERS OR FRICTION WOOD PILES PLACED IN CIRCULAR CONCRETE SUPPORT THE WOOD STAIRWAY

SEA CLIFF STABILIZATION AREA. EROSION, SHALLOW BLOCK FALLS, AND EXTENSIVE GROUNDWATER SEEPAGE ADJACENT TO AND UNDER THE PROPOSED STAIRWAY SHALL BE MITIGATED BY THE INSTALLATION OF ROCK BOLTING WITH WIRE MESH AND HORIZONTAL SLOPE DRAINS AT THE CLIFF FACE.

WOOD GUARDRAIL & HANDRAIL RESTRICTS PEDESTRIAN ACCESS ALONG THE STAIRWAY.

LOCATION OF THE EXISTING BEACH ACCESS. ACCESS SHALL BE DEMOLISHED, REMOVED FROM SITE AND ALL DISTURBED AREAS HYDROSEEDED WITH A DROUGHT TOLERANT HYDROSEED MIX.

ROCK BOLTING COVERED WITH COLORED REINFORCED CONCRETE EXTENDS ALONG THE BASE OF THE SLOPE. CONCRETE COLOR TO MATCH BLUFF.

GLUE-LAMINATED BEAM SUPPORTED STAIRWAY SPANS BETWEEN THE INTERMEDIATE AND LOWER LANDING FOR ACCESS TO THE BEACH.

TOE OF SLOPE

WOOD STAIRWAY AND LANDINGS SUPPORTED BY WOODEN PILES DESCENDS FROM THE BLUFF FOR ACCESS AT THE BEACH

EXISTING LIFEGUARD TOWER MAINTAIN EXISTING UTILITIES TO TOWER

ELEVATED WOOD PLATFORM UNDER THE STAIR LANDING PROVIDES AREA FOR A ROOFED SHOWER OUT OF THE MAIN STAIRWAY TRAFFIC

CONCRETE LANDING AND STAIR EXTENDS INTO THE SOIL TO ALLOW ACCESS AS THE BEACH LEVEL FLUCTUATES

PACIFIC OCEAN

SAND/COBBLE

Figure 2-59: *Illustrative site plan*

tive. The oxidation of galvanized steel hardware, such as all brackets and bolts, imparts a green patina to the metallic elements.

As one looks up from the beach below, native plantings soften the massive profile of the structure. Orange-flowering California fuchsia (*Galesia speciosa*), bush California tree mallow (*Lavatera assurgnentiflora*), and bladder pod (*Isomeris arborea*) create a composition of greenery that recedes into the vegetation of the bluff. (See Figure C–23.)

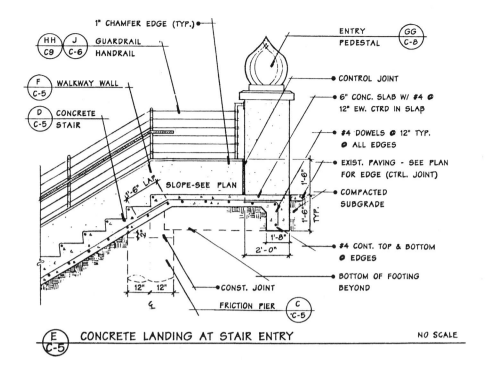

Figure 2-60: *Detail section of concrete landing at stair entry*

Figure 2-61: *The steps sweep down towards the beach in a graceful curve. The pastel color of the handrail mimics the everchanging hues of the ocean waves.*

Figure 2-62: *The entrance is punctuated with an ornament modeled after one at the adjacent property.*

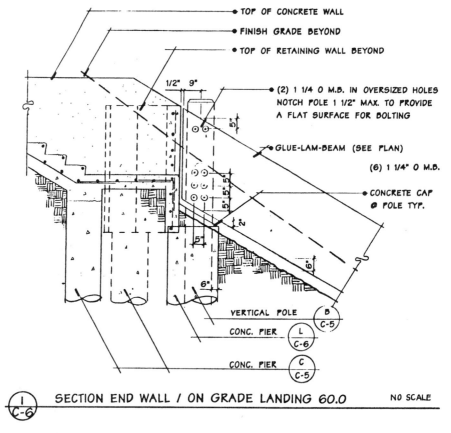

TOP OF CONCRETE WALL

FINISH GRADE BEYOND

TOP OF RETAINING WALL BEYOND

(2) 1 1/4 Ø M.B. IN OVERSIZED HOLES
NOTCH POLE 1 1/2" MAX. TO PROVIDE
A FLAT SURFACE FOR BOLTING

GLUE-LAM-BEAM (SEE PLAN)

(6) 1 1/4" Ø M.B.

CONCRETE CAP
Ø POLE TYP.

1/2" 9"

5"

5" 5" 5"

2"

5"

6"

6"

VERTICAL POLE B / C-5

CONC. PIER L / C-6

CONC. PIER C / C-5

1 / C-6 SECTION END WALL / ON GRADE LANDING 60.0   NO SCALE

Figure 2-63: *Detail section of end wall for landing at elevation 60.0*

Figure 2-64: *A surfer studies his board. Surfers helped the landscape architects site the best place for the access structure.*

PROJECT: *Eagle Crest, California Gnatcatcher Mitigation and Revegetation*
CLIENT: *City of Escondido Department of Parks and Recreation*
LOCATION: *Eagle Crest, CA*
DATE: *1995*
CONSTRUCTION BUDGET: *$120,000*

In contrast to the highly technical construction methodology used at Swami's Beach, the mitigation at Eagle Crest consists of plantings of shrubs and seedings of native materials in order to re-establish habitat for the Coastal California Gnatcatcher (*Polioptila californica californica*) on rolling terrain. An insectivorous bird, it gleans bugs off shrubs and coastal sage scrub, a low-growing open assemblage of shrubs and drought tolerant, primarily deciduous materials. A small finch-like bird, it nests in the lower shrubs, within about three feet of the ground, and uses higher shrubs for territorializing and singing.

Therefore, both layers are required for its habitat. These include California sagebrush, flattop buckwheat, and black sage, which grow up to about three or four feet high, and laurel sumac, which grows up to six feet high. This songbird establishes breeding territories as early as December, and nests in March. It may produce several clutches per season. During the non-breeding season, the birds tend to stay in the same general habitat, but move down the slopes. Therefore, it was important to try to plan the restoration so that vegetation would become established in time for the gnatcatchers to establish new territories.

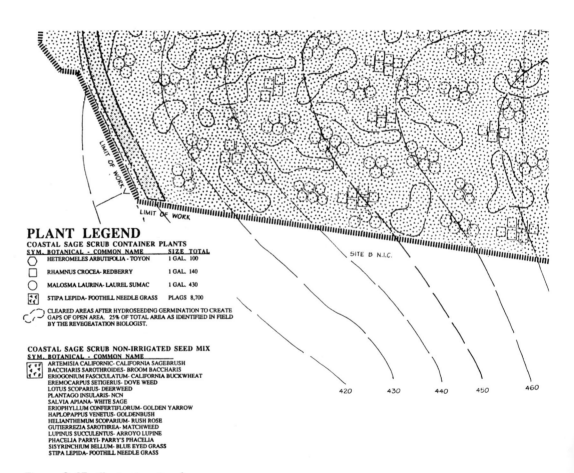

PLANT LEGEND
COASTAL SAGE SCRUB CONTAINER PLANTS

SYM.	BOTANICAL - COMMON NAME	SIZE	TOTAL
○	HETEROMELES ARBUTIFOLIA - TOYON	1 GAL.	100
□	RHAMNUS CROCEA- REDBERRY	1 GAL.	140
○	MALOSMA LAURINA- LAUREL SUMAC	1 GAL.	430
▨	STIPA LEPIDA- FOOTHILL NEEDLE GRASS	PLAGS	8,700

CLEARED AREAS AFTER HYDROSEEDING GERMINATION TO CREATE GAPS OF OPEN AREA. 25% OF TOTAL AREA AS IDENTIFIED IN FIELD BY THE REVEGEATATION BIOLOGIST.

COASTAL SAGE SCRUB NON-IRRIGATED SEED MIX
SYM. BOTANICAL - COMMON NAME
ARTEMISIA CALIFORNIC- CALIFORNIA SAGEBRUSH
BACCHARIS SAROTHROIDES- BROOM BACCHARIS
ERIOGONIUM FASCICULATUM- CALIFORNIA BUCKWHEAT
EREMOCARPUS SETIGERUS- DOVE WEED
LOTUS SCOPARIUS- DEERWEED
PLANTAGO INSULARIS- NCN
SALVIA APIANA- WHITE SAGE
ERIOPHYLLUM CONFERTIFLORUM- GOLDEN YARROW
HAPLOPAPPUS VENETUS- GOLDENBUSH
HELIANTHEMUM SCOPARIUM- RUSH ROSE
GUTIERREZIA SAROTHREA- MATCHWEED
LUPINUS SUCCULENTUS- ARROYO LUPINE
PHACELIA PARRYI- PARRY'S PHACELIA
SISYRINCHIUM BELLUM- BLUE EYED GRASS
STIPA LEPIDA- FOOTHILL NEEDLE GRASS

Figure 2-65: *Illustrative site plan*

This essentially Mediterranean climate has cool winters and hot, dry summers. When things dry out, the plants shut down; in August, the plants look dead.

The property is in a dramatic region of California featuring rolling hills forming a valley between them. A very mild climate has encouraged many surrounding acres of avocadoes and citrus groves. The property is ideal for development, which has threatened the habitat of the gnatcatcher and coastal sage scrub, consisting of grasslands with shrubs specific to California. Development pressures are very high on the coastal plain so that there has been both significant loss and fragmentation of habitat. The site, in a rural, undeveloped part of San Diego County, was chosen partly because it is adjacent to other open areas so that it is more defensible for wildlife. The gnatcatcher has suffered serious depletions since development in the region really picked up in the last decade. The existing vegetation on the site consisted primarily of invasive, non-native species, and was attracting birds and other animals inimical to the gnatcatcher.

Large sheets of polypropylene were spread and anchored over the site to kill the existing non-native vegetation and weeds. An ultraviolet-stabilized, two mil plastic was used. The soil of the five-acre site was first saturated with water, using an irrigation system, and then covered with the mats. Soil solarization is a common agricultural practice, but has never been used in a mitigation and revegetation project. Sunlight striking the plastic heats the soil underneath it to a very high temperature and essentially sterilizes it. This method was preferred to using repetitive cycles of "weed and kill" treatments of herbicides, such as Round-Up™ or methyl bromide, sprayed on invasive weeds. The ideal time to place the polypropylene mats is from June to September, for a period of approximately ninety days. At this site, even though the process did not begin until September, it was quite successful. The work started at the top of the site and proceeded downhill. In uphill areas where the plastic was in place longer, there were less weeds than in the lower areas where the plastic was placed at a later date.

After careful research of appropriate habitat for the gnatcatcher, the landscape architects developed a planting plan for the newly raw site. It was entirely reseeded with a coastal sage scrub mix for non-irrigated sites. Additionally, scattered, irregularly shaped clearings encompassing 25 percent of the site were created and kept clear except

Figure 2-66: *A view of the site*

Figure 2-67: *Large sheets of polypropylene fabric were used to kill weeds. The heat build-up underneath it essentially sterilized the soil.*

for native herbaceous plants. To complete the revegetation, containerized stock of four perennial materials was planted over the entire site in clumps between the clearings: Toyon (*Hetermeles arbutifolia*), a large, eight-to-ten-foot evergreen shrub; laurel sumac (*Malosmia laurina*); redberry (*Rhamnus crocus)*, a mid-sized shrub evergreen, and foothills needle grass (*Stipus lepida*). A revegetation biologist, Larry Sword, worked with the city's project manager, Neil Osias, and directed all operations in the field. Sword was also the expert on the bird's habitat: What does this animal need to survive? The biologist educated the landscape architect about the habitat of the birds, and Mr. Harms translated this knowledge into construction plans.

Mr. Sword recalls an achievement of the landscape architects. "One of the niftiest things that the Schmidt Design Group did was to devise the irrigation system to provide the water necessary to establish the moist heat necessary for solarization. He came up with a nifty irrigation set-up, put in a backbone system with quick couplers, irrigating one section at a time." Parks department people use the system to maintain the plantings until they are adapted to the site. The best method of irrigation is to water one area at a time manually using attachments to the quick couplers.

Most of the containerized stock has become well-established in just one growing season. In a few locations, washouts destroyed the new plantings so replanting was necessary. The hydroseed mixture used on the slopes contained 15 native species, including California sagebrush (*Artemisia californica*), California buckwheat (*Eriogonum fasciculoeum*), golden yarrow (*Eriophyllum confertiflorum*), arroyo lupins (*Lupinus succulentius*), blue-eyed grass (*Styrinchium bellum*), foothill needle grass (*Stipa lepida*), and others. Since the solarization destroyed much of the living organisms in the soil, the site was also "mycorrhized": the soil was inoculated with a "starter kit" containing fungi and microbes typical of what would occur in the soil in which the native plant materials would grow. Mycorrhizae is a type of fungus that forms a symbiotic relationship with native plants. As Mr. Sword explains, "Habitat restoration is part art and part science. One of the lines of thought is that, in disturbed soils, all native microbes are lost, creating conditions more favorable to non-native species. It's like a foundation of a house, if the foundation is lousy, the house will be lousy." By reestablishing microbes in the soil, the foundation is solidified. As several biologists in the field have quipped, "Habitat restoration without mycorrhizae is like putting lipstick on a corpse."

There are two methods of establishing the fungus, either the ground itself is inoculated or all container plants are inoculated with spores. The latter method was used. The Tree of Life Nursery in San Juan Capistrano provided much of the inoculated plant material. Native grasses, bunchgrass (*Nassela pulchra*), and foothills needlegrass (*Stipus lepida*) were planted 5' on center. The fungus travels about 1' per year on a favorable host.

The land for the development was a tradeoff negotiated between the cities of San Diego and Escondido. Escondido was permitted to build a golf course on one property, which would result in the depletion of gnatcatcher habitat, in return for the mitigation of developing five acres of gnatcatcher habitat in an adjacent area to create a habitat of replacement value.

In California and some other states, developers are increasingly relying on this method of landbanking. They jointly assemble properties with other developers and offer them as mitigation in return for the right to develop for housing or other purposes, areas with more limited natural resources. At Eagle Crest, the results of the mitigation will be monitored for five years by Escondido and Sweetwater Environmental Biologists, a consultant to the city. The results will be watched carefully in order to determine how readily a habitat can be created that would provide adequate open space for a threatened species while still accommodating intensive development and agricultural uses.

MARTHA SCHWARTZ, INC.

Cambridge, MA

Martha Schwartz gained instant notoriety with the publicity surrounding her bagel garden for a client in Beacon Hill. Bagels were dipped in pine tar to harden them for use as a paving material, and set in a formal knot garden of purple gravel and low evergreen hedges. A photograph of the garden was on the cover of the January, 1980, issue of *Landscape Architecture Magazine*, and the story generated more mail than any previous article. Many writers objected to what they considered an affront to the profession—bagels indeed! Since that time, she has continued to explore the use of materials found in our culture in unusual ways, often with wonderful results. On February 2, 1994, I was fortunate to interview her in her office in Cambridge, MA.

SC: You have a background as a visual artist that you bring to landscape architecture; your work is on the cusp between the art and design worlds; you try to embrace technology to develop your landscapes and there is a modernist approach or sentiment as opposed to a romantic concept of the outdoors. Could you summarize your background and your approach in general?

MS: In terms of my background, ever since I was a little girl, all I ever wanted to be was an artist; my dad is an architect, my uncle is an architect, cousins and sisters are architects, designers, and artists. Artistic talent runs in the family; it was an example that was set out for me. I was trained in art from the time I was little and basically grew up in the basement of the Philadelphia Art Museum. As a high school student, I would go to the Philadelphia College of Art for classes on Saturdays and went right on to art school at the University of Michigan. I didn't want to go to professional art school because I felt that the other courses available were too limited. I was always interested in science—biological science—so I wanted to go to a school that had a solid art school but also had solid academics, and that wasn't so easy to find in those days. Yale was a possibility, but since I was a woman, I couldn't go. Then the Ivy league schools really had inadequate art schools. They were art schools for dabblers so I wasn't interested in them. So I went to the University of Michigan. They had a really good art department; in fact, a lot of very-well-known people have come out of there since I was there [including Doug Hollis, Buster Simpson, and Pat Oleszko]. When I was an art student there, we learned about the earth works artists: Robert Smithson, Nancy Holt, Mary Miss, and Michael Heizer. These guys were really heroes. It was a very radical time (the 1960s) on campus and these artists were anti-establishment as well. These artists were anti-commercial and were anti-art-establishment. They would go out into the landscape and make art which couldn't be sold. Now, in reality, all this art was sold, in one way or another, in galleries. They were photographed and published in books. They were very well documented. So, in retrospect, it wasn't as radical as it seemed, but the idea that you would go out into the wilderness and make these monumental sculptures that really spoke about the environment in a poetic way was very romantic and very compelling.

SC: Can you think of a few of those?

MS: The spiral jetty by Robert Smithson blew us all away, Nancy Holt's Sun Tunnels were primal and mysterious, and the constructions that Mary Miss was making at that time were really quite allegorical and beautiful. Michael Heizer's Double Negative was raw and powerful, Walter DiMaria's Lightning Field was religious. They were really all strong icons, and spelled the beginning of the environmental movement, through raising our awareness of the earth, ecology, balance, and the need to be active in these areas. These weren't pieces that spoke about ecology literally, but the idea that they were out there in these pristine environments that were so beautiful, began the dialogue about our responsibility to our environment. Again, this was early on, at the beginning of the environmental movement. I wanted to learn how to build earthworks. I was interested in them sculpturally and poetically and in their connection to the larger environment. It also appealed to me that they somehow stood outside the gallery world. I liked the Dada aspect of these pieces as being anti-art. So I

wanted to build landscapes, but there was no Environmental Art 101 in art school as there was no such thing as "environmental art" or "site-specific art" or "public art." This was before all that. I didn't want to go and get a master's degree in fine arts since the arts schools didn't offer any instruction about landscape art. So, I looked into landscape architecture. I was surprised; I had never heard of it. My father is an architect, so in a sense it was an invisible art to me since architects feel that they are the master artists. I grew up on the floor of his office, and I had never heard of landscape architecture.

And so I pricked up my ears. I was almost off to medical school, but I decided to go into landscape architecture where I could learn the technical aspects of building landscape art. I wanted to know about the machinery and how to translate ideas into landscape. How do you get the opportunity to make a landscape? How do you get someone to give you land to do your art? I thought it was perfectly logical to go to landscape architecture school in order to learn how to build art. But I hit landscape school at a time when environmentalism in its most religious and pedantic period was king. Issues about art were absent from the curriculum. Also, the profession of landscape architecture was trying to re-define itself as a science in order to gain legitimacy, and working to create separation from both art and architecture.

Michigan was the only design-oriented school at that time. Here at Harvard, the curriculum was pretty much dominated by grants from the National Science Foundation. There was a lot of attention to computer mapping and development of M-Grid. Basically, students could have design courses waived during that period. Nobody was interested in art or its relationship to landscape. They did not feel that it was an important aspect of the field.

SC: I do remember—at Michigan—they had just moved from the Design School some years before.

MS: Right, during that time was when it happened, and from my point of view, that was a terrible thing. I think the school right now is in shambles.

SC: It was unfortunate because it separated the landscape architecture students from all the other design professions.

MS: It was tragic because when the shoe dropped and the economy fell apart in Michigan, which was dependent on the car industry, the University Regents came in and had to examine each department for budget cuts. They saw landscape architects in a School of Natural Resources which created a situation where artists and designers had to measure up against the programs such as wildlife management, forestry, fisheries, and streams, and soil science. Landscape architecture isn't a hard science, and therefore, the Regents felt it wasn't important. The budget was cut deeply, and the whole department was crushed. If landscape architecture had still been in the School of Art and Architecture, it could have been defended. In order to get rid of landscape architecture, one would have to say that *art* is not important. It would have been very difficult to abolish the School of Art and Architecture. Trying to define landscape architecture as a science weakened its position, and it was easy to diminish it.

SC: How long did you end up staying there?

MS: Two years, but I missed the East, and I decided to come finish my graduate work at Harvard. I knew Harvard wasn't strong in design then, but I wanted to come back East. And it was by luck that Pete Walker came back to teach at Harvard at the same time. He set up the design component of Harvard's graduate school. I spent a whole year thinking and talking about art and its relationship to the landscape. I was very lucky because if I had come a year earlier, there wouldn't have been any such opportunity. Pete had a rogue's gallery of students who had fallen out of the computer system . . . we were the oddballs that year, but doing some interesting and seminal work in landscape. It was the beginning of Harvard's Renaissance in design.

At Michigan, even though it was known as the "design school," there was only one other student who had an art school background. And they took people from different backgrounds, but it meant that people

had never really learned the fundamentals of art. Because I knew how to sharpen a pencil, I was immediately taken on as a teaching assistant. I went around and showed students how to sharpen a pencil this way, how to put on tape that way. I realized then that I had had such a rich background in visual language and art. As artists, we usually don't give ourselves credit for the information and skills that we have developed. This is because it's not information that society values or rewards. But when you get into situations . . . it was like I was Superperson, because I knew how to sharpen a pencil, used pastels, and knew about color and color theory. I knew how to model form on paper. I knew about proportions, texture, and line weight. I knew this language. Most of the people around me didn't have a clue; they had a lot of catchup to do. It was like being on the moon where you have this extra muscular strength and you bound up because you have extra strong muscles. That's what it felt like. Also, I came with a whole backlog of ideas, visual ideas, and knew what other artists were doing. I don't know what I would have done without all the information that I arrived with. As an artist, I was also used to the "blank page," the necessity to create something out of nothing. To be able to do that is a great resource. Many people face a blank page for the first time when they go off to graduate school in landscape architecture. They learn how difficult it is to generate an idea. It takes training to teach people how to approach that problem. Having an analysis or understanding of a site's ecological system is not the same as having an idea about it. I came to landscape architecture with great tools and a kind of agenda. I just had something I wanted to do.

SC: Talk more about your agenda.

MS: Well, my agenda is basically very personal. I have not approached it in a pedantic way. I don't think that everybody else should do and see things my way. I am very project oriented. I like making physical things. That has been an essential piece of knowledge about myself. That's all I've really wanted to do. I like to give form and make sculpture, to make a product. The process is incredibly absorbing and rewarding, more so than anything else. I want to be able to express ideas, feelings, and attitudes in the landscape. I want to be able to approach the issue of the environment in my own way. I'm not a savior, the salvation of the world. I focus on trying to get a project—get somebody to give me some land and some money to make a landscape. That really is it. Besides making landscapes, figuring out strategies to get people to give me those opportunities has really been the gist of my professional career. I find it somewhat funny that I would be in the situation that I'm supposed to tell people what to do and how to think. I just basically stick to what it is that I do—it's hard to say why I'm motivated to do it. Some people just have this flywheel going that makes them do these things without much of a grand plan. I don't have a grand plan at all.

SC: In terms of the body of your work, the three projects that we are talking about, the jailhouse garden, the residence in Santa Fe, and the Citadel, can you put them in some sort of perspective? The Seattle one was much earlier, but how did it get started?

MS: In some ways, they are totally related; in other ways, they are not related at all. I deal with what comes my way. The sequence is very random. When you're working in doing the landscape as a medium, you depend on other people to give you projects; it's like the old sculptors who used precious materials, they needed a pope to give it to them, and were told what to do. It's the cumbersomeness and the expense of the medium itself which results in the randomness of opportunity and your subsequent reaction. Even though the projects are random in their nature, I think there's something which links them in their attitude and form. They all deal with geometries, have a minimal quality about them layered with a "pop" sensibility. The Jailhouse Garden is more baroque. But the other two (the Santa Fe residence and the Citadel) have a minimal, repetitive seriality to them and are better.

The King County Jail project was my first Art Commission. It was very, very important to me; I felt it was a major coup,

as other competitors included Richard Artshwager, Joel Shapiro, and John Mason, all great artists. It was a big deal for me to win that commission. (See Figure C–24.)

SC: What I am struck with, in what I have read, and in the slides that I've seen, is that you created a garden with materials that one does not normally associate with a garden, ceramic tiles and precast concrete units; there are no plant materials. How did you conceive of that? Was it an idea that popped into your head? Was it something you wanted to do? Was it partly your social reaction to what was happening there?

MS: One of the ideas that does run consistently through the projects is to depict a garden without creating the conventional image of a garden we all carry with us. From my own point of view, a garden is a state of mind, a kind of sanctuary. People make gardens for the purpose of escape and fantasy; it's a metaphor for heaven or paradise. A garden can be a metaphor for many things. In any case, it functions as a break from your daily life and takes you into this other realm. Many cultures express this other realm in different ways, depending on the values of the culture, religion, how people live. A garden is an artifact like sculpture and painting, which is connected to a particular culture and history. Gardens can be many things—they don't have to be romantic and sentimental, as in English landscapes. They can be a Zen garden made of materials that are not even living. The garden is a space which allows your mind release—to daydream, to fantasize and to be someplace else. I am interested in that aspect of a garden in your own mind. Gardens also always connote a connection to nature. It is the nature of that connection which interests me. Most people feel that this connection must be in a form which literally copies or mimics nature. Also, the beauty of our natural landscape is a part of our American heritage. However, we are not a garden culture. We have developed a cult-like fervor about nature. We have this need to re-create or to redress that which we have pretty much trashed. When people come to you to design a landscape, they want you to re-create nature. But what really angers me, is that our culture does not really value nature. Everybody gives it tremendous lip service, but we have, by and large, given nature up. I often hear, "Oh, this is a great landscape opportunity," or "We really care about the landscape" or "This is *really* a landscape project." When it comes down to it, money is a direct signifier of what our values are. Most often, the landscape budget decreases as a project progresses. Often, there are no budget provisions to create a landscape in an urban setting. You need to spend a lot of money for that. A landscape must be cared for the way you care for a pet; you need to have light, water, structure, and soil. You usually need a lot more of these things if you want a naturalistic landscape. But nobody wants to pay the money for landscape. So I sit there and listen to how important the garden is, but there is no money for it. You go into a building and you see that the luxury bathroom fixtures have cost you your landscape. It angers me—I have a head of steam about that. Instead of saying "Well, I'm not going to do this," I said "OK, you want a garden, I'll make you a garden; you want a landscape, I'll make you a landscape." But you are going to end up with something that may be a little different than the English rolling landscape you have in your head, because, after all, that would take $35 a square foot, and you've got $5. If I entertain the notion of making landscapes on the cheap, the client must be willing to suspend his/her preconception about what a landscape is. I will see what I can do with $5 a square foot—to re-create a client's vision of what a landscape is—and to create the sense of a garden in my own imagery.

SC: That's quite helpful, that's an approach I could take, about how these are three different conceptions of creating a garden in three entirely different types of settings.

MS: Well, amongst those three gardens, there's a gradient. The Jailhouse Garden gave no hope for doing anything with "raw" landscape. Even though everybody thought it was important, there was no room for it on this very urban corner. The building had been designed so that you traversed the site diagonally to get into the building. There was no commitment to maintenance, so there was nobody to take care of it. With zero money and commitment to take care of a landscape, you can't have anything that is living. I gave them something that required no maintenance. It's a lot of concrete and ceramics. They don't maintain it, and it still looks good. Still, I wanted the plaza to be perceived as a garden. It has a simple plan which is more like a symbol of a garden. It has an axis, cross axis, water element, parterres and topiary. Even though there was nothing remotely connected to nature, you could still read it as a garden.

The Grand Allee of the Citadel project is a glorified service entry transformed into a grand civic plaza. We were very limited in terms of budget and palette; we were given a certain kind of paving with a limited color range and even simpler shapes. Because there was some budget for planting, it is somewhere between the Jailhouse Garden and Dickinson Residence. The Dickinson Residence had a good budget. It therefore has more plants, and is built from more solid materials. It is made of stone, brick, gravels, trees, and fountains. It's extravagant and beautiful, based on a traditional form of garden (Islamic). It requires maintenance. You have to rake up the leaves, clean out the fountains, fertilize the plants, and trim them up. Where there's life, it's messy. (See Figure C–25.)

SC: Could you talk generally about your interest in using modern technology and your techniques of making materials?

MS: Yes, in one sense, I'm not high-tech at all. Most of my projects are low-tech, and made from off-the-shelf products. I usually have very bad budgets. High-tech stuff is always more expensive, because it's more risky, and it costs more money to research. My stuff tends to be not at all high-tech. I like to use artifacts found in the culture— like a collage of found material. I consider myself more modernist in my approach to materials. I like to use materials honestly. I particularly like to use fake materials openly and honestly. If it's fake, I like to make sure that people understand that it's fake. In fact, we embrace fake stuff so much, we think it's real. We eat fake food; we see fake reality on television and in the movies; we wear fake fur, get fake tans. We embrace fakeness. We're used to it. It's part of who we are, and I don't really see it as bad. For example, I would never use "Bomanite" in a way to trick people. I would use "Bomanite" in an honest way. It is just stamped, colored concrete. Instead of seeing fake brick, you can see it as color and texture. But I'm always insulted when someone has used it in order to make you think that you're walking on brick. You'd have to be brain-dead to think that you're walking on brick. Anyone knows you're walking on stamped concrete. So why can't we just be honest about it? It's just that I hate the pretense about it. Veneer is veneer—it's not real stone. We know how much that costs—we know that there hasn't been a financial commitment to it, so why fake us out? That's where I'm moralistic: I believe that we should both tell and face the truth. That is the only way we can see clearly—if we don't fool ourselves. I am also very interested in "pop" art. The pop artists take the stuff that we see as lowly common culture and use it in a way that makes you see it differently. Taking those materials and using them beautifully is a more constructive approach to the future than reminiscing, like Prince Charles, about the good old days of better building materials and craftsmanship. If you were an imperialist, you had slaves as workers and artisans, and wealth in order to employ these people. All the major European empires ended up with really great stone buildings, but so what does that do for us? We've got to figure out how to build cheaply because that's where we are in space and time. Our distribution of wealth is different—in part, we've gone forward with a democracy and it means different things. That's why the States look different from Europe. But what can we do now that poured concrete is all we have? What can we do now that faking brick is the best that we can do? Can we do anything better within those constraints? It was a modernist's ideal that manufacturing, standardization and mass production could produce something of beauty and dignity. As an extension of this thought, one would hope that you can get well-designed, off-the-shelf materials—cheap stuff that looks great. That's the democratic utopian ideal.

SC: I think that theme runs through all of these works, using materials for what they are; even when one of them is more extravagant, it's not pretending to be what it's not.

MS: I also like doing funny twists and things that people don't really expect. A lot of times, there's a Dada aspect of what I do. I like to be irreverent, to shock and to make you a little uncomfortable. I like to go against what everyone's preconceived notion of what landscape is because I think our general preconception of what it is is constraining and boring. We treat the landscape like it's either a virgin, where it's holy, or like a whore, where we misuse and desecrate it. It's very Victorian. So I always try to put a twist on it in order to make you see the landscape in a different way. I want to make it visible, or make it an experience that you remember after you leave.

SC: I understand your sense of interpreting a garden in a lot of different ways—as a departure, as a type of artistic construction. As to landscape architecture in general, is it a medium with other applications beyond which most practitioners don't pursue it?

MS: Yes, I think so. If you got 20 artists to design a median strip in a boulevard or an apron around an existing building, or a landfill or a corporate park, or any of these things, I guarantee the artists would present a tremendous range of possibilities. They are more free to think about the landscape because of their training as artists. Landscape architecture has a whole set of pre-conceived ideas which discourage people from questioning ideas. But I think the tendency is to churn out people who are not tremendously creative or inquisitive and often have no visual background. I think that artists have a much more open view about what a landscape or anything could be. They also are not afraid of personal expression and exposing what is important to them. I think that having a personal committment to the work is at the crux of doing interesting work. Work must be personal to convey meaning. In order to make a contribution to the culture, design and art demand a personal commitment and risk. This may result in work which questions the status quo and therefore makes people uncomfortable at first. Nothing that pushes culture forward is easily accepted at first.

SC: That's really true. I agree with you that so much of what we do has become so homogenized, and it's dull and predictable, and it also gets so hard to challenge bureaucracies that are so used to dealing with the same vocabulary.

MS: I agree. It's not entirely our fault, as very little is expected from us. As a matter of fact, it's expected that we'll give very little; the firms that usually give very little, and don't present challenge are those that do very well. Our office is just hanging on by our fingernails, and probably always will be. It's because people don't want to be challenged; they like the status quo. They don't want to move forward, they don't want to change. Change is undesirable, dangerous, unpredictable. We as a profession are an appendage of the culture, whereas the artists remain somewhere a little outside it. They don't get rewarded, there's no ladder, there's no net for artists. They consequently are more free.

Martha Schwartz's work is a synthesis of the visual arts and landscape, of artistic and practical concepts, of the avante garde and the status quo. In these terms, the three projects discussed here can be conceived as different interpretations of the idea of a garden, based on applying it to different sites at different times for different clients with different budgets. This common thread organizes the following materials.

PROJECT: *The King County Jailhouse Garden*
LOCATION: *Seattle, WA*
CLIENT: *King County Arts Commission*
DATE: *1982–87*
CONSTRUCTION COST: *$120,000*

This site-specific artwork was the first major art commission executed by King County under its one percent for art ordinance, a program in which this minimum percentage of public funds for new buildings is mandated for public art. Responding to an institution designed without a lobby or foyer, Ms. Schwartz designed a plaza that provides a place for attorneys, families, and other visitors to wait and to meet. The plaza is an artwork, yet also a formal landscape: its design addresses the political implications of a prison. While the new jailhouse strives to emulate an office building, the landscape reflects the need to recognize the building for what it houses, the underclass of society for whom the system has broken down.

The artwork is a formal garden complete with hedges, topiary, parterres, and fountain, all constructed of pre-cast concrete and ceramic tile. The beautiful colors and patterning of this garden evoke a sense of light-heartedness. In contrast, the jagged, shattered quality of the tile-work, the somberness of the "topiary" forms and the erratic placement of these dreamlike shapes convey a sense of ominous surrealism.

The plaza is paved in broken tile. Colors gradate from yellow to green, blue to lavender, alternating with stripes of exposed aggregate concrete. Approaching from Fifth Avenue, one enters the plaza past a "planter" covered with green ceramic suggestive of a clipped hedge. The yellow and blue stripes which shoot diagonally across the floor allude to formal pathways. The scattered, geometric three-dimensional forms covered in green ceramic tile suggest topiary which have fallen from grace. Suggesting open space, a predominantly blue ceramic tile mural runs up the wall of the building behind the plaza. A simple arched shape is a garden gate and the implied exit. The mural is paradoxical, since it suggests the fantasy of escape and simultaneously is a wall which imprisons.

Figure 2-68: *The intricate tile patterns sweep through the plaza and flow up the walls of the jailhouse. The complex geometries and contrasting textures and colors of the groundplane more than compensate for the lack of living plant materials. (Photo by Martha Schwartz)*

The diagonal striping of the space and the arrangement of the topiary forms create the illusion of extended space. The design focuses attention on the ground plane and away from the overwhelming bulk of the building. The color and human scale of the objects bring comfort to a harsh, cold space. Repeating the lighthearted interplay of the real and the surreal, the "topiary" forms require no shearing, watering, or fertilization, and provide sitting places. The "topiary" elements are precast concrete covered in tile. Their exact placement was achieved through a study model that was translated into the working drawings.

There were some unusual contractual arrangements for this project. Even though public funds were involved, the execution of the work was entrusted to the designer. Martha Schwartz who was designated "sole artist" for the project, chose as contractors Fabrication Specialties, owned and operated by Larry Tate and Gerald McGuinness, two Seattle artists. They developed a business specializing in high quality fabrication for artists' endeavors. When the City of Seattle legislated funding for art as part of the requirements for any public building they started their own general contracting company focused on building art works. They executed "Nine Trees, Nine Spaces" by Robert Irwin, and many other works. Ms. Schwartz was introduced to them by the Kings County Art Commissioner. She first hired them to help estimate the cost of the work and finally to do the installation.

Even so, the work was so unusual that it went considerably over the $120,000 budget. Ms. Schwartz, in a labor of love expressive of her commitment to the arts, raised funds and spent some of her own funds to insure the completion of the work. The funding came from a new city law that required that one percent of the budget for publicly funded projects be designated for art. However, there was considerable controversy, as some people objected that one percent of the $40 million budget for the jail—or $400,000—be spent on art. In response to the public furor, the city council drafted a codicil to use less for a jail, or about 1/4 of one percent, resulting in slightly more than $100,000.

The construction drawings were a set of nine or ten remarkably concise and precise drawings that detailed everything. When landscape architect Marty Poirier of Martha Schwartz's staff started to manage the detail construction of the project, the essential layout was completed. He was directed to finish the detailing and find a tile setter for the broken tile mosaic. He also worked to confirm all the tile colors and production runs, and came up with the heat ceramics.

The jail is located in a part of town that is not a high traffic area. The design featured a broken tile mosaic, but Ms. Schwartz was concerned that this not become a liability in its execution: there could be no jagged edges extending above the plane of the pavement, nor could there be an uneven surface. Such errors would become a minefield for women

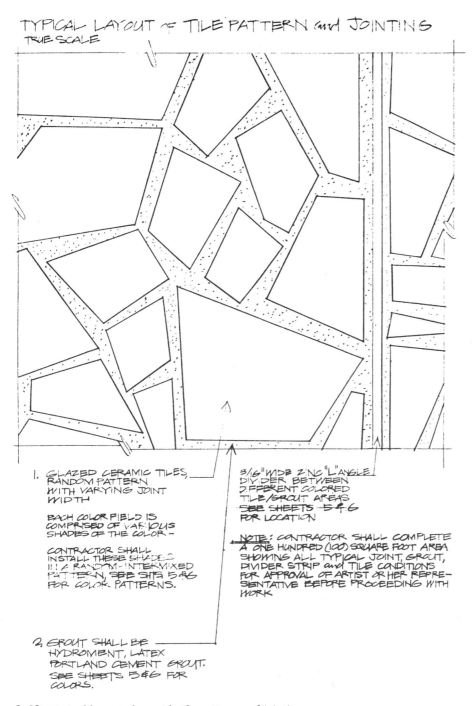

TYPICAL LAYOUT OF TILE PATTERN and JOINTING
TRUE SCALE

1. GLAZED CERAMIC TILES, RANDOM PATTERN WITH VARYING JOINT WIDTH

EACH COLOR FIELD IS COMPRISED OF VARIOUS SHADES OF THE COLOR -

CONTRACTOR SHALL INSTALL THESE SHADES IN A RANDOM-INTERMIXED PATTERN, SEE SHTS 5 & 6 FOR COLOR PATTERNS.

2. GROUT SHALL BE HYDROMENT, LATEX PORTLAND CEMENT GROUT. SEE SHEETS 5 & 6 FOR COLORS.

3/16" WIDE ZINC "L" ANGLE DIVIDER BETWEEN DIFFERENT COLORED TILE/GROUT AREAS SEE SHEETS 5 & 6 FOR LOCATION

NOTE: CONTRACTOR SHALL COMPLETE A ONE HUNDRED (100) SQUARE FOOT AREA SHOWING ALL TYPICAL JOINT, GROUT, DIVIDER STRIP and TILE CONDITIONS FOR APPROVAL OF ARTIST OR HER REPRESENTATIVE BEFORE PROCEEDING WITH WORK

Figure 2-69: *Typical layout plan with tile pattern and jointing*

in high heel shoes coming to visit their husbands and boyfriends in jail. It was also intended that the space be used by children, playing, sitting, and waiting, and their safety was an important concern.

To execute the complex pattern of shapes and colors, two different patterns of broken tile shapes were stamped and dyed: an organic design of irregular shapes, and a flagstone shape. The pattern of each of these designs was pressed into 12″ × 12″ squares to a depth that was two-thirds the thickness of the clay. The tiles were then glazed and fired. Therefore, the finished tile was nominally 1/4″ thick, with joints 1/6″ deep, similar to stamped concrete designs like bomanite. Smooth edges along the cleavage lines made an excellent bonding surface for grout. Since the tiles were cast in squares, they were easy to handle. Any breaks occurring in shipping to the site, tended to be along the cleavage lines, forming the desired joints; or they were easily broken on the site. All the tiles were grouted flush with the adjacent pavement surface.

Some special tiles were created for unusual locations. The pattern was created in two sizes, with the smaller one for areas where a denser concentration was desired. Elements that had 90-degree corners were beaded on the corners with 90-degree quarter rounds with standard trim. These tiles had beveled radii with a bullnose like those used in shower corners. Some of the smaller pieces were up to 1″ long, others were 6″ long. A "hardcore" artisan piece would have had sharp corners, but to fit the 3″ × 5″ × 7″ pattern, beveled edges were used, and some tiles half that size.

The initial intention, prior to budget restraints, was to use terrazzo, which consists of marble chips, stone, and coloring agent mixed with cement and ground down with a diamond polisher. The design was changed to accommodate less expensive tile. Each area of separate tile colors is bordered by a metal edging of a matching color. Contrasting grout colors abut one another, adding to the wonderfully colorful palette. The grouts were all standard colors that approximate the tile colors. The grouts were batched for

exterior use. They were more typical of colors for interior use, but additives, epoxies, and other chemicals, used as hardening agents made them appropriate for outdoor use.

It was necessary to fit the new terrace garden into the existing exposed aggregate concrete plaza. Even though the jail building was new, it had not been possible to build the garden at the same time. Therefore, sawcutting of new concrete pavement was necessary. Basic demolition was done, then the exposed aggregate concrete slab was removed. A new sub-slab was poured with hold-back for grout and tile. Also, new bands of exposed aggregate concrete were set, using a mixture and specification that matched as closely as possible to the original design.

Ms. Schwartz's concept was to brighten the gray site with a lot of color. One goal was to have the colors vibrate. She completed the color palette and Mr. Poirier related the PMS (Pantone Matching System) colors specified on the drawings to tile colors. For each major color of tile, he picked several tones: 2 to 3 shades of yellow (main yellow, lighter, and darker), 2 or 3 shades of green, blue, etc. The sculptural objects in the garden are rendered in dark green with mauve and lilac highlights.

The tile-setter was excellent, but the process was very slow. A sand box was set up to break the 12-inch-square tile modules along cleavage lines. An assistant mixed up the tile pieces in the proper color assortment.

Typical of the excellent working relationship between the contractor and the designer was the construction of a large raised circular area with concrete walls and edges, and a tile pattern with a concrete border on top. Its design was intended to represent a fountain or a pool of water. It was poured in place fairly early during the construction process. The detail had called for a three-inch lip on the top surface that ran around the entire perimeter and would be flush with the tile bed, but the contractor forgot to form the depression for the tile bed. When Mr. Poirier arrived to inspect he immediately saw the

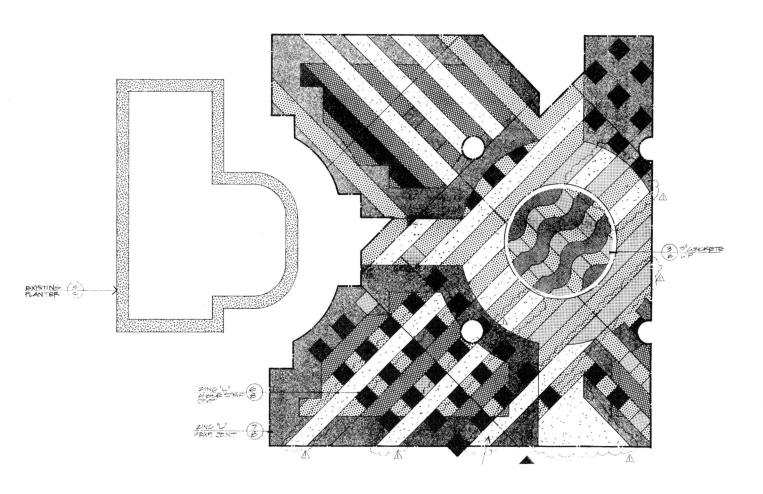

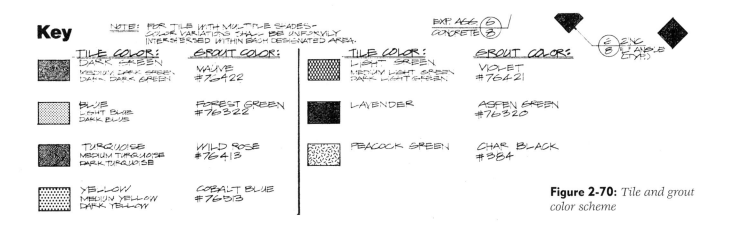

Key

NOTE: FOR TILE WITH MULTIPLE SHADES-
COLOR VARIATIONS SHALL BE UNIFORMLY
INTERSPERSED WITHIN EACH DESIGNATED AREA.

TILE COLOR:	GROUT COLOR:	TILE COLOR:	GROUT COLOR:
DARK GREEN / MEDIUM DARK GREEN / DARK DARK GREEN	MAUVE #76422	LIGHT GREEN / MEDIUM LIGHT GREEN / DARK LIGHT GREEN	VIOLET #76421
BLUE / LIGHT BLUE / DARK BLUE	FOREST GREEN #76322	LAVENDER	ASPEN GREEN #76320
TURQUOISE / MEDIUM TURQUOISE / DARK TURQUOISE	WILD ROSE #76413	PEACOCK GREEN	CHAR BLACK #384
YELLOW / MEDIUM YELLOW / DARK YELLOW	COBALT BLUE #76513		

Figure 2-70: *Tile and grout color scheme*

problem. He did not want the tile to extend to the face of the concrete wall because the concrete border was required with no joints. He also wanted to maintain the integrity of the design calling for a monolithic concrete. Rather than demolish the entire new pour of concrete, the contractor erected a small Makita™ saw, rigged up like a compass to scribe a circle. Then, using a repetitive oscillating impact hammer, like those used for bush hammering, the contractor removed enough concrete to create a slab on which to set the tiles. The problem was solved satisfactorily.

PROJECT: *The Citadel Grand Allee*
LOCATION: *Commerce, CA*
CLIENT: *Trammell Crow Company*
ASSISTING LANDSCAPE ARCHITECT: *Peridian Group*
PRIME ARCHITECT: *The Nadel Partnership, Inc.*
RETAIL ARCHITECT: *Sussman/Prejza*
DATE: *1990–1991*
CONSTRUCTION COST: *$1,300,000*

The Citadel site, formerly the Uniroyal Tire and Rubber Plant, has captured the imagination of a generation of southern Californians. Like an ornate movie set, the decorated Assyrian temple and bas relief front walls have exuded a sense of mystery and awe since the factory's construction in the 1920s. The developer of the site preserved the front wall of the factory's exterior but de-

molished the remainder of the site in preparation for a multi-use development including four office buildings, a retail mall, and a hotel. The challenges Ms. Schwartz faced included how to retain the existing Assyrian wall while creating a compatible context, how to maintain the fantasy and mystery created by the 70-year-old wall, and how to create a strong design infrastructure that would attract people to the building complex. Her firm, in collaboration with the other consultants, designed the master plan for the 35-acre site and performed the full scope of services for the central mall.

All of these goals were accomplished by means of a 150-foot-wide breach in the center of the historic wall adjacent to the Ziggurat temple. An Assyrian theme is used to create a strong visual axis that unifies the different uses within the site. At a museum in Berlin, Ms. Schwartz saw the "entry gate into Babylon and took drawings of this gateway as a starting point for the design. I really didn't envision this as an oasis as much as I did a kind of grand entrance. Materials of the original factory building were incorporated in other areas of the project." Inside the opening in the wall is revealed a courtyard of Date Palm trees aligned in rows on a patterned plaza 150 feet wide by 700 feet long. Evoking the feeling of a civic or ceremonial space, it is formed by buildings located along two sides and at the terminus of the axis. Specially designed tire shaped rings which surround each of the palm trees separate pedestrian and vehicular zones. The checkerboard paving is com-

Figures 2-71 and 2-72: *The rectangular pavement patterns, the rows of precisely aligned and evenly matched trees, and the fanciful repetition of the white rings resonate with powerful rhythms, like an army of giant featherdusters at ease. (Photo by David Meyer)*

posed of a series of colored concrete paver retangles which visually slide under the plantings and other plaza features. The proposed hotel and entrance to the retail area are on a cross axis framed by buildings and palms. A different pavement pattern is used for the axis to contrast with the cross-axis. The retail court re-creates a Middle Eastern bazaar, a space of shade trees and paths, awnings and water. All of these design elements create an environment evoking the mystery of another time and place. The entire landscape portion of the work has been completed, and the remaining buildings may be constructed in the future.

Before Ms. Schwartz became involved with the project, the Peridian Group had been working on the design with the architects. "During the course of the design process, the tire factory became registered as an historic artifact. The team was directed to go back and to look again at the site plan that was generated by the architects at Peridian to see whether they might improve upon it. The team was to try to incorporate the ideas of the wall in the building into their initial scheme. In this manner we became the design master planners and landscape architects for the overall site plan. We basically revised the existing site plan that had the building fairly equally spaced in the parking lot. Each building was surrounded by parking in a fairly conventional type of plan which emphasized accessability and an equal distance walk from the cars to the buildings. The entry that we have now was really just a service drop-off. We took the

buildings and actually placed them on the site so as to create this central mall with parking out to the sides and with the cross axis of the hotel and the mall. We divided the scope of services with the Peridian Group very cleanly down the line. We took responsibility for the area surrounding the Grand Allee where our firm was involved in the design, design development, construction documents, and field implementations. Outside the Allee, the Peridian Group interpreted our master plan, and was in charge of the design and implementation for the rest of the project." This arrangement worked well. The only constraints on the project were money and "preconceived ideas about what relation parking had to have to a building, as well as just getting beyond the prejudices and opinions of the other designers."

A formal allee of flowering trees connects the central space to the hotel. Special pavement links the plaza to the hotel motor court. Parking is designed to recall the agricultural groves of southern California and the Mediterranean. Row plantings of gray olive trees contrast dramatically against the green palm oasis.

This design "incorporates some minimalist principles of repetition and seriality which helps to create rhythm and visual interest. The design really explores the minimalist truth that anything repeated enough becomes interesting unto itself. We also needed to do something that was very simple and strong. We thought the repetition would help to illustrate the strength of the space itself."

PROJECT: *Dickenson Residence*
LOCATION: *Santa Fe, NM*
CLIENT: *Nancy Dickenson*
ARCHITECT: *Steven Jacobson*
DATE: *1990–91*
CONSTRUCTION COST: *$150,000*

The Client called Ms. Schwartz to provide complete landscape development services for this existing residence. New elements included a house addition, guest house and swimming pool as well as a motor court, entry and roof gardens,

site plantings, pathways, and steps. Ms. Schwartz sought to respond to Mr. Jacobson's expansive and traditional adobe architecture.

The house sits atop the crown of a hill and commands an expansive, undeveloped site with spectacular views to the horizon in

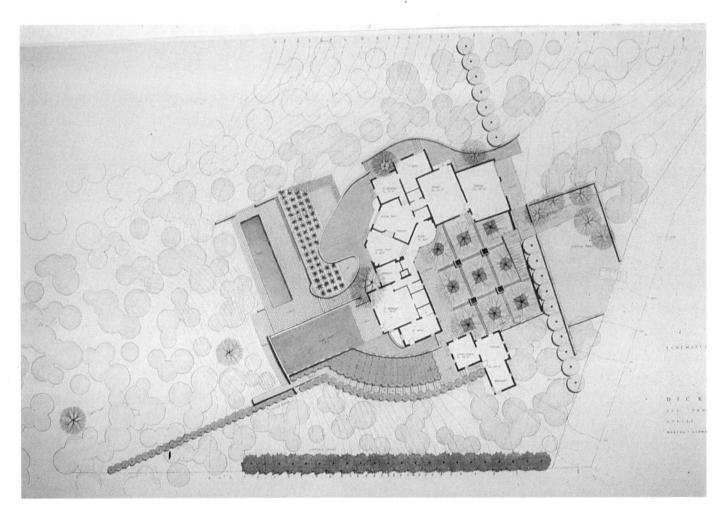

Figure 2-73: *Illustrative site plan*

Figure 2-74: *A view along the axis of the swimming pool juts towards the mountains*

Figure 2-75: *Courtyard*

several directions. Responding to these views, Ms. Schwartz has organized a landscape composed of a series of gestures oriented outward into the native landscape. A central spine is defined by an ornamental wrought iron fence which asserts itself at the front of the house. This fence, 42 inches high, aligns at the back of the house with a long line of purple leaf plum trees which intervene into the indigenous scrub landscape.

The swimming pool and terrace and a turfed roof terrace gesture outward and orient towards impressive views. The siting of the swimming pool and its basic form were already on the site when Ms. Schwartz arrived. "My contributions really had to do with the choice of materials and the design of the paving around it, as well as the cutting of a hole through the wall that extended the gesture of the pool to the mountains." For the planting of the roof terrace, a standard lawn grass mixture was used, planted in "a sandwich of approximately 14 inches of soil and green rock on top of the roof."

In contrast, the entry landscape is self-contained and intimate. A series of stucco, walled enclosures create a sequence of landscape rooms and corridors leading to the front of the house. A walled motor court leads to a walled corridor which contains a line of poplar trees which traverse to a sunken entry garden. It contains six apple trees and four fountains. A gravel panel defines the floor of the room which is divided by an orthogonal series of tile-clad runnels which interconnect the fountains. Rocks define a series of square and circular spaces at the base of each tree. The rocks are boulders of Colorado marble, 12 to 14 inches in diameter. The trees are 3-1/2- to 4-inch caliper apple trees irrigated by drip irrigation.

Moorish garden themes underpin the design: water, fountains, courtyards, and rivulets. "The use of water is essential to all Moorish gardens because water was seen as the source of life and was a symbolic source of life. In fact, water was also often integrated as the irrigation system to the plants that were growing in these gardens. Often

the sound of water became a major element in areas where water itself was very precious. Instead of being used as a strong visual element, the container of the water, the sound of the water, the sense of presence of the water is really what is important."

Mr. Schwartz used the courtyards "as a way of trying to create a sense of sequence going from where you parked through an inner courtyard into the house and out to the back. This was a way of creating space that could be gardened or planted without dealing with a physical transition between the garden and the rest of the natural landscape, which is very tough and rugged and would be virtually impossible to make a transition to. The couryards were really used as a series of rooms in which anything could happen."

Figure 2-76: *This fountain uses tilework in a strong, formal manner, in contrast to the fracturing of the Jailhouse Garden*

Outside them, the site was left in its existing, rugged state. With a construction budget of $150,000, the work was so concentrated in a small area that the cost per square foot was significantly greater than the Citadel project.

There is quite a bit of elevation change on the site. From the parking area down to the front door is appoximately a change of five to six feet. From outside the back portion of the house (the back deck) down to the pool is approximately another eight feet, and down to the end of the site could be another ten feet. The extent of the elevation changes and the ruggedness of the site required the concentration of the design into a small area.

In contrast to the sprawling Citadel site, this garden is not necessarily minimalist in conception. "Its basically an historical garden in its tic-tac-toe configuration. I would say that the garden is constructed from a very simple plan in a simple way so I'm not sure that I would say it was a minimalist garden."

ANDREW SPURLOCK/MARTIN POIRIER, Landscape Architects

San Diego, CA

The diverse work of the firm ANDREW SPURLOCK/MARTIN POIRIER Landscape Architects, in San Diego, CA has ranged from planning projects such as studies of scenic river corridors and canyons, to small scale site designs with unusual features. The firm's two principals have interesting backgrounds. Andrew Spurlock received a B.A. degree in urban and environmental studies in 1970 from Case Western Reserve University in Cleveland. His particular focus was on participatory planning. He subsequently earned a MLA from the University of Michigan, Ann Arbor, in 1975. He worked for a number of major landscape architecture firms in California, including the SWA Group in Laguna Beach and P.O.D. in Santa Ana before starting his own firm. Martin Poirier earned a BLA from Michigan State University in 1976 and an MLA from Harvard in 1986. Prior to forming a partnership with Mr. Spurlock, he was a Design Associate with the Office of Peter Walker/Martha Schwartz in their New York and San Francisco offices. Both of these landscape architects have been involved in complex collaborative projects for a number of years, often site-specific projects in urban areas. Projects with artists are a major focus. The firm has worked with Jackie Ferrara at the Molecular Biology Research Facility and Alexis Smith for her Snake Path—both for the Stuart Collection at the University of California San Diego. The firm has collaborated with Robert Irwin on many projects, ranging from development of proposals to providing design and technical support services for his garden for the J. Paul Getty Center in Brentwood, CA, the Fallingwater project, Frank Lloyd Wright's spectacular house in Pennsylvania, and the Des Moines Art Center. ANDREW SPURLOCK/MARTIN POIRIER have also worked with Newton and Helen Harrison, of San Diego, for the Santa Monica Arts Foundation in developing and implementing a competition-winning project for a beach access property. Additionally, Mr. Poirier oversaw the construction of Martha Schwartz's Jail House garden at the King County Correctional Facility in Seattle, discussed in another section of this book. The two projects included here are notable both for their unusual details and also for the design process that led to their development.

PROJECT: *Snake Path*

LOCATION: *San Diego, CA*

CLIENT: *The Stuart Collection, University of California at San Diego*

ARTIST: *Alexis Smith*

CONTRACTOR: *Klaser Tile Company, Inc.*

DATE: *1990–1992*

In 1989 Alexis Smith was selected to produce an artwork for the Stuart Foundation as part of its collection on the campus of the University of California at San Diego. The Stuart Collection is the group of exterior art pieces, often sculptures, specifically commissioned by the foundation for sites on the university campus. Smith chose to work on the site of an addition to the Central Library, a building designed by William Pereira with the underground addition by Gunnar Birkerts.

After Smith had developed her concept, the Stuart Foundation enlisted ANDREW SPURLOCK/MARTIN POIRIER Landscape Architects to assist her with technical support for the implementation of the piece. The firm worked with the artist and Mathieu Gregoire of the Stuart Foundation to select materials, develop construction details and coordinate grading and planting with the existing site conditions.

Alexis Smith lives in Venice, CA, and is well known for her installations and public projects addressing romance and nostalgia. She recently completed two terrazzo floors for the Los Angeles Convention Center that cover 80,000 square feet. For the Stuart Collection, Smith conceived of a work that "alludes to the complex relationship between nature and culture, or, in the context of the university, between knowledge and the landscape. Her *Snake Path* consists of a winding 560-foot-long, ten foot wide footpath tiled in the form of a serpent whose head ends at the terrace of the Central Library. The tail wraps around an existing concrete pathway as a snake would wrap itself around a tree limb. Along the way, the serpent's slightly rounded body passes a monumental granite book carved with a quote from Milton's *Paradise Lost*: "Then wilt thou not be loth to leave this paradise, but shalt possess a paradise within thee, happier far." The granite is etched with a filigree pattern, like a fleur-de-lis, similar to the decorative patterns that might be found on an old book cover. There is also an ornate, baroque, carved granite bench within the small garden. The snake then circles around a small tropical garden representing Eden. "These pointed allusions to the biblical conflict between innocence and knowl-

edge mark an apt symbolic path to the university's main repository of books." (the Guide to Stuart Collection.) The artist, in creating a sculptural object as well as a pathway, sought construction methods by which she could create beautiful pavement as well as impart the image of a snake. The sheer size of the piece provides dramatic views from many campus vantage points. Walking on the path provides an interesting physical experience, a direct sensual touching of the snake's intricate slate "scale" pattern and arched body. (See Figure C–26.)

During the design development there was a great deal of discussion about the degree of abstraction versus realism desired for the snake path. The repetitive quality of the reptilian scales and the voluptuousness of the body were attributes of "snakeness" that the team focused on. The scales were interpreted in multicolored pieces of hexagonal slate. An exaggerated crowning of the path creates a powerful sense of the snake body. The landscape architects developed technical details and drawings to communicate the artist's solution to the contractor. Three colors of slate pavers were cut into hexagons to suggest snakeskin and set in 1-1/4″ mortar bed on top of a concrete slab. The walk varies from eight to ten feet wide. The concrete is four inches thick at the sides and crowned at the center to a thickness of eight inches, and is continuously reinforced with 2 × 2 by 16 × 16 welded wire mesh. The longitudinal gradient and the cross slope are as steep as 1:6. Since many alternative routes to the library exist, the facility conforms to the accessibility requirements of the Americans With Disabilities Act. Therefore, the *Snake Path* could be built with such steep grades.

The stone selected has a particularly rough surface texture to reduce slippage when wet. The roughness also discourages skateboarders. There is a beautiful range of color: Silver Blue, from South Africa, Rajah Red from India, and Desert Rose from China. The slate pavers were field cut from 12 inch squares into two sizes of elongated hexagons: 11-1/8″ by 5-27/32″ and 10-9/32″ by 5-13/32″ by approximately 1 inch thick, both with 108 degrees and 144 degrees angled corners. The two sizes resulted from extensive experimentation by Smith to find

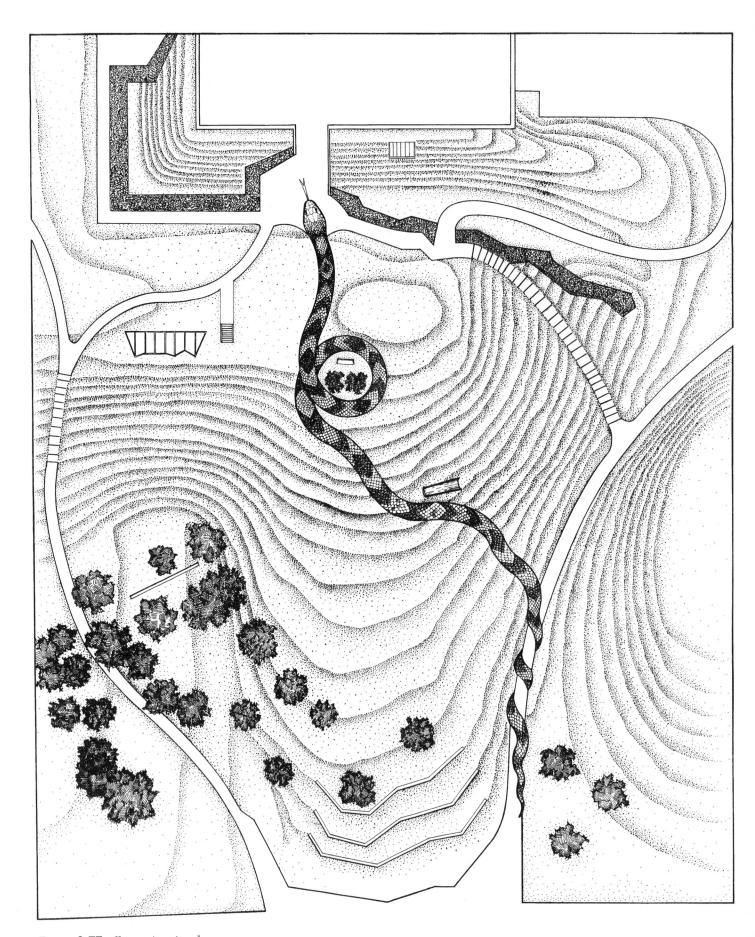

Figure 2-77: *Illustrative site plan*

Figure 2-78: *The tail wrapping around itself (Photo by Phillipp Scholz Rittermann)*

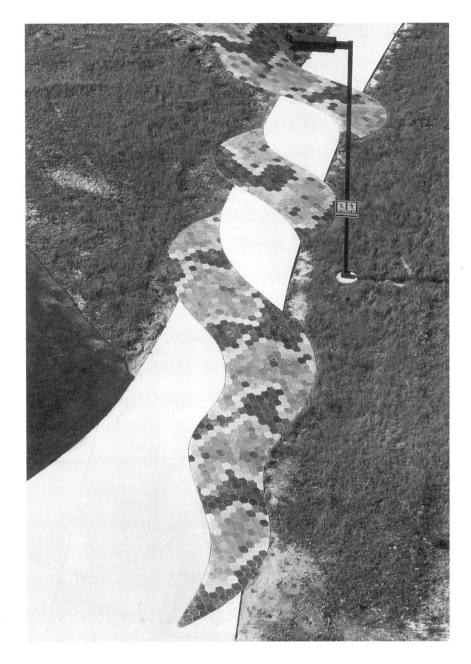

a module that would allow for the many changes of direction in the scale pattern as the snake turns and twists. A cleavage membrane of continuous 15 lb. felt paper separates the mortar bed from the concrete pavement. The grouted paver joints vary between 3/16″ minimum to 5/16″ maximum. To prevent any staining of the pavers by water draining over the surface, the finish grade on either side of the walk is 1 inch lower than the surface elevation of the pavers. In addition, there is a 2-percent slope away from the walk for a distance of 30 feet on both sides.

Much attention was paid to creating rapid transitions back to existing grade so that the snake would glide over the existing slope rather than appear cut into or backfilled like a typical road or path. The grading was carefully supervised in the field by the artist and landscape architect. A dual system of expansion joints was located every 8 feet on center for the tile surface and 16 feet on center for tile and concrete subgrade. These joints in the slate follow the hexagonal edge of the pavers and were filled with a custom-colored black caulk mixed with black sand to match the color and texture of the adjacent grout. In the location where the snake coils around itself, the sharp edge of an expansion joint serves to accentuate the overlap.

ANDREW SPURLOCK/MARTIN POIRIER was Smith's consultant for the detailed design, grading, and construction of the snake. She also worked with the landscape architecture firm WYA Inc., also of San Diego, who had previously done site planning and planting design for the library building. As advised by WYA Inc., Ms. Smith selected plants with biblical references for the tropical garden, located where the snake coils around itself, squeezing a piece of paradise. Among the plantings are pomegranates, pygmy date palms, edible figs, hibiscus, lavender, rosemary, lilies, and narcissus. The graceful slope through which the snake climbs is a mixture of native grasses and chaparral.

The artist spent considerable time working directly with the contractor, Klaser Tile, who brought an enthusiasm and a commitment to quality craftsmanship that contributed immensely to the success of the work. The time commitment to projects of this nature, with their attention to detail and research, inevitably exceeds customary budget allowances. The landscape architects ended up spending more than twice the time allowed by their contracted fee. Nevertheless, much is gained, and indeed, only possible in this type of work. The point of view of the artist—in exploring ideas and personal forms of expression, and that of the land-

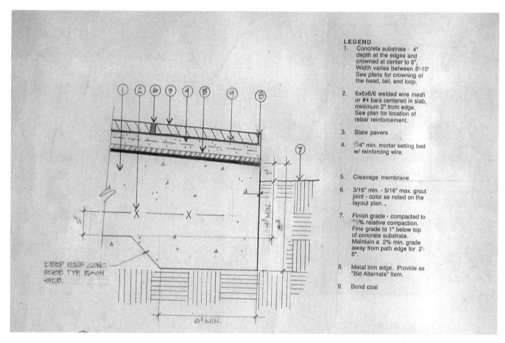

LEGEND

1. Concrete substrate - 4" depth at the edges and crowned at center to 8". Width varies between 8'-10'. See plans for crowning of the head, tail, and loop.

2. 6x6/6/6 welded wire mesh or #4 bars centered in slab, minimum 2" from edge. See plan for location of rebar reinforcement.

3. Slate pavers

4. 1¼" min. mortar setting bed w/ reinforcing wire.

5. Cleavage membrane

6. 3/16" min. - 5/16" max. grout joint - color as noted on the layout plan.

7. Finish grade - compacted to 95% relative compaction. Fine grade to 1" below top of concrete substrate. Maintain a 2% min. grade away from path edge for 2'-6".

8. Metal trim edge. Provide as "Bid Alternate" item.

9. Bond coat

Figure 2-79: *Detail cross-section of path construction*

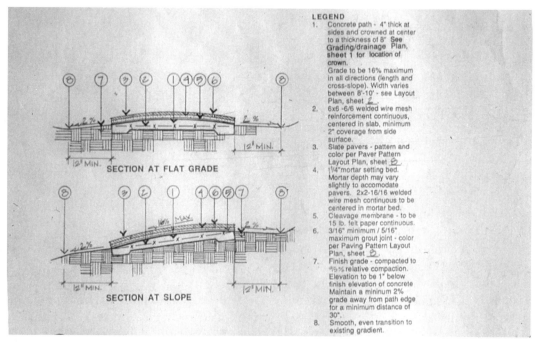

SECTION AT FLAT GRADE

SECTION AT SLOPE

LEGEND

1. Concrete path - 4" thick at sides and crowned at center to a thickness of 8". See Grading/drainage Plan, sheet 1 for location of crown. Grade to be 16% maximum in all directions (length and cross-slope). Width varies between 8'-10' - see Layout Plan, sheet 2.

2. 6x6 -6/6 welded wire mesh reinforcement continuous, centered in slab, minimum 2" coverage from side surface.

3. Slate pavers - pattern and color per Paver Pattern Layout Plan, sheet 2.

4. 1¼" mortar setting bed. Mortar depth may vary slightly to accomodate pavers. 2x2-16/16 welded wire mesh continuous to be centered in mortar bed.

5. Cleavage membrane - to be 15 lb. felt paper continuous.

6. 3/16" minimum / 5/16" maximum grout joint - color per Paving Pattern Layout Plan, sheet 2.

7. Finish grade - compacted to 95% relative compaction. Elevation to be 1" below finish elevation of concrete. Maintain a minimum 2% grade away from path edge for a minimum distance of 30".

8. Smooth, even transition to existing gradient.

Figure 2-80: *Detail cross-section of the crown of the path*

scape architect—in creating landscape space and experience—have combined to form a memorable place on the University of California San Diego campus.

FEES:

Artist—Expenses and Technical Support	$107,000
Landscape Architect (plus $19,000 in extra fees)	17,000
Construction Costs for Path and Landscape	$250,000
Granite "book" and bench	43,000
TOTAL PROJECT COSTS	$417,000

Figure 2-81: *Slate pavers as installed (Photo by Phillipp Scholz Rittermann)*

PROJECT: *The J Street Inn (Single Room Occupancy Hotel)*
LOCATION: *Downtown San Diego, CA*
CLIENT: *197 Partnership*
ARCHITECT: *Ron Wellington Quigley, FAIA*
CONTRACTOR: *Pacific Sun Landscape*
DATE: *1989–91*

The J Street Inn, a single-room-occupancy hotel in downtown San Diego, is a 221-unit, four-story building on a trapezoidal site. With rooms renting for as little as $400 per month, the hotel is intended for temporary service and professional workers and active senior citizens who want comfortable and affordable surroundings. The architect and owner had developed a very efficient building plan that had, in their minds, one big flaw, a long (200′), narrow (8′ wide), central courtyard that functions as a lightwell and is the only view from half the rooms. The landscape architects disagreed, and produced a design that further accentu-ated the linearity of the space. The idea evolved into a garden of lines: lines of plants, steel, concrete, and water.

Materials and details were kept simple so that the owner could use a design/build arrangement to expedite the construction. Minimal drawings were produced—only schematic designs, with no construction documents. The details use commonplace materials and were clarified with the contractor in the field. The most complex details are the tension cable and water feature, the final construction for which was negotiated with the architect, contractor, and owner on the site.

Figure 2-82: *Photo of the site in downtown San Diego (Photo by David Hewitt/Anne Garrison)*

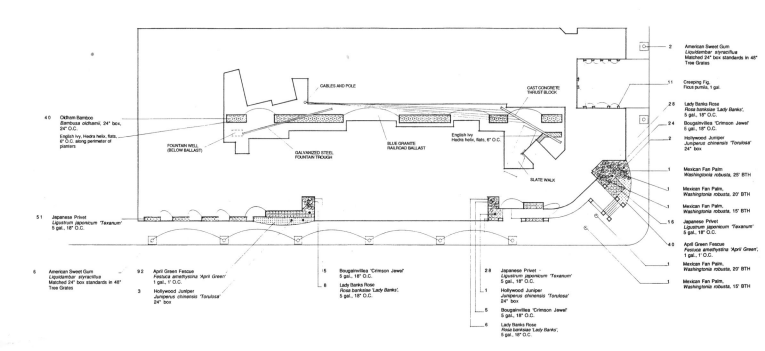

40 Oldham Bamboo
Bambusa oldhamii, 24" box,
24" O.C.

English ivy, *Hedra helix*, flats,
6" O.C. along perimeter of
planters

CABLES AND POLE

FOUNTAIN WELL
(BELOW BALLAST)

GALVANIZED STEEL
FOUNTAIN TROUGH

BLUE GRANITE
RAILROAD BALLAST

English Ivy
Hedra helix, flats, 6" O.C.

CAST CONCRETE
THRUST BLOCK

SLATE WALK

2 American Sweet Gum
Liquidambar styraciflua
Matched 24" box standards in 48"
Tree Grates

11 Creeping Fig,
Ficus pumila, 1 gal.

28 Lady Banks Rose
Rosa banksiae 'Lady Banks',
5 gal., 18" O.C.

24 Bougainvillea 'Crimson Jewel'
5 gal., 18" O.C.

2 Hollywood Juniper
Juniperus chinensis 'Torulosa'
24" box

1 Mexican Fan Palm
Washingtonia robusta, 25' BTH

1 Mexican Fan Palm,
Washingtonia robusta, 20' BTH

1 Mexican Fan Palm,
Washingtonia robusta, 15' BTH

16 Japanese Privet
Ligustrum japonicum 'Texanum'
5 gal., 18" O.C.

40 April Green Fescue
Festuca amethystina 'April Green',
1 gal., 1' O.C.

1 Mexican Fan Palm,
Washingtonia robusta, 20' BTH

1 Mexican Fan Palm,
Washingtonia robusta, 15' BTH

51 Japanese Privet
Ligustrum japonicum 'Texanum'
5 gal., 18" O.C.

6 American Sweet Gum
Liquidambar styraciflua
Matched 24" box standards in 48"
Tree Grates

92 April Green Fescue
Festuca amethystina 'April Green'
1 gal., 1' O.C.

3 Hollywood Juniper
Juniperus chinensis 'Torulosa'
24" box

15 Bougainvillea 'Crimson Jewel'
5 gal., 18" O.C.

8 Lady Banks Rose
Rosa banksiae 'Lady Banks',
5 gal., 18" O.C.

28 Japanese Privet
Ligustrum japonicum 'Texanum'
5 gal., 18" O.C.

1 Hollywood Juniper
Juniperus chinensis 'Torulosa'
24" box

5 Bougainvillea 'Crimson Jewel'
5 gal., 18" O.C.

6 Lady Banks Rose
Rosa banksiae 'Lady Banks',
5 gal., 18" O.C.

Figure 2-83: *Illustrative site plan*

ANDREW SPURLOCK/MARTIN POIRIER was faced with the typical challenges of low-cost housing: how to create an attractive, dignified environment with minimal budget for construction and maintenance. Additionally, the entire courtyard was itself a structure over a parking garage. The designers hoped to resolve the aesthetic and functional issues in a way that would be interesting enough to engage the residents with a play of light and shadow, sounds of rustling leaves and water, and unexpected uses of materials.

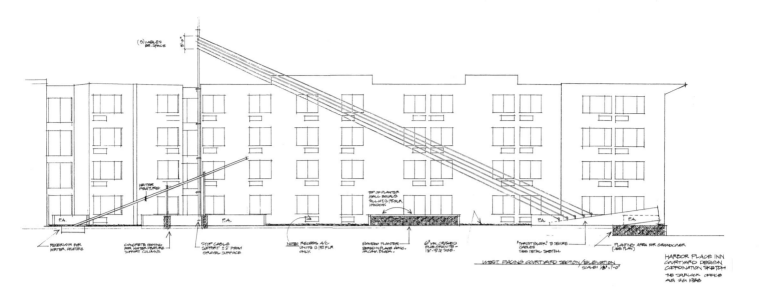

Figure 2-84: *Section/elevation of courtyard*

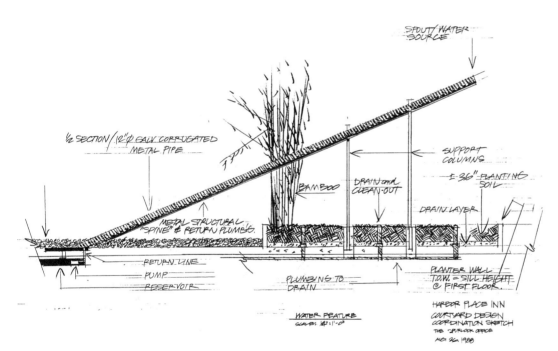

Figure 2-85: *Elevation of water feature*

The landscape architects' solution was to design the space almost like a shadow box for the framed views from the 100 windows, with elements that both reinforced and opposed the geometry and design style of the architecture. A principal element is a simple planting of bamboo running the entire length of the courtyard. Five three-foot-wide planters, the tops of which are the same height as the sill of the first floor of the buildings, contain vigorous stands of Giant Timber bamboo (*Bambusa oldhamii*) in three feet of soil depth. They are all of uniform width but various heights. This creates a rhythmic sense of movement and forms a row parallel to the length of the courtyard, but off center. The bamboo is the only plant material in the entire courtyard, yet the repetitive use of it unifies the space and adds a strong color accent.

ANDREW SPURLOCK/MARTIN POIRIER

Figure 2-86: *Bamboo in the courtyard soars vertically several stories. (Photo by Phillipp Scholz Rittermann)*

Contributing to the play of lines is a web of five equally spaced steel cables secured to a 35-foot-long concrete "thrust block" at one end of the courtyard and stretched to the other end. They are attached to a six-inch diameter galvanized steel tube bolted vertically to the building and rising 75 feet above the courtyard floor. The tube appears to be a pivot for some strange davit: The shadows of the cables move through space, scribing lines and shapes, like two giant abstract triangles.

The line of water is made by a fifty-foot-long, 18-inch-diameter galvanized steel flume held above the floor of the courtyard with a single thin steel column and cables. The flume channels a constant flow of water to the far end of the courtyard where it disappears into the gravel floor of the courtyard. A reservoir is concealed beneath the gravel surface of the courtyard. The water is not only visible but also audible. The corrugations in the chute create a turbulence that mimics the sound of a rushing

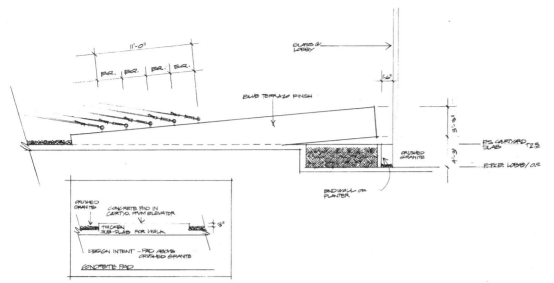

Figure 2-87: *Elevation and detail of thrust block*

Figure 2-88: *Corrugated pipe (Photo by Phillipp Scholz Rittermann)*

ANDREW SPURLOCK/MARTIN POIRIER

189

stream. A concealed tube under the flume mysteriously brings water uphill. The volume of flow is approximately 50 gallons per minute, using a standard swimming pool pump with a one-horsepower motor.

From the courtyard floor, a long slab of concrete thrusts upward at what seems to be a random angle. (See Figure C–27.) This 29-1/2-degree angle, bearing no discernible Cartesian or orthogonal rhyme or reason with the building, is, however, the precise angle required to terminate the cables in this recessed corner of the courtyard without touching any of the building walls. The thrust block's natural concrete is visible through the glass wall of the lobby and draws visitors' immediate attention. The courtyard pavement is crushed blue-gray rock of fairly coarse dimensions, 1-1/2″ to 3″ diameter, so that its textural qualities can be seen from as far as four stories above the surface of the gravel. The gravel plane and bamboo provide a neutral backdrop for the eccentric geometry of the concrete, cables, and flume.

The entrance design of the courtyard playfully jokes with the geometry of the space. Three rectilinear platforms at random angles to one another with one overlapping into the lobby, draw people into the courtyard. The tension generated between the randomness of the ground plane pavement forms, the linearity of the planters, and the jutting kineticism of the cables, creates a powerful potential energy that finally spills forth in the kinetic quality of moving water at the other end of the space.

The sculptural elements are designed to be seen as vignettes in that only in the drawings can one see all of them at once. The view into the courtyard is obscured by the narrow confines of the space and the intervening thickets of bamboo. From the guest rooms wrapping around the courtyard, a mystery unfolds as each room offers a different view, ranging from water shooting by to sections of cable seemingly suspended in air. A guest is bound to wonder about the source and destination of the water and the anchor and mast for the cables.

The simplicity, normalcy, and durability of the materials used contributes to ease of maintenance. As with all water features, the fountain with its equipment and evaporative mineral deposits, produce the most intensive maintenance requirements. Access to the courtyard is restricted to limit nuisance noise into the living quarters. Only the soothing sound of rushing water is allowed to fill the space.

The exterior building facades were modulated and disjointed to express the discrete spaces inside. The street facing planting areas emphasized these breaks by appearing to ooze out from the cracks in the facade. Here, as with the courtyard, the intention was to use the budget sparingly by reinforcing architectural themes rather than watering them down with competing gestures. The plant materials are hardy and simple: bougainvillea (*Bougainvillea braziliensis*), horse-tail reed grass (*Equisetum hyemale*), Hollywood junipers (*Juniperus chinensis*

Figure 2-89: *Plan of courtyard entrance*

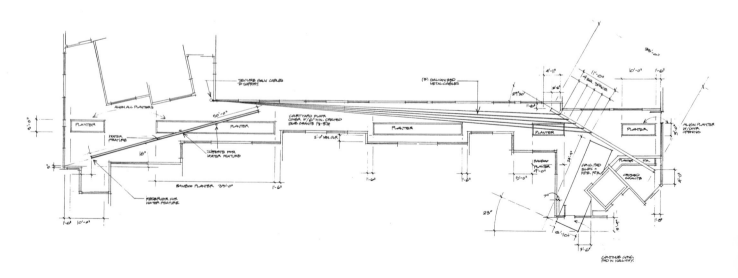

Figure 2-90: *Hollywood junipers and equisetum in sidewalk planter on 2nd Avenue (Photo by David Hewitt/Anne Garrison)*

torulosa), and Mexican fan palms (*Washingtonia robusta*). The very tall and skinny palms tower over the junipers, which will eventually form a massive thicket 18–20 feet tall by 12 feet wide. The dark green, fine texture of the juniper forms a backdrop for the brilliantly colorful flowers of the densely blooming bougainvillaea vine. The horsetail contrasts in texture and character with its prehistoric appearance, like giant green spikes 3 feet high and 3/8 inch in diameter. The result is a beautiful, dignified living environment—bringing a delightful play of light, sound, and landscape to each resident and making no excuses for being low-budget.

FEES: Landscape architect: $ 6,000
CONSTRUCTION COSTS: $ 50,000
   (On-site planting, irrigation
   water feature, cables, concrete)

CHAPTER THREE

THE PUBLIC
AND ACADEMIC SECTOR

The most diverse area of practice in landscape architecture is the public and academic sector, including all of the types and applications of practice not performed by private firms. Three organizations in New York City are presented as examples of many that occur across the country. The Abyssinnian Development Corporation of East Harlem was founded by a reverend in the Abysinnian Baptist Church and landscape architect Karen Phillips in order to provide design and development services to members of its own community. The Central Park Conservancy and the Prospect Park Design Alliance are remarkably energetic organizations responsible for the ongoing efforts to completely restore Central Park and Prospect Park in a manner that is historically accurate but also responsive to the constraints imposed by millions of visitors, limited funding by the city government, and the continuous evolution of New York City into the 21st century. Boston Urban Gardens (BUG) is a notable pioneer in providing community gardens in usually poor neighborhoods with few design amenities.

Also represented here, for example, are those landscape architects in university settings where the stimulus of the design studio and interactions with students contribute to unusual directions and departures from more traditional practice. Mira Engler and Gina Crandell, faculty at Iowa State University, conceived of an art installation as an aesthetic and political statement about the relationship of a new slaughterhouse and food laboratory to a serene campus. Architect Thomas Navin used a studio in design at the Newark Institute of Technology as an opportunity to explore with his students possible designs for the Olympics in Sydney, Australia.

THE ABYSSINIAN DEVELOPMENT CORPORATION

Harlem, NY

PROJECT: *Various community projects in Harlem, New York City*
CLIENT: *Central Harlem community*
LANDSCAPE ARCHITECTS: *Karen Phillips, Elizabeth Kennedy*

The Abyssinian Development Corporation (ADC) was organized in 1987 by Reverend Calvin O. Butts, III, then Executive Minister of the Abyssinian Baptist Church, by Karen Phillips, landscape architect, and other members of the congregation. In 1989 the ADC was incorporated as a non-profit organization whose goals were to provide affordable housing, improve the delivery of community and social services to residents, and foster an economic revitalization to build a strong community. The partnership between the pastor and the landscape architect, though unusual, strikes at the heart of the matter. The institutional strength of the church in combination with the strength of vision of the Reverend Butts, the pastor, and Karen Phillips resulted in dramatic changes in central Harlem. Founded in 1808 by a group of Ethiopian and African American merchants, the church has long been known for its activism in improving the quality of life for its congregation and the surrounding community.

Some notable figures have been pastor of the church, including Adam Clayton Powell and his son Adam Clayton Powell, Jr. Starting in 1908 the Reverend Dr. Adam Clayton Powell preached and promoted the idea of a model church in Harlem in a community in which his congregation would not have to tolerate racial and economic oppression by white property owners. The last few decades of the 19th century and the first decade of the 20th century saw an unprecedented building boom in New York City, including Harlem. Builders were unable to sell the glut of new housing, and became willing to rent to a growing population of black workers, many of whom migrated to New York City from small rural towns and farms of the South. Harlem was one of the few areas open to a large influx of blacks.

The Reverend Powell sought a home in Harlem for a new church building that would not be a renovation of an outdated building sold to them by white businessmen. The new edifice would be built from the ground up within a community in which many blacks could settle and participate as fully empowered citizens. Property was acquired on 138th Street between Lenox and Seventh Avenues. A new church and community center were built in 1923 at a cost of $335,000. Money for the construction and the 12-year mortgage was raised through a tithing campaign in which 2000 members of the congregation, many of whom were domestic workers and servants, pledged one-tenth of their weekly income. In less than 4-1/2 years the mortgage was paid. The congregation next undertook the purchase of a home for the aged, which was operated continuously for 12 years near the church on St. Nicholas Avenue.

Adam Clayton Powell, Jr., succeeded his father as pastor and served from 1937 to 1971. Like his father, he sought to create a viable community in Harlem. The problems in Harlem were enormous: As late as the 1950s there were no black bus drivers,

Figure 3-1: *The logo of ADC captures the spirit of its goals*

ABYSSINIAN DEVELOPMENT CORPORATION

and no blacks worked in any of the stores along 125th Street, the main shopping and business street of Harlem. Elected in 1944 to the House of Representatives, he served 14 terms in Congress. At a time when Congress had only a few black members, he was supremely self-confident about what he wanted to accomplish. He was so courageous and persuasive in articulating clearly what needed to be done that he almost always succeeded. To the white-dominated Congress, he was a dilemma: a man who looked white was shaming them into acknowledging and confronting racism in American institutions, and doing something to rectify it. A forceful champion of social justice and public education, he became chairman of the House Committee on Education and Labor, and managed or initiated almost sixty public laws to benefit the disenfranchised of the country: the blacks, the aged, the handicapped, Hispanic-Americans, women, and poor whites. During his five year chairmanship of the committee, he *never* had a bill defeated on the floor of the House of Representatives once it had been voted from his committee. His legislation provided significant funding for programs in fair employment practices, public educations, aid to public schools, manpower training, fighting discrimination against women, and the war on poverty.

After Powell's retirement in 1971 (he died in 1972), Samuel DeWitt Proctor became the next pastor of Abyssinian. Upon his retirement in 1989, Dr. Calvin O. Butts, III, became the pastor. Under his leadership the church has continued to be a spiritual and political force and increasingly an economic force for positive change in the community. The Abyssinian Baptist Church has had a pervasive impact on community development activities and in addressing homelessness, racial discrimination, and the urban problems so common in large American cities.

The challenge that Dr. Butts and the Church face are as great as ever. Many of the blacks that moved into Harlem in the early 1900s during the tenure of Dr. Adam Clayton Powell, Sr., were able to find jobs in public service, corporations, and other areas that finally opened up to them. They became so successful that they followed the dream of the 1960s and went to Long Island. Poor people replaced them but there were no manufacturing jobs available in a failing economy. A welfare system became the main source of money within the community; everyone else with money left. Increasingly desperate and poor people scrounged in apartments whose owners lived outside the community. A gradual deterioration of much of the housing ensued, along with an increase in crime and drugs. Programs were sorely needed to rebuild the community, provide affordable housing, and improve the delivery of services.

Karen Phillips moved to New York City in 1982 and to Harlem in 1988. Born in Ocilla, Georgia, a small rural town not far from Jimmy Carter's home in Plains, she grew up in a family that was active in the civil rights movement. From her childhood she was inspired by her family to nurture in herself the ideal of using her fair share of power in a democracy to affect change in her own community. Her uncle, Ernest Davis, tried to run for public office in 1956. The town police chief and a group of officers shot at him, and tried to intimidate him. They were upset at his arrogance in attempting to file to run for office. Rather than be intimidated, the Davis family organized and continually worked through the federal court system to fight for justice. Her uncle's courage inspired her. Like many returning veterans of World War II, the five Davis brothers started businesses in order to earn a living for themselves and their families. Her uncles eventually succeeded in establishing a funeral home, a dry cleaning business, a construction company, and a septic tank business. It was not until the mid-1980s that a black was elected to public office in Ocilla. The family continued to be active in the Civil Rights movement of the 1960s with the next generation leading the integration of the Ocilla public schools.

Ms. Phillips earned an undergraduate degree in landscape architecture from the University of Georgia in Athens. From the beginning her professional career was marked by her notable interest in city planning and community development. Her first job was with the City of Atlanta Bureau of Planning. Her responsibilities included providing planning and landscape architectural services for the parks system. She then worked for several years for the Shenandoah Development Corporation which designed and built a new town, Shenandoah, south of Atlanta near Newnan. This large community was intended to provide housing and jobs for diverse income groups. One major aspect of Ms. Phillips' job was to implement the new town's master plan, to maintain the original design guidelines, and to enforce them. Due to its location some distance from the north side of Atlanta, where most growth had occurred, and as a result of a poor economy, Shenandoah's success was limited. The development of the residential community stalled. However, the industrial park thrived, as its location near the Atlanta airport assured excellent access for delivery and shipping of goods.

By 1980 Ms. Phillips had a clear career goal of wanting to be involved in decision-making and to have more control in the development process than typically was the case in planning and design. She sought further training at Harvard Graduate School of Design in a program developed to prepare designers for guiding the real estate development process. She earned a master's degree in landscape architecture in 1982 and moved to New York City shortly after earning her degree. Ms. Phillips worked first for the Port Authority of New York and New Jersey, and later the New York State Urban Development Corporation. At the Port Authority she managed urban planning and real estate development proposals. These included the Port Authority Fishport, the Inner Ring Strategy (a study of the communities in the New York metropolitan area surrounding and supporting the central business district), and the Brooklyn Piers Redevelopment Project. At the Urban Development Corporation she was a project manager for several economic development projects, typically large commercial developments in urban areas, as well as some statewide projects such as the Commercial Revitalization Program.

She became a member of the Abyssinian Baptist Church in 1986, and as she created a home for herself, became more and more involved with community activities. She volunteered with several groups dealing with neighborhood development (community board committees, neighborhood homelessness, NYC Parks Council, historic preservation). During the late 1980s some funding from government and private foundations became available for community organizations seeking to provide housing for the homeless and middle income housing. Compelled by her family history of social involvement, she sought an opportunity to bring her years of experience in planning and real estate to use in her own community. Knowing the Reverend Butts' and the Abyssinian Baptist Church's longstanding commitment to the Harlem community, she joined forces with this institution after working with other groups on political and community development issues.

The Local Initiative Support Corporation (LISC), a community development group established by the Ford Foundation in 1979, provided Abyssinian with seed money to build the capacity of a community-based organization doing physical development. Prior to this grant which paid her a salary, Ms. Phillips at first worked for the Abyssinian Church as a volunteer while continuing to work for the Port Authority and then the Urban Development Corporation. By 1989 she started working full-time managing the real estate development project and organizing a structure for the Abyssinian Development Corporation that would attract more money. The ADC was set up as an entity to function as an umbrella for the development of real estate projects and programs.

A large percentage of all properties in Harlem are owned by the City of New York, and few of the stores are owned by people living in Harlem. Many apartment buildings are in a terribly deteriorated condition with an abundance of vacant structures. The City had attempted various restorations of buildings for the homeless and paid millions for huge numbers of people to be warehoused in hotels. Ms. Phillips had volunteered in one such program for families only to observe poor results: horribly designed and sparsely furnished apartments with limited support services. People were just placed in them and left to themselves. The Abyssinian Baptist Church, which had begun applications in the early 1980s to provide housing for senior citizens, was critical of the city's use of federal money for the homeless. The ABC sought a more comprehensive approach to redevelopment than merely building housing units, and that led to the creation of the Abyssinian Development Corporation.

The funding for her first project in Harlem, transitional housing for 24 homeless families, came as the result of her response to a "Request for Proposal" from New York Department of Housing Preservation and Development (NYCHPD) in 1986. Named the Abyssinian House, this restoration included three buildings on Odell Clark Place, and was completed in March, 1991. The Abyssinian Development Corporation provided the city a community-based, non-profit organization which could direct the restoration of abandoned buildings into fully equipped apartments and operate transitional housing for the homeless. The housing is referred to as "transitional" because it serves as a transition point for relocating a family back into society. As the family is supported by social and community services, they are provided assistance in obtaining permanent housing. ADC provides complete on-site social services, including child care and recreation for the 24 homeless families in the Abyssinian House, who are referred by New York City.

The Abyssinian Baptist Church had been working on creating housing for the elderly. A high percentage of the church congregation was primarily elderly and would benefit. The church had been working with a consultant since 1982 in planning for the development of city-owned property on 131st Street. After becoming executive director of the Abyssinian Development Corporation, Ms. Phillips began to oversee the development of a newly con-structed building to include 100 apartments for senior citizens on the site under a Federal Housing and Urban Development (HUD) 202 program. The housing, called the Abyssinian Tower, was completed in 1990 and contains ten studios and 90 one-bedroom apartments. On the ground floor is office space for social workers and administrative staff. The basement houses a laundry, recreation, and community rooms. Complementing the scale of the five story tenements in the area, the building is eight stories and steps back from the street. Simple plantings of street trees and fenced plantings of shrubs and perennials welcome visitors at the entrance. Planter boxes of marigolds are still doing well late into the fall. From the lobby, there is a clear view through a round window into a rear garden that extends the whole width of the building. The garden features comfortable benches and a shaded pyramidal wooden trellis which shades hanging plants in the summer. Many of the older residents prefer to sit in front of the building and watch activities on the street.

However, the Abyssinian Tower is on 131st Street while the Church is located at 138th street. Not all residents of the Tower are members of the Church. It was clear to Ms. Phillips that one can't just construct a building in isolation: Not everyone in the neighborhood is elderly and interested in the Abyssinian Baptist Church. What is needed is a comprehensive approach to development. Besides the physical structures; a mixture of income levels; and a complete range of community, social, and educational services are essential. Economic development within the community is crucial. There has to be an influx of working and middle class families to help stabilize the community: Doctors must be nearby, as well as grocery stores and good schools. Where would the residents of the Abyssinian Tower and other residents go for basic services (groceries, entertainment, laundry, etc.)?

It was not that such complete facilities had not been planned before. For example, in the 1970s Leon Sullivan was one of the clear thinkers in Philadelphia who provided centers for job training as a part of an economic development strategy for black churches to be involved in redeveloping communities. Also, many churches had been involved in providing housing for senior citizens or low-income people. However, usually the churches were just the sponsors. A developer, usually not from the immediate neighborhood, controlled the housing development and construction, and then left, leaving the church without any real control of maintenance and operations of sometimes substandard construction.

By contrast, the Abyssinian Baptist Church and the Abyssinian Development Corporation sought to build up their own capacity to guide the redevelopment of the neighborhood, and be directly responsible for whatever development took place. The Board of Directors of the ADC consists of about sixteen people, professionals, who live and/or worship in the community. As individuals, they sweep the crack vials off the steps, volunteer to work with youth, or teach in adult literacy programs. One board member living in a brownstone insisted that the crack addicts living next door paint over the graffiti they had done. Faced with such intensive scrutiny and dedication to the community, the crack addicts moved.

Because of its mission to develop a diverse and prosperous community, the ADC, even after its first major successes with transitional housing for the homeless and the elderly, is more focused on the development of low moderate and middle income housing in Harlem, rather than only housing for the homeless. Ms. Phillips has often had to argue forcefully for what she and her board feel is needed: housing attractive to a diverse-income community, rather than re-creating a ghetto by building all low-income housing and housing for the homeless. A city bureaucrat or banker with funds to give to an organization that has successfully provided homeless services

Figure 3-2: *Front view of 51 West 131 Plaza: 38 condominium units for sale to moderate and middle income families and individuals funded through the New York City Housing Partnership and completed in partnership with the Madyus Corporation*

THE PUBLIC AND ACADEMIC SECTOR

does not want to be told, "No thank you." Ms. Phillips bridles at condescension, particularly from people outside her community, who feel that they know what is best for Harlem and wish to impose it. As she responded to one banker, "We want to help homeless mothers with children, but we don't do homeless projects. We don't have any homeless people here. Once we put people into housing, they are not homeless. They are our new neighbors because we live here. I don't have to keep them homeless so that you can say, 'Here are my homeless children. See them?'"

Consistent with its comprehensive approach to community redevelopment, the ADC set up a meeting in a church on West 131st Street in order to start a block association. Through the institutional strength of ADC, the membership was able to have the police attend and their forces aggressively address drug activity. ADC's development on the block encouraged some building owners to invest money in restoration. Quite a few fixed up the facades of their buildings and initiated other renovations. Since its inception, the block association has gained strength and influence, and regularly organizes clean-up campaigns, block parties, and regular monthly meetings to address issues facing the neighborhood.

ADC developed several other housing rehabilitations on West 131st Street. There is West 131 Plaza, a condominium with 38 units (four one bedroom, 30 two-bedroom, and four three-bedroom duplexes) for sale to moderate- and middle-income families and individuals. The maximum income for an individual owner is $66,000 to obtain loans with low down payments and subsidies available through New York City and State. The New York City Housing Partnership created this program and paired the Abyssinian Development Corporation with a minority developer/contractor, the Madyus Corporation. The total cost for the units is $56,000 for one-bedroom apartments, a range of $75–80,000 for two bedroom apartments, and about $105,000 for the 3-bedroom duplexes. Finished in 1992, most apartments are sold. ADC also carried out the rehabilitation of 71 rental apartment units on West 130th and West 131st Street that are now fully occupied. These units were financed through the low-income tax credit program funded by NYCHPD, the Enterprise Foundation (set up by James Rouse) and LISC.

In addition to its housing developments, ADC has three major community services underway: a Pathmark Supermarket, the Renaissance Ballroom and Theater complex (each to cost about $10 million) and a child-care center on 138th Street. Many residents drive to Yonkers or New Jersey for groceries since the only stores in Harlem are small grocers and convenience stores that sell a limited range of products at high costs. Many of these small stores or markets are typically owned by Korean and Arabic families, who tend to live outside the community. Therefore the money they take in is not recycled within Harlem but sent elsewhere. On the other hand, many of the small markets are owned by Dominicans and Hispanics who comprise more than half of the population of East Harlem. Although many blacks were at one time immigrants to New York City, those suffering in poverty have rarely had an opportunity to buy into the system that they helped build.

The Abyssinian Development Corporation's belief is that by creating commercial ventures like the Harlem supermarket it will not only greatly increase the quality of goods available to residents at a reasonable price, but stimulate opportunities for economic development within the community. Residents will still use corner stores for purchasing orange juice or milk or occasional groceries when convenience is important, but will also benefit from the major inventory of a large supermarket (about 53,000 square feet). It would be the largest in upper Manhattan, and would also include a delicatessen, a pharmacy, and a flower shop. To be located on a block of city-owned land on 125th Street, between Third and Lexington Avenues, the store will hire about 200 local residents as employees. Part of the $12 million financing is being provided by LISC. It is likely that other stores and businesses will locate to the same general area to be near the magnet store that draws a lot of customers. As these stores will all be financed through local banks and capital, the dream of an economically viable community which includes local merchants could become reality.

Still, the project is not without opposition, including Councilman Adam Clayton Powell, IV. It is ironic that, as the son and grandson of the former ministers of the Abysinnian Baptist Church, he strongly opposed what the Church firmly endorsed.[1] With a political base drawn largely from Hispanic residents of East Harlem, he argued that Pathmark was receiving unfair tax advantages in the newly created Federal Empowerment Zone at the expense of small businesses that have been established in the community for generations. East Harlem is 39 percent African-American and 53 percent Hispanic. Dominican and Hispanic small market owners are worried about the competition a large supermarket will bring. Final approval had to be given by the Manhattan Borough Board, composed of the borough's ten City Council members, the chairman of Community Board No. 11, Eddie Baca, and Borough President Ruth W. Messinger as chairwoman who votes only in case of a tie. Mr. Baca, who is Hispanic, is one of Pathmark's staunch supporters, and tried to placate some of the bodega owners who would be affected by finding city subsidies for them. As of February, 1995, three of the Board's ten City Council members firmly opposed the project. Ms. Phillips calmly pointed out—to whomever would listen—that a regional shopping center is a service typically available to people in the suburbs, and Harlem residents deserve exactly the same. Opposition was so heated that the Board's final vote of endorsement of the project, in the spring of 1995, was by the thinnest of margins. A deciding vote was cast by Councilman Linares, who previously opposed the project. He changed his mind after long deliberations, and became convinced that the Pathmark could help the residents of East Harlem without undermining the network of bodegas.

Mayor Giuliani, mindful of the considerable support among Hispanic small business owners that helped elect him, waited for months before finally endorsing the project in early August, 1995. However, the mayor engineered—some would say imposed in an aggressive show of power—a management arrangement in which the city will keep a 49-percent stake in the enterprise until a local group, most likely a Hispanic organization from East Harlem, can be found to assume control. The remaining stake in the project continues to be the Abysinnian Development Corporation, and the group of organizations under its auspices who painstakingly nurtured the project over several years. After months of inaction, during which it seemed the project might die, the mayor gave Ms. Phillips and Reverend Butts an ultimatum. They had less than a day to accept the mayor's terms or see the project fail. After some tense negotiations, they accepted. The mayor also firmly rejected as an unfortunate and politically dangerous precedent Pathmark's offer to contribute $25,000 annually to a development fund for East Harlem, which would have aided Hispanic businesses. The mayor advised that such a contribution was an undesirable business practice.[2]

The Abysinnian Development Corporation is completing the property purchase from the City the spring of 1996, and will lease the property to Pathmark. Construction is scheduled to begin in the fall.

The Renaissance Ballroom and the adjacent theater complex were designed by Harry Creighton Ingalls, a specialist in theater architecture, and were completed in 1922. During its heyday in the big band and swing periods, it was the center for large celebrations and dances. Popular black intellectuals, musicians and writers such as Louis Armstrong, James Baldwin, Count Basie,

---

[1]Jonathan P. Hicks, "Mayor Gives Final Approval for East Harlem Supermarket," *New York Times,* Vol 144, August 2, 1995: B1, B3.

[2]Brett Pulley, "In Store Fight, Mayor Gets Tough," *New York Times,* Vol. 144, Aug. 12, 1995: L25. *See also* Aug. 3: A24, Aug;: A36.

Harry Belafonte, Duke Ellington, Langston Hughes, Sidney Poitier, Leontyne Price, and Paul Robeson all celebrated special occasions and performed there. Former Mayor David Dinkins held his wedding reception there. Based on its cultural significance to the Harlem community and its proximity to other landmarks like the Harlem Hospital, Strivers Row, the Schomburg Center for Black Culture and Research, and City College, and its history as a traditional community center, the New York City Landmarks Commission is currently considering designating the Renaissance Ballroom as a landmark.

Through a $500,000 grant from the Federal Department for Health and Human Services Office of Community Services Grant Program, the Abyssinian Development Corporation has planning underway for the renovation. The facility will provide

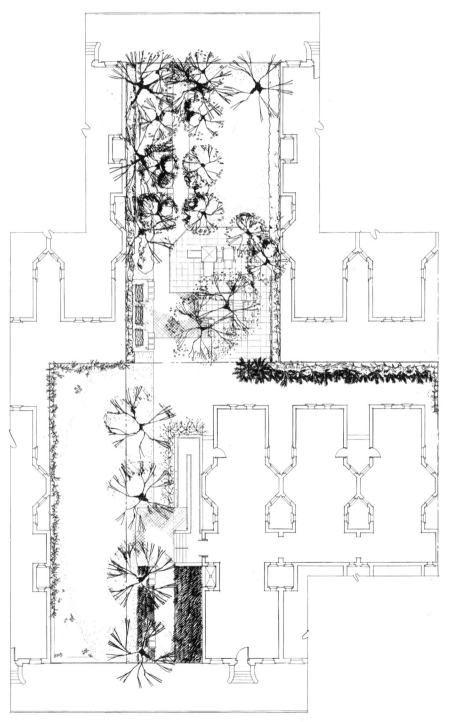

Figure 3-3: *Illustrative plan, ADC headquarters playground for Head Start Program*

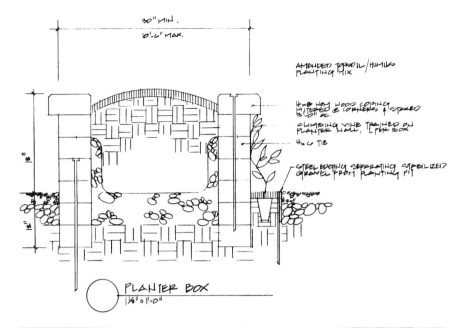

30" MIN.
6'-6" MAX.

AMENDED TOPSOIL/HUMUS
PLANTING MIX

4×6 HDWD WOOD EDGING
MITERED @ CORNERS & STAKED
@ 4'-0" OC.

CLIMBING VINE TRAINED ON
PLANTER WALL, 1 PER BOX

4×6 TIE

STEEL EDGING SEPARATING STABILIZED
GRAVEL FROM PLANTING PIT

PLANTER BOX
1/2" = 1'-0"

banquet and catering services to accommodate as many as 700 people. The Abyssinian Development Corporation has founded with eight local business leaders the Renaissance Complex Redevelopment Corporation to undertake the development, lease the commercial spaces, and establish a food services training program to prepare community residents for jobs generated by the facility.

Across the street from the Church, the childcare center is an $800,000 renovation on the first floor and cellar of three former tenements. It will have a staff of 16 and will service 100 children from three to five years old in a Head Start Program which also addresses issues important for parents. Landscape Architect Elizabeth Kennedy has been ADC's design consultant on this project. A registered landscape architect in New York, she has been an advisor to the Abyssinian Development Corporation on several projects over the last five years.

The tot lot for the Head Start Program is located on four rehabilitated vacant lots adjacent to and behind the Abyssinian Development Corporation's headquarters. The building houses the offices of ADC in the basement, residential units on the upper stories, and the Head Start Program on the ground floor. The outdoor space will ultimately provide recreation space for as many as 100 children, but usually in smaller groups. The property encompasses four former lots that originally held tenement buildings. When assembled for development by ADC, the total parcel, extending between 138th Street and 139th Street, was just under 1/4 acre, or 52 feet by 200 feet. Three of the lots were available with long term leases, but one lot was available on an interim basis. It is anticipated that the interim lot will eventually be redeveloped for housing. This "temporary" lot was leveled, topsoiled, and sodded, and is used as one of

Figures 3-5: *Entrance to the site from the building is from a ramp down to the level of the site. The circulation space for people going through to the next street is separated from the play areas. (Photo by Elizabeth Kennedy)*

Figure 3-6: *Dr. Deborah Allen, a member of the ADC Board of Dicrectors, speaking at the opening ceremonies of the Annie G. Newsome Headstart Center*

the free play areas in the playground. Ms. Kennedy's design concept integrated the four lots, but allows for the future loss of this one lot. In order to accommodate handicap access according to the requirements of the Americans With Disabilities Act of 1990, it was necessary to move the entrance to the building for the Head Start Program to the side, away from the 138th Street entrance for ADC and residents. The side yard becomes part of the permanent circulation system for the block and the permanent entrance to the building's Head Start program. The development of the circulation system and the concentration of safe spaces for different activities essentially resulted in a lay out of the principal design elements. Ms. Kennedy prepared the schematic design for the facility. Architect Andrea Lightman of the New York City Department of Housing Preservation and Development developed construction bid documents. There was competitive bidding and the work was implemented for a total cost of approximately $200,000.

A final focus of ADC is the development of open space. As Ms. Phillips states, "Open space is a tool for empowering the commu-nity. It allows people who live here already and new people moving in to work together, regardless of income levels. Once you get out here digging in the ground it doesn't matter. It's an organizing tool with which to focus people on positive changes. It's a way to get a block association going by making a park together." The creation and renovation of open space is an easier and faster way to change the environment than housing because everyone can see it. Its visibility is one way to bring people together working toward a concrete, common goal of creating and protecting their open space.

With the visibility of this resource comes the potential for community control. Illegal dumping of garbage, sometimes, hazardous materials, into abandoned or otherwise "available" open spaces is a problem in Harlem. By helping set up a block association on 131st Street, Ms. Phillips was able to enlist participation in a New York City Department of Sanitation program in which the reporting of illegal garbage dumping to the police results in the group receiving a share of the fines imposed by the city.

As ADC finishes with the restoration of a group of buildings and all apartments are occupied, it plans to set up a corporation which will become a managerial agency. In one sense, ADC will go from being an advocate to a landlord. However, the landlord is based in the community, usually in one of the buildings which the corporation is managing, and hires community residents. This community business entity helps to sustain the economic viability of housing development. There are clear opportunities for regular communication and clear formats for the resolution of complaints. Due to the success of this community-based approach, the city has renovated city-owned buildings and turned them over to ADC or one of its affiliate corporations to manage. Programs are being created by New York City to transfer occupied city-owned buildings to non-profit organizations and local entrepreneurs.

With her experience in historic preservation, Ms. Phillips has tried to set guidelines to preserve and enhance the integrity of the architecture of the structures in Harlem. The ADC works whenever possible to save or replace the existing cornices, even when considerable restorative work is required, since they give so much character to the architecture. Many of the buildings have decorative lobbies found in various states of disrepair. Whenever possible, many of the elements, like marble steps and wall panels, are restored. In some situations when funds must be focused on structural elements and creating safe and comfortable apartment layouts, elements such as the details of lobbies are left incomplete even though the space is completely useable. It is preferable to anticipate a more authentic restoration at a later date rather than completely reconstruct a lobby with no trace of its historic character. Sometimes painting has been postponed or delayed while funds are raised for accurate restorations. For example, the original marble lobby of one building was kept, even though there were not enough funds yet to recast all its plaster ceiling and moldings or restore the limestone facade of the entire building.

One of ADC's current projects, the restoration on West 130th Street of the northside of Astor Row, developed by Jacob Astor at the turn of the century, is a comprehensive approach to restoration. The street is unique in that the south side features the Astor Row houses with 20-foot setbacks and wooden porches on brick rowhouses. These structures are designated historic by the NYC Landmarks Commission, while the north side, with its handsome, typical brownstones, is not. Due to its historic status, the south side is eligible for grants through the Historic Properties Fund and NYC Capital Funds, but the north side is not. In Harlem the landmark designation has tended to discourage restorations as owners perceive it as imposing bureaucratic obstacles on tight budgets. Working with the ADC and block association, the New York City Landmark Conservancy moved forward and secured funding for rehabilitation from New York State, banks, HPD, and the Vincent Astor Foundation. For Ms. Brooke Astor, seeing the project is a prerequisite for possible funding from her charities: "she won't fund what she can't touch," says Ms. Phillips. Ms. Astor also recognizes the importance of a strong community base, which has been a founding principle for ADC. At 91, she is fast reaching her goal of giving and donating all of her money before she dies.

To heal rifts between neighbors on different sides of the street, a garden is being designed by Ms. Kennedy to be built in the space left when one building that was too deteriorated to save was removed. This open space will be used by the whole block for neighborhood events and gardening. One of the houses is city-owned, but in disastrous condition; ADC is negotiating taking it over from the city because another "hole" would risk destroying the linear strength of the Row.

At Astor Row, Ms. Kennedy conceived a design that would respond to an infill situation created as a result of a 20-foot-by-100-foot vacant lot that had previously contained a row house. Between two standing brownstones, the volume of this narrow slot of space opens up to the rear yard. She sought a design treatment that would "ostensibly continue the massing of the building across the space." The garden will feature a trellis whose wooden poles will mirror the design of the posts on the Astor Row houses. In combination with dense massing of understory vegetation, she created a sculpture garden as "a sponge of vegetation with a meandering path wandering through it." The linear structure of an axially located wooden arbor is superimposed over the less rigid layout of the path. Ms. Kennedy prepared schematic drawings and developed working drawings. Originally, the design called for an eight-foot-high chain-link fence to enclose the rear yard and an eight foot high iron fence across the front. A neighbor in an adjacent

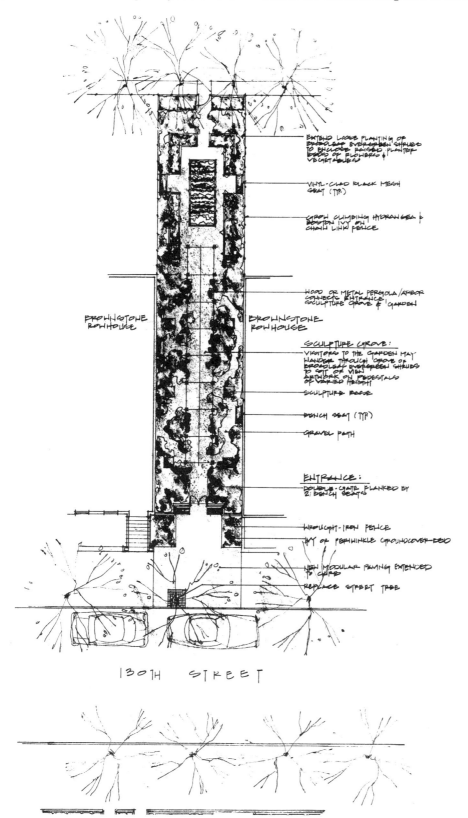

Figure 3-7: *Illustrative, conceptual plan of Astor Row garden in the space vacated between buildings*

building was able to broker an arrangement in which it was agreed to add an iron fence between the community garden and the neighboring garden to the east. The fencing and stabilization of the site are complete. The Abyssinian Development Corporation is raising funds for the arbor, planting, and walk. The planting will be carried out by community residents.

The Astor Row houses feature compact front gardens with beautiful ornamental wood porches that are being restored. ADC and the Landmarks Conservancy are creating limited equity cooperatives in two buildings. Three stories high in the front and four stories in the back, these buildings will house four apartments when totally rehabilitated. The row of them restored will anchor the eastern end of this block with considerable charm and elegance.

Restorations of some old tenement buildings into larger modern apartments is difficult. Many of these old buildings had numerous, poorly arranged apartments with minimal ventilation and light. By renovating several adjacent buildings at once, it has often been possible to restore the facades and exterior ornaments, but create

Figure 3-8: *Front view of Lillian Upshur Houses—the rehabilitation of 66 rental apartments for families and individuals funded through HPD/LISC low-income tax credit program*

THE PUBLIC AND ACADEMIC SECTOR

new apartment layouts that cut through the walls of the buildings. This technique has been particularly successful with some of the narrow, railroad style apartments. Instead of restoring them with the original layout, the adjacent buildings are merged into one new building with a longitudinal hallway. ADC's Abyssinian House is an example of this technique.

ADC is also becoming involved in properties that have existing tenants prior to renovation. On West 138th Street, work is just beginning on a few such buildings where checkerboarding will be used. Checkerboarding is the process of moving existing tenants from floor to floor while renovation or rehabilitation takes place.

Originally working in office space in the Abyssinian Baptist Church on West 138th Street, the Abyssinian Development Corporation finally relocated into a building across the street that they are now rehabilitating, the same one housing the childcare center described earlier. Under the leadership of Ms. Phillips as Executive Director, the ADC has grown to a staff of six for the core efforts and 30 for the total organization, with its own offices and a substantial budget and clout. ADC has directed the rehabilitation of 320 units of housing for low-, moderate-, and middle-income families. ADC continues to emphasize the importance of comprehensive social services. Programs are available for individuals and families in all ADC housing developments and local residents, including children, adolescents, seniors, and family support services. ADC continues to promote community empowerment through organizing members of the community. ADC assists in the establishment of block associations and participates in their activities including block clean-ups, crime preventions programs, meetings, neighborhood improvements, and open space development.

What challenges face ADC in the future? Ms. Phillips feels that "I'm at a crisis; it's time to grow exponentially." However, ADC can't grow so large that she loses touch or gets overextended. She now has professional staff whom she can trust; so that it is not necessary for her to know and be completely in charge of everything that is going on. Answering a question about the specifics of a particular project, she responds, "I don't know, and because I have efficient staff, I don't have to know. It's very refreshing." Still, her heart is set and her goals are clear. For her, community development is "not people coming from the outside to do it to you, or for you, but people doing it with us."

In the end, Ms. Phillips is a communicator or translator. She straddles the world between the banker and the homeless, between nervous residents and expectant newcomers, between any two groups that tend not to communicate with one another, but must in order to develop a thriving community. Her mission is to be in touch with the community and impress on everyone the responsibility of being involved with their own community. It is hard to imagine that she will ever stop.

BOSTON URBAN GARDENS, BUG

PROJECTS: *Various community gardens and related projects*
LOCATION: *Boston, MA*
LANDSCAPE ARCHITECT: *Michael Immel*
BUDGET: *approximately $100,000 each*

Michael Immel, originally from California, worked for many years in the offices of the SWA Group, California. An opportunity arose in 1987 for him to relocate to the Boston office, which needed a person experienced in construction management.

He continued at the SWA Group, Boston, for a number of years in the role of field observer and landscape architect. He worked on a range of large projects including office parks and regional headquarters facilities, often for corporate clients. Seeking a change of pace from this work environment, he sought a position with the Boston Urban Gardeners, of which he was the staff landscape architect for 3-1/2 years. The following interview about his work with BUG was recorded in February, 1994. Mr. Immel practices landscape architecture in New England; he consults to design firms as a specification writer, and as design consultant to community based organizations.

SC: Discuss the design process you used for one of these gardens.

MI: What I would do came out of a need grounded in each neighborhood, and we worked in several neighborhoods throughout Boston. There was no way we could know each neighborhood really well, so I wanted to create a method to get to know the neighborhoods for myself, as well as for the gardening group. With a person from the site as an insider, we would set up meetings with interested people in the neighborhood or the gardeners and talk about redesigning the garden. I developed a set of exercises to demystify and make visible the design process in an effort to make design available to the gardeners.

SC: And what were the exercises?

MI: The first one I called Get to Know Your Neighborhood. What I would do is go get maps of the neighborhood, trying to locate the site roughly in the center, and piece those together. They are big, four-foot-square drawings. I'd set those down and we would talk about the neighborhood in a general way. In my mind, it was divided into two categories of discussion, one was a discussion of the kind of social infrastructure around the site, because the gardens need a social infrastructure to survive. They need patrons and they need partners, organizational as well as individual, in the neighborhood. Those would be graphically located on the plan, the map. Then, also the physical infrastructure of the neighborhood, in terms of its physical details or qualities like trees and plants, for example; is it a neighborhood defined by

wood structures or brick structures? Is it a neighborhood that has a Hispanic presence, and the kind of cultural design details that go with a culture of Hispanic descent, or an American kind of culture with a different kind of appearance and vernacular? So we would go through exercises that identify favorite places in the neighborhood, beautiful places, sacred places, ugly places, and listen to the people around the table define where things were that they liked in the neighborhood, things that they wanted to change, and discuss the neighborhood in a broad way. I did have them define their cognitive maps of the neighborhood: I would ask, "How do you define the neighborhood?" They would draw circles around what they thought was the neighborhood, their boundaries. Then I'd ask, "How do you define the area this garden serves?" and there would be another loop. You get ten people drawing these different loops and it looks kind of interesting and it leads you to a critical zone. We would also draw where people lived, what routes they took to the site. A lot of good stuff came up about people who weren't at the table, who should have been there, business partners, individuals, institutional partners who help with the garden in the long run. People realized neighborhood connections from the mapping exercise. They identified shelters in the areas where they could take their extra produce.

SC: Would you have more than one of these basic beginning type meetings, or one per garden?

MI: One per garden.

SC: For instance, in terms of people who should have been there but weren't, would there be an opportunity for them to show up later?

MI: Yes, there would be other meetings but we wouldn't go through this exercise again. What we would do is bring that plan to every subsequent meeting and put it on the wall. Every meeting, you'd bring everything and put it up. So you'd always have everything visible.

SC: Then it's a real political meeting?

MI: One reason to always have all the products of your design visible at public meetings, at all kinds of meetings, is that you trace the development of the design and the course of the work very publically. It's not a piece of work that's done in the community meeting and taken back to the office and reworked; it's done right there in the meeting. So, politically, it's wise to show your process all the time. You don't want to be towards final presentation and someone comes to a meeting and says, "I wasn't informed, and didn't have a say in what's going on." The result of showing all the process is that you have real strong partners in the community who say, "No, we were here, there was wide notice. Look at our process." The community people deal with that issue, rather than the designer. You need a good design process that complements a good community organizing process.

SC: Talk a little about Boston Urban Garden, or BUG? How it was set up and how is it funded? Did you try to get them to hire a community organizer that would help you with the whole process? Would you talk about both of those?

MI: BUG is part of the national community gardening movement, dating from the early seventies. People saw that there was a lot of vacant land in the cites of America and wanted to do something about it. People began to take these vacant lots and appropriate them, and it would sometimes be as small as a flower pot, sometimes as extensive as a community garden. I call those gardens "found object creations"; they are donated railroad ties, they were kind of this-and-that-kind-of-things put together, often in wonderful and delightful ways. That was the beginning of the community gardening movement. Now, it's an organized national movement, and BUG is certainly one of the leaders in that movement. Over time the community gardening movement and BUG in particular have become more institutionalized, in that it's gone from a guerilla movement of community action, to funding, to a non-profit status with funding, then with government funding, and even government incorporating these programs as policy and as services. People throughout the neighborhood see the value of being able to appropriate a site for positive community use; a use that looks good and produces food for people, and is a safe zone in the neighborhood. So, the whole movement is on that

kind of trajectory, and I see it moving into something not along the lines of a parks department. Because community gardening has too strong a grassroots flavor, it will retain its stance against authority. So it's looking for an identity: it doesn't want to be a parks department, but the community gardening movement can no longer survive as struggling non-profits.

SC: Where does the funding come from? You are saying that each of these gardens can have as much as $100,000 in funding? Where would the funding come from and how would it be secured?

MI: Through the city of Boston there is a development arm called the Public Facilities Department. The Department is similar to a redevelopment agency but it is a city department. There are advocates of landscape architecture on the staff of that agency who saw the value of this community gardening movement, and from the advocacy work of the community gardening movement, programs were developed in this agency to have open space components in city development policy. In Boston we have a thing called the Grass Roots Program, which is part of an Open Space Development Program, much like affordable housing programs or economic development programs, but it is open space. A development department is a good location for such a grant program because it tries to connect open space development with other community development. If it is in the parks department, then it becomes a category of parks, and they seem to operate separately from other community development. The community gardening movement is really a piece of community development, not open space all by itself, but a broader community development issue, and keeps itself close to that movement. The funding that comes to BUG and other groups around the country is from Community Development Block Grants, federal money through the United States Department of Health and Human Services.

SC: Once a site has been selected, the funding is done through the granting agency?

MI: It's from the community, the community says we want this site or it's a symbiotic thing between the city and BUG and other green non-profit groups and the community.

SC: And then the first step is to have this community meeting that you described, or one of the first steps?

MI: As you can imagine with urban redevelopment, there is a lot of background legwork that must be done. Can we get this site? How do we get it? How do we roll it over from a private to a public to non-profit ownership? So there is some pre-development work, you might say. But if it is indeed appropriate for it to be a garden site, there is a process it goes through to discover that.

SC: You said that after some years of experience at BUG you recommended that the organization hire some people within the community to do organizing? How did that work?

MI: I am a landscape designer, I'm not a community organizer. I don't know all the communities and neighborhoods of Boston. And a community organizer is a skilled position. You go out into communities and you knock on doors and talk to people, network with agencies and government and get issues together. Design, I think, is another aspect of the work. If you are capable of doing community organizing, fine, but if you're not trained in it you need someone to partner with. So our strategy was to look to the communities where we would be working for a kind of partnership and identify an organizer in that community who would be paid from the development grant to organize the community around the project site. It could be someone in Charlestown or Roxbury, in Brighton or the South End. It's a different kind of person, different culture, different class, in every community. My argument was that it would be very hard to have one centralized organizer do all that, because our cities are very diverse and to be able to relate to an Italian gardening community or an Hispanic one, an African American one, an Irish one, would test anybody. Plus there is great value of having somebody from the neighborhood and being able to pay them. I thought that was important.

SC: So you started doing that? Let's jump ahead. You've had this meeting where you map out the neighborhood. You've broken the ice and you start the plans. How does the process work? What would happen gradually that you would go from having that meeting to going to the site, to going ahead with the development of a plan, and finally building it?

MI: In the first phase, you "get to know your neighborhood." Then, the next one, we would "Measure The Site." I would have a survey done of the area, but the survey wasn't very useful to community people. What we would do is set a table up on site with the survey and a piece of trace over the top of it, and with 100-foot tapes and community people, we would map the site in whatever way it was looking at the time. If it was a garden, we would measure all the plots and paths, the fences and describe everything. If it hadn't been developed, we'd try to describe it as best we could, by measuring things, calling out the names of things, and I think that's always a good exercise to go through. Unfortunately, landscape architects don't get to go to their sites enough to smell them and really experience them in a physical way. The mapping really gave the gardening constituency a chance to transfer their knowledge of the site to paper, rather than it being given to them from a survey or by me. It also validated their understanding and knowledge of the place, and informed me as a designer a great deal. At the same time, they began to learn to transfer scale to the paper, and to begin to see what a plan did and how it worked; maybe to develop a comfort level with manipulating a plan. Then we'd frequently sit down, there'd be food involved, and chat about, well, what do you want to change? What do you want to do? And have informal discussions about programming and taste and design, stuff like that. It was quite interesting, that is, when people see that their garden pathways were two feet wide, yet they would be asking for six-foot-wide paths in a meeting without the mapping exercise. Measuring a site gave them useful experience to size and scale changes, as well as garden elements.

SC: At the end of this second phase, measuring the site, you would have the basics of a site analysis and the map of the site that you would use for coming up with a design?

MI: Then we'd start programming. And the programming happens throughout the contacts with clients. Ideas would come up a lot. And we'd talk about wish lists, brainstorming, mostly just what do you want to do? What do you see, and there'd be a lot of ideas already out there. We'd write those down and list them, and go through exercises like collapsing the list and prioritizing the list. So we had three products now, get to know your neighbor, measuring the site, and a brainstorm list or an articulated program.

The next phase was to put the program on the site. We'd take these words and try to transform them into a diagram with respect to the site. What are the goals? Is the goal to have more gardening space, to reduce the number of paths, to improve garden soil? "We want a secure fence, we need to make it safer, we want fruit trees, we want a better path, we want a structure to shield the summer rain." So all those things would come up and we would start locating them on the site with this bubble diagram. People would be interested in that somewhat, rarely would people pick up pencils and pens and draw. They really want me to do

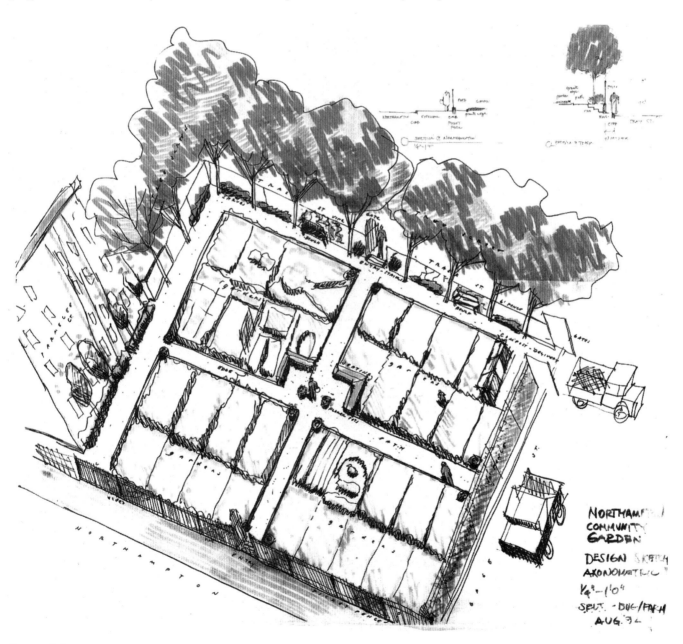

Figure 3-9: *Illustrative sketch of Northampton Community Garden*

that, they don't usually feel comfortable doing that. Frequently we'd be around tables doing that kind of thing with trace, and then there may be a request after that for me to go and take this rough diagram or that rough diagram and turn it into a plan.

Then I would go back and do that at the office, create a plan, inviting anybody who wanted to come. Sometimes clients would come, or a representative, or someone from the funding agency and work with me on that level of work. And we'd come back with a couple of alternatives, with budgets attached to them and the group would tend to pick one or the other and there'd be a budget associated with it and probably they'd have to pick priorities and line items out of the budget, because they had to make some decisions about certain things that always had cost implications so the budget would be right there next to the alternative. We would work that out, and once that was resolved, that was the end of the design, and the request at that time was that the group should appoint one person to act as liaison to the design/build group to work any subsequent issues out, because it becomes too cumbersome to continue with the community meetings. That was the design process.

SC: Then the building of the garden would start?

MI: Right, and we often had an intern on board, maybe a student at a local art school who would build our models, or sometimes this would be done in the context of hiring neighborhood kids for summer work.

SC: Would you often build a model of the whole garden?

MI: Yes. Sometimes an existing conditions model and then the new one. That's when I had an intern for a year, an art student. He had to tackle scale for the first time. He did six or seven cardboard models. People like the models. I thought they would be requisite to understanding the site but they weren't that important, in my estimation, to the people. Some of them read really well, some of them didn't. One model we did of a school, a grammar school was a big success. Then we go into the build phase, which was design/build.

SC: By then, you had a standard vocabulary of details that had to be diagrammed: fencing, places to get out of the rain, edgings, planting, soil additives. Could you talk about those?

MI: We have two projects in a historic district in Boston and we knew we would be required to have design review by the historical commission. And we knew that it was going to cost more than usual, because we would be required to have steel picket fencing, which is typical for that area, as well as granite and brick. In deciding what kind of fence to use, we used the Get to Know Your Neighbor process, and took a tour of the neighborhood of the places people liked. That is an ancillary part of getting to know your neighborhood; you go on a neighborhood walk for those who are interested enough to do it. And someone from the group brought a camera and we would go out and take pictures of all the fences in the neighborhood and what people liked and so on. Security was a big issue. Gardeners

Figure 3-10: *The new fence harmonizes with the existing fence typical of the South End Historic District. This design is similar to the fencing used in the rail corridor that used to go through the District. (Photo by Michael Immel)*

would say, "We want a six-foot fence." Then we'd go out and see it in person and people would say, "Oh, we can deal with a five-foot fence." Once they get out there and realize that a six-footer is over their heads, they don't like it. I thought it was really important that people have a visual experience of the design details, rather than showing slides or my sketches. In the neighborhood there are 10–15 different kinds of fences. Then, we'd go stand next to them and feel them. It also validates their neighborhoods, because a lot of these projects are done in poor neighborhoods or neighborhoods in transition, and people are feeling, you know, things aren't so great. To be able to walk around and validate that there are good things here, there are some quality things, well, I thought that would be useful to do. So the group came up with the idea that they had found some pieces of fencing on an old site and they wanted to do something along the lines of these found pieces of fencing. It happened that these pieces of fencing came from the railroad corridor that came through the district, the southwest corridor and is typical of railroad fencing throughout the Northeast, a strap-and-rivet kind of thing. So we adapted that to the steel picket fence scheme for the site, along with a kind of faux brownstone curb along the edge; with granite posts, and inscriptions written in the granite that identify the garden and local community trust that owns the garden.

SC: And the faux granite curb might be concrete?

MI: Right.

SC: You said that the concrete was tinted to satisfy the Boston Historical Commission?

MI: The Historical Commission wanted granite, which is a typical detail along the stoops of all the houses in the neighborhood. We couldn't afford granite so we offered tinted concrete to look like brownstone, which is also part of what's in the

neighborhood and the commission accepted that.

SC: You said you were able to have the fences executed by a minority firm from the neighborhoods?

MI: Right. Another attitude of BUG is being a part of community development and that means keeping the money in the community. It was important to advocate for money to get into poor neighborhoods and be spent on the local people who live and work there; rather than have outsiders come in and take the money out. So we got connected with some contractors in the neighborhood and had them collaborate on the design development of the fence. Just

Figure 3-11: *The general vocabulary of the community garden: the fence, brick sidewalk, integrally colored concrete curb (to simulate the brownstone used in the District), a gazebo, and garden plots (Photo by Michael Immel)*

like you would in a regular firm, you'd have a general idea for some kind of item and start collaborating with people in the building trades and see if it is possible. We talked about structure and design and all that sort of thing. They were a big help throughout the whole process. We were pleased to have them on board to build it. I think it added immeasurably to our credibility and made us feel good, made everybody who was doing the work feel good. Not to say that it was a totally rosy picture. I think we built three or four fences. They are glamorous projects for these contractors and they liked them a lot, and we are quite proud of them.

SC: You said that their work even improved over the course of the project?

MI: We worked with them initially three years ago and they had just barely begun to start their business, and they were working out of our shop in the winter under really tough conditions. Now, three years later they have their own shop. It's an immaculate place. They have hired several people and they are really coming along in terms of a business. The quality of their work is better. They are building much more difficult projects now than the first ones they built. We changed the design for the first ones they built, since curvilinear designs in fencing weren't appropriate for them and we had to change them.

SC: These fences are five feet high?

MI: I call the barrier five feet, that includes the curb that the fence sits on so, over-all its probably five, four foot six of actual steel with a gap at the bottom.

SC: Talk about the evolution to granite curbing for inside the planting beds.

MI: Remember, historically, community gardens are these found object creations, guerrilla gardens. People found construction materials in the neighborhood and made gardens with them. They could be quite delightful at times, also they were kind of makeshift; they weren't necessarily on stable ground, and some of the materials looked unsightly. People outside the community garden group wanted the gardens to look better. Politically and in terms of community development, grants were given to build gardens.

After going through the design process with the people and through different options for materials, it was clear that people wanted edges to define pathways as different from garden areas. When we started looking at materials, we looked at concrete, pre-

Figure 3-12: *The community garden fits into the context of the neighborhood. (Photo by Michael Immel)*

Figure 3-13: *The Cape Cod berm (curb) is used as an edging to the interior walks. The granite slabs serve as informal benches, but are not so obvious as to attract too much attention from those who typically would not use the garden. (Photo by Michael Immel)*

cast concrete, wood, granite, steel edges. People gravitated toward granite as the solution. We found a cheap ready-made granite product here called Cape Cod Berm, it's a three-and-a-half- by twelve-and-a-half-inch section. It's a common item in all the quarries and runs about six dollars a running foot, delivered to the site. It is just dug into the ground directly without footings, rock or anything. After setting, it has about a three-inch reveal, about nine inches into the ground, with a dry joint that gets buttered.

The granite curbs go in with a stone dust path, with gardens on the other side. These curbs go around a big area. The gardeners divide up their own plots; they range from ten by twelve feet, to ten by fifteen. The gardeners seemed pleased with them. The funding agency loved them. They certainly fit into the Boston vernacular, in terms of being a regional material and appropriate for the neighborhoods of the city. We think it's a real stable material, especially in the direction community gardens are headed towards permanence;

moving away from the found object situation to something permanent. Not only are gardens becoming more permanent physically, but now they are permanent open space, deeded sites that are owned by community land trusts. Administratively, also, gardens are on a path of institutional vision, though a community based level.

SC: What about the soil preparation?

MI: Redevelopment in cities, especially the older cities, faces certain difficulties. Urban soils are anybody's guess as to what they are. Lots of sites where gardens are, were building sites. These sites weren't necessarily cleaned up properly when the buildings were taken down. Gardeners over the years have been faced with lots of debris problems in the soil. The most difficult problem is lead in the soil, which can be a toxic problem. Debris clean-up doesn't address that. There is always soil testing for lead, because the paint off the houses has created some toxic levels in the soil. Kids play in the soil and air-borne lead dust can create problems for youngsters.

Figure 3-14: *A view through the fence shows a water source with a granite slab as a bench. Gardeners stake separate garden plots in different ways as they see fit. (Photo by Michael Immel)*

debris all the time. At the sites we would typically haul off 80 to 100 yards of brick, stone, wood, and metal, which is a lot for an urban site of 10,000 square feet. Then we'd have to end up importing some soil. Certainly not as much as hauling off a whole site. We found a machine out in the trades that is just a sifting machine with a one-inch screen. A tractor pushes all the soil into a big hill and then loads it into the machine and all the clean stuff comes out the other side, and on one side is all the debris. Then you just regrade the site. It was well received by the gardeners. They are battling with things no larger than an inch, which can be a problem. If you are dealing with seedlings, it's a problem. And you used to see at the old gardens that there were bricks and rocks and debris that lined the garden everywhere. So maybe this is one way of taking care of that complaint.

SC: What about the benches?

MI: At one design meeting I almost had two people come to blows over whether we should put a bench on the site or not. It's a real touchy problem I think everywhere. You know William Whyte addresses it in his plaza studies (*The Social Life of Small Urban Spaces*). Some people think that benches are going to attract undesirables. But we had these big chunks of granite that were worn soft, so we used them as benches. These benches were strategically placed on-site so people could take a break and sit down, after gardening and allow for the opportunity to socialize. People accepted granite benches much more readily than any other material that looked like a real bench that said "bench" from the street. So if you walk by on the street it doesn't say, "come and sit on me," as much as people understand a bench to do. And strangely enough these are real comfortable, we get them from the quarry and knock off the hard edges; they are fairly cheap and they are comfortable. And they fit in with the rest of the scheme with the granite curbing and the stone dust paving and they are nat-

SC: As well as growing edible produce.

MI: Right. Especially the leafy vegetables. In fruit trees, the lead doesn't seem to move that far into the plant, but lettuce and leafy things are a problem. And the dust and playing in it is a real problem. In terms of the debris, what we thought we would do is, dig down about eighteen inches, which is a rough depth we thought someone might dig down if they were gardening, you know, double-digging or something when gardeners turn over the soil, and sift the top eighteen inches of the site, the whole site. That would get rid of the debris and allow us a fairly clean site for us to put our minor site improvements on without having to run into

Figure 3-15: *The water source becomes a common gathering spot in the garden. (Photo by Michael Immel)*

ural materials that are, of course, permanent. We are real happy with them and certainly the gardeners like them a lot and certainly the funding agency does as well.

SC: Well, what about the stone dust path?

MI: We're lucky in Boston that we have a quarry, a stone products quarry. It has a reddish product of stone, everything from two-inch rock to stone dust. So we used that for all the pavements. It's a real soft, earthy look, when it dries out it dries to a kind of powdery, lavender color, so it brings some color into the site that contrasts nicely with the greenery. It also creates a firm enough finish for physically challenged people, and it's very inexpensive. It's just a four-inch section of stone dust over compacted earth. We are real happy with it. It allows water to penetrate without destroying it, and we think it compacts great. It looks beautiful, and we're just real happy with it as surfacing for pathways.

SC: And the basic infrastructure for each garden, you told me a little about that, that it includes six water outlets that you tend to scatter wherever you can?

MI: The garden needs water and irrigation. The found garden projects had no water, or guerrilla water, people taking it from taps without the authorities knowing. The Boston Sewer and Water Commission will allow us six outlets per site. We try to distribute those so everyone has equal access to water. Sites for hose bibs are social points in terms of design, just as where pathways take you to or maybe a bench or a tree, it is a natural zone where people would connect. Negotiating who is going to use the water next, who is going to roll up the hose and all that sort of thing. So water is certainly a real basic piece of the program.

The site preparation is also critical; fencing is a great big issue in community gardening, security, and also the fence is a basic piece of vocabulary in the city in terms of street side. Then pathways, path edges, then the gardens themselves.

SC: And you're saying generally, that once the main paths and the water sources are located you recommend that the gardeners themselves subdivide the space at a regular, comfortable rhythm, and put up alot of additional barriers or enclosures.

MI: Right. Put the granite curbs up, and you know the granite curbs may be fifty by fifty, but inside that area the gardeners decide how they break things up. That depends on the garden constituency at the time, how many gardeners there are, what sort of horticultural styles, botanical approaches people take, and it gives them some freedom rather than having it all divided up and it becomes a cumbersome bunch of hardware out there. My inclination as a designer was to keep it as simple

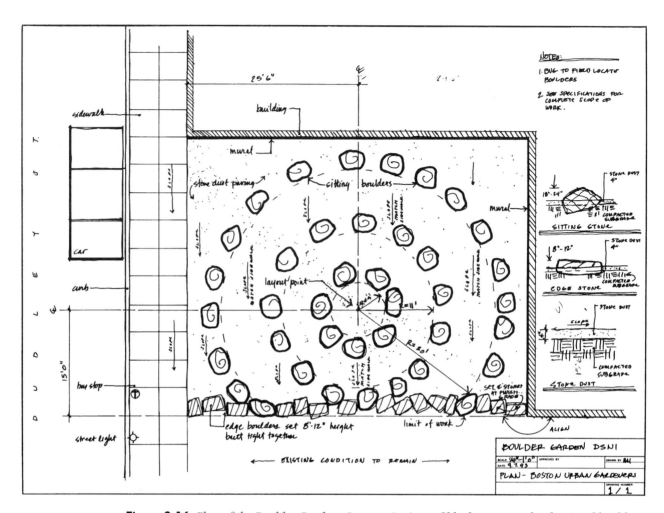

Figure 3-16: *Plan of the Boulder Garden: Concentric rings of black, green and red painted boulders set in a field of purple stone dust are the foil for a community mural*

as possible, make the materials permanent, and as much as possible let the gardeners have control over the shape.

SC: Lets go look at the drawings. Tell me the history of this and what you did.

MI: This we call the Boulder Garden, for Dudley Street Neighborhood Initiative, which is one of the strongest community based development organizations in the nation. They have unusual power of "eminent domain," which is rare for community based development organization to have. They have the ability in their target community area to actually take land through a legal procedure, that is real unusual. They've approached their community development from a human side first. It's like the human thing they look at first, then the physical, not just going and putting buildings up. So they've got a lot of process about that, and for a couple of years, BUG has tried to work with them on open

spaces; just in the last year or so we've started doing some projects together. One of the first ones we did was a quick vacant lot rescue at a site featuring a mural on two sides of a grocery store on Dudley St., the main street of the neighborhood.

SC: It's a big mural, 50 feet long on one side by about 30 feet on the other.

MI: Yeah, its real big. It's about fifteen, twenty feet high. And it was designed by a real good artist. There are pictures of heroes in the neighborhood, such as women who have run day care centers in the neighborhood for years and Reggie Lewis, the Celtic basketball player who died suddenly. He died during the development process of this mural and the kids painted his jersey up there. So lots of local fame and really strong, vibrant colors, and when they had finished the mural they asked us, "Mike, there's just this ugly vacant lot at the mural, what shall we do there?" And so my intern for the sum-

Figure 3-17: *The Boulder Garden (Photo by Michael Immel)*

mer, Jenny Cheng, and I decided that what it needed was a plaza program to complement the mural. Plantings weren't a possibility because of maintenance and cost and that it needed some kind of pavement solution.

A couple of blocks away we were developing interim use of two large community center sites for the same agency and moving these boulders around that are typically used to keep people from dumping on vacant land, so we thought what we'd do is take these boulders and put them on the site in some pattern along with that purple stone dust paving. So the solution was to grade the site, put some pattern of boulders out and then put the colorful paving down. And then get the muralist to come in and paint the rocks in one or two colors that came out of the mural. So we worked on the scheme and Jenny and I came to the conclusion that we needed some sort of geometric form because the site was so small and the type of boulder was unknown so we couldn't control that so we needed a simple kind of solution. We came up with concentric rings of boulders, with a kind of sunken boulder edge over here, be-

cause this is a big vacant lot where trucks turn around for delivery to the grocery. And there is a bus stop here. What we have now is a really colorful mural with this program of a kind of purplish reddish field with boulders three foot plus or minus in three concentric rings that are painted the three nubian colors that were included in the mural: red, black, and green.

SC: You said Nubian?

MI: They're African colors: red, green and black. Those are strong colors, lots of black in the mural, and they come out of the mural and work on the site. It's a tilted plane. Its used for hanging out for the bus stop, the boulders can be used for sitting, kids play on it, they jump from one to the other, it's a soft surface, and we think it's real successful. It was done for four thousand dollars total, hired, all the work done by a local, minority, earth-moving contractor.

SC: What kind of paint do they use to paint these boulders?

MI: Waterproof latex. No special thing, and they did that on their own. What kind of stone do you think this is? Mostly granite, some big puddingstone, which is a regional stone, looks like aggregate through the matrix. Olmsted used puddingstone in his buildings and projects and bridges: typical stone of the region and you'll find big chunks of it. I think it's one of the kind of fun things you can do when you when you are a designer who is perceived to be an insider in the community, not an outsider. I feel a great deal of trust was given to me to come up with a design without a process. They trusted us enough to be aware of where people were at and what people's needs were. Jenny and I actually drew this up on a found piece of paper with a few crayons, then took it to them in their office and presented it to them on the spot at their lunch where they have lunch from different cultures. We presented and they said, "Yeah, let's do it." And then we just went ahead and did it. It was a lot of fun, and Jenny, being an intern for the summer, was set up to do certain projects, and when they got delayed, it was great to see something get done so quickly from start to finish. So it's satisfying for the intern to see how that happens.

It was a lot of fun. I liked the Boulder Garden because it's not a garden. It also made the people in the city real nervous because some of them felt that painting the rocks was a vulgar thing. But it's been very successful.

CENTRAL PARK CONSERVANCY

New York City

Two projects are presented here; the first, the Harlem Meer, was executed primarily in-house by the Conservancy's versatile design/build/maintenance staff. The second, the reconstruction of the Concert Ground, was done by a team of consultants.

PROJECT: *The Harlem Meer*
LOCATION: *Central Park, New York City*
LANDSCAPE ARCHITECT: *Central Park Conservancy*
CONSULTING ENGINEERS: *Weidlinger Associates (NYC) structural for Dana Discovery Center, Ebasco Services Inc. (NYC) for the site*
CONSULTING ARCHITECTS: *Buttrick White and Burtis (NYC)*
DATE: *1993*
CONSTRUCTION COST: *$8.55 million (1.8 million—Dana Center; 2.9 million—dredging; 3.3 million—landscape construction; 0.3 million—planting; 0.25 million—playgrounds)*

The Central Park Conservancy was founded as a not-for-profit organization in 1980 "to help restore Central Park. Working in conjunction with the New York City Department of Parks and Recreation (NYCDPR), the Conservancy funds and carries out projects which are beyond the means of available public funds, but nevertheless, provide restoration, maintenance, and security necessary for the Park's survival. The Conservancy supports its work through contributions from corporations, foundations and individuals." Its staff includes 15 landscape architects.

In 1985 the Conservancy published *Rebuilding Central Park: A Management and Restoration Plan*. Under the direction of Elizabeth Barlow, then the Central Park Administrator, a team of landscape architects and other professionals including primarily Marianne Cramer, Judith Heintz, Bruce Kelly, Phillip N. Winslow, and Pamela Tice carried out a three-year planning study. Their recommendations are carefully summarized in the text of the report which was written by Ms. Barlow and John Berendt. Remarkable for its breadth and thoroughness, the report sets management and restoration goals and principles for the entire park, and then identifies specific priorities for restoration within each of the 21 precincts of the park. In addition, three distinct historically named sites, the Great Hill, the Ravine, and the rugged landscape surrounding the Blockhouse, are treated separately in the report. In order to "establish an identity for the woodlands as places with a unique set of characteristics, problems, and opportunities," Marianne Cramer and Leslie Sauer of Andropogon Associates, a consultant to the Conservancy, coined the phrase North Woods to apply collectively to this urban woodland of 90 acres in the northern portion of the park. Immediately east of the North Woods is the Harlem Meer.

Since the master plan for the restoration of the park was adopted in 1982, a great deal of improvements have been constructed. During the early 1980s, the Conservancy customarily hired private consultants to design major restorations in the park. For example, Bruce Kelly/David Varnell designed the Shakespeare Garden. The conceptual design for the reconstruction of the Concert Ground was done by Phillip N. Winslow. The construction documents were developed by Clarke + Rapuano, Inc. and finalized by the Conservancy, with construction inspections by the consultant in response to requests from the Conservancy's on-site construction supervisor. In contrast, by the late 1980s Tim Marshall, the Deputy Administrator of Central Park, had organized the Conservancy's staff into a design/build/maintenance operation in which most projects were done in-house. Two examples are the restorations of the North Woods and Harlem Meer. The North Woods project was directed by Marianne Cramer, the Central Park planner. The Harlem Meer project was one of the first done in-house, and was directed by Laura Starr, Chief of Design for the Conservancy. She was assisted by staff landscape architects Patricia McCobb and Jeff Poor, Douglas Blonsky, the Chief of Construction and Preservation, and landscape designer Chris Nolan.

Ms. Starr joined the Conservancy in 1985 and has been Chief of Design since 1990. Following a liberal arts degree with a major in architecture from Washington University in St. Louis, she earned a MLA from the University of Pennsylvania in 1984. After working in architecture a few years

Figure 3-18: *The cascade at Glen Span Arch in the North Woods is one of several restoration projects already completed there (Photo by Sara Cedar Miller)*

The Upper Park
Central Park, New York City

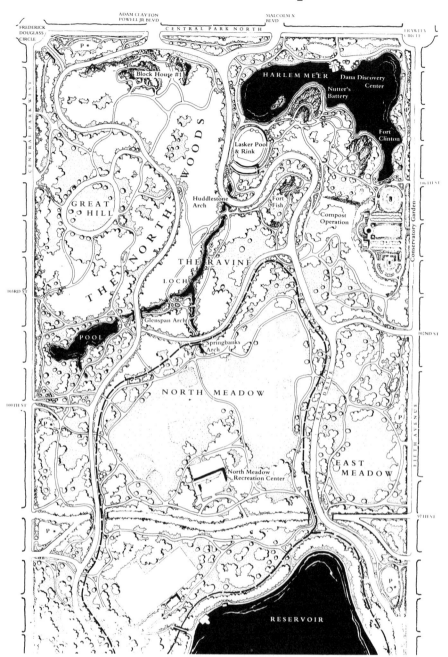

Figure 3-19: *Plan, the upper park. The Harlem Meer is in the northeast corner of the park, adjacent to The North Woods*

for a firm that specialized in restorations, she found that "the need for well-designed open spaces greatly exceeded the need for buildings." She developed an interest in the land: how it is allocated, manipulated, and used; as well as where buildings should be and how infrastructure systems should be handled within open space systems. These specific interests eventually led her to the

Conservancy and its work with Central Park, one of the most highly manipulated and well used pieces of land in the country.

Located in the northeastern corner of the park, the Harlem Meer is an 11-acre waterbody defining the lowest point of the park. (See Figure C-28). Its boundaries are Central Park North on the north and Fifth Avenue on the east; these two streets intersect to form Frawley Circle, at the northeast corner of Central Park. The Meer's boundary on the south is the Conservatory Garden and on the west is the eastern edge of the North Woods. The original purpose of the Meer was as a free-form water body with an informal soft edge in a picturesque landscape. In the mid-nineteenth century when Olmsted and Vaux designed the park, the city had yet to develop around the park, so that few people visited the site of the Meer. The Meer was designed as a very rustic landscape, without the facilities that were included in the more heavily trafficked southern end of Central Park.

In the 1940s in response to the greatly increased use of the northern end of the park, Robert Moses, then the City's Parks Commissioner, drastically altered the soft shoreline of the Meer by replacing it with a thick concrete wall adjacent to a wide asphalt path. Since there was a need for facilities, in the 1940s he added a boat house and restaurant along the northern shore and two characteristically oval-shaped playgrounds on the northern and eastern edges of the Meer. In 1966, he directed the construction of the Lasker Pool and Ice Skating Rink by the southwestern shore. Built in the middle of a major drainage corridor, the rink immediately had seepage problems. Its construction required the five-foot culverting of the once picturesque stream from the Loch that fed the Meer, thus severing the most important visual and physical link between the Meer and the North Woods. The Lasker development reduced the size of the Meer from 14 acres to 11. Although all of these amenities were popular, they destroyed the pastoral character of the site and degraded its environment.

Throughout the 1970s as Central Park's budget shrank in response to the city's severe fiscal crisis, maintenance became more lax. By the early 1990s, when the Conservancy undertook its restoration, the Meer was badly degraded. The water was eutrophic and covered by a mat of algae over its entire surface every summer. In the summer of 1987 the mechanical removal of surface weeds was required on three occasions. The 110th Street Boathouse was severely vandalized, particularly over

the last decade, when there was no concessionaire or management of any kind. The entire area was poorly used and often abandoned, and had become a haven for drug dealers. The local community avoided the site as unpleasant and dangerous. The walks and edges of the water were badly deteriorated. The stones capping the concrete wall had been dislocated, the banks were littered with broken pavement and debris. Engineers calculated that as a result of its reduced size and the hard perimeter edge, the Meer had the capacity to absorb only a ten-year storm. The pedestrian paths were crumbling and the surrounding landscape had lost much of its vegetative cover.

The rehabilitation of the Meer required the dredging of its approximately 11 acres and the removal of approximately 1/2 mile of the concrete retaining walls and the pavements along the edge of the water. The design team reevaluated what visitor services were needed. The program was expanded to include a new visitor center and adjacent terrace on the north side of the Meer and an island for wildlife in the southwest portion of the lake. Corrective action was planned to stabilize eroding banks to prevent future siltation of the lake. Planting was desired which would provide the visual delight and horticultural variety of Olmsted's original design, and function to provide wildlife habitat and shoreline stabilization while withstanding the stresses caused

Figure 3-20: *Before the reconstruction, the Meer was surrounded by a paved edge (Photo by Sara Cedar Miller)*

by the anticipated increase in the number of visitors.

Borings of the lake revealed an intact clay layer that held water in the lake. An eight-inch sand layer protected the clay. Rather than dredge the lake, the design team decided to drain the lake and excavate the sediment. Using seine nets, the Parks Department rounded up the fish and relocated them to different water bodies within the park. The Meer was then drained and allowed to dry. Leaving the clay and sand layers intact, bulldozers excavated approximately 34,000 cubic yards of deposited materials and hauled them off site. Since the demolition of the perimeter walls was planned, a method to prevent leakage at the edges of the lake was required. A new

Claymax™ (bentonite) liner was installed with one edge meeting the existing clay bottom of the Meer and the other fastened to the base of the edge treatments. When the excavation and restoration process was completed, the average water depth in the restored lake was six feet.

Knowing that the site was on the doorstep of a populous community, the design team faced the challenge of how to restore the naturalistic edge of the previous century in a sinuous form that could accept intense use, yet be stable and flexible. Severe siltation from the steep, eroded slopes to the west had created mud flats. The Meer drains the largest watershed in the park, almost 200 acres, including the North Woods.

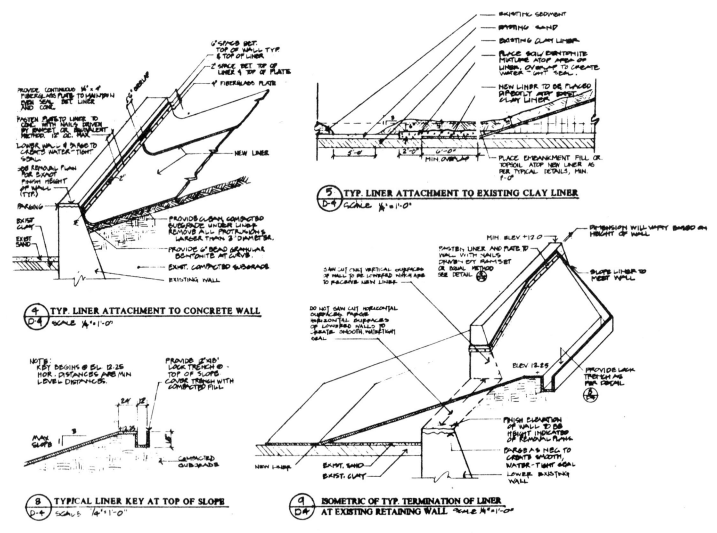

Figure 3-21: *Construction details, showing the installation of the Claymax liner and different attachments of the liner to the edge of the Meer*

In general, the tops of existing walls were cut off to a stable elevation below finish grade. In some locations, where possible, substantial portions of the existing walls were removed; in other locations, only the capstones were removed, and these were salvaged for reuse. Many of the shoreline details use a bentonite mixture or Claymax™ liner as a waterproof extension of the existing clay layer. The Claymax™ liner was placed to overlap the edge of the existing clay layer and firmly anchored either to the faces of new wall construction or to a specially constructed key. A minimum of twelve inches of cover is maintained over the Claymax™. Then a structural fill embankment at a slope no steeper than 3:1 was placed over the location of the old wall and the Claymax™. The top of the embankment transitions to meet the new finish grade which dovetails to existing grade.

At most locations along the perimeter of the Meer, a naturalistic shoreline is created through the placement of skillfully sculpted fill embankments, the artful clustering of boulders, and appropriate plantings. Four types of boulder treatment occur. In some locations boulders are laid flat as stepping stones along the shoreline. These boulders are placed so that only the top face is exposed. Another method of boulder treatment is for stabilization, in which the front face and no more than 1/4 the height of the top face is exposed. These boulders help to prevent re-erosion into the Meer as a result of fluctuating water levels and wave action. In a third method, boulders are clustered in ornamental groupings to create a visually appealing, continuous rocky shoreline. Two thirds of each boulder are buried, leaving the irregular top third obtruding from the ground in a naturalistic manner. A final boulder treatment is installation in a linear manner as a gutter to direct storm drainage. Adjacent to walks, these boulders were placed in compacted stone screenings in a swale with a minimum gradient of two percent to assure positive drainage.

The design team carefully tested different arrangements and sizes of boulders in the field. During construction, the boulders were placed under the direction of the field engineer and landscape architect. A schedule of sizes and quantities for each type of boulder treatment was developed to give the contractor a clear prescription for bidding and installing these materials. For example, four sizes of boulders were required, based on the volume of the stones in cubic feet with the smallest dimension being twelve inches.

Where the gradient at the lake's edge was steeper, dry laid stone walls were built into the embankment fills in order to stabilize the slope in a naturalistic way. Special care was

Figure 3-22: *Detail showing shoreline treatments*

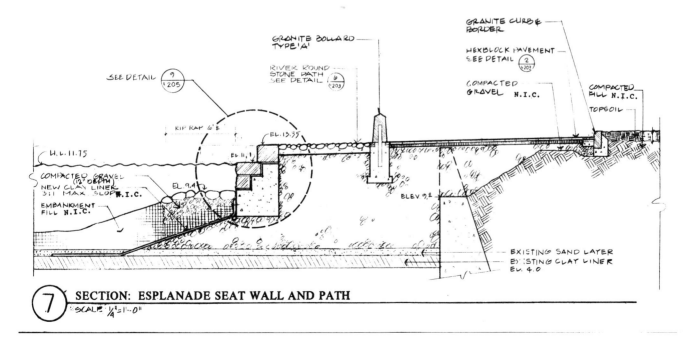

SECTION: ESPLANADE SEAT WALL AND PATH

Figure 3-23: *Historic photograph of 1873 showing the view towards Fort Clinton from the eastern edge of the Meer (Central Park Conservancy)*

Frawley Circle and may wish to walk around the entire lake. Other visitors walk northwards from the Conservatory Gardens or eastward from the North Woods. The most important area to stabilize was at the base of the steep bluffs at the south shore of the Meer. Historically, there was not a path, but one was needed to accommodate people who would walk around the lake. The design team developed a detail for a path that would be low-key and dissolve into the landscape, invisible from the other side of the Meer. A reinforced soft surface path was designed with a concrete grid block paver. Blended stone screenings are placed over the grid blocks, which in turn rest on a gravel sub-base and a layer of sand. The gravel sub-base acts as a detention reservoir to hold run-off, filter it, and allow it to percolate slowly into the ground and into the Meer.

The entrance from Frawley Circle uses the park vocabulary of Hastings hexagonal block pavers and granite block pavers in a particularly rich treatment. At the main entrance to the Meer, granite threshold stones, cut radially to follow the curve of the Circle, announce the entry. A basketweave pattern of granite blocks contrasts to squares of herringbone patterns that appear as accents.

From the north end of the Conservatory Garden, the visitor is drawn towards the arrival space at the southernmost shoreline of the Meer. A broad set of bluestone stairs widens and flares as they approach the edge of the water. Two intermediate landings accentuate the effect of a stately progression towards the water. The lower treads disappear below the surface of the Meer and draw the visitor's view. The lowest sets of bluestone treads are 4-1/2 inches thick on a 1/2-inch mortar setting bed and 20 inches wide. Each adjacent tread over-

exercised near large existing trees to avoid cuts or fills for the lake edge restoration. In some cases near trees, the existing concrete walls were left in place and concealed with earth, a process which prevented cutting or filling over major tree roots. Within the dripline of specimen trees along the shoreline, the finish grade, whether topsoil or amended pond sediment, does not exceed existing grade by more than four inches. Where existing trees were not impacted, a twelve-inch thick layer of pond sediment, amended with standard horticultural materials, was consistently used as the top layer of the fill embankment at the water's edge and other locations where planting was to be established.

A great deal of pedestrian traffic occurs at the Meer. People enter the park from

Figure 3-24: *The same view after reconstruction. Notice the boulder treatment. (Photo by Sara Cedar Miller)*

Figure 3-25: *The south shore steps under construction (Photo by Sara Cedar Miller, Central Park Conservancy)*

laps the following one 2 inches, creating steps with 18-inch treads and 5-inch risers. The stairs begin about 17 feet wide and flare to 45 feet in width at the water's edge. The upper sets of treads also create steps 5 inches high, but the treads are constructed of a full size bluestone tread 2-1/2 inches thick stacked on top of another 2-1/2-inch bluestone only 5 inches wide that is notched into the reinforced concrete footing. Cheek walls veneered with split-faced schist with a bluestone capstone parallel the two sides of the steps. Triangular bluestone capstones rest atop stone piers accenting the top of the last run of steps.

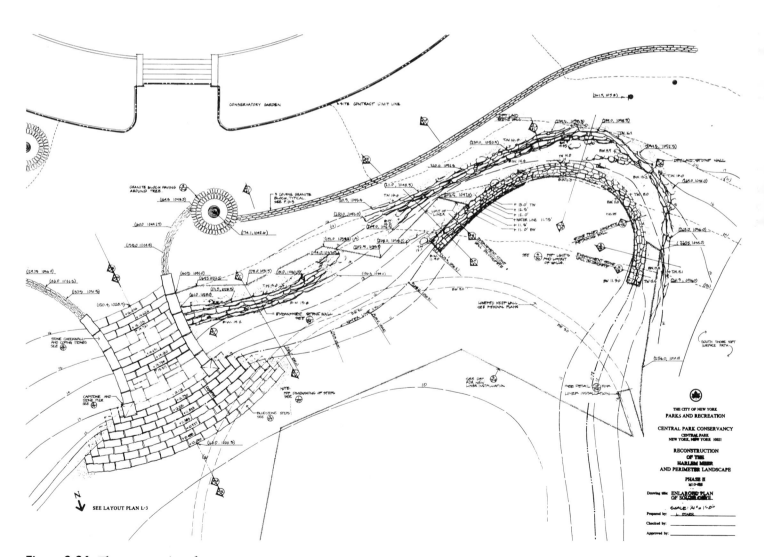

Figure 3-26: *The construction plan*

Figure 3-27: *The south shore after construction and planting (Photo by Sara Cedar Miller)*

A similar but less formal treatment of steps occurs at the northern shoreline of the Harlem Meer. The continually curving edge to the Meer is constructed of granite coping stones approximately 12 inches square set on a concrete footing. Adjacent and flush with the coping is a 5-foot-wide band of pavement consisting of riverrounds set in concrete that leads to a set of three granite steps, constructed of three 6-inch risers and 14-inch treads. The broad arc of stone steps exactly parallels the alignment of the coping of the wall. Farther away from the building the steps are broader, 22-inch-wide slabs of Deer Isle granite, forming a seatwall that dovetails with the granite coping stones so that visitors may sit on the granite and put their feet into the water.

At the northern edge of the lake is the new visitor center, the Charles A. Dana Discovery Center and Lila Wallace–Reader's Digest Terrace. The Fragile Forest, the interactive exhibit inside the building, gives visitors a hands-on introduction to the history and ecology of the entire 90-acre North Woods area, including the Harlem Meer. Other changing exhibits will be developed about themes relating to the history and ecology of the park.

A bluestone terrace provides a gathering place for visitors prior to their entering the building or a place to sit and enjoy the views of the Meer and the sights of people fishing and strolling. Although the terrace is only about 10,000 square feet, it is gracefully subdivided into several different spaces, each defined by different pavements. Equally spaced granite bollards accent the entrances to the terrace and separate it from the perimeter walk of hexagonal asphalt block pavers. A striking element is a bronze and granite compass plaque, a handsome sculpture, set in the center of a circular bluestone pattern, 40 feet in diameter, inside the main entrance to the terrace. Inside a 24-inch-wide circular granite border, concentric rows of bluestone are cut radially to emphasize the circle. This pattern contrasts to the hexagonal block asphalt pavers that are used on the exterior walk leading around the Meer and to the random irregular pattern of bluestone that is used in adjacent areas of the terrace nearer the Meer. Dry laid stone retaining walls hold back mounded landforms on either side of the circle. Planted with native shrubs and large shade trees, the effect of these areas is to squeeze the view, creating an intimate entrance into the terrace, which opens up after one passes between the mounds and walks through the circle.

Even though different materials and patterns are used, the strong geometry unifies the space. The outer edge of the terrace, a granite seat wall or granite coping, is defined by a radius of 61'6" with the same centerpoint as the central bluestone circle. The irregular random bluestone pattern terminates at a flush granite border that marks the beginning of granite steps. It is again concentric to the bluestone circle. The three steps lead down to a stone pavement consisting of crushed bluestone and river gravel pressed into concrete.

Throughout the site the design team showed a remarkable sensitivity to the diverse construction materials used. Attention was paid to each transition, both at locations where contrasting materials and design functions occurred, as well as those locations where the same material was used in different ways. For example, the transitions at the perimeter of the Meer between the Claymax™ liner details and the concrete walls and between the various boulder treatments and walls are subtle and strong.

The Harlem Meer was seeded with 40 catfish and 50,000 mixed fingerlings including bluegilled sunfish, carp, and perch. The staff of the Discovery Center has instituted a program of fishing events to teach children and other park visitors the rudiments of casting and fishing, as well as to educate them about the inhabitants of the Meer and its ecology.

Four objectives guided the planting design: to use plants with the ability to survive in a difficult environment, yet not be invasive; to stabilize the water's edge where the treatment with boulders was deemed insufficient; to use indigenous species which would provide food and habitat for wildlife; and, finally, to return to the origi-

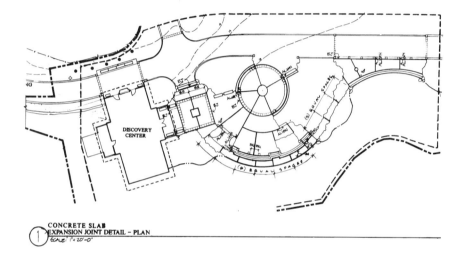

Figure 3-28: *Layout plan of the esplanade and edge treatments by the Discovery Center*

Figure 3-29: *The esplanade and edge treatment under construction. (Photo by Sara Cedar Miller)*

Figure 3-30: *A view across the Meer to the Discovery Center (Photo by Sara Cedar Miller)*

nal Olmstedian design. The design team used historic documents, both photographs and descriptions of the park, as aids in researching the original planting design. Constraints—concerns about safety, visibility, and maintenance—dictated some departures from the Olmsted design. For example, the south edge of the Meer originally was a wooded slope. A path running along the base of the rock outcrops was added when the Meer was given a hard edge. In the reconstruction, the path, though not a historic feature, remained, and concerns about safety along the shoreline path and maintenance of the water's edge resulted in this area's development as a tall, grassy edge featuring bayberry, sedges, and grasses. Planting for the entire project was done incrementally so that the design team could evaluate what worked the best and implement planting mixtures that had grown well in other areas of the site.

At the Dana Discovery Center the planting reinforces the design concept of a plaza and terrace system carved from an existing landscape. Dense stands of red maples (*Acer rubrum*) and bald cypresses (*Tax-*

odium distichum) will envelop the terraces and extend the wooded park landscape at the northern boundary of the park to the edge of the Meer. One specimen weeping willow (*Salix babylonica*) is used as an accent by the entrance to the building. Massings of deciduous and evergreen shrubs separate the spaces without blocking vision, and together with an array of perennials, ferns and ground covers, contribute to a simple but varied palette of plantings. Shrubs used are the following:

Fothergilla gardenii	Dwarf fothergilla
Ilex glabra compacta	Inkberry
Ilex verticillata	Common winterberry
Leucothoe catesbaei	Coast leucothoe
Myrica pensylvanica	Northern bayberry

The bayberry, used structurally, is thriving, particularly in the early stages of the planting when there is more direct sun. As the trees mature and the amount of shade increases, the bayberry will fade. It is anticipated that the fothergilla and the leucothoe will spurt in growth as the bayberry fades. Two species of ferns add contrasting textures in the planting, lady fern (*Athyrium* filix-femina) and ostrich fern (*Matteuccia struthiopteris*). Three groundcovers are used: andropogon (*Andropogon scoparius*), drooping sedge (*carex pendula*), and purple wintercreeper (*Euonymus fortunei*). In addition to iris and dalylily varieties, the perennials chosen are bigleaf goldenray (*Ligularia dentata*) and leopard plant (*Ligularia tussilaginea*).

Among the plantings to stabilize and beautify the water's edge throughout the Meer are blue flag iris (*Iris versicolor*), black needle rush (*Juncus roemarianus*), Virginia arrow arum (*Peltandra virginica*), and pickerel weed (*Pontedaria cordata*). The durability of the fleshy plant materials, particularly the latter two, in the face of a great deal of fishing and pedestrian activity along the water's edge, has been encouraging to the Conservancy's staff.

Near the entrance from the Conservatory Garden, Jeff Poor, the landscape architect, sought to transition the plantings from the cultivated varieties used in the Conservatory Garden to looser, more native material as one moves farther into the Meer's landscape. One of the attractive trees that he specified is the sweetbay magnolia (*Magnolia virginiana*), native to river bottoms and swamps, but adaptable to diverse wet or dry conditions and hardy in typically compacted urban soils. The sweetbay magnolia is used in part because its upright, ovoid form recalls the similar character of stewartias planted in the Conservatory Garden. In keeping with his concept, crimson pygmy barberry (*Berberis thumbergii 'crimson pygmy'*), bluewave hydrangea (*Hydrangea mariesii 'Bluewave'*), lily turf (*Liriope muscari 'Big Blue'*), and other ornamental plantings cluster near the top of the entrance steps to the Meer. As one moves closer to the water's edge and farther from this entrance, more native materials in looser arrangements are used. Along with native red osier dogwood (*Cornus sericea*), inkberry (*Ilex glabra*), winterberry (*Ilex verticillata 'Harvest Red'*), and native oakleaf hydrangeas (*Hydrangea quercifolia*), three varieties of roses were originally planted, two cultivars and one native species: Fairy Rose, Sea Foam Rose, and swamp rose (*Rosa palustris*). The two cultivars were

stolen, while the swamp rose, not appearing to potential thieves as a typical rose, has thrived. The two cultivars have been replaced by bayberry, red osier dogwood, and winterberry, which have all grown well in other parts of the Meer. The ground covers include tussock sedge (*Carex stricta*), Virginia arrow arum, and four species of ferns: hayscented (*Dennstaedtia punctilobula*), ostrich (*Matteuccia struthiopteris*), cinnamon (*Osmunda cinnamomea*), and royal (*Osmunda regalis*).

Three sweetbay magnolias are also planted at the south peninsula, along with northern bayberry and swamp rose (*Rosa palustris*) as the structural materials, in the midst of massings of grasses such as little bluestem (*Andropogon scoparius*) and red switchgrass (*Panicum virgatum 'Rehbraun'*) and a range of herbs. The planting design is looser than at the entrance to the Meer from the Conservatory Garden. Joe Pye weed (*Eupatorium fistulosum 'Gateway'*), cinnamon fern (*Osmunda cinnamomea*), and blackeyed Susans (*Rudbeckia fulgida 'Goldsturm'*) are notable plantings. Tussock sedge, blueflag iris, Virginia arrow arum, and pickerel weed grace the water's edge.

The Meer Island features thickets of planting to create a secluded wildlife habitat and also screen the Lasker Rink. Built largely of sand with a six-inch layer of topsoil, the irregularly tapering island of about 1/3 acre rises about 7-1/2 feet above the water level of the Meer. The planting concept was to use a palette of plant materials native to the sandy coastal plain. Three sizes of pitch pines (*Pinus rigida*), 18"–24" in height, 2'–3' and 3'–4' are planted with thickets of shrubby scrub oak (*Quercus ilicifolia*). Along with northern bayberry and inkberry, widely used throughout the Meer, are red chokeberry (*Aronia arbutifolia brilliantissima*), red osier dogwood (*Cornus sericea*), and highbush blueberry (*Vaccinium corymbosum*). Perennials include sedges and bulbs such as tussock sedge, blue flag iris, and pickerel weed. Grasses and rushes are also prominent, such as manna grass (*Glyceria canadensis*), black needle rush (*Juncus roemarianus*), cutgrass (*Leersia orysoides*), and switchgrass (*Panicum virgatum 'Rehbraun'*).

The planting design is a work in progress. Additional plantings are carried out in response to specific needs. The two most frequent that have arisen are stabilization of the water's edge and screening. Tussock sedge and blue flag iris have proved very successful along the water's edge. Bullrush (*Scirpus validus*), which has volunteered itself into the park landscape, has been found to work quite well for screening, in combination with red osier dogwood.

Since opening in 1993, the Meer has been heavily used and appreciated by thousands of visitors of all ages for fishing, education (ecology, birdwatching, and plant identification), walking, sitting, and relaxation. The pedestrian path system links the Meer to the Conservatory Garden and the North Woods, while continuing to provide access to the much maligned Lasker Rink. The careful restoration of the Meer—so much in evidence through the attention paid to the re-creation of the original, undulating water's edge and the rich vocabulary of design detailing—underscores the intrusion and harshness of Robert Moses' legacy into this otherwise serene and undulating landscape.

PROJECT: *Concert Ground at Central Park*
LOCATION: *New York City*
DESIGN TEAM: *Phillip Winslow, landscape architect*
   Clarke and Rapuano, Inc., Consulting engineers and landscape architects
   Central Park Conservancy
CLIENT: *Central Park Conservancy and the New York City Department of Parks and Recreation*
DATE: *1989–1993*
BUDGET: *$4,000,000 (1/2 from the New York City Department of Parks and Recreation, and 1/2 from the Central Park Conservancy)*

The reconstruction of Central Park's concert ground, a formally designed space for outdoor performances, is the figurative exclamation point at the end of the mall. Lined with double rows of elm trees, the mall leads from the Dairy (north of the park entrance at Grand Army Plaza) to the concert ground and Bethesda Terrace and Fountain, just north of the 72nd Street transverse road, a distance of about one half of a mile. A grand staircase descends from the concert ground under the transverse road to Bethesda Terrace. Although elm trees have been affected by Dutch elm disease, greater damage has been done by the environment. However, many of these grand, stately trees continue to hold their own and are rigorously monitored and maintained. Although there are gaps in the continuous canopy, the effect is still of a grand procession. New and vigorous disease-free young elm trees have been planted to replace those that have died.

Landscape Architect Phillip Winslow was hired by the Central Park Conservancy to develop conceptual plans for the reconstruction. Along with Marianne Cramer, Bruce Kelly, and Elizabeth Barlow Rogers, he helped initiate the efforts to restore Central Park in the 1970s and was part of the design team that developed the restoration master plan for the park. Together with Bruce Kelly and the historian James M. Fitch, they prepared a case study of The Ramble, the 34-acre romantic wilderness accentuated with large rock outcroppings and majestic trees. Their restoration plan for the Ramble was incorporated into the master plan for the restoration of Central Park, and their methodology for historic landscape restoration was used as a model for many other projects. While analyzing all of the random footpaths worn into the terrain of the Ramble where people naturally tend to walk, Mr. Winslow is credited with inventing the term "desire line." He implemented several of the most significant projects in the park, most notably the planting restoration for the Bethesda Terrace, Cherry Hill, and The Mall.

THE PUBLIC AND ACADEMIC SECTOR

Typically, Winslow would develop preliminary plans, revise them and present them, until they were approved by all jurisdictions such as the local community boards, the New York City Arts Commission, the Landmarks Board, the Parks Department, and the Conservancy. After these approvals, he would work with a consultant—in the case of the concert ground, Clarke + Rapuano, Inc.—who would prepare the construction documents. Initial planning began in 1987. In 1989, as Mr. Winslow was dying of AIDS, he approached all of his design partners and consultants in order to expedite the orderly continuation of projects that he initiated. "Recent events affecting my health have made it impossible for me to remain actively involved in my landscape architectural office and therefore, prevent me from continuing to serve as a consultant," he announced. It was agreed that the remaining work, primarily the construction documents and site inspections "be completed by Clarke and Rapuano in direct relation with the Central Park Conservancy." Initially, the project manager for Clarke and Rapuano, Inc. was engineer Andre Martecchini, but as the project moved forward, that role was assigned to myself. Although I hardly knew Mr. Winslow—we had participated in only three or four meetings on the project before Mr. Winslow's untimely death—a gay man myself, I was inspired by Winslow's honesty and integrity in dealing with such a tragic situation.

The work was awarded to the low bidder, the Audax Construction Company. Jennifer Monahan from the Central Park Conservancy was the resident construction supervisor. She periodically scheduled inspections of my work and that of the project engineer, Kevin Maher, from Clarke + Rapuano. Since the Conservancy's funding is partially provided by the NYC Department of Parks and Recreation, that department also sent representatives to inspection meetings at the site. An unusual aspect of construction management was reaching an accommodation with the resident population of the existing band shell. After a series of break-ins into the construction trailer on the site, Ms. Monahan was able to negotiate with several of the homeless individuals occupying the site to protect the trailer for $30 a week. There were never problems after this agreement was reached.

As the park's only formal landscape architectural element, the mall was its historical centerpiece, used for parading, promenading, and gathering. There was a strong axial relationship between the mall and the concert ground, at its north end, and a continuing connection to Bethesda Fountain and Terrace. Changes over the years had had a severe impact on the appearance and usefulness of both the mall and the concert ground. In 1923, most of the original features of the concert ground were removed, including the bandstand, special benches, and ornamental fountains. Large planting islands encircled with benches and containing large American elms, were also removed, and replaced with small concrete-curbed circular shapes. A band shell was built on the slope at the eastern edge of the concert ground in 1929, and funded by donations from the Naumberg family. When initial planning for the restoration began, the concert ground had the character of a large asphalt parking lot in which floated a few rows of elms, many of which were in a stunted condition. Several different species of elms were present: Siberian, English, and some hybrids.

The master plan for the park by the Central Park Conservancy shows the re-creation of a formal space for concerts. It would be implemented with the vocabulary of design elements and materials that have been used historically in the site, including: hexagonal asphalt pavers, slate edgings and curbs, granite and bluestone pavements, asphalt drives, lawn and trees, and the traditional Central Park light post, but with a more efficient metal halide bulb in the Central Park light luminaire. Interestingly, the hexagonal pavers are so well established as part of the park's vocabulary that the Hastings Pavement Company manufactures one called the Central Park paver with a particular ratio and mixture of aggregates and sands. Like many materials, the size of the paver has shrunk over the years: the original hexagonal pavers measured 8-1/2" across (flat to flat), whereas the currently manufactured ones are smaller, 8". As various conceptual and preliminary plans were prepared, Phil Winslow and Marianne

Figure 3-31: *The concert ground, prior to reconstruction, was a large, derelict, flat space with areas of poor drainage (Photo by Sara Cedar Miller, Central Park Conservancy)*

Figure 3-32: *During the initial phases of reconstruction, the site took on the appearance of a giant mud hole (Photo by Steven L. Cantor)*

Cramer shepherded the project through various approvals by the Art Commission, community boards, and the Parks Department.

The program for the restoration called for the reintroduction of planting islands in order to re-establish the axis and also provide a well-drained horticultural environment for the trees. Existing pavement and lighting was to be removed. The layout and design of benches around the perimeter of

THE PUBLIC AND ACADEMIC SECTOR

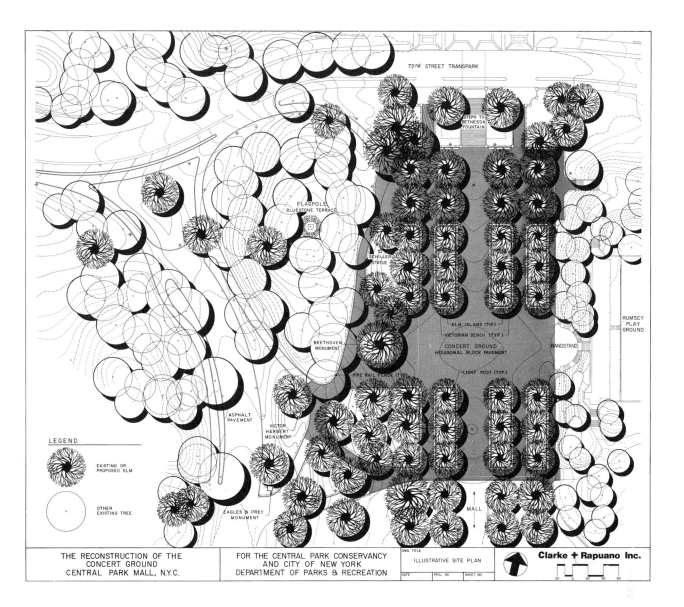

72nd STREET TRANSPARK

STEPS TO
BETHESDA
FOUNTAIN

FLAGPOLE
BLUESTONE TERRACE

SCHILLER
STATUE

RUMSEY
PLAY
GROUND

BEETHOVEN
MONUMENT

ELM ISLAND (TYP.)
VICTORIAN BENCH (TYP.)
CONCERT GROUND
HEXAGONAL BLOCK PAVEMENT

BANDSTAND

LIGHT POST (TYP.)

ASPHALT
PAVEMENT

PIPE RAIL FENCE (TYP.)

VICTOR
HERBERT
MONUMENT

MALL

EAGLES & PREY
MONUMENT

THE RECONSTRUCTION OF THE
CONCERT GROUND
CENTRAL PARK MALL, N.Y.C.

FOR THE CENTRAL PARK CONSERVANCY
AND CITY OF NEW YORK
DEPARTMENT OF PARKS & RECREATION

DWG. TITLE
ILLUSTRATIVE SITE PLAN

DATE: PROJ. NO.   SHEET NO.

Clarke + Rapuano Inc.

the islands were to reinforce the form of the new islands. New lighting was to integrate with the design of the whole site. It was also necessary to regrade the site for better drainage, since there were substantial areas that puddled, and replace the asphalt with a new paving material. The bandshell, although attractive in its form and character, was too small for the types of concerts that typically would occur. Therefore, it was proposed that a portable, temporary stage be designed that could fit at the other side of the site and be hauled into the concert ground by truck. It was likely that the Naumberg bandshell would remain. A particularly daunting challenge was to save the existing grove of elm trees, ranging in size from 6 inches to 48 inches in diameter. Some were declining, but many were quite

healthy. A new storm drainage system was also desired, since the century-old system in the park, amid a spaghetti network of water tunnels, gas lines, abandoned utilities, and active lines, was in poor condition. The site was graced with a number of historical monuments including statues of Beethoven, Schiller, and Victor Herbert. These were scattered through the site and could not be moved, yet needed to fit into the landscape, so that they appeared neither too obvious nor too unobtrusive. It was also desired to relocate four historic Victorian urns, removed from the park for safekeeping, back into the concert ground. Two new ones were also to be placed. A concrete terrace supporting a flagpole that accented the hilltop to the west of the concert ground was badly deteriorated and needed

Figure 3-33: *Illustrative site plan*

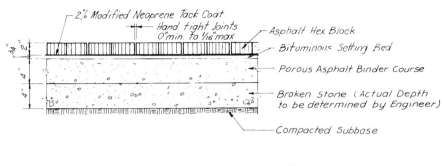

ASPHALT HEX BLOCK PAVEMENT ⒣
Scale: 1½"=1'-0"

Figure 3-34: *Detail of hexagonal block pavers*

Figure 3-35: *Detail plan and section of Victorian style bench*

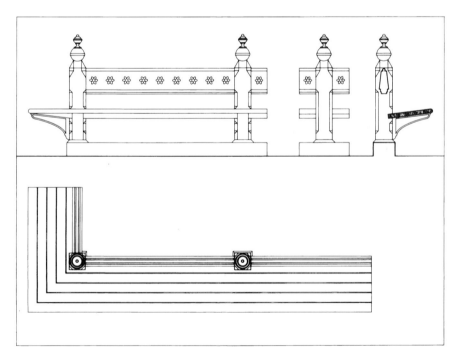

to be removed and repaved. As a focal point at the end of the mall, it was important to develop a design that would harmonize with and tie together the adjacent, diverse surroundings: Bethesda Terrace and the 72nd Street Transverse Road to the north, the Rumsey playground and arbor to the east, the mall to the south and major pedestrian walks to the west.

The existing site included several species of elms, from a gigantic English elm more than four feet in diameter, one of the few original Olmsted plantings, to numerous American elms of varying form and character. Some were the traditional vase shape, even though young, while others, even though mature, were distinctly eccentric. Many of the trees in the central space of the concert ground, the "parking lot," showed

obvious signs of stress. As a result of poor drainage and ponding, the existing asphalt pavement was badly deteriorated. There were also problems with erosion on the slopes to the west and east of the concert ground and some of the walks leading into the space. There was almost no seating at all in the entire space.

The design created three rows of elm islands, each about 27 feet wide and 107 feet long, all parallel to one another to direct pedestrians from the mall either to the concert ground or through it to Bethesda Terrace and Fountain. Anticipating the tremendous amount of foot traffic that this area can receive, the Central Park Conservancy decided to design a Victorian style bench that would fit the perimeter of the major elm islands and protect them from pedestrian traffic. Each elm island has two corners with square intersections and two corners with 4-foot radii. The design and alignment of the benches follow this geometry. In this way a well-aerated horticultural environment could finally be created for the elms and related groundcovers, while ample seating could be provided for people wanting to sit informally in the grand space. Portable seating would be provided for scheduled concerts in the center of the space, a large rectangular area between the existing bandshell and the portable stage opposite it on the western edge of the plateau. The design was carefully laid out so that the statue of Beethoven is absorbed into a small island directly across the space from the bandshell, adjacent to the proposed location for the portable stage.

Usually in Central Park remnants of earlier designs can be found in storage somewhere, but not even old slats could be found from the original benches. Old photographs were studied carefully by the planning staff, led by Tom Giordano, and used as a basis for the reconstruction. Four mock-ups of benches with different dimensions were made to assess the comfort of seating and aesthetic criteria. Although it seemed that the original benches support posts were constructed of wood, it was likely that the elbow joint supporting the wood slats was what had failed. The design team decided to consider aluminum with a finish to simulate cast iron in order to minimize the weight of the benches and avoid excessive shipping costs. Three fabricators bid on the work, based on careful drawings by the design team. The aluminum posts treated with an electrostatically applied black paint were supplied by a firm in Alabama, Gaintime. The white oak slats were made by a company in Manhattan called Building Block. The original slats were probably a softer cedar, not as durable as the white oak selected by the designers. The Central Park Conservancy developed a stainless steel press for the wooden flower ornaments inlayed into the backs of the benches. The Conservancy's in-house restoration crew assembled the benches on site, including the painting and final staining of the wood.

Hastings pavers are the groundplane for the formal plateau that composes the flatter space of the concert ground. As walks lead away from this plateau on steeper slopes the pavement changes to asphalt. A steel rather than slate or bluestone edging is used around all of the elm islands and other planting areas. Although the steel is less accurate to the historical vocabulary of

Figure 3-36: *A Conservancy worker tries out a mock-up of the bench (Photo by Sara Cedar Miller)*

the site, it lends itself as a material to the curving forms that are created. Adjacent to the formal plateau, the Central Park standard piperail fencing, painted black, is installed as a means of deterring pedestrians from walking across the lawns, and directing them, instead, via the walk system to their destinations. The flagpole pavement was replaced by a symmetrical design of

Figure 3-37: *The concert ground after development: existing elms are retained, with new paving, lighting, and benches (Photo by Sara Cedar Miller)*

Figure 3-38: *The Victorian urns were relocated to a prominent axis of the space*

eight panels of rectangular shapes. (See Figure C-29.) The flagpole rises from the center of this pattern. It serves as a monument commemorating city employees who died in past wars.

The existing grading for the site was extremely flat, primarily about 1 percent, with some areas less than 0.5 percent. Significant puddling had occurred over the years, and there was extensive sedimenta-

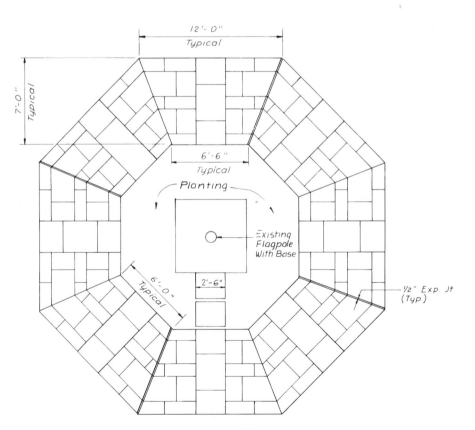

BLUESTONE PAVING PATTERN
Scale: ¼"=1'-0"

Figure 3-39: *Detail of bluestone paving pattern. The planting area was deleted, as the existing concrete pavement around the base of the flag pole was left in place.*

238   **THE PUBLIC AND ACADEMIC SECTOR**

Figures 3-40 and 3-41: *Two views of the blue-stone under construction. It was necessary to cut stones in trapezoidal shapes to match the required pattern, which was conceived to avoid small, impractical slivers. (Photo by Steven L. Cantor)*

tion in the storm drainage structures. In order to minimize the impact of grading operations on the often weakened existing elm trees it was decided to follow the existing grade wherever possible. Several different grading plans were developed before a final plan evolved that met existing grade near all of the existing elm trees. High points approximated the existing high points. Since the agreed gradients in the formal plateau are quite flat, from 0.5 percent to about 1.5 percent, it was agreed that some puddling of water might occur in the flatter areas of the site, as slow moving water would settle around low points and also deposit some sediment. Since the goal of the grading was to minimize impacts on the existing elms, the occasional puddling of water was considered acceptable. During construction, the contractor was required to shoot elevations on the subgrade for the entire plateau to verify that the whole site drained.

Another factor besides gradient that affected the pavement was the proposed use of the concert ground. Since the portable stage would be pulled into the site by heavy duty tractor trailers, the layout of the islands had to accommodate their large turning radii. In addition, the cross-section of the pavement had to be designed in order to withstand the heavy weight of these trucks. The Central Park Conservancy emphasized the desire for a porous pavement, both to minimize puddling after large rainstorms and to direct storm runoff to the roots of the elm trees throughout the site. Clarke + Rapuano balanced the engineering criteria for the pavement with the horticultural requirements of the trees. The

Figure 3-42: *The major circulation routes through the concert ground occur on the flat routes through the elm islands so that the grassy hillside with the flagstone terrace serves as a passive space from which to watch the people below. (Photo by Steven L. Cantor)*

Figure 3-43: *The concert ground can readily accommodate large crowds, such as these from the annual Gay Pride parade, with minimal disturbance to the major trees in the islands. Compare this to Figure 3-32. (Photos by Steven L. Cantor)*

hexagonal pavers are set standardly with hand tight joints on a bituminous setting bed (see Figure 3-34). The binder course, however, is a porous asphalt four inches thick, and the base course is recycled concrete aggregate, also four inches thick. Even though the pavers have tight joints, water will percolate through the joints and continue through the porous asphalt and aggregate layers. Since some of this percolated water will move parallel to the subgrade towards low points, holes were drilled in the sides of the manhole and catchbasin structures in the flattest areas of the site. In that way, excess water is drained from the site both at the surface and underground.

All of the existing storm drainage system on the plateau was removed, and a new system designed. Many storm drainage lines had to be removed because they had badly deteriorated over many years of use. To minimize the impact on the existing trees, new storm lines were located in the trenches of the existing lines wherever possible. It was important to drain the water properly while minimizing the number of catch basins, since each additional basin might require digging on tree roots. Clarke + Rapuano and the Central Park Conservancy used the services of an expert arborist, Dr. Terry A. Tartar, the director of the Shade Tree Laboratories at the University of Massachusetts, Amherst. Dr. Tartar helped determine the best locations for new catch basins while minimizing the total required on the site. At an on-site meeting, Mr. Maher, Dr. Tartar, Central Park horticulturalist Neil Calvanese, Chief of Construction and Preservation for the Conservancy Douglas Blonsky and I agreed on the final configuration of the storm drainage system.

Planting on the site is as simple as possible. Despite the risk of Dutch elm disease striking new trees as they mature, it was decided to plant uniform specimens of American elms in order to harmonize with the existing elms already established on the site. The disease does not strike trees until they reach maturity; and healthy trees tend to offer some resistance. It is hoped that on-

Figure 3-44: *A festive crowd parades through the concert ground on Gay Pride Day. Notice the flagpole in the background, the flowers in the urn, and how most people avoid the cobblestone tree islands even though there is only a slight rise in elevation above the smooth hexagonal block pavement. (Photo by Steven L. Cantor)*

going research may yield effective treatments and deterrents to this disease by the time these newly planted trees reach maturity. Since American elms are rarely grown in nurseries, the largest size available was only about 2″ caliper, but these trees have been growing well. The ground plane is simple. Groundcover in the elm islands is purple wintercreeper euonymous (*Euonymous fortunei v. coloratus*). (See Figure C-30.) Turf is used in all the other areas adjacent to the pavement.

Theresa Yap, the coordinator of the Soil Conservation Program, in association with Mr. Calvanese, developed a sandy, well drained soil mix for backfilling the elm islands. It consists of 70–71 percent sand, 19 percent silt, and 10 percent clay, with 5–10 percent organic matter and a pH of 6.0 to 7.0. By comparison, the older soils in the park tend to be 65 percent or less sand with an organic content of less than 5 percent. The standard soil specification used by the Conservancy for most projects in the park is 60–70 percent sand, 9–18 percent clay and 12–31 percent silt, with an organic content of 5 percent. At the elm islands, both a high organic and sand content was desired to retain moisture for the new elm planting while also promoting good drainage.

One condition that surprised the design team and the contractor was the extent of schist near the surface of the plateau. Some of the trees were stunted because their roots over many years had not been able to penetrate it, and had been severely limited in their amount of growth. Approximately 4000 cubic yards of schist had to be excavated from the top of the plateau in order to give the elm islands adequate depth for good planting conditions. Although some of this rock was bedrock, a great deal of it was rubble backfill, perhaps dating from the 1923 construction on the site. Unfortunately, since the layer of rock

near the surface was so deep, water tended to pond without draining properly. An underdrain system of perforated polyvinyl chloride pipes, wrapped in a geotextile fabric, Mirafi™ 140N, was installed. Each pipe connects to a clean-out and ties into the new storm drainage system. The new soil mixture was backfilled over the underdrain system.

At the northern end of the site, as the visitor approaches the steps leading down towards Bethesda Fountain and Terrace, were eight elm trees kept in solitary locations, each growing or surviving in a small concrete island similar to the others on the site. To allow ample pedestrian space at this

Figures 3-45a and 3-45b: *Old cobbles were left in place around the roots of existing elms. A low curb was built to absorb the grade change to the new pavement. The curb, even though low, deflects traffic so that many people walk around the island rather than through it. (Photos by Steven L. Cantor)*

Figure 3-45b: *(Cont.)*

transition as people approached the edge of the site, these elms were not contained within large elm islands. The roots of some of these trees had grown into and around a pattern of cobbles that were originally placed to protect them from pedestrian traffic. Rather than cut the roots to extricate the cobbles, they were left in place and the size of each island was increased in diameter by the placement of concentric bands of cobbles around each of these trees. The outer few courses were mortared in place, but the interior courses were set in sand to allow percolation of water to the roots.

The storm drainage system eventually directs water through a large pipe into the lake just north of the 72nd Street Transverse Road. The lake will be one of the last elements restored as part of the complete overhaul of the park. As all of the areas within the watershed of the lake are restored and reconstructed, the loss of soil due to erosion and unstable conditions should be minimized. At that point the lake will be dredged and the edges re-established. The amount of water draining from the concert ground into the lake is kept as small as possible through the porous pavement design of the plateau. The outlet sys-

tem crossing under the 72nd Street Transverse Road had to consist of three pipes placed side by side, rather than one large pipe, because the layout had to thread the needle between two existing utility systems that could not be disturbed. Mr. Maher designed this system and meticulously inspected it to insure that the system would be viable and sustainable. Quite a lot of handwork was required by the contractor at the transition chambers at each end of this utility crossing.

Mr. Maher and Ms. Monahan jointly supervised the installation of the drainage pipes across 72nd Street to the lake. Since the transverse road is a vital transportation link between the east and west sides of Manhattan, it was agreed that the work be performed on a weekend, but it was necessary to move ahead with the work as quickly as possible in order not to delay other work on the storm drainage system above this crossing. Unfortunately and unavoidably, the weekend chosen happened to be the weekend of a major New York City road race. Thousands of runners were treated to a spectacular view of an exposed excavation site as they jogged by. Steel plates covered the excavation over the roadway. Although there were no incidents with runners, a few emergency vehicles had closer than desirable encounters with the excavation, including a large pumper truck which almost fell into the excavation despite the steel plates and all normal precautions.

The completion of the concert ground stabilized one end of the watershed draining into Wagner's Cove at the southern end of the lake. Therefore, the cove was dredged and its shoreline planted with wetland material. Common reed (*Phragmites australis*) was removed and a range of plants was established, including juncus, curex, shadblow (*Amelanchier canadensis*), cinnamon, and ostrich ferns.

A final complication occurred unexpectedly. The design team and contractor felt that the drainage work would proceed quite rapidly once the crossing of the 72nd Street Transverse Road had been completed. The backhoe doing the excavation unexpectedly encountered the brick exterior of an existing underground tunnel. Arch-shaped, it measured approximately eight feet wide with an accumulation of silt several feet deep. Unfortunately, no accurate records of existing utilities were available. An accurate survey of all utilities would be a major help in planning for capital improvements, reconstructions, and maintenance. It was determined in the field that this tunnel was some sort of sediment trap as several old existing catch basins were connected to it. Both sides of the tunnel opening were sealed where the new pipe crossed it. All upstream catch basins were connected to the new system.

In the lower part of the site, the walk system from the plateau descends the hill and parallels the 72nd Street Transverse Road. A standard Central Park wooden guardrail separates the walk from the edge of the road. The walk is very wide to accommodate the large numbers of people who congregate and use the park. To scale

Figure 3-46: *The design team did not anticipate the tremendous popularity of skaters and their desire for a smooth, bump free surface on which to stage their own events (Photo by Steven L. Cantor)*

down the effect of a walk that wide, a three-foot-wide median of cobblestone pavers, flush with the asphalt pavement on either side, was designed to divide the walk into two segments, each ten feet wide and parallel to one another. The median, like a roadway median, tends to separate people walking in opposite directions. The median ends where the walk diverges, one part leading along the road and the other heading away from the road and into the heart of the concert ground.

The reconstruction has been quite successful, but not without some unanticipated results. Only one elm tree, already

weakened by Dutch elm disease, died. The new elms are growing well, and the groundcover has become a solid mat. At one time during the construction process, a large plaque honoring the donor to the Conservancy of the funding for the site was installed in the center of the concert ground, but it was removed because plaques set at the bases of the Victorian urns were deemed more attractive. The benches add the warmth of the white oak slats and the scale of the flower ornaments, and are popular resting places for visitors. However, the large formal hexagonal pavement has become a favorite in-line skating area. If problems with roller-bladers persist, even with police enforcement, it might be possible to introduce a rough textured pavement into the space that would further define its character and discourage its use as an in-line skating racetrack.

PROSPECT PARK ALLIANCE

Brooklyn, New York City

PROJECT: *Reconstruction of the Vanderbilt Street Playground in Prospect Park*
LOCATION: *Brooklyn, NY*
LANDSCAPE ARCHITECTS: *Rex Wassermann, conceptual design; Christian Zimmerman, working drawings, specifications, inspections*
DATE: *1992–1994*
BUDGET: *$750,000*

Restoration of Frederick L. Olmsted and Calvert Vaux's masterpiece Prospect Park is now underway. Many elements have been completed, such as the Boathouse, several major arches, and the carousel. The development of a master plan for the restoration started in the late 1970s, when the park was at its nadir. Most buildings were abandoned and there had been widespread vandalism and deterioration of the park landscape. Exhaustive reports were compiled on each of five regions of the park, but only one has been published, on the Ravine. It is officially called the Historic Landscape Report (HLR), and is the first exhaustive historic study for any public park in the United States. Published in 1986, it uses methods first developed by preservationists for historic structures. Including history, inventory, analysis, and a synthesis of phased reconstruction alternatives and recommendations that are quite specific, the report recommends discrete capital projects. In more recent years, work in Prospect Park has been guided by an ecological approach to the restoration and management of the park. The Parks Department's Administrator's Office for Prospect Park, with a staff that includes an ecologist, a forester, maintenance personnel, and landscape architects, is gradually implementing restoration projects according to ecological principles.

The other four areas studied in the historic landscape reports, as a basis for a master plan, are the park perimeter (from the drives outward), the Long Meadow, Litchfield Villa including Grace Hill, and Prospect Lake. The reports for Litchfield Villa and Long Meadow are completed, but not published. The documents for the park perimeter and the lake are incomplete. These reports are extensive and quite dense, and are geared to a professional audience. Most of the capital reconstruction that has been done since the early 1980s has been based on recommendations of those reports. The Prospect Park Alliance, founded in 1987 to raise private funds for the restoration of the park, has directed many of these restorations. However, since the park has been derelict for so long, there is a need for the

Prospect Park Alliance (PPA) to communicate its goals clearly to the public and politicians. PPA is directing the preparation of a refined and updated master plan for broader audiences. The new master plan will in many ways be a departure from some of the recommendations of the Historic Landscape Reports because the PPA has available more sophisticated information about park users and is committed to an ecological approach to restoration.

Of major cities in the United State, New York City is among the lowest in terms of the percentage of its budget allocated to parks and recreation, about .3 percent. Even though its total operating budget far exceeds that of any other city, New York City's parks system is suffering. The next lowest percentage is Philadelphia, at 1.0 percent. At the highest end are San Diego and Phoenix at 8 percent, although a significant portion of funds in these two desert climates goes for irrigation. Professional planners and landscape architects have argued for some time that if NYC's percentage could be consistently maintained at 1.0 percent, then the city's parks could be properly managed. But even that amount represents more than triple the current levels of funding. Over decades, such low expenditures have resulted in the deterioration of New York's extensive 26,000 acre parks system.

The New York City Department of Parks and Recreation has two budgets: a capital budget raised from the sale of bonds and an operational budget raised from general tax revenues. There is generally never enough in the latter, as competing political and economic interests are always vying for these funds. Since the city's fiscal crisis of the 1970s, every capital project in Prospect Park has been funded by either the Borough President's office or local City Council members.

The New York City Department of Parks and Recreation (NYCDPR) has a capital budget set city-wide. In the fiscal year, June, 1994 to June, 1995, NYCDPR has a $200 million capital funds commitment for the fiscal year. This amount is much higher than usual, as the new mayor, Rudolph Giuliani, is seeking to pay off political debts from his recent election as well as underscore his belief that a lot of investment in capital will create a rippling effect throughout the city's economy. Expenditures on the parks will result in jobs in the construction, manufacturing, and nursery industries. Each of the five boroughs is awarded an amount of the total capital budget, and the borough president directs the authorization of funds among competing projects.

Under the recent reorganization of the city charter, the City Council now provides funding for many smaller projects. In addition to the capital budget, the Borough President and Council members have discretionary funds that are made available for particular projects. Nevertheless, funds for both capital construction and maintenance of parks and recreation facilities in New York City are the subject of fierce political battles and tugs-of-war. Many groups compete to win approval for pet projects when funds are not available for most of them. At least for the current year, capital funds are relatively plentiful, but funds for maintenance are always scarce. The maintenance staff for Prospect Park's 526 acres consists of only 30 people, or one per 17.5 acres, so it is crucial that the designers of any restorations or reconstructions in the park anticipate bare-bones maintenance of facilities and planting.

The sheer size of the city and its system further complicates matters. In an effort to promote efficiency and avoid parochial interests, the city has tried both centralized and decentralized administration of the parks. Robert Moses centralized five formerly separate borough parks departments into one regional office, located in the Arsenal in Manhattan. Since 1980, the Mayor has appointed the Park's Commissioner, currently Henry Stern, who, in turn, appoints park commissioners for each borough. Julius Spiegel is the Parks Commissioner in Brooklyn. The larger parks in the city system, Riverside, Flushing Meadows-Corona, Pelham Bay, Forest Park, Van Cortlandt, Prospect, and Central Park each have their own administrator. The administrators function both in management and fundraising.

The organization of the Prospect Park Alliance (PPA) was modeled after the Central Park Conservancy. Tupper Thomas, like her Central Park equivalent Betsy Rogers, wears two hats, serving as both the

President of the Alliance and the Prospect Park Administrator. In her office, employees of NYCDPR, publicly funded, and of PPA, privately funded, are completely integrated. Salaries are paid jointly by funds privately raised for the Alliance and from grants and salaries paid by the NYCDPR.

PPA bids as a consultant to do work for NYCDPR (either for the Office of Management and Budget or the Office of Construction) and almost always underbids private consultants since PPA's salaries and overhead are relatively low and it operates as a non-profit organization. Turnover is low, as the employees are quite dedicated to the restoration efforts in Prospect Park. PPA provides quality services at low prices for work essential to the restoration of Prospect Park. Serving as a consultant to the NYCDPR, PPA's staff functions like a private practitioner. Since they literally spend almost every day in the Park and interact regularly with maintenance staff and police, the PPA employees are in a unique position to know the park better than anyone. They invest heart and soul in all of their endeavors in the park.

As part of a new master plan effort, the PPA has computer-mapped the location, size, and condition of 10,000 non-woodland specimen trees throughout the park. These are defined as trees *not* in woodlands except those that are within ten feet of a major path or facility. Based on research of historical documents, the master plan proposes to plant new trees based on precedent. Partly funded through a grant that the city received from the Leila Acheson Wallace Foundation (*Reader's Digest*), the restoration of the park includes stabilizing woodland slopes and planting native herbaceous materials. The tree survey and restoration are led by Ed Toth, the director of Landscape Management, and Ainsley Caldwell, the director of Natural Resources. Christian Zimmerman, originally from North Dakota, holds degrees in both horticulture and landscape architecture. As Assistant Director of Design and Construction for Prospect Park, he is the lead designer and oversees all day-to-day operations for the park. After working for the New York City Department of Parks and Recreation's design office in Flushing, New York, landscape architect Rex

Wassermann joined the Prospect Park staff on Halloween, 1988. He functioned as the park historian, archivist, and jack-of-all trades until his death from AIDS in November, 1995. He conceptualized the design for the restoration of the Vanderbilt site, while Mr. Zimmerman directed and produced the construction documents.

Unfortunately, lack of information has been a problem in developing a basic database for Prospect Park. There is no accurate utility information, nor has there ever been a comprehensive drainage study, nor geological or soil studies. There is no sophisticated user information, and no accurate topographic survey. Planning and design for the park's natural areas have been assisted by Andropogon, a firm in Philadelphia, that has also been a consultant to the Central Park Conservancy. This firm has considerable experience in directing restoration efforts in public parks.

Reconstruction of the Vanderbilt Street Playground is recommended in the Park Perimeter Historic Landscape Report. Since the site is used by so many people, this project was strongly supported by the Brooklyn Borough President's office and the Brooklyn representatives to the New York City Council. As with all major parks, there are political realities. In the larger scheme of things, Vanderbilt's reconstruction might or might not have been done at this point; in an ecological and practical sense, its restoration does not adversely affect anything.

By contrast, the planning for the restoration of the ravine is proceeding very slowly. A once spectacular and mysterious woodland approached by grand granite staircases that still manage to fit the grades of its steep slopes, it is badly deteriorated and avoided by most park users. Therefore, its restoration is a lower political priority. From a park management viewpoint, since it is practically the top of an entire watershed within the park, its restoration is critical. Since erosion and sedimentation occurring as a result of overuse or deterioration moves down into the watercourses and valleys, it is important to restore the outlying areas of a watershed first. Once they are stabilized, the bottom of the watershed can be addressed. This principal has been followed in Central Park where the dredging and rehabilitation of the lake will be the last phase of work. Planning and design for the rehabilitation of the Ravine is proceeding, but it is a fundamentally more complex project than the playground. The original consultant to NYCDPR was terminated when the approach changed from being horticultural in nature to a carefully developed ecological restoration.

In Olmsted's original design, Prospect Park included an informal children's playground near Flatbush Avenue. In subsequent years, its use was changed into a rose garden. This flat area across from the main branch of the Brooklyn Public Library and above the Vale of Cashmere is sunken below the surrounding open landscape of the park. Intended as a natural companion to the children's playground above, Olmsted planned the Vale of Cashmere like the Conservatory Water for children's boating in Central Park. However, the design was significantly altered by McKim, Mead, and White, and made more formal in order to accommodate the rose garden. The pool became neoclassicist and romantic, and was given an exotic name. Olmsted had simple macadam walks around it; McKim, Mead, and White added marble balustrades and paved walks.

By the 1920s there was a national reform movement to create state of the art play facilities for inner city children. Some prominent landscape architects such as Jens Jensen were involved. In New York City, for example, the Hekscher Playground in the south end of Central Park was built in 1927–29. Satellite playgrounds were created at the perimeter of Central Park after a lot of criticism about the size and impact of the Hekscher Playground. In Prospect Park, three major playgrounds were built during the late 1920s: Lincoln Road playground, one outside the Picnic House, and the Vanderbilt Street playground, which opened in 1929.

The original playground was essentially trapezoidal, a rectangle that tapered at one

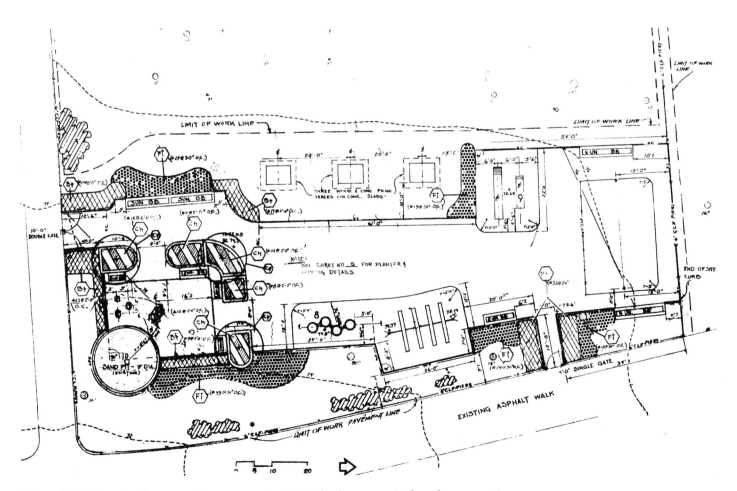

Figure 3-47: *Plan for playground improvements, 1962. The forms are rigid, and pavement is brought close to major trees as well as the major walk on the eastern edge.*

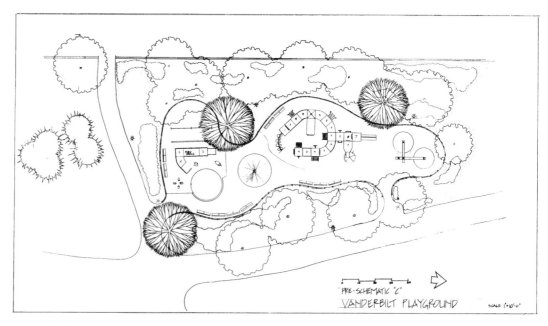

Figure 3-48: *Concept plan for reconstruction, 1989. Trees that are hollow are existing. The goal is to fit a new outline to the playground within the existing major trees and to create some breathing room between the playground and the major walk. (Prospect Park Alliance)*

end. The site had been a lawn with mature specimen trees: horsechestnut, sugar maple, tulip tree, and ailanthus. Naively and unfortunately, in the 1929 reconstruction, pavement was brought right up to the trunks of some of these trees, many of which were irreparably harmed. Only two large horsechestnuts and one ailanthus have survived. The largest tulip tree and sugar maple died slowly over a 60-year period, succumbing just before the restoration had begun. In 1975 the form of the playground was retained, but everything inside was updated. New play equipment and new chain link fencing were installed. However drainage problems were not properly resolved, so they persisted. Landscape Architects Rex Wassermann and Christian Zimmerman achieved a new layout based on saving the remaining historic trees, and worked out forms that allowed people to walk and play *around* them, not *through* them. A new sugar maple and tulip tree were planted to replace the originals.

The Prospect Park Alliance (PPA) has found that, in most cases, specimen trees, even significant ones, are too easily vandalized. It's as if, by their very isolation in being planted well away from most other vegetation, they attract vandals. Most trees planted in the park are 3-1/2 inches to 4 inches minimium in caliper. Trees much larger are slow to adapt to park conditions, and also strain often limited budgets. By planting trees of this minimum size in groups or clumps, the PPA has found that the individual is obscured by the mass, which is absorbed by the park landscape. As a result, vandals tend not to notice and the trees survive.

The project started as a reconstruction of the playground, with a budget of $750,000. This was a rare case in which more money was allocated than was required. As preliminary design drawings and the cost estimate were developed, it became clear that the restoration of the playground would cost $500,000, making $250,000 still available. The estimate was developed during the fall of 1989 when construction materials and costs were plummeting, so that it appeared that a great deal could be accomplished with the additional funds. The PPA petitioned the NYCDPR for permission to spend the additional funds on landscape restoration. The NYCDPR agreed on the condition that PPA did not raise its fee for design and inspection services. The area of the work ex-

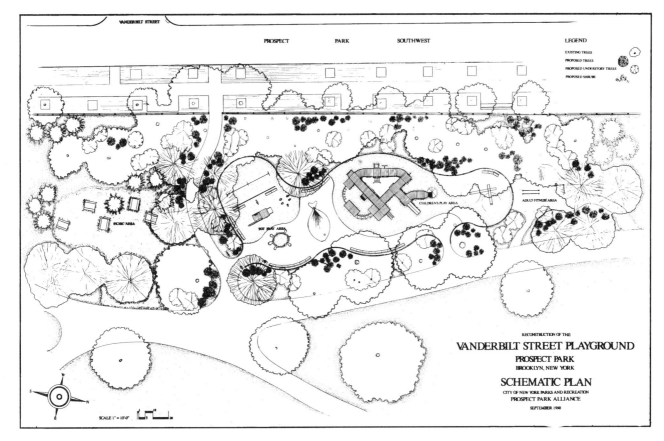

RECONSTRUCTION OF THE

VANDERBILT STREET PLAYGROUND

PROSPECT PARK
BROOKLYN, NEW YORK

SCHEMATIC PLAN

CITY OF NEW YORK PARKS AND RECREATION
PROSPECT PARK ALLIANCE

SEPTEMBER 1990

Figure 3-49: *Illustrative schematic plan, 1990. The curving forms are set. The woodland between Prospect Park Southwest and the playground is enhanced as a buffer. The secondary entrance from the street is also further refined as part of the curvilinear vocabulary, so that people may enter the playground before seeing the main pedestrian route through the park. (Prospect Park Alliance)*

panded from 1.4 acres, the general space for the playground, to seven acres. The restoration of the surrounding perimeter landscape included the planting of over 350 trees and shrubs in the areas adjacent to the playground, in an open parkland that still included some magnificent specimens of tulip trees, maples, and horsechestnuts dating from the original design. All plant materials were field located by PPA staff landscape architects. The results of this process helped to emphasize to NY-CDPR the advantages of working with PPA rather than a consultant in the private sector.

Typically, these plantings are individually staked and further protected by snow fencing. There has been some vandalism, but the public generally respects the need for the modicum of protection offered by this fencing that could easily be destroyed, and the trees have done well (see Figure

C-31). Tree and shrub species native to the region and typical of the woodland ecosystem were selected.

Size at planting and the general rate of growth and health are carefully monitored to aid in future plantings. For example, three beeches were planted in a group: all about 3-1/2 inches to 4 inches caliper. Two were not pruned (one quite dense and the other more open) and one was limbed up. Growth has been significantly faster in the unpruned ones, and the more open unpruned one has filled in considerably compared to the one that was pruned.

Reflecting the diversity of a landscape transitioning into a woodland, the designers have included many plant materials not presently growing in the park perimeter landscape, but which could be expected to be part of a more complete and healthy ecosystem, and also a few more exotic cultivars that are known to do well in city conditions.

Figure 3-50: *The forest restoration project flanks the wide gravel walk leading to the playground. A snow fence has been adequate to protect new plantings of trees and shrubs. (Photo by Steven L. Cantor)*

Liriodendron tulipifera	tulip tree/yellow poplar
Magnolia soulangeana	saucer magnolia
Magnolia virginiana	sweetbay magnolia
Ostrya virginiana	hophornbeam
Quercus sp.	oaks (pin, red, white, scarlet)
Picea glauca	white spruce
Pinus sp.	pines (white and some non-native)
Tilia sp.	lindens (American, Redmond, little-leaf)

Additional shrubs and perennials include the following:

Aquilegia sp.	
Aronia melanocarpa	black choke-cherry
Aronia arbutafolia	red chokecherry
Calycanthus floridus	sweetshrub
Comptonia peregrina	sweetfern
Dicentra sp.	Dutch-man's breeches and bleeding heart
Kalmia latifolia	mountain laurel
Rhododendron maximum	rosebay rhodo-dendron
Rhododendron sp.	native azaleas (roseshell and pinxterbloom)
Rhus aromatica	fragrant sumac
Sambucus canadensis	American elder
Viburnum cassanoides	witherod vibur-num
Viburnum prunifolium	blackhaw

A layer of herbaceous perennials and wildflowers, including hayscented and cinnamon ferns, Indian grass, bluestem, rudbeckia, and indigenous bulbs has also been established.

The only plant materials that have not grown well are the *Rhododendron maximum*, for reasons still not understood (root competition and pollution are suspected culprits), and the tulip poplar, most of

Among the trees planted are the following:

Abies concolor	white fir
Acer sp.	maple (primarily sugar and red)
Amelanchier canadensis	shadblow
Carpinus caroliniana	ironwood
Cercis canadensis	redbud
Chionanthus virginiana	fringe tree
Cornus florida	American flowering dogwood
Fagus grandifolia	American beech
Franklinia altamaha	franklinia
Gymnocladus dioicus	Kentucky coffee tree
Hammamalis virginiana	witch hazel
Ilex opaca	American holly
Liquidambar styraciflua	sweetgum

which have been decimated by oyster scale that was noticed too late to treat effectively.

Landscape management goals in Prospect Park must address the safety of park users, as well as the limited resources and budget of the park's maintenance staff. Generally, plantings are in large clumps rather than scattered individual specimens. The finish grade of areas being planted is often mounded to promote better drainage, to make areas of planting appear larger, and to deter people from shortcutting through them. There is sometimes a conflict between those maintenance personnel who wish to minimize crime by removing vegetation and the landscape architects and natural resources staff who seek to fill in the existing tree canopy with understory and herbaceous materials. Clear site lines through existing and proposed plantings are maintained to minimize the potential for crime.

To integrate the playground within a naturalistic setting, the designers sought to cut it back into the edge of the perimeter landscape where it would appear as recessive as possible. The larger play structures were sited away from the park's main pedestrian route and closer to Vanderbilt Street. The mature tree canopy tends to scale down the size of the largest play structure significantly. Only two site-planning changes were made to the 1929 design of the Vanderbilt Playground. One was the relocation of its entrances to two points that tie into the existing walk system more effectively and also integrate with the geometry of the graceful curves around the fenced perimeter. The other was the realignment of the entry walk for the same reasons.

Normally, fences in New York City Parks can be quite dominating as visual elements and barriers. In this playground, the fence is only 2-1/2 feet tall and painted black so that it recedes into the landscape. The fencing is also a New York City standard, but restrained to be only as high as the back of the continuous benches that fol-

low the curving play edge. The curving forms that move around the three large existing trees alter the psychology of the space: in some locations, one feels inside the space even when outside the fence. In time, if the new trees continue to grow, the tree canopy will be continuous and heal the wounds caused by the decline and removal of major trees.

The programming goal for the playground was to create a more interesting playground for different age groups. There had been nothing for older children. The site, only 1/3 acre, was too small for megastructures. One larger unit for older kids was provided along with tire swings near

Figure 3-52: *The playground equipment is pushed into the slope, away from the main pedestrian activity on the opposite side. (Photo by Steven L. Cantor)*

Figure 3-53: *The low, curving fence is adequate for enclosure and comfortable in scale. Seating for adults and supervisors is nestled into the curves of the fence. The curving edge of the poured-in-place surface for the play equipment is consistent with the vocabulary of forms used by the designers. (Photo by Steven L. Cantor)*

Figure 3-54: *The turtle sandbox is quite popular with children. (Photo by Steven L. Cantor)*

the north end. A turtle-shaped sand pit, mini-climber, and mini-swings for younger children are all grouped near the entrance at the south end, where there are also many benches for parents and supervising adults. All furnishings and play elements are standard. A four-foot fence is required by law at the swing set.

Playgrounds must have a resilient and bouncy surface to absorb the impact of children's falls and accidents. Several treatments were tried. After considerable experimentation and comparison with efforts in Central Park, a successful pavement has been developed, a rubberized material that is actually poured in place against the edges of adjacent pavements. A skillful design detailing results in a curving edge to this material that is concentric to the curving forms of the fence. The slight color change between the asphalt pavement and the mat is noticeable, yet the curving joint line blends into the design vocabulary of the space.

Installation of the poured-in-place mat is fairly simple, requiring a cement mixer, rubber, urethane, trowel, and squeegee

gun. The thickness of the material varies, depending on the height of the fall against which it is protecting. Typical is about a 2-1/2-inch-to-3-inch thickness. A base course mixture of 2-5/8-inch black shredded rubber and urethane is applied, with the texture and consistency of cedar mulch. A wearing course, also a shredded mixture of rubber and urethane, but more granular, is also applied. It can be colored like an aggregate pavement.

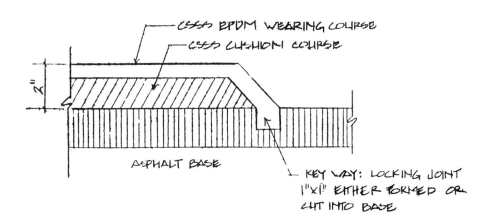

Figure 3-55: *Construction detail of poured-in-place safety seal.*

The New York City Department of Parks and Recreation discontinued the poured-in-place safety surface due to quality control—it wears out too quickly. If the wearing course is too thin, or the proportions of urethane to rubber are not correct within tight tolerances, or the temperature is too hot or too cold, the material does not work. If it dries too quickly, it cracks. Rubber matting is now used: premanufactured in squares, it cannot readily be adapted to curving edges. Its beveled edge (45 degrees) can be cut into a curving pattern only if it is set on a firm subbase and its edges meet flush with concrete curbs or some other rigid material that provides an unyielding border. Nonetheless, this material is being installed at several other playgrounds in Prospect Park.

Compared to other surfacing materials, the unitary synthetic materials, as the rubber/urethane mixtures are called, have a relatively high installation cost. They are also subject to vandalism, in that they can be cut and defaced and even may be flammable. However, the rubber matting is proving to be fairly durable with low maintenance. Unlike other surfacing materials, such as sand, gravel, or wood mulches, the material is not displaced by children during play activities, nor does it spread into adjacent areas and clog drains. It provides consistent shock absorbency and uniform footing and is accessible to the handicapped. One final advantage is that foreign objects, such as glass and metal fragments, do not readily adhere to the rubberized mats nor become embedded in the material.

Throughout the site, particularly for the walk system through the landscape restoration area that was added to the project, it was desired to develop a pavement that would be modeled after the original macadam. It was desired that the aggregate be impregnated into the asphalt. The first attempt was an exposed aggregate pavement on a full depth asphalt base. A three layered asphalt was applied over a prepared subgrade: first a 2-1/2-inch asphalt concrete base course, then a 2-inch top course, and finally an asphalt emulsion binder. The aggregate consisted of a surface treatment of crushed bluestone, graded so that "100 percent would pass a 1/2-inch square opening sieve and 100 percent would be retained on a 1/4-inch-square opening sieve." In other words, the aggregate was of a size range so that all stones were larger than 1/4 inch in diameter and smaller than 1/2 inch diameter. It was also specified that "the aggregate shall be roughly cubical in shape" and that "flat or elongated aggregate will not be accepted." The aggregate was spread at a rate of 25 to 30 pounds per square yard of pavement, and then compacted by use of pneumatic tired rollers. Unfortunately, this treatment did not work. The aggregate was too large and would not adhere to the asphalt. A heavy tack coat was applied, and the stone placed and rolled on it. However, regardless of the quality of the tack coat, the stone would not adhere to the asphalt, even though there was a considerable dimensional variation.

A second approach was tried, in which the composition of the bluestone aggregate was redefined: "50 percent will consist of stone, 100 percent of which passes a 3/8-inch sieve and is retained on a 1/4-inch sieve" and "50 percent will consist of bluestone screenings." This was clearly an aggregate that was denser and smaller. It was again applied at the same rate, and was much more successful. Through additional testing, it was found that by adding dolomitic limestone to the aggregate, the bluestone would bind to the asphalt better and be less likely to wash off.

A third approach has been more successful: the top course (#7F) or wearing coarse has been deleted altogether. Instead, two layers of a thicker base course are applied. The effect is to create a material similar to porous asphalt. An oil truck spreads a layer of tack coat on the surface, and the aggregate is rolled into place with a rubber tired roller, not a conventional roller.

A timber curb, consisting of No. 2 Southern yellow pine, was incorporated to form a clean edge to which the asphalt would be placed. The curb, with its top surface set flush with the pavement, remains following paving. Thinner lumber is used for curved sections, compared to tangents. Three bracing pins or stakes to each ten linear feet of timber curb are used to hold it steady so that it resists the pressure of the pavement and the impact of the roller. The timber is thoroughly oiled before the asphalt is placed against it in order to prevent the absorption of asphaltic substances into the wood, which would deteriorate it. Another important design detail has been to depress these paths lower than the surrounding landscape, a technique that Olmsted followed throughout the major walk system in Prospect Park.

The reconstruction of this playground succeeds in transforming an eyesore so that it recedes into the overall structure of the park. Although the design vocabulary consists of New York City Parks Department standards, they are arranged in an artful way and used functionally. There is effective segregation of different age groups with ample space allocated for parents and socializing. The park landscape has been dramatically enhanced. A modern interpretation of Olmsted and Vaux's dense perimeter landscape has been created which transitions between the Windsor Terrace neighborhood and the interior landscape of the park.

INTERIOR GARDEN
Iowa State University

Ames, IA

PROJECT: *Interior Garden*
CLIENT: *Iowa State University*
LOCATION: *Ames, IA*
LANDSCAPE ARCHITECTS: *Mira Engler and Gina Crandell*
DATE: *1991*
COST: *$40,000*

Mira Engler, with degrees in landscape architecture from the Technion in Haifa, Israel, and the University of California, Berkeley, is an Assistant Professor of Landscape Architecture at Iowa State University. "The complex and hybrid nature of the profession of landscape architecture—the integration of living systems and artifacts, ecology and art, nature and culture—attracted me to become a landscape architect, and promised a fertile ground for inquiry and practice." Her practice in Israel from 1981 to 1987 produced several traditional and highly crafted landscapes. Among her built projects abroad are "The Rock Garden," in Hayarkon Park, Tel Aviv, Israel and "The Rose Garden" and "Music Hall Garden," both in Yavnhe, Israel, in collaboration with Gideon Sarig. Graduate work at Berkeley "freed me to explore, in another culture, how cultural images and values determine physical form and aesthetics. I was also able to deepen my understanding of the social, ethical, and ecological implications of design." Her areas of scholarly focus are "mundane and rejected cultural landscapes, landscape aesthetics, and public art." In the United States, in collaboration with Professor Gina Crandell of Iowa State, she has designed and had built "Rail Interior" in St. Louis, MO. and "Interior Garden" on the campus at Iowa State. "Interior Garden" explores "the power of public art to extract and distill the meaning and narrative of a place, while also investing and encoding a place with new meanings."

In 1978 legislation was enacted in Iowa allocating one half of one percent of every new state building for art. The Art-in-State Buildings program at Iowa State University has commissioned an impressive range of public art at sites throughout the campus. In 1990, landscape architects Mira Engler and Gina Crandell were contracted by the

Art-in-State Buildings program at the University to develop proposals for public art for the new "Linear Accelerator Facility" at Iowa State University. Adjoining an existing slaughterhouse, this building is not an experimental structure for theoretical physics, but a facility to irradiate pork as part of an ambitious program in agricultural research. The irradiation is achieved by a high powered X-ray "gun" that emits invisible short waves to reduce or eliminate bacteria from

Figure 3-56: *Slaughterhouse dock, plan and elevation, 1991*

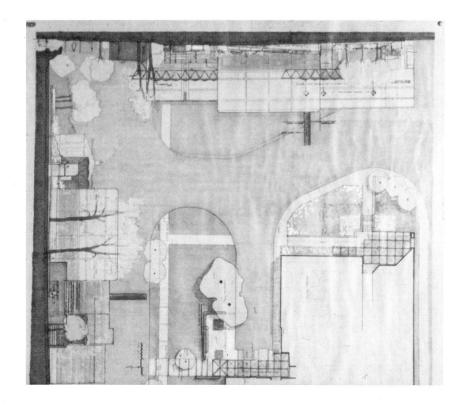

food and feed. Since the high energy electrons and X-rays that are generated are dangerous, the interior walls of the facility are ten feet thick and only conveyor belts travel inside it.

The facility is generally quite inaccessible. Neither the slaughterhouse nor the linear accelerator has any windows or design connection to the adjacent campus. The stainless steel slaughterhouse and kitchen are secluded from students passing by. However, the slaughterhouse and linear accelerator facility appropriately adjoin the Meat Laboratory Building where teachers in the fields of animal science and meat research are trained. The architects designed a new screen wall to hide the loading dock where the animals were delivered to the slaughterhouse. Therefore, the two landscape architects saw as their goal for public art "to create visual, physical, and, most importantly in this situation, psychological access" to a facility that would otherwise be unknown.

Selected by the Art-in State Buildings Program, a review committee, composed of university administrators, animal scientists, and designers, evaluated the proposals of the designers. Their first proposal, called "Slaughterhouse Dock," was rejected as too controversial because it might have generated debate about animal rights issues. The proposal focused on the essential nature of the facility as a place where animals are transformed into food for people. As described by the two landscape architects,

"Bright red enamel fences, like those farmers all over Iowa use to mark the entrance to their fields as well as to contain livestock, lead from the street to the proposed screening wall. Like gates, the fences are lined up behind one another, but they enclose nothing. One can climb or simply walk around them. The screening wall has been pulled open to form a doorway inviting entrance, and two metaphorical windows have been cut out to further stimulate the passersby. Behind the wall are brightly painted transformers and a bill-

Figure 3-57: *Slaughterhouse dock, model, 1991*

board size quotation by Iowa State writer Jane Smiley."

Acclaimed in her home state, Smiley is perhaps best known for her Pulitzer Prize-winning book, *A Thousand Acres*. On the billboard, an excerpt from her work *Ordinary Love and Good Will*, (Alfred A. Knopf/Random House, 1989) proclaims,

> "I think it is good to experience one's power over the animal, to treat it well, house it properly, give it a good life and a painless death, to feel with one's own hands the

bloody cost of one's appetites, and to know viscerally what one is like, one is like an animal, one lives in nature, where death is."

The lettering on the billboard and its positioning on the site make only the first line and part of the second visible from the street or sidewalk. If the pedestrian's interest is engaged, then he or she must make a decision to read the rest of the quote, and as a result, see the unloading dock and discover the activities that occur there. The

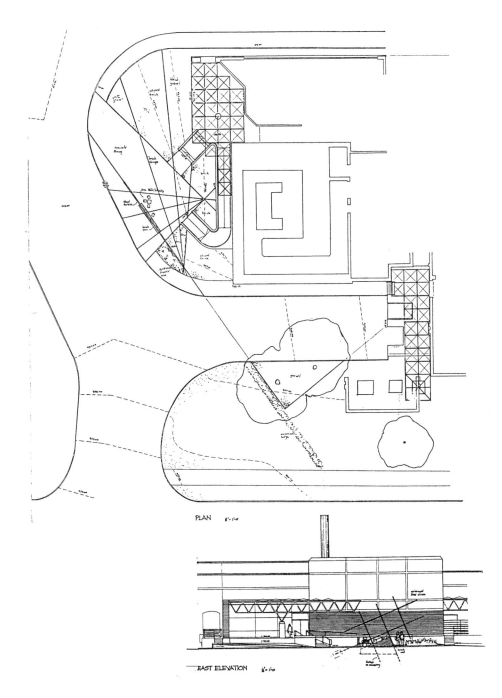

PLAN

EAST ELEVATION

Figure 3-58: *Interior garden, plan and elevation, 1991*

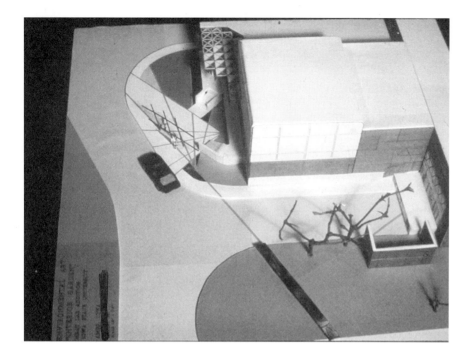

Figure 3-59: *Interior garden, model, 1991*

Their second proposal, called "Interior Garden," was accepted. The designers proposed the creation of a garden outside the ten foot thick walls of the building. In the final design, the facade of the building wall is deconstructed: it is expressed as a stainless steel skeleton 20 feet tall and 40 feet long, recalling the recessed grid in the concrete facade of the building. The stainless steel frame is not parallel to the building, but placed at a 30-degree angle to it, as if pointing towards the unloading dock of the slaughterhouse. Stainless steel is used to mimic the materials of the irradiation and slaughterhouse equipment inside the building. In elevation, when viewed from in front, the stainless steel is rotated downward towards the ground, and a low brick wall at the same angle appears to rise from the ground on one side of it, as if the weight of the structure is causing it to sink into the ground. Perhaps, it appears to some to be rising from the ground plane. The transparent wall, in front of the opaque wall of the building, opens a psychological window and becomes a gateway into the garden space. (See Figure C-32).

The engineer for the stainless steel screen and the brick wall was K. F. Dunker, a professor of engineering at Iowa State. The stainless steel screen is made of 6 inch by 6 inch by 1/4 inch tubes, forming a grid of 42′ × 18′. The brick wall measures 14′-0″ long and 1′-4″ wide with a four inch thick concrete cap. The wall extends from grade to a height of 5′-0″.

The design of the ground plane reinforces the distinctions between what is inside and what is outside the building. A four inch wide, narrow band of brick pavement extends from the base of the stainless steel skeleton, crosses the service drive to the site of the existing screen wall in front

quotation is powerful imagery that gives animal slaughter a context within the processes of nature that encompass humans as well. The farmer and the consumer, as well as the animal, exist as a part of this ecology. The quotation was the pivotal element in the committee's rejection of the proposal. The committee directed the artists to focus their work away from slaughter and towards the process of linear acceleration.

Figure 3-60: *The garden is bound by the ten foot thick walls of the building and the stainless steel skeleton recalling the recessed grid in the concrete facade*

of the slaughterhouse. The band turns abruptly at a right angle and leads to the door of the slaughterhouse. The band forms the boundary of this garden that symbolizes life and death for the animals that enter. Another set of brick bands seem to radiate from the irradiation facility itself. "Inside" the garden all pavements are inert materials: concrete, brick chips, black and grey gravel. The gravel beds were filled with 12 tons of clay-colored chipped brick, 850 pounds of chipped blue and black slate and four tons of white marble chips. Immediately outside the band of brick are dense volumetric plantings of shrubs and perennials to symbolize life. The plantings include a bed of red bee balm or Oswego tea (*Monarda didyma*) and a linear hedge of arborvitae (*Arborvitae thunbergii*).

Additional brick bands in the ground plane project from the linear accelerator and intersect with the line of the stainless steel screen, as if the bands on the ground represent lines of x-rays radiating from equipment inside the building. The two series of intersecting lines visually connect the new facility with the existing laboratory. The same treatment is used for the entrances for people and those for other animals.

Passing underneath or around the screen wall, the visitor comes across bizarre furnishings for a picnic. Silhouettes, punched from stainless steel, of pigs, cows and a chicken, give form to a skeletal iron table and chairs. The imagery is stark: one is reminded that these animals enter alive, are irradiated, and exit as food. The table and chairs are not ergonometrically conceived; they are not for sitting. "This is not a place to have lunch; it is a place to feed one's thoughts."

As if to emphasize the irony of the setting, the set of chairs with table could possibly be "part of your own dining room or porch furniture. Manufactured by Guild Master Imports, Inc., the furniture can be bought through your local furniture store, similarly to the slab of meat from the super-

market shelf." The furniture was ordered unfinished, in raw iron without upholstery, and was sandblasted and primed. Mounted atop the backs of the chairs are iron profiles of pigs. The table design is a hollow iron box on four sturdy legs. A stencilled design of a cow has been cut in each of the four sides of the box. "Industrial Maintenance Coating Paint," manufactured by Sherwin Williams, was specified. "Ebony," a dark grey, was used for the chairs and exterior of the table, and a safety red for the interior surfaces of

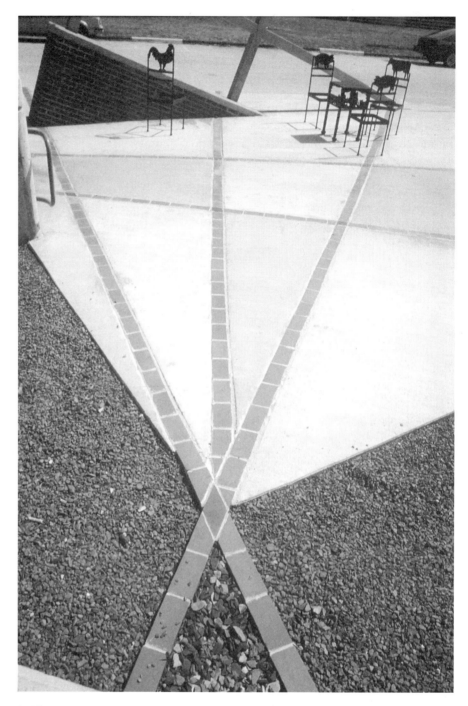

Figure 3-62: *Another set of brick bands seem to radiate from the irradiation facility itself*

the table. The contrasting colors in the table highlight the symbolism of the animal images, as if one is looking through a dissected cow.

The differences between the proposal that was accepted and the one that was rejected are instructive. Environmental art demands its viewers "to think about and experience a very specific place in unexpected ways." The "Slaughterhouse Dock" was more direct, in that it provided an unimpeded view into the loading dock for animals brought for slaughter. By contrast, the "Interior Garden" is more subtle, and as a result, more successful in creating a room that is invested with symbolic meanings.

Figure 3-63: *Inside the garden and behind the "screen" wall, the visitor comes across bizarre furnishing for a picnic. However, this is not a place to have lunch; it is a place to feed one's thoughts.*

The incorporation of the table where food is consumed, in contrast to the dramatization of the ramp leading to slaughter, is still a powerful image full of meaning about life and death, should the passerby wish to participate. Just as the quotation by Jane Smiley was too direct for the committee, the imagery it contains is brutal but certainly powerful. By removing the concreteness of the language and substituting a more fanciful image, the designers achieved their goal without offending sensibilities.

Art-on-campus tours as well as design classes and daily users frequently visit the

Figure 3-64: *A view of the chairs and table along the wall.*

Figure 3-65: *Detail, chairs and table.*

site. The art invokes varied questions and interpretations. The most common reaction to "Interior Garden" is the exclamation of surprise that the building is a slaughterhouse and a linear accelerator and that such facilities exist on campus. There is also surprise that landscape architecture can integrate such telling and multiple forms into the subject of the site.

SYDNEY, AUSTRALIA OLYMPICS
New Jersey Institute of Technology

Newark, NJ

PROJECT: *Sydney Olympics*
LOCATION: *Sydney, Australia*
ARCHITECT: *Thomas Navin, AIA, New York City, Adjunct Professor*
STUDENTS: *Carl Dahlquist, Jeffrey Gerhard, Gary Saitta*
DATE: *1992*

Architect Thomas Navin, AIA, also Associate ASLA, combines his own small practice in New York City with teaching. He is an Adjunct Professor in the School of Architecture at the New Jersey Institute of Technology (NJIT) in Newark, where he teaches both an architecture design and an all-encompassing lecture course entitled "Landscape Architecture," a requirement in the undergraduate architecture curriculum. Also an instructor in the Education Department of the New York Botanical Garden in the Bronx, he teaches an intermediate level landscape design studio and a lecture course on the history and theory of landscape architecture. Finally, he has worked as an associate with Eric R. Kuhne and Associates in the design for a new public park in Fort Wayne, IN, called Headwaters Park and projects in Sydney, Australia.

For the spring, 1992, upper-level Architecture studio at NJIT, Navin sought a timely problem that would challenge and excite his students as well as tie into his own interest in the relationship between architecture and landscape in the creation of civic spaces. His choice was to have the class members prepare master plans for the Olympics in the year 2000. Perhaps clairvoyant, his students finished their work well before the vote was taken in 1993 in which Sydney was selected the host of the Olympics at the turn of the century.

Mr. Navin began the 12 week course with a presentation to the students of the site proposed by the city of Sydney. The boundaries of the proposed Homebush Bay site are the Parramatta River to the north, Homebush Bay itself to the east, the F4 Freeway to the south and Silverwater Road

to the west. Much of the area, including the sites of the former State Brickworks and the Homebush Abattoirs (slaughterhouses), was government-owned but no longer in productive use. In addition to being attracted to the site by its availability for development and its access to existing transportation, the Olympics 2000 Bid Team, which included architects from five of Sydney's leading architecture practices, saw an opportunity to create a 20-minute ferry service following the Parramatta River from Sydney's Harbour Bridge to the Homebush site. Homebush, an industrial and residential community located 14 kilometers (8.7 miles) west of Sydney's central business district, provided a site of approximately 660 hectares (1637 acres) that was mostly vacant, except for the remains of a magnificent, 150 foot deep pit for brick excavations. However, there were considerable constraints to development on this flat and gently rolling topography. Parts of the site were wetlands associated with meandering Haslams Creek. The mangroves, marshes, and other areas had been the site of landfill and dumping, including toxic wastes from a Union Carbide plant formerly located across Homebush Bay.

The second major task was an intensive investigation of site-planning strategies employed in previous Olympics and related recreational parks, such as world's fairs and amusement parks. Site concepts were analyzed, such as Bernard Tschumi's Parc de La Villette and Thomas Jefferson's Academical Village. The goal was to give the students a background in site-planning issues that would enable them to "translate conceptual ideas into the organization of the landscape, with buildings as a mere component within this large composition and space conception." The Olympics are a celebration of the highest aspirations of mankind in an international forum in which the vicarious experience of the spectators is as important as the participation of the athletes. Therefore, site planning for the Olympics must focus on the modulation of space to create not only athletic venues, but also forms which lend themselves to civic processions and other rituals.

Navin assembled and distributed to the students a complete packet of information about the venues for the Olympics 2000. He had contacted the Sydney Olympic Games Committee and Win Zeliff of Sizemore Floyd Ingram, a joint venture which was doing architecture and facilities programming for the Atlanta Olympics. These materials included a list of all the sports events that would occur together with the capacities of their facilities, and whether they were existing or proposed. The program included the locations of all of these facilities at either Homebush Bay, the major site in Sydney, or Darling Harbour, the secondary site in the city, and several scattered locations some distance from the city where other facilities were indicated. The proximity of each proposed facility to two central locales—the city center of Sydney and the location of the proposed village to house the athletes—was an important criterion as well. For example, the hotel to house the members and staff of the International Olympic Committee, and the media facilities including housing and offices for the press and media, had to be immediately adjacent to the Athletes' Village and reasonably close to the city center and major transportation facilities. Some sports venues could be considerable distances from both the city center and the Athletes' Village. Some existing facilities, such as the Sydney Football Stadium which seats 40,000, required no adjustments. Others required considerable upgrading, temporary modifications, or temporary *fitout*, an Australian term referring to programming changes. For example, the existing soccer stadium, to be used for a warm-up space for the athletes, required the fitout of additional bleachers. Some facilities were already under construction as part of park development in the city, and some had been proposed but never built.

HOMEBUSH BAY VENUES

FACILITY	OLYMPIC USE	CAPACITY	STATUS
Olympic Stadium	Opening and closing ceremonies Football (finals) Individual showjumping	80,000	Bid dependent
Sydney Internat'l Athletics Center	Athletics warm-up and training	15,000	In construction
Gymnastics Pavilion (Coliseum)	Gymnastics Handball (Finals) Volleyball (Finals)	16,000	Proposed
Sydney Internat'l Aquatic Center	Swimming, Diving Water polo (Finals) Synchronized swimming Modern pentathlon (swimming)	10,000+	In construction (temp. upgrading required)
State Sports Centre	Fencing Modern Pentathlon	4,500 and 2,000	Existing

State Hockey Centre	Hockey	20,000 and 5,000	Existing (upgrading req.)
Velodrome	Cycling	6,000	Proposed
Volleyball Pavilion 1	Volleyball (prelims)	7,000	Proposed
Volleyball Pavilion 2	Volleyball (prelims)	3,500	Proposed
Handball Pavilion	Handball (prelims)	7,000	Proposed
Badminton Pavilion	Badminton Rhythmic Gymnastics	5,000	Proposed
Judo Pavilion	Judo	10,000	Proposed
Wrestling Pavilion	Wrestling	5,500	Proposed
Olympic Tennis	Tennis	10,000 and 5,000	Bid dependant
Archery Centre	Archery	5,000	Proposed (temp. upgrading req.)
Showring	Modern Pentathlon (equestrian)	10,000 +	Proposed
Bicentennial Park	Modern Pentathlon (cross country)	?	Existing (temp. fitout req.)
Pistol Shooting	Modern Pentathlon (shooting)	?	Proposed

The Athletes Village and Technical Officials Village are also proposed for Homebush Bay.

DARLING HARBOR VENUE

Sydney Entertainment Centre	Basketball	12,000	Existing (temp. modificatn req.)
Sydney Convention Centre	Weightlifting	3,800	Existing (temp. fitout required)
Exhibition Hall 1 and 2	Table tennis	10,000	Existing (temp. fitout required)
Exhibition Hall 4 and 5	Boxing	10,000	Existing (temp. fitout required)

The International Olympic Committee Hotel, the Media Centre, Hotel and Village, and the City Centre are also proposed for Darling Harbor.

Still other facilities are proposed for other areas of Sydney. Many of these take advantage of existing facilities, such as yachting at Rushcutters Bay and Sydney Harbour, and soccer at Parramatta Football Stadium. Additional soccer venues will use existing facilities in Melbourne, Brisbane, and Adelaide.

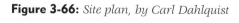
Figure 3-66: *Site plan, by Carl Dahlquist*

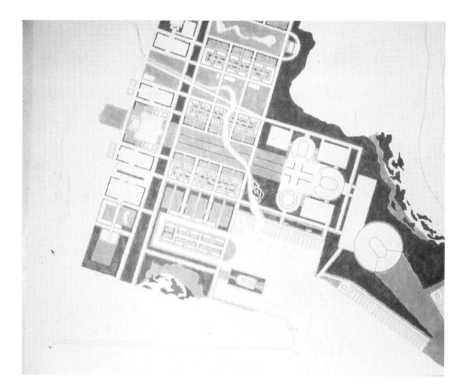

within the site. The class mapped the location of the landfills and dumping sites, the large mangrove wetland on the eastern border and the salt marsh on the northern edge of the site. An existing bicentennial park of 102 hectares (253 acres), squeezed between the mangrove and one of the landfills, is located in the southeast corner of the site. Finally, there is a botanical garden to the north, bordering a large area of polluted bay sediments.

After the class as a whole studied different types of planning approaches to ordering large sites, and developed a site analysis and program development, each student prepared a master plan. After a presentation of each master plan, each student, in consultation with Mr. Navin, selected a particular focus for further study. These additional design studies were presented either as models or as additional drawings. Dramatically divergent designs by three students are presented.

Carl Dahlquist applies a rectilinear geometry to the site, with great potential for prominent processional spaces that would offer dramatic sequential experi-

The class concentrated their design efforts on the Homebush Bay site, located 12 kilometers due west of the city center. Using existing topographic maps, photographs, and other materials provided by Mr. Navin, they prepared a schematic site analysis showing constraints due to incompatible adjacent land uses and flood plain conditions. Several historic properties occur

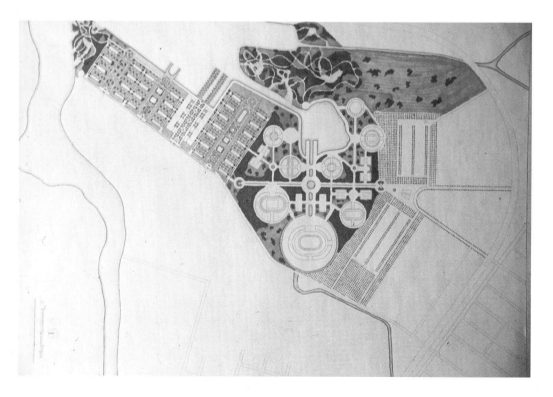

Figure 3-67: *Focused development plan, by Carl Dahlquist*

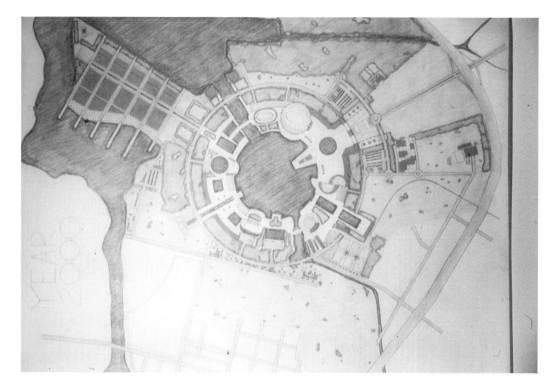

Figure 3-68: *Site plan, by Jeffrey Gerhard*

Figure 3-69: *Site model, by Jeffrey Gerhard*

Figure 3-70: *Site plan, by Gary Saitta*

Figure 3-71: *Site model, by Gary Saitta*

ences for both the athletes and visitors. He studied in further detail the edge of the waterfront and the procession into the site from the waterfront to the main Olympic Stadium.

The other two students explored curving geometries with different defining characteristics. Jeffrey Gerhard created a vast, formal, circular geometry in which all buildings, roads and systems are concentri-

Figure 3-72: *Model of Headwaters Park, Fort Wayne, IN, the design for which was informed by the work on the Sydney Olympics. The Terrace Garden, with its curved grass terraces, links park to river as one of a series of landscape rooms. The Garden restores a waterfront ignored by the city for over a century. Designed by Eric R. Kuhne and Associates, New York, NY and Grinsfelder Associates Architects, Fort Wayne, IN (Photo by Jack Pottle/Esto)*

cally placed around a large interior lake, the Olympic Quay, created by flooding the site of the existing brick pit. He chose to study in detail the main access into the site via highway and marina facilities. Finally, Gary Saitta wed concentric circular forms to dynamic axes which intersect the circle at pivotal geometric points in the design. His design retained the brick pit as a central element around and through which processional events would occur. The Olympic torch, the pit, and the Olympic stadium are aligned on one axis that terminates with a spectacular view over the bay. This axis is perpendicular to another organizing axis that is terminated at either end by large buildings that accept the rectilinear geometry on one face and the circular geometry on the other. He chose to study further the three major components of the first axis, and the circulation system leading to the Olympic Village, located off the other axis.

As site planning and development moves forward with the Sydney Olympics, it will be fascinating to see how final designs evolve and respond to the opportunities and constraints of the site. For Mr. Navin, the studio project gave him an opportunity to explore with his students large-scale site-planning issues, in contrast to the small-scale architectural projects which he typically handles.

A serendipitous advantage has been the project's unexpected application to his work as part of the design team for Headwaters Park, in Fort Wayne, IN with the New York offices of Eric R. Kuhne and Associates. A 22-acre site in what had been a light industrial area built up in the floodplain and gradually abandoned, the park is

a three-phase restoration with a total construction budget of $8 million. The program includes what is called the Festival Center, a permanent home for diverse festival groups that had previously located their annual events in various parts of the city. The design of this space within the park has required the study of parades, processions, and rituals in civic spaces. The final plans call for ceremonial spaces with viewing stands for the public and city officials, so that both participants and spectators can fully appreciate and be intimately involved with the arrival, passage, and exit from special spaces in the park. In addition, a rich mix of trees and understory planting restores the floodway to the St. Mary's River. The Terrace Garden, with its curved grass terraces, links the park to the river as one of a series of landscaped rooms. Riparian habitats along the waters' edge redeem the river for wildlife and aquatic life. The combination of large-scale planning concerns and small-scale design details explored in Mr. Navin's studio on the Sydney Olympics have rewarded him with a design vocabulary utilized in the development of this river park.

CHAPTER FOUR

CONCLUSION: PROJECT MANAGEMENT

One of my goals in this book has been to give the reader a sense of some of the covert personal, political, and social processes that contribute to the success of a major project. A good design, if it is well-constructed and in tune with the dynamics of its site, is self-evident. However, there is something mysterious, even magical, about the process whereby a group of diverse and often egotistical design professionals join forces to produce a creative, cogent result that satisfies both the articulated and unstated desires of a client, either an individual or a group of people. This process is the art of project management. In my experience as a professor at two universities and a landscape architect in four distinctly different landscape architecture firms, certain factors, attitudes, and guidelines expedite a good design process and contribute to a quality result. The following twelve guidelines are my rules of the game.

The discussion that follows is highly subjective based on my experience. To make it as concrete as possible, I have included some examples that are taken primarily from my work at Clarke + Rapuano, Inc., and other professional experience that is noted. I feel certain that every project presented in this book includes numerous additional examples that

would best be told, and of course, embellished, by those people who resolved the problems or foresaw solutions. A few of these have been described in some detail in the previous sections, but most go unnoticed because they are so rarely documented. Perhaps the compliment often paid to landscape architecture projects— "It looks as if it has always been that way"—is also applicable to project management. The project manager of a well-managed project often goes unnoticed. Often one is only aware of the project manager when there are problems.

Even though wonderful designs are created and constructed in violation of these guidelines, such results are a credit to the talent of the designers and their dedication and professionalism in overcoming obstacles, some of which are created by the people who employ them. Project management *in a vacuum* eventually takes a severe toll in battered and warring egos, plummeting office morale, mental and physical exhaustion, high turnover rates, and frequent bankruptcies.

Sadly, the landscape architecture and design professions seem besieged by project managers and even principals who undermine, whether consciously or unconsciously, their own best intentions. In a field in which uncertain economic conditions intensify the competition for limited potential projects, a natural tendency is for employees to be always on the cusp between being full-time and part-time, or between being part-time and laid off. Insecurity and masochism become merit badges for employees, who, never having experienced anything better, grow to expect as normal appallingly stressful and abnormal conditions and treatment. It does not have to be that way. Think what could be accomplished if these situations were the exception, not the rule.

1. Communicate

An argument can be made that all of life is about communication: The need to communicate is a basic instinct. Design, too, is about communication. Before the concept for the design can be developed, one's qualifications must be communicated to a prospective client, who is likely listening to presentations or reviewing similar materials from competing design teams. To com-

municate clearly, in all ways, whether written, oral, computer-aided, or graphic, is an essential skill. It is rare to have equal talents and skills in all such areas; therefore, it is crucial to know one's limitations.

Someone must communicate with the client consistently, clearly, and directly. All design and contractual aspects of the project must have organized documentation. Depending on the size of the firm and the role it is playing in a particular project the communicator is as crucial as the designer. One must communicate with consultants, colleagues, and those being supervised. One must deal with a responsible member of the bureaucracy, as high up as possible, without stepping on anyone's toes. The results of all of these efforts must be carefully organized in correspondence files, the bulk of which should be backed up by computer files.

An important aspect of this documentation often overlooked is the need to photograph works during and after construction. In New York City, the Department of Parks and Recreation requires that all contractors

Figure 4-1(1), 4-1(2), and 4-1(3): *Wall reconstruction at the Harlem Meer; the mowing of algae by the Central Park Conservancy's workforce; and the construction of the Victorian style benches at the Concert Ground are all documented carefully by Sara Cedar Miller, the staff photographer for the Conservancy. A huge photographic library is available for each project.*

provide photographs of the work in progress. The Central Park Conservancy has its own staff photographer, Sara Cedar Miller, to document all construction efforts during the restoration of the park. For private firms and others, an accurate photographic record is crucial in publicizing the work and recalling what was done in order to inform contemporary practice. It is far preferable to be organized about photographing in a timely manner during the progression of the work, rather than in a frantic rush to meet a publisher's deadline or to gather evidence in a lawsuit.

In larger firms, the role of communicating is often assigned to a person deemed the project manager. He or she may also be a designer, but his or her principal role is not necessarily to design but to keep the project on schedule and within budget. This person is responsible for all communications with the client, discussing and negotiating contractual issues, arranging meetings, distributing documents, and trying to free the time of the design team members to do what they do best. Often, if there is friction between different participants, the project manager is needed to instill confidence in insecure personalities, assuage bruised egos, and tantalize other members with the goals. The project manager may be a very capable designer and may actually contribute in major ways to the design, yet it is not likely that credit will be given for that function. Instead, the other skills are what are most needed: business sense, common sense, and an ability to listen and communicate. For the balance of this discussion I will refer to the project manager, although the role may be taken on by the principal-in-charge, a landscape architect, or someone entirely different.

Clarke + Rapuano was originally hired by the Maryland National Capital Parks and Planning Commission to develop parkway studies for the Rockville right-of-way. As part of the public participation required for this project, we made presentations to the Montgomery County Board of Commissioners. Public opposition to a road of any kind, no matter how sensitively designed, became pronounced. In order to present the broadest range of alternatives to the client,

and by extension, to the public, it became clear that a no-build alternative should be considered. I communicated with the client, and for an additional fee, we produced a third concept for the right-of-way, a conceptual plan for a linear park. Along with the two-lane and four-lane parkway plans, the park plan was presented at public meetings and became a critical part of the discussion about the eventual resolution of the use of the right-of-way. Including the park study in the final product also had the effect of responding effectively to the criticisms of some citizens convinced that the client's only goal was to build a road.

Figures 4-1(2) and 4-1(3): *(Cont.)*

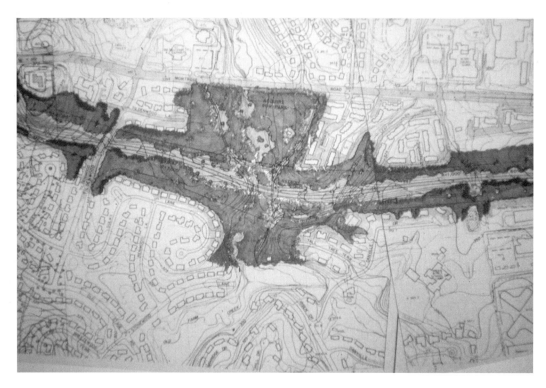

Figure 4-2: *Two lane parkway study at the western entrance to the Rockville Facility.*

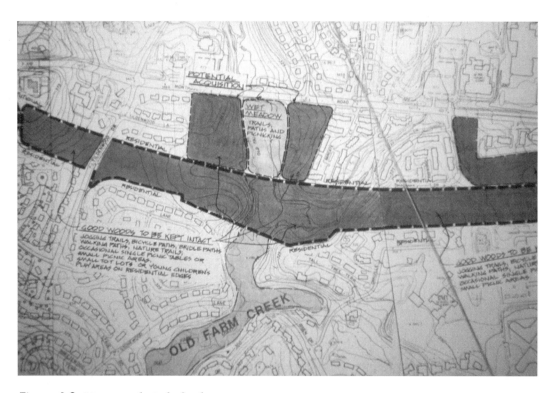

Figure 4-3: *Linear park study for the same area.*

Although there are clearly times when a project manager must make recommendations to a client, give clear directions, and tell people, usually the staff, what to do, there are also times in which it is important to listen. Active listening in a non-judgmental manner is an aspect of communication often overlooked. This refers to evincing clear expressions from others, rather than asking leading questions. There is a

PROJECT MANAGEMENT

tremendous difference between the questions, "What do you think?" and "Don't you agree?" The difference in responses is likely to be even more compelling. For example, in the initial conceptual phases of a project when a team is becoming familiar with the site and design issues, a design process often used is brainstorming. Random ideas are generated without any evaluation. A project manager participating in this process should be helping participants to generate as many ideas as possible, not short-circuiting it with narrowing strictures before it even begins.

As a volunteer I benefited from training and participation in the Gay and Lesbian Switchboard. Members receive thousands of calls a month in which people are simply asking for information, such as an organization's name and phone number, a referral to a travel agency, or a bar that appeals to the caller's interest. However, a significant number are in the category of peer counseling, in which the caller has a specific problem, sometimes not even that well articulated, and needs help. We were trained never to offer advice or judge. After all, it is arrogant and dangerous to tell a person who is a complete stranger what to do. The goal is to ask questions in a manner that enables the caller to define the problem, sort out his or her options, and begin to reach a solution. For example, the simple questions, "How do you feel about _____?" or the statment, "I hear what you are saying; what do you think about _____?" may evoke a tremendous range of response that can gradually be focused in an effective way. Many project managers and designers would benefit from an empathetic approach to communication in which they help others articulate their needs or concerns about a design or management issue before pontificating their own.

The most notable change during the period of my employment at Clarke + Rapuano has been the transition from manual to computer-aided drafting and design. The Merck Headquarters facility and the Rockville Facility Right-of-Way Study were among the last projects in the firm that were done entirely without computer-assisted drafting. As a project manager working with some of the "old-timers" on these projects, I found it fascinating to see how they worked and how similar types of drawings or tasks of work would be done by computer. However, regardless of the means of production, communication among key personnel is critical. For example, the elevation of one entire section of the road system for the Merck facility was raised several feet as a result of architectural changes and site planning concerns. Redrawing manually the grading plans was a major task that could have been done easily by computer. Yet, this onerous task was made manageable by the principal engineer, William Wild, who directed the work methodically, communicated with the draftspeople, provided graphic standards for all of the changes, and checked preliminary grading plans carefully for errors.

The Rockville project (see Figures 1–29 through 1–39) did not progress to a working drawings phase. Even so, many alternatives were explored for certain sections of the corridor. Although alternative horizontal alignments and grading plans could have been prepared by computer, it might not have been a significant savings in time over the relatively quick and consistently applied manual drafting techniques that were used to study alternatives.

On the other hand, there are significant time savings in plotting vertical profiles of roads, particularly when alternatives are being explored. Also, the computer offers considerably more efficient and accurate means of calculating elevations of points along the centerline and other points on cross sections of proposed roads. We take the information from such computer print-outs to locate proposed contours and complete grading plans. For more final drawings, existing and proposed contours tied into specific cross-sections of a road may be plotted quickly and accurately. The computer is also indispensable in calculating and plotting the final horizontal geometry of road systems. Finally, the computer is a remarkable aid in calculating volumes of excavation and fill for roadwork, particularly roads that have uniform cross sections. However, none of these applications substitutes for clear communication between the designers and engineers, on the one hand, and the computer staff, on the other. In fact, since there is a tendency not to be able to see the results of revisions until they are replotted, compared to a more immediate visual confirmation from manual drafting, it is all the more important to stress communication.

2. Organize

The primary way to keep a project on schedule is to organize the time of everyone participating. For a large project involving many consultants, this may not be possible; but the project manager can help consultants organize their time by being certain that they have all information, documents, and schedules in hand and are completely aware of deadlines and requirements.

The most important aspect of organization is planning the production of the work in increments that do not involve repeating or redoing steps once they are completed. Obviously, doing this maximizes the efficiency of the operations and also boosts morale. No employee, whether at the highest or lowest level, finds satisfying the prospect of redoing a plan because critical information available at the time it was done was somehow not distributed promptly and properly. In the end, there can be no excuse for this omission. Due to circumstances beyond anyone's control and the nature of the design process, there are many times when the design evolves and the drawings must be revised. Therefore, every effort should be made to limit rework to those situations in which it is absolutely necessary.

Organization according to critical path is important whether documents are being produced by manual drafting or computer aided drafting. How much time should it take to produce a drawing? Which drawing comes first, and what work must necessarily precede it and follow it?

Particularly on larger projects, the project manager may be responsible for seeing the larger picture, while civil or structural engineers, for example, may focus on particular details or problems to such a degree that they have no sense of the overall picture. It is therefore critical that the project manager know what everyone on the design team is doing at any given time, to be certain that what is being produced reflects the most current design decisions.

One of the most difficult aspects of project management is the challenge of being certain that all key staff that are preparing the schedules are working from the most current plan sheets and using the correct, standardized language and symbols. For the project manager, a sense of the critical path is essential in this task since many, but not all, of these plans, profiles, and detail sheets must be nearly complete before most of the various schedules can be compiled. Some schedules can be started earlier, and a few must wait until the very end. Therefore, the organization of this information for all members of the design team is a critical part of an efficient design and production process.

3. If the Timing's Wrong, Nothing Else Matters.

In some ways, this idea is a corollary to communication and organization. If one does both well, the timing falls into place. Often the design team can be so excited about the work being done, and so distracted by pressures of production, and sometimes so irresponsible, that they forget to bill the client. Similarly, no matter how wonderful the product, if it is submitted a month late without careful explanation to the client, the job may be over.

Billings, submittals of milestone documents, and major communications must be submitted in a timely manner. Clients, particularly government agencies, often have specific requirements for billings. They may occur on the first of the month, with appropriate back-up of employee time sheets, for example. A description of the work performed should accompany any bill as a frame of reference for both the client and the landscape architect. If there is a question about a bill months after submittal, it is helpful to both to see a summary of the services for which the client was being billed. The time to ask for payment for extra services is before they start, or at worst, as they are starting, but not after they have been completed and submitted. It seems obvious, but too many designers overlook the simple notion that a client, no matter how generous and fair-minded, will be less likely to pay for extra service that he or she needs if the completed drawings are submitted before there is any discussion of them in contractual language.

The submittals of milestone documents can sometimes become delayed as a result of numerous last minute changes. Except for final contract documents, it is important to remember that a particular drawing is only as final as the revision date noted on it. It is often better to submit design development drawings, for example, on time, rather than withhold the submittal while waiting to resolve two or three issues. If these are major issues, there is the likelihood that extra services will be involved. In addition, important issues require careful study. To include sketchy information about them in an otherwise comprehensive submittal may create problems during the review, as if the client is being insulted rather than accommodated. Therefore, it is better to submit the documents and discuss the extra services in a separate communication. Too often, if the project manager withholds a submittal indefinitely on a complex project while the last issues are being resolved, additional problems will be discovered by the client or the designers that will further complicate the design, delay its completion, and end any hope for a review in a timely manner.

4. Review the Payroll for the Project on a Regular Basis

"Good" design that results in a huge monetary loss to the firm is *not*, in fact, good at all, but inept. The human costs in staff layoffs, deadline pressures, and overtime without compensation are very real and very significant to the people subjected to them. It must be the project manager's responsibility to know, at any time, where the project is in relation to the budget. In addition, he or she must be able to project what this relationship will be in the future. When financial problems arise, they must be addressed immediately, whether this means a conference with the staff to discuss how to work more efficiently, a discussion with the client about the fee structure, or both. There can be situations in which the fee agreed upon is found to be low, but there are no options for financial salvation. These are obviously the situations in which it is most crucial to be able to project what is left to do, and how it can be done as efficiently as possible, while still serving the client's needs. I am familiar with a mythical project, for example, in which the fee negotiated was woefully low, and even though the scope of work increased by millions of dollars, the client refused to acknowledge that the fee should be increased. The project manager, horrified at this situation, was too embarrassed about the negotiations and so dedicated to doing a perfect job that he neglected to inform the principals. Years later, the client is still asking for the completion of the work for the same fee, the drawings for this wonderful design are still not finished, and hundreds of thousands of dollars in payroll are gone.

5. Trust

Just as it is crucial to communicate with clients and colleagues, it is equally important to trust one another. Everyone on the design team, from the most senior to the most junior person, must have equal access to information about the project. There is no room for controlling personalities or insecure people who secretly hoard information with the fear that they would become obsolete if it were available to those who needed it. Although every member of the design team has a different role, each cannot function synergistically if the lines of communication are short-circuited.

Lawrence Halprin in his book, *RSVP Cycles*, introduced the idea that design is a cyclical process, that the four major functions of the design process as he defined it, research, scoring, valuaction, and performance, may occur anywhere within the cycle.[1] Design is not a linear process. Similarly, imagine being a musician in a chamber music ensemble. Usually, at the first rehearsal of a new work, all the musicians have the music for their instruments; occasionally a conductor or pianist has a complete score showing all the parts. At any point in the rehearsal process, any musician may stop in order to orient himself or herself to the cues in the parts for the other musicians, or to discuss how to phrase passages, or interpret score markings or dynamics. This is a joyous, but difficult process, made possible by everyone trusting one another. Too often in design offices, some people are asked to perform without ever having seen the score, or others are expected to contribute to the whole even though they are missing an entire part or have no context for

where their part fits. To subject employees to this is nonsensical, childish, and stupid.

Clients can also be caught in these situations. It is not uncommon for a client to hire a consultant for his or her expert advice, and then find reasons to ignore every recommendation that is made. This seems not so much a result of the client's expertise in areas unknown to the consultant, as a matter of the client not trusting the consultant to do what he or she was hired to do in the first place.

The most difficult aspect of the design work that Clarke + Rapuano, Inc. performed in the reconstruction of the concert ground at Central Park was the grading plan. The existing site was extremely flat, with many gradients less than 1 percent. The client, the Central Park Conservancy, was extremely concerned that any signifi-

Figure 4-4: *Some sedimentation and puddling occur in the flattest part of the newly graded concert ground pavement. This photograph was taken before construction was complete; as the work progressed, the amount of sedimentation was reduced as the plantings became well established and began filtering the soil particles and retarding soil erosion. Note the newly planted American elm tree in the background. (Photo by Steven L. Cantor)*

---

1 Halprin L: *RSVP Cycles, Creative Processes in the Human Environment,* George Braziller Inc., NY, 1969, pp. 2–3.

cant change to the existing grading of the site might result in excavation on the roots of the rows of spectacular elm trees, the defining elements of the space. However, a problem with the site was drainage: the flat gradients resulted in puddling. It was extremely challenging to achieve a workable grading plan without increasing the gradients to a more reasonable percentage. Finally, we were satisfied with a plan in which most of the gradients were between 1-1/2 to 3 percent. The plan did require some small areas of cut and fill. The Conservancy's representatives remained unconvinced that these could be minimized enough to spare an impact on the trees. We therefore re-did the grading plan with flatter gradients and devised some methods to facilitate drainage in the flattest areas near the drain inlets, where gradients were as low as 1/2 percent. This plan was executed successfully, although we warned the client that some puddling would occur: After rain storms, the runoff would move so slowly to the drains in the flattest areas that some sediments would settle and leave a visible residue on the pavement. Perhaps, this is a minor limitation to accept in the course of protecting a grove of trees. Hindsight revealed that most of the trees had limited root systems as a result of being severely constrained by a schist layer near the surface. Of course, no one knew this initially. However, it is still provocative to stand in the site and visualize how the other grading plan would have been executed to eliminate the puddling and sedimentation that now occurs.

6. Delegate

It is only human to have gaps in one's knowledge about any subject, particularly complex areas of design. When faced with such situations in the course of a project, a design team member must have enough self-confidence and trust in others to acknowledge that he or she does not know all the answers or even know the right questions. Therefore, it becomes critical in moving forward with the work to delegate tasks to members of the design team, the staff, or to other consultants. This is not only a matter of delegating to others tasks that one is ignorant or uncertain about, but also tasks that are very simple, but time-consuming, that should better be accomplished by a person in a lower position in the firm.

Some offices are organized vertically, in which each person is expected to carry out all duties relating to a job, while others prefer a horizontal organization, in which each person has one principle area of responsibility. In complex projects, it is more efficient to assign people to what they do best if at all possible. Occasionally, this means that someone who is making a valuable contribution to the project may not be as stimulated as if he or she were assigned a totally different task from the previous project. On the other hand, landscape architecture projects are diverse. Any two projects are distinct enough from one another that grading plans, specifications, construction details, or graphic techniques vary widely. A person with a specific area of responsibility can learn a great deal and maintain continuity by carrying out similar tasks on several projects.

One way to avoid developing staff that are too specialized is to be certain that each has at least one major area of responsibility and also a secondary area. Ideally, each person should be working in both areas on the same or different projects. For example, William Wild, the senior civil engineer at Clarke + Rapuano handled all of the civil engineering responsibilities for the extensive road system at the Merck International Headquarters Building. (See Figures 1-16 through 1-28). The architecture firm for whom we were working became so confident of his abilities to discuss the general grading concepts of the roads near their approaches to the building and the specific elevations of storm drainage structures that the architect's project manager would regularly communicate with Mr. Wild, and free one of the Clarke + Rapuano principals to handle the most critical matters. Conversely, during a very busy period, one of the principals did not direct someone to order new three-hole-punched pads for use in doing estimates. He therefore spent hours talking with printers and suppliers in order to arrange for this service, rather than delegating the work to one of the people who could have assisted him.

7. Take Responsibility

The project manager must take responsibility for success and failure of all communications and results. Regardless of the reasons for problems, the only way to solve them is for one person to have the responsibility of answering to the client and facing difficult situations. Complex projects can involve incredibly torturous and convoluted problems, with ramifications that take weeks or months to sort out. However, the client and the staff respect someone who is willing to take charge of a situation, whether good or bad. That's one reason the project manager must be the sounding board for the whole office and the contact person for the client, regardless of the circumstances.

Over 20 years, Domenico Annese has been the principal project manager or principal for all of the projects that Clarke + Rapuano, Inc. has performed for the Calverton National Cemetery for the National Veterans Administration. (See Figures 1-40 through 1-47). He brings years of experience and expertise in all of the design and engineering issues of relevance to the cemetery, so that the client has complete confidence in him.

Another important aspect of this principle is to hold others to a standard of accountability. If the project manager is responsible for direct, clear, and timely communications with the client or the client's representative, then reciprocation is essential for a successful result. It can be quite satisfying indeed to tell a client, "Yes, we submitted the design development documents for review as you requested. We did not incorporate the changes we received from you last week, because as was agreed at the last review meeting (see the memorandum of the meeting) two months ago, we would need responses from you within a month's time in order to incorporate into the next submittal." This is not being combative, but merely encouraging the client to be timely and responsive.

8. Practicality, Common Sense, and Flexibility

These are design issues as well as project management issues. Just as the designer should not promise a client the reincarnation of Versailles when the budget only permits a color garden, the project manager cannot promise the client the delivery of a complete set of working drawings in two weeks when at least five to six weeks are necessary. The results of such efforts are disastrous: drawings full of inconsistencies that incur the wrath of the client and inevitably require time-consuming revisions. How much better to determine from the beginning a realistic design for a realistic budget with a realistic delivery date!

Landscape architecture deals with fluid subjects, anything *but* the immutable, hardline drawings that some draftspeople and project managers insist on producing. Landscape architect Edward L. Daugherty of Atlanta, GA for whom I was fortunate to work for five years, insisted that planting plans (and many other drawings) be done in pencil, rather than ink, to underscore and mimic the softness of the palette the drawings represent. He also sought to emphasize that just as designs evolve, so can the drawings to represent them. It is not a crime to change one plant material to another in deference to the client's wishes, or to erase a line that is incorrect or to correct a misspelled word without replotting an entire drawing. Nor is it a criminal act for the computer plotter to draw on a grading or layout plan a chain link fence as a simple line symbol, rather than some perfectly exact representation of a black, vinyl-clad, eight-foot-high fence with posts six feet on center. No one who is sane would use this literal symbol to determine the number of posts required. That is why scales were invented.

9. Share the Credit

When things go right, include everyone in sharing the credit. No complex landscape architecture project is conceived entirely by one person, nor is it ever realized by one person. It is so easy for a project manager to thank every one who has participated in an award-winning project: Be certain that the names of all design team members are included in publications, press releases, articles, and other media contacts. The good will that such inclusion generates more than compensates for the time spent learning how to spell and pronounce everyone's name.

10. Honesty and Respect

More than a matter of following the golden rule, honesty is simply a matter of self-interest. On complex projects that can last for months and even years, the project manager cannot be in a position of rehashing more than one account of important events. If careful notes are taken at meetings and incorporated into the contractual records, these notes must be used to reconstruct chronologies and develop responses to questions from the client or the staff. If one is in the habit of being truthful, even if it may be embarrassing, then one does not have to remember more than one version of any important event. Project management built on fabrications, no matter how skillful, will eventually indict itself.

Designers draw upon complex information about how people behave in the environment and what types of facilities will make them comfortable and evoke the results desired by the client. It is completely hypocritical to think of ourselves as erudite designers if we do not treat one another with respect, acceptance, and dignity. There is no room for bigotry against minorities—women, ethnic groups, lesbians, gays, people with disabilities—in our profession. It insults everyone and undermines what we do. The person who has great expertise in grading plans that meet ADA standards but then tells jokes about cripples does not belong in a landscape architecture office, nor does the person who works on a garden for an AIDS hospice, but

tells faggot jokes. Acceptance, respect, and courtesy are essential traits of comfortable people, and will be appreciated by colleagues and the client.

One of the more unusual experiences I have had was in working on the design of the Rushmore community in Woodbury, NY, a planned residential development in Orange County. The beautiful site featured many natural areas, including rocky forested slopes that were to be left undisturbed. Clarke + Rapuano was hired by the developer to prepare an Environmental Impact Assessment and preliminary plans for the first phase of development. During initial discussion about the timber rattlesnake population on the site, the client's representative asked me to meet Robert Zappalorti, the herpetologist hired as a consultant, at the Rushmore mansion a few hours north of New York City. He was to meet us there and lead a tour of the site to examine its wildlife habitats.

This meeting is still a vivid memory for me. About seven o'clock that evening as I was sitting in an old armchair and waiting for him in the somberly lit, spacious living room with its huge fireplace, I realized why his name was so familiar to me. Just a few days previously I had attended a meeting of

Figure 4-5: *Herpetologist Robert Zappalorti examines wildlife specimens found at the edge of a wetland habitat in the Rushmore property (Photo by Steven L. Cantor)*

the Lambda Independent Democrats, a Brooklyn lesbian and gay political organization of which I am a member. The program had focussed on the aftermath of the murder of a gay man named Jimmy Zappalorti, a Vietnam veteran, on Staten Island. I realized that the name was so unusual that there may be a connection. When Bob Zapporlorti arrived, I shared my experience at the Lambda meeting, and Bob acknowledged that the murdered man was his brother. What a tragedy for him! My honesty about my situation set me in a position to hear his story, express sympathy to him, his wife, and his family, and to begin a professional relationship with him in a direct manner. As events unfolded during the following months, the murderers were arrested and convicted. Although my relationship with Bob Zappalorti was (and continues to be) a professional one, my direct and honest approach gave me the opportunity to acknowledge his courage and express my gratitude—he endured a great deal of bigotry while educating the public and fighting for justice. Being sensitive, direct, and honest pays many dividends in developing professional relationships.

11. Separate Contractual and Design Matters

Project management is about both design and contractual matters. Although the distinction between the two areas is often clear, at times it can be fuzzy. The project

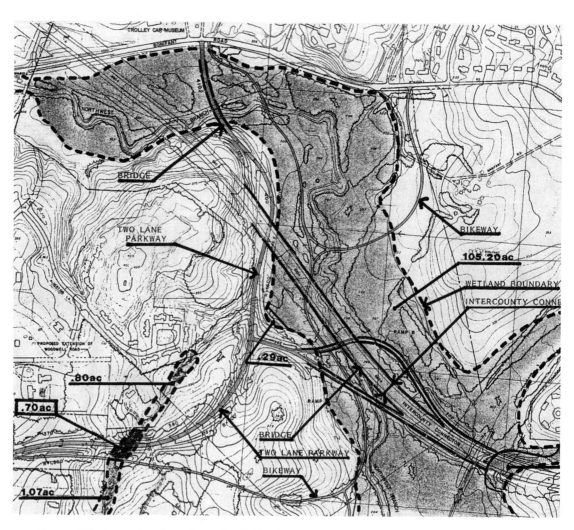

Figure 4-6: *An excerpt from the Rockville flooding impact study showing the route of the two-lane parkway at the intersection with the Intercounty Connector. Wetlands of .70 and 2.35 acres would be filled. The parkway (and Connector) either bridge or avoid all other wetland areas in this sector. The bikeway would travel through the wetlands.*

manager must draw the line. The project manager must know what is required under the terms of the contract, and be certain that what is being produced is within those parameters. At the same time, if the design process uncovers new directions that should be pursued, it is the responsibility of the project manager to communicate with the client at the proper time for additional compensation under the terms of the contract. It is important to rely on previous experience, particularly when working with a regular client. If a client has responded favorably to a particular approach, then such a strategy merits repeating when a similar situation arises. On the other hand, don't repeat mistakes. Finally, if contractual matters become difficult, it is important not to make idle threats. For example, never write or tell a client that you will have to stop work if payment is not made, unless you are absolutely certain that you will be able to do so. Bluffing can be disastrous.

The Maryland National Capital Park and Planning Commission was a very reasonable client on the Rockville project. With Thomas Robertson, a highly skilled and articulate planner as our point of contact, communications were consistently good. As the design process on the parkway progressed, it was necessary to have them evaluated by the Montgomery County government. One of its branches felt that it was important to evaluate the impact of the proposed parkways on the existing wetlands: How much flooding might occur and how much wetlands would be destroyed? We agreed that this was critical information, but that it represented additional work beyond the scope of our original proposal. The client agreed, and we negotiated an extra fee for completing this analysis.

Some firms have the policy that the project manager be responsible for both the design and the management of a project. If practical, this is the preferred method, because she or he can immediately be aware of changes in the scope of work and fee structure, for example, that will have a bearing on the design. In larger and complex projects, this may not always be possible; therefore, there must be clear communication between the principal designer and the project manager. The designer does not deserve to find, for example, that there is no more fee to finish the work, nor should the project manager endure a situation in which a great deal of beautiful design drawings have been done that have nothing to do with the listed items in the scope of work in the contract.

12. Tenacity

Tenacity in the face of lethargic bureaucracies is sometimes required. Similarly, one must be clear on the basic principles governing the design and management of a project and be prepared to fight hard if they are being compromised. The more one develops good rapport with staff and the client on routine matters, the less traumatic it becomes to challenge the client or staff on critical matters. One must learn how to push, without pushing too hard. One cannot be afraid to push or afraid to say no.

Clarke + Rapuano's work with the Central Park Conservancy on the Concert Ground was rewarding in terms of interacting with a group so dedicated to the noble task of the complete restoration of the Central Park. The management of storm drainage became a critical issue in which there was some disagreement. We tended to favor a plan which called for five or six more drain inlets than the Conservancy's staff, who were focused on minimizing the impact on the stressed elm trees. We tried different approaches, made some compromises, but still disagreed. I was convinced that to do without that many drain inlets would result in major drainage problems, while the Conservancy was convinced that to include so many would endanger at least five or six important trees. Finally, since each believed strongly in the validity of his own approach, we agreed to bring in an arborist, in this case Dr. Tartar from the University of Massachusetts, to meet at the site with representatives of the Conservancy and Clarke + Rapuano, in order to evaluate the situation. In walking the site again, I could point out three critical locations where water needed to flow into drainage structures, and not be expected to flow around corners in very flat areas of the site. This was accepted by all parties. I was also persuaded that by adjusting the grading slightly, we could forego two proposed drain inlets at locations where excavation on tree roots might cause considerable damage. This meeting resulted in a successful compromise solution to the original storm drainage and grading plan. However, in order to affect the solution, it was necessary to be quite stubborn and tenacious about the limits to which we could reasonably adjust the plan and achieve the desired goals.

Fortunately, I have learned about tenacity over the course of managing many projects. This requires persistent communication with clients and consultants. Some would criticize, and call this tendency pigheadedness, singlemindedness, or stubbornness. However, results speak for themselves. There are situations in which it is much better to accept such criticism if, as a result, an important decision is reached with a client—for example, a client whose schedule is so busy that the consultant must call frequently in order to communicate.

In completing this book, an arduous task over several years, it has been necessary for me to be persistent with contributors in order to receive materials and comments. Many of the contributors were equally persistent with me, resulting in what I hope are thorough, informative, and stimulating accounts of diverse landscape architecture projects.

APPENDIX

This section lists the names and addresses of all contributors, along with team members who participated in the projects discussed. If individuals have been listed in the text, they are not always listed again.

Please note the following affiliations:

ASLA = American Society of Landscape Architects
FASLA = Fellow, American Society of Landscape Architects
AIA = American Institute of Architects
OLGAD = Organization of Lesbian and Gay Architects and Designers

1. **Anshen + Allen, Inc.**
   2526 St. Paul St.
   Baltimore, Md. 21218
   t 410-467-7011
   f 410-467-3966
   Carol Macht, ASLA
   Lee Coplan, AIA

PRIVATE RESIDENCE
Design principals: Carol Macht, ASLA; Lee
   Coplan, AIA
Project manager: Tim Moshier, ASLA
Contractor: Nelson/Donofrio, Inc. (J.
   Patrick Donofrio, President)

CHURCH HOME AND HOSPITAL
Client: Church Hospital Corporation,
   Baltimore, MD
Design principal: Carol Macht
Project manager: Darragh Brady, AIA
Other key personnel: Joan Floure, ASLA

NORTH PLAZA
Client: public university
Design principal: Carol Macht
Project manager: Joselito Tongson
Consultant: Morris & Ritchie Associates,
   Inc.; Engineers and Landscape
   Architects: Timothy Madden, ASLA
   (principal) and Steven McCurdy

2. **Central Park**
   The Arsenal
   830 Fifth Avenue
   New York, NY 10021
   t 212-628-1036

Doug Blonsky, Chief of Operations and
   Capital Projects
Neil Calvanese, Horticulturalist

3. **Central Park Conservancy**
   1 E. 104th St. Room 224
   New York, NY 10027
   t 212-360-2700
   f 212-360-2754
   Laura Starr, ASLA, Chief of Design
   Jeffrey Poor, Landscape architect
   Sara Cedar Miller, Photographer
   Marianne Cramer, Central Park Planner

4. **Jack Chandler & Associates**
   P.O. Box 2180
   Yountville, CA 94599
   t 707-944-8352
   f 707-944-0651
   Jack A. Chandler, ASLA
   Jennifer Chandler, ASLA and photogra-
      pher
   Chris Moore, ASLA
   Jared Chandler, photographer

ISGUR RESIDENCE
Key personnel: Brodie McAllister, Jennifer
   Chandler

CAKEBREAD WINERY
Project manager: Chris Moore

DANFORTH RESIDENCE
Project manager: Chris Moore
Contractors: Josh Chandler Landscaping,
   T & O Masonry

5. **Guido Ciardi and Jane Herman**
   San Francisco Recreation and Park Department
   McLaren Lodge
   Golden Gate Park
   San Francisco, CA 94117
   t 415-666-7070 or 753-7041 or 42

   Deborah Learner, Planner
   t 415-666-7087
   f 415-666-7130

6. **Clarke + Rapuano, Inc.**
   Consulting Engineers and Landscape Architects
   71 W. 23rd Street 9th floor
   New York, NY 10010
   (The firm closed its New York City operations in August 1996, and may re-open.)
   Raymond J. Heimbuch, President, PE
   Domenico Annese, FASLA
   Steven L. Cantor, ASLA, OLGAD
   Charles Gardner, ASLA
   William Wild, PE
   Bernd Lenzen, environmental engineer
   James Utterback, PE
   Lou Cardi, PE

MERCK
Principal: Raymond J. Heimbuch
Landscape architects: Steven L. Cantor, James Coleman, Charles Gardner, Al Vetere, Shirley Way
Project Engineers: William Wild, Lou Cardi, Peter Martecchini
Consulting landscape architects: Edmund Hollander Design P.C.: Edmund Hollander, Maryanne Connelly, 21 East 4th Street, Suite 608, NY, NY 10003 212-473-0620 212-473-1104 (FAX)
Principal architect: Kevin Roche Dinkeloo: Howard Lathrop, John Carr
C + R Architect: Jaime Vasquez
Client: Fran Cashes, Merck Co;, 1 Merck Drive; PO Box 100, Whitehouse Station, NJ 08889

ROCKVILLE RIGHT-OF-WAY
Principal: Domenico Annese
Landscape architects: Domenico Annese, Steven L. Cantor, Charles Gardner
Landscape designers: Jason Brotter, Stephanie Gash

Project Engineers: Bill Mysak, Barbara Thayer, William Wild
Client: Thomas Robertson, planner; Montgomery County Planning Department; 8787 Georgia Avenue; Silver Spring, MD 20907; 301-495-4563

CONCERT GROUND AT CENTRAL PARK
Project manager: Steven L. Cantor
Landscape architects: Steven L. Cantor, Al Vetere
Project engineers: Kevin Maher, William Wild, Andre Martecchini
Contractor: Audax Construction Corp., Long Island City, NY
Client: Central Park Conservancy and NYC Department of Parks and Recreation

CALVERTON CEMETERY
Project manager/principal: Domenico Annese
Landscape architects: Steven L. Cantor, James Coleman, Charles Gardner, Al Vetere
Landscape designer: Jason Brotter
Project Engineers: William Wild, Lou Cardi, Peter Martecchini
Project Architect: Jaime Vasquez
Client: Mike Riordan (and others); Department of Veterans affairs; Office of Construction Management; 811 Vermont Avenue; Washington, DC 20420

7. **DHM, Inc.**
   1660 Seventeenth St.
   Suite 1400
   Denver, Co. 80202-1282
   t 303-892-5566
   f 303-892-4984
   Robert Smith, ASLA, President

RUSHMORE, YELLOWSTONE,
AND THE PRESERVE
Project manager: Bill Newmann
Other key personnel: Charles Elliott
Architect: Anderson Mason Dole, P.C. (for Mt. Rushmore)
Contractor: Valley Crest (for The Preserve)

8. **Professor Mira Engler, ASLA and Professor Gina Crandell**
   Department of Landscape Architecture
   146 College of Design

Iowa State University
Ames, IA 50011
t 515-294-5676
f 515-294-9755

Gina Crandell, ASLA
117 Stedman Street
Brookline, MA 02148
t 617-731-0503

9. Hargreaves Associates
539 Bryant Street 3rd Floor
San Francisco, Ca 94107
t 415-543-4957
f 415-543-0516
Glenn Allen, ASLA
George Hargreaves, ASLA
Mary Margaret Jones, ASLA

BYXBEE PARK
Client: City of Palo Alto, California
Design principals: George Hargreaves,
  Mary Margaret Jones
Project manager: Peter Geraghty
Collaborating artists: Peter Richards,
  Michael Oppenheimer
Other key personnel: Pariya Sheanakvl,
  Sam Williamson
Contractor: Granite Construction

CANDLESTICK POINT CULTURAL PARK
Client: George Rackelman (retired);
  California State Department of Parks and
  Recreation; 1050 20th Street;
  Sacramento, CA 95811
Design principals: George Hargreaves,
  Glenn Allen
Collaborators: Mark Mack, Architect; 246
  First Street, Suite 400; San Francisco, CA
  94105; 415-777-5305
Douglas Hollis, Artist; P.O. Box 411105; San
  Francisco, CA 94141-1105; 415-826-4582
Other key personnel: Hiroki Masegawa,
  Brian Costello, Laurie Romano
Contractor: Bauman Landscape

10. Michael Immel, ASLA
5 Pico Beach Road
Mattapoisett, Ma. 02739
t 508-758-6310

11. Jacobs/Ryan Associates
1527 N. Sandburg Terrace

Chicago, Ill. 60610
t 312-664-3217
f 312-337-1550
Terry Warriner Ryan, ASLA

GURNEE SWITCHING STATION
Project manager: Scott Mehaffey, ASLA
Consultants: Ross Barney + Jankowski,
  architects; Teng & Associates, engineers
General Contractor: Camosy
Landscape Contractor: Landscape Concepts
Photographer: Nick Merrick for Hedrich
  Blessing and Jacobs/Ryan

VERNON HILLS SWITCHING STATION
Project manager: Daniel Heuser
Consultants: Ross Barney + Jankowski,
  architects
  Teng & Associates, engineers
General Contractor: F.W. Landensky
Landscape Contractor: D.R. Church
  Landscape Company, Inc.
Architectural drawings by Ross Barney +
  Jankowski

12. Carol R. Johnson Associates, Inc.
1100 Massachusetts Ave.
Cambridge, MA 02138
t 617-868-6115
f 617-864-7890
Carol R. Johnson, FASLA, President
Harry S. Fuller, ASLA, Executive Vice
  President

CHARTER OAK PARK
Client: Riverfront Recapture Incorporated,
  Joe Marfugg, Director
Client manager: Ellen Miller-Wolfe
Design principal: William Taylor, ASLA
Project manager: Joanne Hiramura, ASLA
Other key personnel: Pam Shadley, ASLA
Consultants: Childs Engineering, marine
  structural
Haley and Aldrich, geotechnical
Peter Dalton, electrical and mechanical
Bruce Fink, artist
Contractor: Managort Brothers, Plainfield,
  CT

LOGAN AIRPORT
Design principal: Carol R. Johnson
Project manager and photographer: John
  Gustausen

13. **Jones & Jones Architects and Landscape Architects, PSC**
105 S. Main St.
Seattle, WA 98104
t 206-624-5702
f 206-624-5923
Grant Jones, FASLA
Ilze Jones, ASLA
Maren Coleman, publicity

14. **Elizabeth Kennedy**
66 Overlook Terrace #3-K
New York, NY 10040
212-568-7505

15. **Thomas Navin, Architect, Associate ASLA, AIA**
315 E. 68th St.
New York, NY 10021
ht 212-517-8705
wt 212-966-6332
f 212-535-0647

16. **Karen Angell Phillips, ASLA, Executive Director**
Abyssinian Development Corp.
132 W. 138th St.
New York, NY 10030
t 212-368-4471
f 212-368-5483
Mark V. Flowers, Assistant

17. **Prospect Park Alliance**
95 Prospect Park West
Brooklyn, NY 11215
t 718-965-6565 and 965-6566
f 718-965-6595
Mary Fox, Director
Rex Wassermann, ASLA, OLGAD
Shirley Way, Landscape Architect
Christian Zimmerman, ASLA

18. **Royston, Hanamoto, Alley & Abey**
225 Miller Ave.
Mill Valley, CA 94942-0937
t 415-383-7900
f 415-383-1433
Asa Hanamoto, FASLA
Robert N. Royston, FASLA

Barbara D. Lundburg, ASLA
Douglas M. Nelson, ASLA

19. **Elena Saporta, landscape architect and John Taguiri**
102 Ellery St.
Cambridge, MA 02138
t 617-547-2138
t 617-547-5093
t 617-547-6892

20. **Schmidt Design Group, Inc.**
Landscape Architecture
2655 Fourth Avenue
San Diego, CA 92103
t 619-236-1462
f 619-236-8792
Glen Schmidt, ASLA
Joel Harms, ASLA

SWAMI'S BEACH ACCESS
Project manager: Joel Harms
Consultants: Woodward Clyde Consultants
Travis, Verdugo, Curry & Associates
Contractor: Baldwin Construction
Other key contributors: Swami's Surfer Association
Coastal Conservancy

EAGLE CREST CALIFORNIA GNATCATCHER MITIGATION
Project manager: Joel Harms
Key personnel: Jim Shipton, Linda Smith
Consultant: Larry Sword, Sweetwater Environmental Biologists
Contractor: Heffler Company

21. **Martha Schwartz Inc.**
167 Pemberton St.
Cambridge, MA 02140
t 617-661-8141
f 617-661-8707
Martha Schwartz, landscape architect

22. **SPURLOCK/POIRIER**
Landscape Architects
710 13th St. No. 315
San Diego, CA 92101
t 619-233-3324
f 619-233-6256
Andrew J. Spurlock, ASLA
Martin Poirier, landscape architect

INDEX

casting process, 150–51
chess set, 154–56, C22
    competition, 154
    sheet metal components, 154–55
Lafayette Park, 144–48
    sculpture, 146
Re-Vision House, 152–53
Salem Walkways, 148–152
Tartar, Dr. Terry A., 240, 283
Tate, Larry, 172
Teng & Associates, 135
Thomas, Tupper, 245–46
Tice, Pamela, 220
Toth, Ed, 246
tulip tree, 248, 249, 250–51

U
underdrain system, 241

V
Valders stone, 140–42, C20
Vasquez, Jaime A., 53
viticulture, 88–90, 92–93

W
Walker, Peter, 167, 180
Walls
    dry laid, 27–28
    retaining, 28–30, 71, C2
    seat, 118
    wood/plaster, 109–110
Washington
    Columbia River Gorge National Scenic Area
        (*see also* Jones & Jones), 79–80
    Jones & Jones, 75–87
    Nooksack River Study, 75–79

Woodland Park Zoo (*see also* Jones & Jones),
    80–83
Wassermann, Rex, 244, 246, 248
water feature
    bubblers, 111
    corrugated metal chute, 187–89
    echo chamber, 111–12
    fountains, 112–13, 116, 179, C25
    pools, 7, 9, 109, 112, 118, 177–78, C1, C13
    rills, 112
    steam effect, 112–13
    two pump method, 116
Weidlinger Associates, 220
wells, 54, 104, 106, 127
Whyte, William H., 216
Wild, William, 53, 279–80
Winslow, Phil (*see also* Central Park
    Conservancy), 232–33, 234
Woodland Park Zoo, Seattle (*see also* Jones &
    Jones), 80–83
Worden, W. Nikolaus, 75
Wright, Frank Lloyd, 135, 180
Wyoming
    Yellowstone National Park (*see also* DHM,
        Inc.), 58–60

Y
Yap, Theresa, 241
Yellowstone National Park, WY (*see also* DHM,
    Inc.), 58–60
Young, Andrew, 46

Z
Zappalorti, Robert, 281–82
Zimmerman, Christian, 244, 246, 248